PRAISE FOR
HOW NOT TO INVEST

"Barry Ritholtz's *How Not to Invest* is a well-written, invaluable guide to what to do—and not do—in investing."

—**Ray Dalio, Founder, Bridgewater Associates**

"*How Not to Invest* uses striking stories and abundant evidence to show that most of us, including market 'experts,' are limited in our ability to divine the future and would be better off sticking to a simple strategy."

—**Michael J. Mauboussin, Head of Consilient Research, Morgan Stanley Counterpoint Global, and Adjunct Professor, Columbia Business School**

"An invaluable field guide to the varieties of BS investing advice coming from Wall Street and the media, and a practical intro to investment strategies proven to work."

—**Scott Galloway, Professor, NYU Stern, and Co-Host, Pivot and Prof G Markets Podcasts**

"Barry Ritholtz takes readers on a wildly entertaining journey through the pitfalls of the stock market. His humor and wit will help you navigate through this unprecedented time."

—**Molly Jong-Fast, Host, FastPolitics Podcast, Special Correspondent,** *Vanity Fair***, Political Analyst, MSNBC**

"A hugely entertaining investing book. Barry uses stories from throughout his 30-year career to illustrate the pitfalls to avoid if you want to build long-term wealth."

—**Nick Hanauer, Second Avenue Capital**

"A radically brilliant takedown on everything that's wrong with Wall Street, financial media, the advice industry, and the human beings who must navigate this thorny morass of nonsense."

—**Anthony Scaramucci, Founder, SkyBridge Capital**

"In *How Not To Invest*, Barry Ritholtz shows that success is not so much about the good decisions that make you, but the bad decisions you avoid. Winning at investing is about cutting out errors—Barry shows you how."

—**Annie Duke, Author,** *Quit, How To Decide,* **and** *Thinking In Bets*

"I've now finished *How Not to Invest* and come to recognize the biggest investing mistake for me to avoid in the future. It is failing to implement the excellent lessons of this book."

—**Robert Cialdini, Author,** *Influence* **and** *Pre-Suasion*

"This is a unique book, maybe the best I've ever read, and I've read a lot."

—**Ed Hyman, Founder and Chairman, Evercore ISI**

"Ritholtz warns against several mistakes in investing—blindly listening to the 'doom and gloom' and taking big numbers out of context. Then, he drives the point home with vivid anecdotes. Pay attention or you may show up in future editions of his book."

—**Claudia Sahm, Chief Economist, New Century Advisors**

"Read this book. Barry's insights are clever, candid, and, simply, great counterpoints to the conventional wisdom that's far too prevalent today."

—**Jack Brennan, Retired Chairman and CEO, Vanguard**

"Barry's fresh and unfiltered exploration of how not to invest leads the reader to clearer perspectives on how to invest."

—**Perth Tolle, Founder, Life + Liberty Indexes**

"I loved this book! Sure, *How Not to Invest* is filled with solid market advice that will make you a smarter (aka less dumb) investor, but the real kicker is that it's a blast to read."

—**Jack Schwager, Author,** *Market Wizards* **Series**

"Wonderful! *How Not to Invest* is a great read; as addicting as a great novel."

—Rob Arnott, Founding Chairman, Research Affiliates

"The best way to build wealth is to not make dumb mistakes. Barry Ritholtz tells adult investors they need to understand that in this great, fun read from one of the smartest people in finance."

—Sheila Bair, Former Chair, FDIC, and Author, *Money Tales* and *How Not to Lose $1 Million*

"Sometimes, knowing what NOT to do is far more valuable and enlightening than traditional how-to books. *How Not To Invest* should be in every investor's library."

—Jim O'Shaughnessy, Founder, O'Shaughnessy Ventures

"A seriously good book on investing that doesn't take itself too seriously."

—David Dunning, Ann and Charles R. Walgreen, Jr., Professor of the Study of Human Understanding, and Professor of Psychology, University of Michigan

"Investment is easier than surgery. So why do investors make so many more errors than surgeons? You will know the answer to this question and many more when you read Barry Ritholtz's insightful and entertaining book. You might even find your own bad ideas there, and learn to dispose of them."

—Meir Statman, Glenn Klimek Professor of Finance, Leavey School of Business, Santa Clara University

"Barry Ritholtz is one of the most passionate and entertaining writers in finance today. Knowledgeable and unafraid, Barry is a must-read for all serious investors."

—Eddy Elfenbein, Portfolio Manager and Editor, Crossing Wall Street

"In *How Not to Invest*, Barry teaches that avoiding common mistakes is more effective than chasing complex strategies for financial success. As a lifelong believer that some complexity can be very useful, I still think Barry is giving the right advice for most investors."

—Cliff Asness, Founder, Managing Principal and CIO, AQR Capital Management

"Conventional wisdom is a foreign language to Barry Ritholtz and he cuts right through commonly held beliefs that actually inhibit and hurt one's investing journey and portfolio."

—**Peter Boockvar, CIO, Bleakley Financial Group**

"Barry holds up a mirror to our own idiocy with a fun, provocative tone. He's a genuinely smart guy who delights in sharing what he knows. The best way to accumulate wealth is to stop throwing money away. Listening to Barry Ritholtz is a good start."

—**Jeff Macke, Investor, Author**

"For about two decades Barry Ritholtz has been my go-to thinker when it comes to investing, markets, irrationality and human behavior. *How Not to Invest* is a distillation of his wit and wisdom in an easy-to-understand package."

—**Om Malik, Veteran Technology Writer and Technology Investor**

"Barry has been the voice of cognitive market reasoning, behavioral economics and evidence-based results for three decades. *How Not to Invest* is historic! He teaches us what he's learned from his own investment mistakes and the blunders of others, how to be less stupid and avoid unforced errors."

—**Jeffrey A. Hirsch, Editor in Chief,** *Stock Trader's Almanac*

"Barry is one of the best and most insightful financial writers of the last few decades. *How Not to Invest* is as entertaining as it is useful. Barry's wit and insights shine through on every page!"

—**Dan Greenhaus, Chief Strategist, Solus Alternative Asset Management**

"In a world increasingly flooded with garbage masquerading as information, Barry continues to be the ultimate straight-talking guide we're fortunate to have in this treacherous journey that we call investing."

—**Sam Ro, Founder and Editor, TKer.co**

"*How Not to Invest* skips the lectures and hero worship and tells real stories of how money and markets work, and can work for you if you're careful. Barry manages to be serious and funny at the same time, and very, very clearly on the reader's side."

—Dave Nadig, Financial Futurist

"Barry is one of the most brilliant minds in all of finance. Any time he produces content, I'm always amazed by his insights and his ability to speak so well on many different topics. It's a strong quality that should inspire all of us to do the same."

—Joe Fahmy, Portfolio Manager, Zor Capital LLC

"Barry distils decades of wisdom into *How Not to Invest*, showing that avoiding mistakes is the key to long-term success. With clarity and wit, he offers practical advice to help you sidestep bad information and emotional traps—a must-read for anyone looking to navigate markets more confidently."

—Lakshman Achuthan, Co-Founder, ECRI

"No one has done more to educate modern investors than Barry Ritholtz. *How Not to Invest* is witty, smart, insightful, and humble—just like its author, and is a must-read for today's educated investor."

—Caleb Silver, Editor in Chief, Investopedia.com

"*How Not to Invest* is a highly entertaining reveal of the secret to smart investing. Barry Ritholtz shows that simply by avoiding dumb mistakes, you will outperform 90% of investors."

—Jim Wiandt, Founder, ETF.com

"*How Not to Invest* is that essential work of service journalism that does something still too rare: de-exoticizing Wall Street for the Everyman. I'm going to buy a bunch for friends and fam."

—Roben Farzad, Host, Public Radio's Full Disclosure

"Barry details many of the bad ideas and seductions we all fall for over and over again. If this book helps you avoid just one such mistake in the future, it's worth its weight in gold."

—**Meb Faber, Co-Founder and CIO, Cambria Investment Management**

"Barry Ritholtz turns his years of professional money management and fascination with human behavior towards a contrarian view of personal investing."

—**Jonathan Miller, CEO, Miller Samuel, HousingNotes.com**

"Barry's direct communication style and sharp wit are on full display as he breaks down the flawed thinking and misguided data that lead investors astray. The first step to avoiding investing pitfalls is to recognize them when you see them, and this book serves as a great guide."

—**Peter Mallouk, President & CEO, Creative Planning**

"A how-to investment book based around what not to do may seem contradictory. But in Barry Ritholtz's highly capable hands, it positively sings. Authoritative and humble, earnest and wry, funny and deadly serious—Barry shows exactly how counterintuitive thinking can yield powerful results."

—**Daniel Gross, Author,** *Pop!*, *Dumb Money*, **and** *Better, Stronger, Faster*

"Barry is the OG of helping investors avoid the traps commonly found on Wall Street and in financial punditry—and in themselves. If you take Barry's wildly entertaining investing tips in this book to heart, you'll make a lot of money and save yourself a lot of trouble and heartache along the way."

—**Nir Kaissar, Bloomberg Opinion**

HOW *NOT* TO INVEST

HOW NOT TO INVEST

THE IDEAS, NUMBERS, AND BEHAVIORS THAT DESTROY WEALTH—AND HOW TO AVOID THEM

BARRY RITHOLTZ

Harriman House

HARRIMAN HOUSE LTD
3 Viceroy Court
Bedford Road
Petersfield
Hampshire
GU32 3LJ
GREAT BRITAIN
Tel: +44 (0)1730 233870

Email: enquiries@harriman-house.com
Website: harriman.house

First published in 2025.
Copyright © Barry Ritholtz

The right of Barry Ritholtz to be identified as the Author has been asserted in accordance with the Copyright, Design and Patents Act 1988.

Hardback ISBN: 978-1-80409-119-7
Paperback ISBN: 978-1-80409-134-0
eBook ISBN: 978-1-80409-120-3

British Library Cataloguing in Publication Data
A CIP catalogue record for this book can be obtained from the British Library.

All rights reserved; no part of this publication may be reproduced, stored in a retrieval system, or transmitted in any form or by any means, electronic, mechanical, photocopying, recording, or otherwise without the prior written permission of the Publisher. This book may not be lent, resold, hired out or otherwise disposed of by way of trade in any form of binding or cover other than that in which it is published without the prior written consent of the Publisher.

Whilst every effort has been made to ensure that information in this book is accurate, no liability can be accepted for any loss incurred in any way whatsoever by any person relying solely on the information contained herein.

No responsibility for loss occasioned to any person or corporate body acting or refraining to act as a result of reading material in this book can be accepted by the Publisher, by the Author, or by the employers of the Author.

The Publisher does not have any control over or any responsibility for any Author's or third-party websites referred to in or on this book.

This book represents a lifetime of learning and experience, distilled from many sources, but none stand out more than this wisdom:

Charley Ellis, who showed us that the way to win in investing was to approach it like tennis—make fewer unforced errors, and your performance will go way up.

And Charlie Munger, who taught us how to think about investing: Don't try to be smarter than everyone else, just be less stupid.

CONTENTS

Foreword by Morgan Housel — xv

Preface: Consistently Not Stupid — xvii

How to Use This Book — 1

Part 1: Bad Ideas — **5**

  Section 1: Poor Advice — 7

  Section 2: Media Madness — 53

  Section 3: Sophistry: The Study of Bad Ideas — 91

Part 2: Bad Numbers — **117**

  Section 1: Economic Innumeracy — 119

  Section 2: Market Mayhem — 163

  Section 3: Stock Shocks — 211

Part 3: Bad Behavior — **255**

  Section 1: Avoidable Mistakes — 257

  Section 2: Emotional Decision-Making — 301

  Section 3: Cognitive Deficits — 343

Part 4: Good Advice — **377**

Conclusion	**445**
Acknowledgments	**447**
Endnotes	**449**
Index	**473**

FOREWORD BY
MORGAN HOUSEL

I FIRST HEARD OF Barry Ritholtz in 2010. I was at an investing conference in Vancouver, Canada, where he was a keynote speaker.

Have you been to some of these conferences? The bar for speakers can be quite low, with a dry slog through 45 minutes of PowerPoint charts and self-promotion. The audience claps at the end because they are relieved.

But Barry. I'll never forget Barry's talk. It changed how I think about not just money, but communication.

It's easy to forget, but for most of modern history financial commentary consisted of professional journalists who quoted experts. The experts themselves rarely had an opportunity to speak unfiltered, unedited, at length, for a big audience.

Barry was one of the first who did. I'll date both of us by pointing out that he's been blogging about investing since I was in high school. His Big Picture blog was years ahead of its time, and it upended how we now consume financial news for two reasons:

- **It's fun to read.** Barry isn't afraid to lay his opinion on the line even when it's controversial. Better yet, he's a *storyteller*. Presenting investing as a wild story about human behavior rather than a black hole of sterile data makes it something you look forward to. Historian David McCullough once pushed back on critics of "pop" history, saying, "No harm's done to history by making it something someone would want to read." Barry did that for finance.

- **He knows what he's talking about.** As the founder of one of the fastest-growing wealth management firms in the United States, Barry's views aren't just chalkboard theories—he's been in the trenches, so to speak, dealing with the wild, unpredictable nature of how real people respond to greed and fear. No one is always right, but you cannot accuse Barry of pontificating from an ivory tower.

The result is what so many people want and need out of financial commentary: The feeling that you're having a casual beer with an experienced, wise, and honest friend.

Back in Vancouver, Barry spoke about being bearish on China—a controversial point at the time. Asked why, other speakers would launch into a garble of buzzwords and theories. Barry leaned into the mic and, in a whisper, told the audience, "*Psst, they're communists.*"

What I love about Barry's work is that he views investing as a game of emotions and behavior, rather than one driven by intelligence and data. That's important, because a) it's accurate and b) behavior is messy (if not sloppy), unpredictable, varies from person to person, and—unlike data—doesn't pretend to offer a simple answer. Understanding how our behavior makes us do wrong can be more valuable than data purporting to show us how to do right.

This book offers just that, and I think you'll enjoy it as much as I have.

Morgan Housel
Winter, 2025

PREFACE:
CONSISTENTLY *NOT* STUPID

THIS BOOK IS designed to reduce mistakes—*your mistakes*—with money. Tiny errors, epic fails, and everything in between. If only you could learn how to *avoid the avoidable errors* investors make all the time, your life would be so much richer and less stressful!

That is my charge: To share what I have learned so you can skip the most common mistakes people make with their capital. Avoid these unforced errors and your financial well-being will eclipse 90% of your peers.

Most finance authors don't take this approach. The typical investing book goes the "How-To" route. They want to teach you—in a dozen chapters or so—everything you need to learn to become financially successful. Execute these 100 strategies, and start adding up the dollars!

That approach fails in the real world. Even if you do all the right things, it only takes a few mistakes to undo all your prior efforts.

This truth is counterintuitive: Avoiding errors is more important than scoring wins. This wonderful insight came from Charley Ellis in a 1975 *Financial Analysts Journal* paper titled "The Loser's Game."[1] Investing, Ellis observed, is similar to tennis, in that most people lose by making unforced errors. The way to win the "loser's game" is simply to *lose less*: Make fewer errors, and let the other guy beat themselves. A decade later, Ellis expanded this thesis into his classic book *Winning the Loser's Game*.[2]

How Not To Invest will do that too: In the modern context of social media, Reddit memes, and 24/7 news, I am going to teach you to avoid the many mistakes that undo most investors.

More simply stated: Make fewer errors, make more money.

Berkshire Hathaway's inimitable Charlie Munger phrased it this way: "It's remarkable how much long-term advantage people like us have gotten by trying to be *consistently not stupid*, instead of trying to be very intelligent."

I am going to review the most common errors investors make; I will show you the myths that so many firmly believe to their detriment. I'll include some favorite mistakes, including a few of my own, as well as lessons from the wealthiest and most error-prone investors.

All humans are fallible. That is the very nature of what it means to be human; we have a limited ability to see the future or even understand the past and present. We all make mistakes. This book will help you make fewer of them; those you do make will be less expensive.

The goal is the same as Munger's: "Consistently less stupid."

HOW TO
USE THIS BOOK

OVER THREE DECADES as a trader, strategist, and asset manager, I have been sharing my thoughts about markets in public and in real time. I wanted to organize those ideas and experiences into something *especially* useful for other investors.

Finding a useful structure was the first task: Between *The Washington Post*, Bloomberg, and TheStreet.com, I have written nearly 1,000 columns on money and investing. Add in 43,158 posts published at The Big Picture as of December 31, 2024, and that useful structure proved elusive.

After my last vacation, I was sifting through all these columns and blog posts, and a pattern emerged: I'll be damned if every other piece wasn't debunking some piece of investment bullshit* or another. Since the 1990s, dissecting behavioral errors and revealing money myths has been the heart of my work. If only investors could ignore the doomsayers, forget the predictions, steer clear of Wall Street, lose unreliable sources of information, and skip listening to their brother-in-law's stock tips, they would all be better off.

My list of investing **"Nos"** went on and on: Avoid pricey products, steer clear of most SPACs and IPOs, understand your portfolio (why *do you* own commodities?), be skeptical of active managers. You can't even trust your own brain—it wasn't built for this, and more often than not, it will fool you into making mistakes that will lose you money.

---

* I originally pitched the idea of calling this book *Debunking Investment Bullshit*, but my proper British editors would tolerate none of that American coarseness.

As I plowed through the list of DON'TS, the structure of the book revealed itself: *How Not To Invest*. A simple guide to avoiding the myths, mistakes, and errors investors make all the time.

Despite how much we have learned over the past century about capital markets and risk, about human nature and our behavior, too many people still do quite poorly when it comes to investing.

The short reason is simply *too many mistakes*.

The facts are unassailable: It's not that most investors aren't great, it's that they make too many avoidable errors. In baseball, a low batting average is not caused by the lack of home runs, but rather, by too many pop-ups, groundouts, and strikeouts. Or, back to Charlie Munger, *not smarter, but less stupid*.

That is the subtle but crucial secret to your success as an investor. As I have watched my own investing improve over the decades, I attribute that success to being less stupid rather than to becoming smarter.

More than a few people warned me, "Don't use a negative statement in a book title!" I hope to make up for that *faux pas* by filling this book with lots of good advice as to what you can do to avoid these problems. For each of the lists of *what not to do*, there are just as many suggestions of what *TO DO*. You will find these lists useful.

I divided the book into four parts: *Bad Ideas, Bad Numbers, Bad Behavior,* and *Good Advice*. Each of those *Bad* sections is subdivided into three subsections. *Bad Ideas* looks at money-losing advice, the media through which it spreads, and the sophistry used to deceive us. *Bad Numbers* explains how our discomfort with numbers, statistics, and probability creates a poor understanding of how stocks, markets, and the economy operate in real life. *Bad Behavior?* That is where those bad numbers and ideas show up—in how we think about and act around money.

As we progress through each, we move from problems to solutions, from negatives to positives. Pointing out the mistakes we make is easy—but of the most value to you as an investor are the ways you can avoid making these expensive errors.

The last section, *Good Advice*, offers a summation designed to help you minimize these mistakes, including specific *strategies*. The goal is to put

HOW TO USE THIS BOOK

what you learn in a usable set of solutions. It will be a great improvement to your personal finances and investment success.

Follow the lessons from all four parts of the book, then send me a thank you from your new higher tax bracket and/or your happy retirement.

PART I:
BAD IDEAS

There are so many bad ideas associated with investing. We consider three broad areas: Advice, which is where bad ideas impact investors; Media, which is how bad ideas spread; and Sophistry, the subtly deceptive reasoning and argumentation that so often fools us.

SECTION 1:
POOR ADVICE

We begin our discussion by examining the awful advice that hurts investors. By the time you have finished this section, you will know how to identify and avoid bad advice wherever you encounter it.

Experts have their role, but when it comes to foretelling the future, they are as bad as everybody else. This is true for movies, music, and technology, as well as stocks and the economy.

It's easy to delude ourselves that the pros know what comes next. As we shall soon see, when it comes to the future, *nobody knows anything…*

WHO DO YOU LISTEN TO?

EVERYBODY HAS IDEAS for what you should do with your money. The problem? The quality of this advice is at best unreliable and at worst destructive: Some of it is conflicted, much not relevant to you, and most just plain bad. Sifting through it all is not only time-consuming, but it can also easily derail you from your course.

In the coming chapters, we're going to meet a number of characters: Financial gurus and journalists, fund managers and forecasters. Their advice is often seductive and compelling. In evaluating their words, we have something they did not—the benefit of hindsight. We *know* what happened and how their advice worked out. This gives us an advantage in assessing those claims. The lessons will help you assess people on TV, on social media, or even at a dinner party who want to tell you what you should do with your money.

Spoiler alert: Much of the advice was not good.

The purpose here is not schadenfreude, but to reveal to you just how relentless bad advice is. These are not outliers—they are run-of-the-mill media appearances that can be heard on any given day. Most important of all, none of this "free" advice should ever be the basis of your investment decisions.

There is an endless torrent of media advice. It's an overwhelming firehose of speculation and opinion. Most of it can be safely ignored.

When I see someone confidently declaring why this or that investment is so great—in the media, at a conference, or in published commentary—I maintain a healthy skepticism. I accomplish this by considering the speaker and their advice.

About the advice:

- What risks do I assume when following this advice?
- Is this tailored specifically to me (and my investment plan)?
- How much will this advice cost me—in fees, taxes, and lost opportunities?

About the advice-giver:

- What are they selling?
- What is their track record?
- What conflicts of interest do they have?

Those six questions will help you avoid a lot of financial mistakes.

The bigger issue is not the bad advice, but rather, *the outsourcing of your thinking* to a third party. You need to do your own thinking. I want to enable you to take control of your decisions, by giving you enough confidence in yourself and your capabilities that you are not dependent on what you read in print, see on TV, and encounter on social media.

It's your money—no one benefits from its growth more than you. Be responsible for it.

We give too much credence to confident people, regardless of their track records. What happens when billionaires go on TV to make bold economic predictions and market forecasts?

Let's find out.

THE HALO EFFECT

On December 18, 2015, billionaire real estate mogul Sam Zell said, "There is a high probability that we are looking at a recession in the next 12 months."[3] The culprit, he told Bloomberg TV, was the strong dollar and slowing global trade, the beginnings of layoffs at multinational companies, and a general lack of consumer demand.

Market bears dutifully repeated the forecast, as did the mainstream media. Let's use this as an opportunity to look at the risks *any* forecaster presents to investors.

Zell was a legendary real estate investor. His track record as an opportunistic buyer of "distressed properties" was outstanding. Few understood when to buy or sell real estate better than he. He earned the nickname "Grave Dancer" in the '70s, when he penned an article attributing his success *"to dancing on the skeletons of other people's mistakes."*[4]

But as a forecaster, he was no better than anyone else. His 2015 warnings of a looming recession turned out to be off by five years—there would not be a recession until the Covid-19 pandemic caused one in 2020—and by then, both stock and real estate markets were appreciably higher.

But it reveals two issues: First, people who achieve outstanding success in one sphere are often emboldened to make broad pronouncements in another. (More on *epistemic trespass* in later chapters.) Second, listeners find these forecasts incredibly seductive. Impressed by business success, we tend to believe these forecasts, often to our financial detriment.

Blame the *halo effect*: The tendency to see a person's success or positive traits in one field spill over into unrelated areas. The term was coined by Edward Thorndike[5] in the 1920s, but it rose to prominence in 2007.[6]

Zell's 2015 recession forecast was not his first. "We're Heading for Recession," he said three years earlier in October 2012.[7]

We weren't.

At the time, Zell was supporting Mitt Romney, the Republican presidential nominee, and the election was one month away. Perhaps a bit of political bias was subconsciously at work.

Five years before that, in September 2008—weeks after Lehman Brothers and AIG collapsed—Zell warned that the US economy could "slip into recession next year."[8] That forecast was wrong the moment he uttered it. The US was *already* in the worst recession since the Great Depression, and it had begun nearly a year earlier, in December 2007.

The year prior, in 2007, Zell was at the University of Pennsylvania's Wharton School when he said: "We're not really in a quote 'credit crunch.' I think what we are in is a *'confidence crunch'*."[9]

We were in the biggest credit crunch in decades, and it was getting a whole lot worse. Contradicting what he would claim a year later (2008), Zell added, "Despite the fact that we are in the middle of a recession, the real estate industry balance sheet has never looked better."

Wrong again. Residential real estate was in the early days of a 32% crash—and the banks, homes builders, and Real Estate Investment Trusts (REITs) were all about to have huge problems with their balance sheets.

Zell made his billions patiently purchasing distressed assets at fire sale prices. He assembled a portfolio of real estate properties then held on to them for decades, some for as long as a half-century! He was a brilliant real estate investor—but he did not make one red cent forecasting recessions.

The issue with Zell wasn't that he was wrong—we all are wrong, most of us quite often. The problem is his real estate acumen and financial savvy led people to inappropriately overweight his economic pronouncements.

We pay too much attention to billionaires and other successful businesspeople offering up opinions, despite how little they know about what is going to happen in the future. But what about other experts? What do they actually know?

Let's begin finding out in Hollywood.

NOBODY KNOWS ANYTHING

ADVENTURES IN THE SCREEN TRADE was a scathing confessional on the film industry authored by novelist and screenwriter William Goldman. His 1983 bestseller was filled with great lines, perhaps none more memorable than: *"Nobody knows anything."* This quote is applicable to so much more than the film business.

Goldman was a keen inside observer of Hollywood: He won Academy Awards for *Butch Cassidy and the Sundance Kid* (Best Original Screenplay, 1969) and for *All the President's Men* (Best Adapted Screenplay, 1976). He wrote the novel *Marathon Man*, later turned into a gripping Dustin Hoffman film ("Is it safe?"); his screenplay adaptation of Stephen King's novel *Misery* starred Kathy Bates and James Caan (Bates won an Oscar for her performance). Perhaps most fun of all, he wrote the novel *The Princess Bride*, as well as its screenplay, which became a delightful Rob Reiner cult classic.

Goldman's first mention of "nobody knows anything" referred to the future blockbuster movies all passed on by the studio executives. Every Hollywood studio but one (Paramount) turned down *Raiders of the Lost Ark*. It became one of the highest-grossing films of all time and was nominated for nine Academy Awards.

Columbia Pictures missed the boat with several Spielberg projects—not only *Raiders*, but they passed on *E.T.* because they had another alien film in the works (*Starman*, starring Jeff Bridges). They also passed on *Back to the Future* and *Pulp Fiction*.[10]

Star Wars was turned down by the largest Hollywood studio at the time, Universal. As analyst Trung Phan pointed out, George Lucas' original conception was for six films. He did not trust Hollywood, and so to make sure he had control of the film series, he asked Fox Studios for a modest "directing fee of $150k—a 70% cut on the $500k base pay—in exchange for certain film rights."[11]

It's hard to imagine today what the execs at 20th Century Fox were thinking when they gave up *Star Wars*' merchandise and sequel rights for less than half a million dollars: The novice filmmaker outfoxed the executives at Fox. *Star Wars* grossed $1 billion, and spawned a franchise with five films that are in the all-time top 100 in gross box office sales.[12] Walt Disney Co. purchased Lucasfilm, *Star Wars*' production company, for more than $4 billion. The merchandising for *Star Wars* has brought in more than $32 billion for Disney.[13]

"Nobody knows anything" was Goldman's way of referring to the fact that despite all of their expertise, experience, and focus groups, no one in the entertainment industry has any idea how well a film will do *in advance*. Figuring out what will sell in five years' time is an impossible task, often driven by random luck.

Start with a screenplay, which may or may not translate well from the page into a visual medium. How compelling is the director's vision? How likable are the characters? What special sauce will this or that actor's portrayal add? Is there chemistry between the leads? And most random of all, what will the public's tastes be in five-ish years, when this germ of an idea that gets greenlighted today is finally released as a finished film in theaters or streaming services?

It's not only the films themselves, but where and how they get consumed that is subject to unforeseeable outcomes. Blockbuster turned down an offer to buy Netflix for $50 million in 2000. At the time, the movie rental giant had 9,000 stores, and Netflix's business was renting DVDs by mail. Less than a decade later, Blockbuster filed for bankruptcy (2010), and has one store left in Bend, Oregon. Netflix became the dominant video streamer, with 260 million paying customers, and since 2002 a stock that has risen over 50,000%. Netflix's market cap is over $395 billion.[14]

Hit films are more than just a good story, attractive actors and special effects: There is an enormous degree of serendipity and good fortune that

PART I: BAD IDEAS

turns a good movie into a bona fide hit. The same can be said about every complex human activity where the outcome is unknown until years in the future, from marriage to careers to elections to investment portfolios.

We too easily mistake randomness for skill. We imagine we see the *future* when we hardly understand *today*. We readily convince ourselves we are in control of our own destinies, when nothing could be further from the truth.

Recognizing your own ignorance is an advantage. Most of Wall Street hates this fact.

Professor Robert H. Frank teaches at Cornell's Johnson Graduate School of Management. His economics textbook, co-authored with former Federal Reserve Chairman Ben Bernanke, is widely used in colleges. He also wrote *Success and Luck: Good Fortune and the Myth of Meritocracy*,[15] which analyzes the impact of random chance on success.

Successful people tend to credit their own skill, hard work, and intelligence for their fortunate outcomes. But those are mere table stakes—skill, hard work, and intelligence are what you need merely to enter the arena. They are not guarantees of success. Frank observes that for every big winner, there are scores of people just as skilled, hard-working, and intelligent who came in behind.[16] The lack of a lucky break can be the difference between wild success and a near miss (or worse).

When it comes to luck, perhaps the most insightful person in the world is Michael J. Mauboussin, adjunct professor of finance at Columbia Business School and Head of Consilient Research at Counterpoint Global (Morgan Stanley). The "paradox of skill" is explained in his book *The Success Equation: Untangling Skill and Luck in Business, Sports, and Investing*.[17] Mauboussin writes that as a field becomes more crowded with talented, skillful players, the role of luck becomes ever more important. When everyone is competing at the highest level, personal qualities like skill, hard work, and intelligence cancel each other out. Outcomes are determined by the combination of skill *plus* luck.

It is a fool's errand to predict complex systems filled with random, interrelated variables, and exogenous factors mixed with erratic human behavior.

HOW *NOT* TO INVEST

—

We don't like to admit it, but nobody knows anything about the future—not just you and me, but the so-called experts, too.

Let's have some fun learning how little experts know about music…

"LADIES AND GENTLEMAN, THE BEATLES"

IS THERE ANY greater gap between expert opinion and subsequent history than The Beatles?

AllMusic sums up the Fab Four as: "The most popular and influential rock act of all time, a band that blazed several new trails for popular music."[18] That's obvious today, but it was not the consensus early in their career.

Amusing details were recounted in *The Better Letter*, Bob Seawright's twice monthly take on the world. Nobody skewers humanity's cognitive failings better than Seawright does. He giddily recounted the early reviews of The Beatles when they first came to America.[19] At the time, the band had five singles in Britain's Top 20, three of which hit #1—all in 1963. Their debut album, *Please Please Me*, held the top spot on Britain's charts for 30 weeks, displaced only by their next album, *With the Beatles*.

Despite the sensation they were causing in Great Britain, their record label (EMI) could not persuade its American counterpart (Capitol) to release any of the band's singles in the States. Dave Dexter was the man in charge of international A&R for Capitol, and ostensibly an industry expert on the public's musical tastes. He repeatedly rejected The Beatles singles, calling them "generally amateurish and unappealing." One after another, Dexter vetoed those singles tearing up the charts in the UK, starting with "Please Please Me" and "She Loves You."

Ed Sullivan had also turned down the Fab Four (twice) for his show. By coincidence, he was at London (now Heathrow) Airport, when he witnessed Beatlemania first hand. The band was returning home from a tour in Sweden, greeted by a raucous, screaming mob of teenage girls. That convinced Sullivan to book the lads on his show.

The Ed Sullivan Show was a huge platform for breaking new acts, and

Capitol decided to release "I Want to Hold Your Hand" a few weeks before The Beatles' appearance. This was not some insightful exec reversing Dexter's misguided rejections; rather, it was an attempt to capitalize on the demand one of the country's most popular TV shows might create. Not a change of musical heart, but simply good corporate opportunism.

How did the *Sullivan Show* go?

Notably, "*The Ed Sullivan Show* received 50,000 ticket requests for the 728-seat Studio 50 (now known as the Ed Sullivan Theater) where the band was to perform." This surpassed the previous record of 7,000 ticket requests for Elvis Presley's 1957 debut appearance on the show.[20]

Perhaps the public was telling the experts something?

The Beatles played five songs on two segments, ending with "I Want to Hold Your Hand." Ray Bloch, Ed Sullivan's musical director, was unimpressed: "The only thing different is the hair, as far as I can see. I give them a year."

He was not alone in panning the appearance. Seawright collected a string of headlines and reviews that have not aged particularly well:

> *The New York Herald Tribune*: "BEATLES BOMB ON TV."
>
> *The Boston Globe*: "Don't let the Beatles bother you. If you don't think about them they will go away and in a few more years they will probably be bald."
>
> *The New York Times*: "The Beatles' vocal quality can be described as hoarsely incoherent, with the minimal enunciation necessary to communicate the schematic texts."
>
> *The Los Angeles Times*: "Not even their mothers would claim that they sing well."
>
> *The New York Herald Tribune*: "75 percent publicity, 20 percent haircut and 5 percent lilting lament."

Talk about "nobody knows anything."[21]

It wasn't just that the reviews missed the mark. What is noteworthy is how much bias and personal baggage they reveal among the critics. This is also evident in our next section on "Media" (later on, we explore what causes this).

PART I: BAD IDEAS

Consider *Newsweek*:

> Visually they are a nightmare, tight, dandified Edwardian-Beatnik suits and great pudding bowls of hair. Musically they are a near disaster, guitars and drums slamming out a merciless beat that **does away with secondary rhythms, harmony and melody**. (emphasis added)

Whether you like their songs or not, the musicality and beauty of The Beatles' harmonies and melodies are simply not debatable.

Then there was *The Washington Post*, which revealed a very inside-the-beltway-DC perspective:

> They are, apparently, part of some kind of malicious, bi-lateral entertainment trade agreement. The British have to sit through dozens of dreadful American television programs. In return, we get The Beatles. As usual, we got gypped. Nothing we have exported in recent years quite justifies imported hillbillies who look like sheep dogs and sound like alley cats in agony.

What was the 1960s equivalent of, "Okay, Boomer"?

You probably know what happened next: "I Want to Hold Your Hand"[22] went to number one in the US, quickly selling a million copies. American tastes were not so different than Britain's after all, and Beatlemania became a cultural phenomenon in the US too.[23]

Ironically, these music "experts" missed the biggest cultural shift in generations, and it was happening right before their eyes and ears. How did they blow it? Derek Thompson's book *Hit Makers: The Science of Popularity in an Age of Distraction*,[24] explains Raymond Loewy's concept of MAYA—new products that are "most advanced yet acceptable."

Loewy "believed that consumers are torn between two opposing forces: *neophilia*, a curiosity about new things; and *neophobia*, a fear of anything too new. As a result, they gravitate to products that are bold, but instantly comprehensible." Any innovation too far ahead of the curve gets rejected by much of the public.

But with music, I suspect MAYA varies with age. The receptiveness to new music is different for a critic in their 30s, 40s or 50s than for teenagers. One group is still in its formative age, embracing new things (and rejecting most of what their parents liked); the others' formative years were decades earlier. Once your musical taste hardens, perhaps you are less receptive to the latest sounds.

This might explain the bad reviews from Beatles critics throughout their career. Many of their albums, including some of the best music ever recorded, were initially panned. Musicologist and historian Ted Gioia observed that critics "literally were handed the greatest recordings of their era to review, and blew them off. Every classic song on these albums was not only attacked, but actually mocked."[25]

MAYA helps explain why.

Gioia notes that The Beatles were "punished for how quickly they were pushing rock music ahead… the critics misunderstood the lads from Liverpool for the worst possible reason—namely, that they were constantly learning, growing more ambitious, and absolutely willing to take risks."

Or as UK rocker Elvis Costello said, "Every [Beatles] record was a shock."[26]

The Ed Sullivan appearance was merely a single episode in an explosive career. Throughout the 1960s, bad reviews of Beatles albums such as *Sgt. Pepper's*, *the White Album*, and *Abbey Road* would come back to haunt the critics who penned them.

―

"Nobody knows anything" surely applies to music, but let's return to Hollywood to see if we can find any more billion-dollar mistakes.

HONG KONG GUN FU

As we have seen, novelist and screenwriter William Goldman wrote "nobody knows anything" about the Hollywood of the 1960s and 1970s. Today, we are so much more sophisticated in how we evaluate audience tastes—we have big data and artificial intelligence (AI). We would never make mistakes like passing on *The Princess Bride*.

Just a minute though…

Allow me to tell you about *John Wick*, a 2014 Keanu Reeves movie. The first *John Wick* film was made as an indie film, because none of the major studios were interested in financing it.

It almost wasn't made at all.

Despite being attached to Keanu Reeves, who enjoyed huge box office success with both the *Speed* and *Matrix* franchises, *John Wick* could not find any love from the studios. The film had the stuntmen and fight choreographers from *The Matrix* as directors and writers; despite the insatiable demand for action movies, everyone passed on this shoot-em-up film. *Everyone*.

Danny Boyd, creator of the YouTube channel Cinemastix,[27] explains the challenges *John Wick* faced. Quoting Chad Stahelski and David Leitch, the co-directors of the film, who said, "We were literally turned down by every studio that we went to. It's Keanu Reeves being an assassin, kills dozens of people over a puppy, and it's directed by not one but two crazy stuff [*Matrix*] guys."

Boyd offers more details: "Even after the movie got made, that was far from over. *John Wick* was still a couple of studio execs' beguiled faces away from getting sent straight to Blu-ray. Nobody with any power understood it; nobody with any money wanted to distribute it, and none of the critics in early screenings for it could figure out why they've never heard of it."

Just to get the movie finished, Reeves ended up financing some of it himself. That turned out to be a lucrative decision. Reeves was paid between $1 and $2 million for each of the first three *John Wick* films, but is believed to have negotiated a percentage of backend points.

The first *John Wick* film (2014) was made on a shoestring budget of $20 million, and did $86 million in box office.[28] Then came *John Wick: Chapter 2* (2017), which grossed $175 million;[29] then *John Wick: Chapter 3—Parabellum* (2019), which blew up to $328 million;[30] the latest, *John Wick: Chapter 4* (2023), released over the summer of that year, earned $440 million at the box office.[31]

Total box office for the first film and its three sequels is over a billion dollars. That's before the video games, comic books, television series, and spin-off films from the original are counted. *John Wick 5* heads to theaters in 2026—I wouldn't bet against it also doing big bucks at the box office.

By the time it's all said and done, the *John Wick* franchise is worth over $2 billion. And it almost wasn't made, because none of the studio heads could see the commercial potential of one of the most bankable action stars in history spending two hours kicking ass and killing bad guys.

We have the benefit of hindsight, and so it seems obvious to us: How could *John Wick's* style of Hong Kong Gun Fu not be a hit? How did the studios lack the vision to see its potential? *John Wick* is yet another reminder about how little any of us know about what might happen in the future.

So the experts cannot tell what is going to happen with music or movies. What about television? All of those streaming companies seem to have the public's tastes figured out, right?

Let's see how much they can foretell the future...

SQUID GAMES

SQUID GAME WAS the breakout streaming hit show of the Covid era. Written and directed by Hwang Dong-hyuk, it made its Netflix debut in September 2021. Despite a low budget, violence, and subtitles, it quickly became must-see TV during the pandemic lockdown. *Variety* reported the show was a global phenomenon, racking up 1.65 billion hours of streaming in the first four weeks after its release.[32] Eventually, it became Netflix's most-watched original show, with over 2.2 billion hours viewed. *Stranger Things* and *Wednesday*—in second and third place—are about 500 million hours behind.

It must have been an incredible, obvious success from the onset, with studios tripping over each other to buy such a massive, winning concept, right?

Not even close.

For more than 10 years, the South Korean survival drama was dismissed by the industry as grotesque and unrealistic. *The Wall Street Journal* covered the show's history a few weeks after its debut, after it had become a global phenomenon:

> *Squid Game* creator Hwang Dong-hyuk came up with the idea for the show **more than a decade ago**, while living with his mother and grandmother. He had to stop writing the script at one point: He was forced to sell his $675 laptop for cash. Back then, potential investors and actors bristled at the brutal killings and implausibility of individuals competing to the death for money.[33]

It is amazing how many people with experience, expertise, and capital passed on funding what would become the most popular worldwide show of the 2020s.

Before you credit Netflix for recognizing the show's potential, note that is not the story here. As the *Journal* explained, Netflix used a shotgun approach, spending $700 million to scoop up a giant netful of Korean films and television shows from 2015 to 2020; the US streaming giant dropped another half a billion dollars on Korea programming in 2021 alone. It was less they saw the appeal of a shocking game with deadly consequences for its contestants than it was sheer luck.

By the time you read this, Season 2 of *Squid Game* will be out.

This is all a reminder of how little we know about the future, and how often sheer randomness determines the outcome of events...

The experts cannot tell what is going to happen with music or movies or television. What about economics and policy? Surely they have *some* insights there?

Surely you jest...

BROKE BOOMERS?!

For decades, we have been told that the baby boomers—the generation that began nine months after American GIs returned home from World War Two—would be facing an insurmountable retirement crisis. Experts predicted the boomers would be broke in their old age.

Steven Malanga, a senior fellow at the conservative think tank Manhattan Institute, described the predictions:

> By now, many retired baby boomers should be pinching pennies, at best, or battling destitution, at worst. For decades, the media and the experts they quoted warned that boomers weren't saving enough for a comfortable retirement. Thousands of stories expounded on the inadequacy of private-sector retirement plans and of the government policies regulating them. The bleak future for many boomers, one headline predicted, would be "Work, Work, Work and Die."[34]

How did those expert predictions turn out?

Retiring boomers are the richest generation in history. They hold over $78 trillion in assets. *Fortune* magazine pointed out that during the Covid shutdowns, boomers as a group grew $14 trillion richer.[35] My colleague Ben Carlson dubbed them "The Luckiest Generation."[36]

Broke boomers is yet another forecast that was not merely wrong, but wildly so.

—

The forecasts about the retirement "crisis that wasn't" were made decades ahead of time, difficult under even the best of circumstances. How do the pros do with shorter forecasts—mere months or years?

To answer that, allow me to introduce you to Lawrence Summers.

Universally regarded as a brilliant economist, Summers was President of Harvard University, Director of the National Economic Council under President Barack Obama, and served as the 71st United States Secretary of the Treasury. His name was floated last decade as a potential Federal Reserve Chairman.

We dodged a bullet in his not getting appointed to that role.

The CARES Act was the US federal government's response to the Covid-19 pandemic. At 10% of Gross Domestic Product (GDP), it was the largest fiscal stimulus since World War Two. That massive fiscal spend, combined with snarled supply chains and a consumer shift from services to goods, sent inflation spiking up 9%. (Complex systems like the economy are rarely driven by just one or two factors. As inflation was rising, I detailed 15 factors that were to blame—and even that list was likely incomplete.[37]) You might believe that if anyone would know how to wrestle fast-rising prices into submission, it would be Summers.

You'd be wrong.

Here is the former Treasury Secretary in June of 2022:

> We need five years of unemployment above 5% to contain inflation—in other words, we need two years of 7.5% unemployment or five years of 6% unemployment or one year of 10% unemployment (to bring inflation down).[38]

That bold pronouncement was picked by nearly every media outlet in the country. After all, he was an expert on such things.

Or was he?

As Summers was opining as to why we need to *triple the unemployment rate to beat rising prices*, inflation had already peaked. From the moment he uttered the words "10% unemployment," CPI did nothing but head lower. It collapsed from 9% year over year to 3% over the next 24 months. As this was happening, the exact opposite of what Summers prescribed was also occurring: Unemployment fell to 3.5%, the lowest rate in 60 years. It stayed under 4% that entire two-year period of disinflation. As of this writing, year over year, it's still only 3.8%—the lowest unemployment rate since the 1960s.

PART I: BAD IDEAS

Literally, nothing that Summers had insisted as necessary to tame inflation turned out to be true.

There are two lessons to take away from the *Larry Summers' Inflation Experience*: The first is just how emotional the timing aspect of this was. As inflation was reaching its zenith, a wild claim—*we need 10% unemployment?!?*—was widely spread by the media.

This is par for the course.

Whenever the economy or the stock market hit an extreme, so too do the noise levels. Pundits hungry for the spotlight make outrageous pronouncements during these periods, just to be heard over the din. The media are often all too willing accomplices.

Even more revealing is what these claims tell us about the experts themselves. Tech investor Paul Graham's insight is telling: "When experts are wrong, it's often because they're experts on an earlier version of the world."[39]

Larry Summers came of age as an economist in the 1970s, graduating MIT in 1975. That was an era of structural, not transitory, inflation: Oil embargos and wage spirals were taking place in the middle of a long bear market (1966–82). Sentiment was poor, and the United States was suffering from a post-Watergate and post-Vietnam War malaise.

The 2020s have little in common with the 1970s. A better frame of reference to today is the post-war era of the 1940s. There are obvious parallels between the war on Covid and World War Two, from the huge fiscal stimulus to the pent-up consumer demand once things normalized. Both eras suffered from an inflation spike, and in both instances, it was "transitory." Unemployment fell as well.

It's a reminder that experts are humans, filled with the bias and baggage we all carry. Investors and policymakers should be skeptical about their pronouncements, especially during crises.

If nobody knows anything about the future of economic data, how well do the experts do when it comes to forecasting the future of stock market prices?

Take a wild guess …

DOW 36,000

SOMETIMES WHEN EXPERTS make market forecasts, they can be too bearish—meaning they expect market prices to fall and then prices don't in fact fall. Other times, they are too bullish, expecting prices to rise when they don't.

Then there is James K. Glassman and Kevin Hassett. In September 1999, the pair published the book *Dow 36,000: The New Strategy for Profiting from the Coming Rise in the Stock Market*.[40] At the time, the Dow Jones Industrial Average (DJIA) was hanging around 10,000. Their claim was the Dow would more than triple in three to five years.

Instead, the Dow peaked four months later at 11,722 (January 2000); it would soon fall 37.8%. As for the forecast in the book's title, the Dow Industrials eventually crossed 36,000... 22 years later.

"Dow 36,000" has been called the "most spectacularly wrong investing book ever."[41] It was not wrong merely because its forecasts were so bad, or its underlying premise was hilariously incorrect (it was), but because its authors got caught up in the mania of the bull market. As it turns out, stocks were not actually "less risky than bonds;" nor were investors "overly cautious in demanding a high-risk premium" for holding equities. The claim that stocks were undervalued for decades was also proven laughable.

As Glassman and Hassett claimed in the book's introduction:

> This book will convince you of the single most important fact about stocks at the dawn of the twenty-first century: They are cheap... If you are worried about missing the market's big move upward, you will discover that *it is not too late*.

Narrator: It was way too late.

If you followed the book's advice and bought the Dow in the fall of

PART I: BAD IDEAS

1999, you had to wait until 2012 to recover permanently from various drawdowns along the way (2000–03, 2008–09, 2011). That's 13 years just to get to breakeven.

The book contains other claims that were questionable then and look utterly ridiculous now. Perhaps its greatest sin is the foolish extrapolation during peak boom years that stock prices would triple every seven years. This forecast simply tacked on the *prior* seven-year run—one at a record-breaking pace which was the crescendo of the 18-year bull market that had begun in 1982—and assumed it would continue.

Rather than engage in more schadenfreude, here are ten valuable insights I gleaned from reading (and disagreeing with) the investing and literary disaster that was the book *Dow 36,000*:

1. Every **bull** market is followed by a **bear** market.
2. **Buy & hold** is easy during secular bull markets, but much more challenging during secular bear markets.
3. Returns are a function of **risk**: The greater return you seek, the more risk you must be willing to accept.
4. **Valuation** matters a great deal.
5. "Risk" means that sometimes, you get less than your **expected returns**.
6. The **business cycle** exists, and **recessions** occur regularly.
7. Markets are subject to bouts of **extremes**. They are, after all, just crowds of people, where emotions sometimes prevail over logic.
8. **Behavior** is an important part of performance. Temporary drawdowns become permanent losses if you behave foolishly during inevitable downturns.
9. **Extrapolating** the current trend to infinity or zero is foolhardy.
10. **Politics and investing** make for terrible bedfellows.

Note that these were surely not the lessons its authors intended, but they are what you can discern from the debacle surrounding the *most spectacularly wrong investing book ever*.

Every market gives us an opportunity to learn new lessons. You will find the tuition much less expensive if you can learn from *other people's mistakes*, rather than your own.

We obviously want to pay less attention to people who make forecasts that are terribly wrong, but what about people whose forecasts proved prescient? What about the guy who got the big one right?

Let's find out...

THE BIG SHORT

MICHAEL BURRY HAS proven himself a rare fund manager. He has a great ability to identify a variant perception versus Wall Street consensus, and then find a way to express that view in a market position.

In the years leading up to the Great Financial Crisis, Scion Capital, Burry's hedge fund, bet against the housing market via collateralized debt obligations (CDOs).

As we learned in Michael Lewis's book *The Big Short*,[42] Burry had the courage of his conviction to stay with his position, even as his clients and others opposed it. The result was incredible returns at the peak of the crisis. As real estate fell 32% nationally, and the S&P 500 crashed 57%, Burry's fund made over $725 million, and he personally made a profit of $100 million.[43]

The thing is, making a bet and staying with it is very different than making a forecast. What a manager says in an interview (or a tweet) during the trading day is usually them talking their book, or seeking some free marketing. It costs nothing and is usually forgotten.

Except when people like Adam Khoo keep track of what you have been saying publicly.[44] Burry, since famously nailing the collapse of the subprime mortgage market, has been looking for a replay of that era to no avail, making regular predictions about an imminent stock market crash.

HOW *NOT* TO INVEST

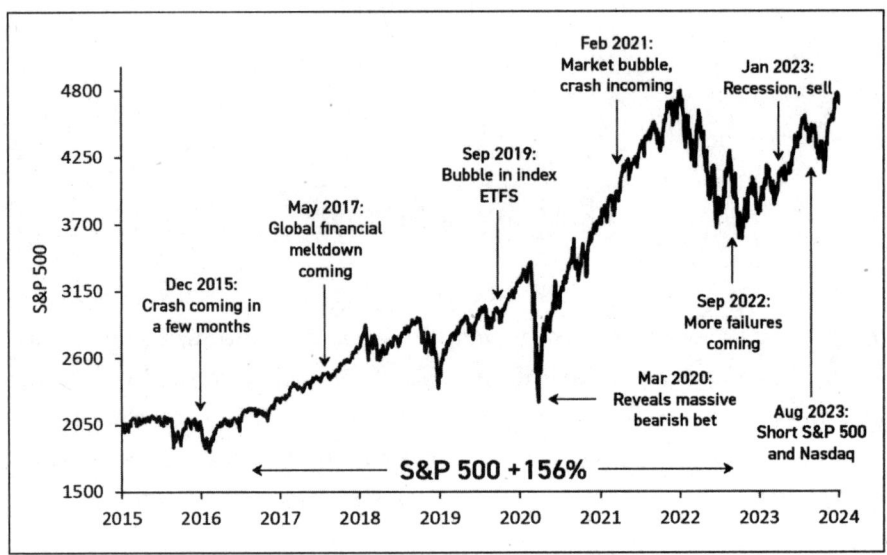

Source: Piranha Profits.

Khoo has tracked Burry's forecasts, and the results are unlikely to land him in another Michael Lewis book anytime soon:

- December 2015, predicted the stock market would crash within the next few months. Next 12 months, S&P 500 +11%.
- May 2017, predicted a global financial meltdown. Next 12 months, S&P 500 +11%.
- September 2019, predicted stock market would crash due to a bubble in index ETFs. Next 12 months, S&P 500 +15%.
- March 2020, revealed a massive bearish bet. Next 12 months, S&P 500 +72%.
- February 2021, predicted a stock market crash due to a speculative bubble. Shorts Tesla. Next 12 months, S&P 500 +16%, Tesla +13%.
- September 2022, warned of more failures, said bottom not hit yet. Next 12 months, S&P 500 +14%.
- January 2023, predicts a recession and new round of inflation. Says "SELL." S&P 500 +25% for the year.[45]

PART I: BAD IDEAS

The *Dow 36,000* guys may have beclowned themselves, but Burry remains a fantastic investor. His net worth has grown to over a billion dollars, and he accomplished that by being a uniquely insightful steward of risk capital. He is willing to fight the crowd, something we will see in later chapters can be terribly uncomfortable. He not only embraces risk, but can withstand vicious, painful drawdowns that have broken lesser traders.

Despite his acumen as an investor, his forecasts have proven themselves to be money-losing. The entire purpose of this exercise is for you to recognize that you should not care about *anyone* else's forecast—even a brilliant investor like Michael Burry.

But there is even more to this for a very specific reason: *Forecasters who make one great outlier call correct tend to make lots more outlier forecasts.* Worse, observers overweight the "rare call," putting even more faith in future forecasts.

This is the paradox of predictions, according to Joe Keohane of the *Boston Globe*:

> How can someone with the insight to be so right about a major event be so wrong about so many other ones? According to a recent study, it's simple: The people who successfully predict extreme events, and are duly garlanded with accolades, big book sales, and lucrative speaking engagements, don't do so because their judgment is so sharp. They do it because it's so bad…[46]

In other words, they keep trying for the next great doomsday call. What should be a once-in-a-lifetime great prediction becomes their standard operating procedure. Keohane was writing about Nouriel Roubini, but it's just as applicable to Burry, or anyone else who nails a big outlier forecast.

I have had a few great market calls in my career, notably the top and bottom of the Great Financial Crisis (GFC). And at the end of Q1 2020, I urged people not to assume that Covid had ended the bull market.[47] But I understand enough about forecasts that I honestly have to admit I don't know if those calls were based on skill or luck. I certainly wouldn't want to sling around $5 billion dollars of client assets based on my gut instincts.

The takeaway for investors is the same: If you are going to put capital at risk, make sure you know why. Understand what you want to get out of markets.

And always, *think for yourself.*

Up next, we meet the greatest-selling personal finance author in history. For sure, the things he says are what we want to hear, and he has been mostly right about many of them, right?

Right?

Oh, dear...

RICH AUTHOR, POOR READERS

ROBERT KIYOSAKI IS the author of *Rich Dad, Poor Dad*.[48] It's one of the most popular personal finance books of all time, having sold 32 million copies. You would assume a guy like him must know a thing or two about investing. Instead, despite all of his personal success, Kiyosaki has morphed into a panicky *doomer*.[49]

I was unaware of this until my colleague Ben Carlson pointed it out.[50] He was wondering what Kiyosaki was up to, and found this from the *Rich Dad* author in December 2023:

> FYI. Bank Credit just sold off like 2008. Get some cash out of banks as you need cash. This may be the start of the biggest crash in history. Hope I am wrong yet no time to play Russian Roulette with your life.[51]

Before you liquidate all of your assets and relocate to New Zealand, you may wish to consider Kiyosaki's track record. Three months after making that call, markets continued rallying; one year later, in December 2024, the S&P 500 was 30% higher than when that warning was tweeted.

"Wait a minute, I feel like I've heard this before," observed Carlson. On September 26, 2021, Kiyosaki issued a very similar market warning:

> Giant stock market crash coming October. Why? Treasury and Fed short of T-bills. Gold, silver, Bitcoin may crash too. Cash best for picking up bargains after crash. Not selling gold, silver, Bitcoin, yet have lots of cash for life after stock market crash. Stocks dangerous. Careful.[52]

The year 2022 was not a great one for equities or bonds, both falling double digits. But the 15% drop from that tweet to the October 2022 lows was hardly a disastrous market crash. For the *Rich Dad* author, it was merely one in a long line of warnings.

Before that was the October 2020 call:

> The EVERYTHING CRASH is coming. Since 1987 world has been in EVERYTHING BUBBLE. Now all crashing. Prices of gold, silver, Bitcoin will crash too. US dollar to rise. Be patient. Massive money printing ahead eventually destroying dollar. Time to buy more gold, silver, Bitcoin coming.[53]

And this a few days earlier:

> CRASH ONLY BEGINNING: Buffett says "When tide goes out you see who's been swimming NAKED." Billions of naked swimmers. SAD. Bankruptcies and bargains floating to surface. SAD. Yet great time to get rich. PENSIONS NEXT CRISIS. Retire now. Do not waste this crisis. Swim for freedom.[54]

Markets screamed 46% higher over the next 14 months; they are 85% higher as of December 2024.

On May 10, 2018, he offered up this advice:

> Another sign that the real estate market in the U.S. is nearing the top before the next crash. #financialeducation[55]

This was truly god-awful, horrific, ruinous advice. Instead of a real estate crash, 2018 was one of the best times *in your lifetime* to buy US residential real estate.

On September 1, 2015 Kiyosaki tweeted this gem:

> I've been predicting since '02 that we would see a stock market crash in '16. #richdad[56]

PART I: BAD IDEAS

For the calendar year 2016, the S&P 500 gained 9.5%, a little over its historical average. The worst drawdown that year was 10.5%, something that occurs once every two to three years. And once again, markets were appreciably higher over the next five years.

A few months earlier on May 23, 2015, we saw the same schtick, different medium:

Rich Dad Radio Show
New show: Cash In On The Crash.[57]

On April 7, 2011, came this gem:

For the educated, an economic crash is the best time to get rich. Guess what? The crashing is not over.[58]

Guess what? It was! Or as Carlson observed, "This guy has been predicting the end of the financial system as we know it for years."

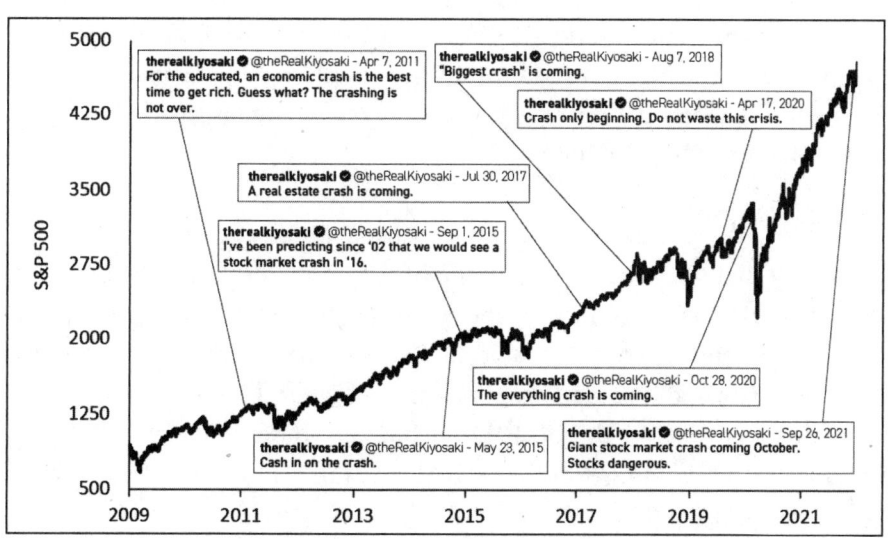

RichDad has 2.5 million Twitter (X) followers. Hopefully, most ignored Kiyosaki's advice. Had they listened to him, they would have missed one of the greatest decades in stock market history.

Despite the success of his book, Kiyosaki didn't seem to follow his own advice. Rich Global LLC, the company he set up to manage his business activities, filed for bankruptcy in 2012.[59] No wonder he has become so dour since.

As neurologist, author, and investor William Bernstein astutely observed, "The reason that 'guru' is such a popular word is because 'charlatan' is so hard to spell."[60]

———

There is always the risk of overreach when people venture outside of their skill set and into other fields.

Such was the case with Tony Robbins, the self-help guru. He has sold millions of books that help many people realize their full potential.[61] I don't know why he ventured into financial advice, but he did. In a video released August 6, 2010, titled "An Important Note of Caution," Robbins, after lots of caveats, said:

> Right now is a time you might want to take some stocks off the table in the stock market. Especially if they are in manufacturing or retail or banking or god forbid homebuilding and housing… I would feel bad if I didn't warn you… One of the biggest bubbles in history is blowing up now.

Bubble? We were at the start of a massive decade-long rally.

The day that video was released, the S&P 500 closed at 1,121.6. It would give up a few dozen points over the rest of August, and then begin an epic tear. By the end of 2010, it would be 12.1% higher. Three years after the video was released, the S&P 500 was 51.3% higher. Five years post-video, the gains were 85.8%. The S&P Homebuilders Index—a sector Robbins recommended avoiding—did even better, gaining 149%. The S&P Retail Index was up 158.2%.

A self-help guru warning of dangers *after* a 57% crash sounds a lot like the recency effect at work. Investors become bullish after they buy stocks, bearish after they sell them; it is part of the process of how we

PART I: BAD IDEAS

rationalize our decisions, and justify our behavior. This tendency to be backwards-looking is hard-wired.

As happens so often with accomplished people, they sometimes believe their achievements in one field carries over to another (and the Halo Effect leads us to follow them). Michael Jordan was the greatest basketball player ever, but switched mid-hoops career to be a mediocre minor league baseball player. Nobel Prize-winning physicist William Shockley practically invented Silicon Valley, turning northern California into a technological hotbed of innovation. He was less successful dabbling in the eugenics of race, proposing financial rewards for the poor and those he deemed genetically disadvantaged (that's code for Black) who volunteered for sterilization. As John Kenneth Galbraith famously observed, "There are two kinds of forecasters: those who don't know, and those who don't know they don't know."

After the past few chapters, you may be wondering what you can do to avoid poor advice. My advice: Stay away from the wrong crowd…

MORE BAD ADVICE: THE WRONG CROWD

HAS THIS EVER happened to you?

You're about to make a new investment—you've done all of your research, you're ready to go—but just before you pull the trigger, someone says *something* to create some doubt about a company, the market, or the economy. They get in your head, create self-doubt, and you hesitate. To be safe, you decide to do a little more homework—and the next thing you know, that stock or market is off to the races without you. All you can think is, "Thanks for nothing, buddy."

It's not just the folks writing dumb books or appearing on TV that offer bad advice—it's *all around you*. To guard against it, stay away from the following people:

- **The Tipster**: The well-connected guy with the hot story: An announcement is *imminent*. He is excited about [fill in the blank], but even more jazzed about his sources. "I know the head trader at a hedge fund/wire house desk/The FDA/Board of directors." For a guy supposedly so plugged in, his track record is stunningly poor.
- **The Articulate Incompetents**: In his book *The Tao Jones Averages*,[62] Bennett Goodspeed described a specific type of Wall Streeter who goes on TV to tout the latest product as "Articulate Incompetents." The more confident they sound on TV, the more likely TV viewers are to believe them. Most are simply slick salesmen using the right buzzwords and sporting very poor track records.
- **The Enthusiast**: He's always breathlessly recounting the latest company on the verge ("Big news due out any day!"); someone is about to "snap these guys up." He's entranced with new

PART I: BAD IDEAS

management ("New CFO was employee No. 12 at Google!"). We've all been bitten by the infectious salesmanship of the enthusiast; its a shame his stories never seem to work out.

- **The Permabear**: The most dangerous clown in the circus, responsible for more wealth destruction than any other player. Any data point has the seeds of destruction within. Every market wobble is a start of the next crash. When things are fine, investors are complacent; when they are less so, it's proof trouble is coming. At least the **Permabulls** have the overall market trend on their side (stocks tend to go up over time). The permabears are fighting a trend in place for centuries, as well as human ingenuity, innovation, and technological progress. That's been a losing bet for millennia.
- **The Doomers**: The world is always on the razor's edge of disaster. Every geopolitical crisis is spiraling into a world war, every credit market hiccup is a new Great Financial Crisis. Economic slowdowns aren't even recessions, they are budding Depressions. Own bottled water, ammo, and farmland far away from the roving murder-gangs? (Hard pass—that's not a life worth living.)
- **The Exotician**: The more obscure, the better: Fascinated by little-known indicators, the exotician flits from style to style like a butterfly seeking nectar. Last week it was Bollinger Bands and McClellan Oscillators, this week it's Elliott Waves. The esoterica masks a lack of conviction for previous ideas. They never stick with any style long enough to test its validity. Instead, they are on a search for a magic bullet that does not exist.
- **The Liar**: All industries have their share of BS artists, but a special type is attracted to trading. They never have a losing position; their buys are always the low tick of the day. And the sells! The best possible print! I can count on one hand the number of times I've top-ticked a stock on the way out;* yet somehow, the Liar manages decades worth of statistically aberrant prices *each day*

---

* Bajillions of trades, and there were just three lucky exits: Iomega, Micromuse, and Qualcomm.

before lunch. Make a mental note of who the Liar is and dismiss whatever statements they make in the future.

- **The Know-It-All**: One of my favorite dudes—and it's *always* a dude—he knows obscure arcana on products and tech companies: Board members, model numbers, useless minutiae. Their unholy knowledge is irrelevant to the investment process. At a BBQ in 1999, I recall overhearing this: "Wait till you see the new 2200 dynamic cross circuitry router—it's going to kick Cisco's ass." Sure, dude, whatever…

Learn to recognize destructive investor personalities—and stay as far away from them as possible.

―

We have clearly seen that *nobody knows anything* and forecasts about the future, in finance and every other field, are fraught with difficulty and prone to error. With that being the case, why do we have so many forecasts in the first place? Let's find out…

THE END OF PREDICTION, INC.?

I COME NOT TO praise forecasters, but to bury them.

After these many years of listening to their nonsense, it is time for the investing community—and indeed, the seers themselves—to admit the error of their ways. Most forecasters are barely cognizant of what happened in the past. And based on what they say and write, it is apparent they often do not understand what is occurring here and now.

There's no reason to imagine that they have the slightest clue about the future.

Economists, market strategists, and analysts alike suffer from an affinity for making big, frequently bold—and typically wrong—pronouncements about what is to come. This has a pernicious impact on investors, who allow this guesswork to infiltrate their thinking, never for the better.

I have been beating this drum for two decades. What say we finally put a fork in Prediction, Inc.?

There is a forecasting-industrial complex, and it is a blight on all that is good and true. The symbiotic relationship between the media and Wall Street drives a relentless parade of money-losing tomfoolery: Television and radio have 24 hours a day they must fill, and they do so mostly with empty nonsense. Print has column inches to put out. Online media may be the worst of all, with an infinite maw that needs to be constantly filled with new and often meaningless content.

Just because the beast must be fed, does not mean you must be dragon fodder.

The other partner in this mutually beneficial dance is the financial products industry. Forecasting is simply part of its marketing strategy. There are two principal approaches to meeting the media's endless demand for unfounded guesses about the future. Let's call them: a) Mainstream; and b) Outlier.

The Mainstream strategy is simple: Take the average annual change in whatever the subject at hand is and extrapolate forward a year. Voila! You have a mainstream forecast. Equities, predict 8% gains in the S&P 500. For any economic data series, project out the trailing six-month average forward. As Lord John Maynard Keynes observed, "Worldly wisdom teaches that it is better for reputation to fail conventionally than to succeed unconventionally."[63]

Then there is the Outlier approach, where a wildly unorthodox forecast is made. The prognosticator predicts 5,000 for the Dow Jones Industrial Average when it's three times that, or hyperinflation, or $10,000 gold, or a 1% yield on the 30-year Treasury bond, or a collapse in the Federal Reserve's balance sheet. Lately, it's been Bitcoin $1,000,000.

If it comes to pass, the forecaster is feted as a rock star. If not, most people forget (though some of us track these outlier forecasts). Those in the prediction industry are pernicious survivors. They understand how to play on the human psyche to great advantage. Like the cockroach, they adapt well to conditions of chaos and uncertainty.

There is a flaw in the human wetware that leads to a demand for predictions. The evolutionary propensity humans suffer from is the desire for specific claims from self-confident leaders.

This is demonstrated in a wealth of academic data about forecasting track records. Research has shown there is a high correlation between a forecaster's appearance of self-confidence and believability. Unfortunately, there is an inverse correlation with accuracy, for reasons revealed by the Dunning and Kruger studies on metacognition and self-evaluation (more later). The more precise a prediction, the more likely it will be believed, and the less likely it is to be right. These factors set up viewers to have the most faith in the people who are least likely to be correct.

History shows us that people are terrible about guessing what is going to happen—next week, next month, and especially next year. We are error machines, a mess of biases and emotions. We prefer to seek out, notice, and remember that which agrees with our prior thinking.

The experts are no better than the public at large. Consider the

PART I: BAD IDEAS

comprehensive examination of expert forecasting performed by Philip Tetlock,[64] professor of psychology and management at the University of Pennsylvania. He studied 28,000 forecasts made by hundreds of experts in a variety of different fields. His findings:

> Surveying these scores across regions, time periods, and outcome variables, we find support for one of the strongest debunking predictions: it is impossible to find any domain in which humans clearly outperformed crude extrapolation algorithms, less still sophisticated statistical ones.

In other words, expert forecasts are statistically indistinguishable from random guesses.

What should investors do instead of paying attention to these unsupported, mostly wrong, exercises in futility called forecasting? At the very least, I suggest three simple things:

1. A well-thought-out financial plan that is not dependent upon correctly guessing what will happen in the future.
2. A broad asset allocation model that is Core & Satellite: Mostly passive indexes, plus whatever ornaments you might want on the tree. Rebalance every few years. Repeat forever.
3. Cut the useless, distracting noise in your media diet.

It is important for investors to understand what they do and don't know. Recognize you cannot know what is going to happen in the future, and any investment plan that is dependent on accurately forecasting where markets will be next year is doomed to failure.

Never forget this simple truism: All forecasting is marketing, plain and simple.

—

Markets are intricate and complex, so it's no surprise predictions are poor. Let's see what makes them so difficult to forecast...

FORECASTING CHAOS

ANYONE IN MY line of work is familiar with the *perils of predictions*. If you appear in the media and occasionally opine on risk assets, the occupational hazard is eventually, someone will ask you for your forecast.

Unfortunately, investors give print and TV predictions more weight than they deserve. A confident-sounding analyst or economist who makes bold, exciting claims is catnip to investors. This can throw off even the best-laid financial plans.

I wish the Securities & Exchange Commission (SEC) mandated the following disclosure to accompany all punditry:

> The undersigned admits that he or she has no idea what's going to happen in the future, and hereby declares that this prediction is merely an unsupported and wild speculation…

I've been tracking pundit nonsense for three decades; I have yet to find *anyone* who consistently forecasts markets with any degree of accuracy. Extrapolating a short-term trend is the best you can hope for with markets or economic data. This truism never dissuades prophets or the press from their fortune-telling ways.

Gains are always relative to potential losses, and higher returns by definition involve greater levels of risk. Your frame of reference for risk is always against the "risk-free" rate of returns that US Treasury bonds provide: Treasury bond yield, minus inflation.

But I really like the definition Elroy Dimson, Emeritus Professor of Finance at London Business School, uses: "Risk means more things can happen than will happen."[65] There are many more potential outcomes than the one that eventually occurs. It is fair for investors with capital at risk to ask: "Am I getting paid enough yield or upside relative to the possibility that a less desirable outcome occurs?" This is the difference between risk-based analyses and predictions.

When making a probability assessment, we don't predict what *will* happen, but rather, assess the range of possible outcomes—what *could* happen. Think of it as war-gaming scenarios, each with a different likelihood of occurrence. You can express an opinion by assigning rough percentages to those outcomes (just maintain humility about your own accuracy). Whether this or that scenario plays out is determined by how the countless variables interact over time.

You will find it useful to think about the future in this way. "As we know in life and in investing, uncertainty and risk are inescapable," said Howard Marks, co-founder and co-chairman of Oaktree Capital Management.[66] When we consider all of the unforeseen actions that might occur between now and even a year from now, it's apparent that forecasting is a low-probability activity.

Chaos theory

What makes markets so difficult to predict? *Chaos theory*.

Professor Stephen Kellert[67] of Hamline University defines chaos theory as "the qualitative study of unstable aperiodic behavior in deterministic nonlinear dynamical systems."

Or in plain language: "Nonlinear" is when small inputs create disproportionately large reactions. (Like a rumor that causes a panic sell-off.) Markets are *nonlinear* and also have a high degree of "instability." Every factor affects every other factor in the system—that's "dynamic"—which has secondary effects, tertiary impact, and so on. "Reflexivity" is how legendary investor George Soros described these interactions.[68] And lastly, "aperiodic"—markets never repeat quite the same way twice. "History doesn't repeat, but it rhymes."[69] There may be similarities from one era to the next, but they are never identical.

And, we haven't even gotten to the *humans* yet. Every one of them trying to generate a return, using biology that evolved to adapt and survive on the savanna, not make intelligent choices in the capital markets. Our limbic systems keeps us alive, but at a cost: Fearful one moment, greedy the next.

Or as the brilliant theoretical physicist Richard Feynman once stated, "Imagine how much harder physics would be if electrons had feelings."[70]

Bad advice comes in many flavors. The best way to avoid it is to ask one simple question. That is what we do next.

WHAT ARE THEY SELLING?

WHY DO WE pay so much attention to the opinions of others? You've read in the previous chapters how much of that advice is terrible. So why do we give folks on TV or in print credit for knowing the future, or seeing what comes next?

In short, why are we so trusting to people trying to sell us something?

Despite a lot of bad advice, this is a difficult habit to break. We are social animals, part of a tribe, and thus have evolved as a cooperative species. Our adaptability and cooperation may have helped us tame the planet, but that same evolution does not help us make intelligent asset allocation decisions. This is especially true during periods of volatility and stress. As we see later on, our own genetic wetware works against us in modern capital markets.

To remedy that, I want you to be more skeptical of other people's advice, and more independent. It is your money, and you must think for yourself. The goal is to move you toward a healthy skepticism—not to be negative about everything, but simply less naïve than you were before. During the SALT treaty negotiations with the Soviet Union, President Ronald Reagan said "Trust but verify;" you should employ a similar strategy with investing.

I want you to be less of a financial sucker than you have been during most of your life. Full disclosure: I was quite a sucker early in my career. I failed to understand what motivated salespeople (duh). I believed the nonsense I heard on quarterly conference calls! I learned expensive lessons being too trusting of the analysts, brokers, traders, economists, fund managers, strategists, regulators, journalists, and even clients I encountered.

Everyone is selling something.

The challenge is there's so much bad advice out there. Some of it is maliciously motivated, or at least motivated by a salesperson's self-interest; some of it is driven by naïve good intentions; and some of it is just "business." At the very least, a lot of the advice you hear is highly conflicted.

To avoid bad advice, you must always ask yourself: "What is this person selling?" Once you figure out what the product is, you can put the sales "advice" into better context.

Allow me to disclose what I'm selling—my product—so you can get a sense of how much weight you may wish to put on my words:

- *Content*: Whether it's this book, my podcasts, or columns, I want you to consume my ideas and embrace my philosophy. Some of this is altruism—I love getting emails from people telling me how much investment angst they avoided due to something I wrote. But do not be naïve: Everyone who does this is engaging in branding and marketing (me included).
- *Time*: Even free blog posts and podcasts have a cost—you pay for that content with your time and attention. I love asking an audience what product radio or TV sells; the answer is invariably "advertising." That answer is incorrect. When something is free, we overlook that *we are the product*. Our attention is being sold to advertisers, along with our data. And that gets cross-referenced to include your web browsing habits, geographic location, credit score, income, purchase history, and a whole lot more.
- *Investment management*: My firm runs ~$5 billion for a few thousand families. We charge a fee for our investment and planning services. If we win your business, our firm's revenues and profits go up. (Sorry to be blunt, but it is a fact.)*

---

* Ritholtz Wealth Management's business model is simple: You can manage your own investments if you can control your own behavior, and we provide a wealth of free, valuable content to help you with that. But if you want assistance, feel free to reach out. We will gladly manage your investments for a modest fee. I have been completely transparent about this since the day the firm launched in 2013.

PART I: BAD IDEAS

Free advice (especially about money) comes with that caveat. Anytime money gets discussed, you should assume a sales pitch is embedded within. That is especially true when it comes to stocks. The problem, as we have seen, is most of that advice is not very good.

We have reviewed a lot of bad advice that hurts investors. The examples should give you a sense of what to look for and avoid. That's what the first part of the book was about.

In the next section, we dive into how this advice finds its way to investors.

SECTION 2: MEDIA MADNESS

In section 1, we looked at bad advice—the terrible ideas spread by professionals and laymen alike that cost investors billions every year.

In this section, we consider the endless torrent of media coverage of markets, the economy, and investing. We see how bad ideas spread through the traditional mainstream and social media. I showcase the worst examples, and show how to safely navigate this dangerous mess.

The challenge is figuring out who to pay attention to and who to ignore. We give way too much credit to media—newspapers, magazines, websites, and television. In the coming chapters, I share successful strategies for figuring how who is worthy of your attention.

24/7 FINANCIAL ADVICE

THERE ARE OCCASIONS when we all flip on the TV and watch live events unfold in real time. National disasters, wars, and big sporting events are the last vestiges of the prior generation of broadcast television. In those olden days, there were only three networks, and mornings in the office led to water cooler discussions of the big broadcast last night.

Note the anachronisms in that sentence: *networks, office, water cooler, broadcast.*

As someone immersed 24/7 in the modern financial mediascape, I have an unusual perspective. Professionally, I have learned how to contextualize noisy distractions. Spend some years as a trader, and you must learn to compartmentalize your emotions. Good traders understand context and framing, seeing the nuances that lead to better decision-making. It is a skill that transfers well as you shift from trading to investing.

As a professional money manager, I never want to lose touch with how Main Street feels about what's going on in the market, especially during high-volatility sell-offs. What the non-professional sees, hears, and especially *feels* affects capital flows—and eventually, prices.

In February 2020, Mr. Market was starting to sniff out the pandemic. I have vivid recollections of my vacation, reading a book on a Caribbean beach. My connectivity was limited, I had no Bloomberg Terminal, and limited internet. I learned what was going on from Twitter and financial TV(!). That experience revealed why Mom & Pop investors have given up on Wall Street, turned off the TV, and migrated trillions of dollars to low-cost index funds.

For many, this is an easy solution to a complex problem that I believe works well (more on this later).

Imagine a cable channel dedicated to gardening. Throughout the day, you can learn about landscape architecture, hear discussions on which plants work best in what climates, learn to create compost, get advice on fertilizers, weed killers, and pesticides. Want to maintain your perennials, annuals, or topiary? Build a greenhouse? All are regular segments. It's inexpensive to produce and relaxing to watch.

The channel's website has remote webcams watching trees grow. Any day you visit the site looks more or less like the previous one. Perhaps every six or 12 months, you might notice some progress on the growth.

Then, a private equity fund buys the channel. The pastoral, ASMR-like broadcast doesn't work for the new owners. They need to attract eyeballs, sell advertising, ramp up viewership numbers. *Not enough people were tuning in*, and they want to flip the property for a profit.

So they rebrand The Gardening Channel with flashy graphics, sound effects, and sexy anchors. Artificial conflicts used to create the dynamic tension all good narratives require—AKA classic reality TV—becomes the focus.

Guests are scheduled so disagreements occur. Viewers see many different gardening approaches, including some that don't work especially well. Arguments over *the* webcam tree (*Not this one, that one!*) are plentiful; the tree was planted too deep (*No! Too shallow!*); it should be there (*No, here!*). They yell about too much or too little watering, what types of fertilizer to use, how much it should be trimmed back each season.

Instead of bucolic imagery, it's now all debates, arguments, and criticism. "Big Garden is repressing the landscape!" It has become an MMA cage match of faux disagreements about flora.

Viewership soars, despite a simple truism: Nothing that ever gets said makes a damn bit of difference to that tree. It just quietly keeps growing over time…

PART I: BAD IDEAS

What do we get from consuming 24/7 coverage of economics, markets, and investing? How does all of this "free financial advice" impact our collective psyche? Is it helping or hurting us financially? How much value do you derive from consuming endless tweets, blog posts, podcasts, YouTubes, and most perniciously, TikToks?

Here's an idea for those folks: Just STFU and let the tree grow…

———

In 2013, I was offered a gig doing a daily financial TV show; I turned it down.

Why? Because my nightly television show would have quickly run into a problem: Each evening, I would come out and say: "Own a globally diversified, low-cost portfolio of inexpensive ETFs; Rebalance every few years; See ya tomorrow!"

The problem: 59 minutes and 47 seconds of dead air.

Instead of a show, I took the opportunity to do something that I thought *would be* valuable: I convinced the nice folks at Bloomberg Radio to let me launch their first true podcast. Every week, I would have an intelligent conversation with a smart, accomplished professional and ask them questions like: "Who are you and how did you get that way? What is your investing philosophy? What can the rest of us learn from you?" I enjoy the audio format a lot, and radio requires less shaving and zero dieting.*

———

This raises a question we will address in this section: Who are you paying attention to and why? What do you get out of this endless stream of opinion? How much actual *signal* do you find buried amidst all that *noise*?

How shall we begin? Tear it all down and start over. *Lose the news.* That's what we do next…

---

* My entire team at Ritholtz Wealth Management operates this way: When investors feel knowledgeable, informed, and rational, they make fewer emotional errors.

LOSE THE NEWS

To BECOME A better investor, you need to do more than eliminate bad ideas and misinformation; you must also be aware of your emotional state.

The barrage of news is emotionally distracting.

How can you defend against that noise?

Start by recognizing how much of media is simply pontificating. When you have 24 hours a day, seven days a week to fill, and an infinite amount of internet space, you end up with a lot of filler. Mostly opinion, much no better or worse than your own. Sometimes it's right, sometimes it's wrong—at times, hilariously so (as we shall see shortly).

Read or watch whatever media you want, but for God's sake, don't base your investment decisions on it.

News is hardly new. It is backward-looking, informing you as to what has already happened. Investing is about what is *going to happen*. The recent past may be of interest, but it's not germane to your investments. By the time news gets published, it's *already in stock prices.*

But news—old or otherwise—can have an impact on your emotions. When I started out as a junior trader, I read *The Wall Street Journal* on the train home—not on the way to work. Why? It prevented the news from influencing my decision-making process during the day. Emotional headlines affect us on a subconscious level, and we are often unaware how this impacts our thinking.

"If it bleeds, it leads" was the expression decades before social media. Personal finance author Andrew Feinberg writes that to financial television producers, "Anxiety is your friend, viewer hypervigilance your bread and butter."[71] Keeping viewers "engaged by keeping them on edge, worried and confused about what might happen next" is the path to higher ratings.

PART I: BAD IDEAS

The simple fact is the majority of what the media churns out is irrelevant to your portfolio. Data points are occasionally important, but most of the time, much less so than many believe. If you are investing for retirement or generational wealth transfer decades in the future, what happened on Tuesday at 10:43 am is of little importance. Even if you find your favorite publication or financial channel entertaining, it should not be the basis of how you allocate capital, full stop.

Any "Alpha" in news flow is already being harvested by high-frequency trading hedge funds deploying big data and AI to catch short-term price movements. How can you compete with that? *You can't and shouldn't*. As my colleague Josh Brown likes to say, "The way to win against Wall Street is to not play their game."[72]

What matters more than breaking news—including SEC or FDA decisions, takeovers, litigation outcomes, earnings reports—is the *reaction* to the news. That reflects how much of that info is already priced into market expectations and stock prices.

As I discuss later on, even when events of great geopolitical significance occur, markets tend to shudder, then go back to whatever they were doing before. It is very counterintuitive.

News organizations try to appeal to lots of people, so they have the disconcerting tendency to catch various trends just as they are peaking. Neal Frankle[73] explains why media should not be the source of your investment strategy. As we shall see in the next few chapters, they can even be contrary indicators.

HOW *NOT* TO INVEST

PART I: BAD IDEAS

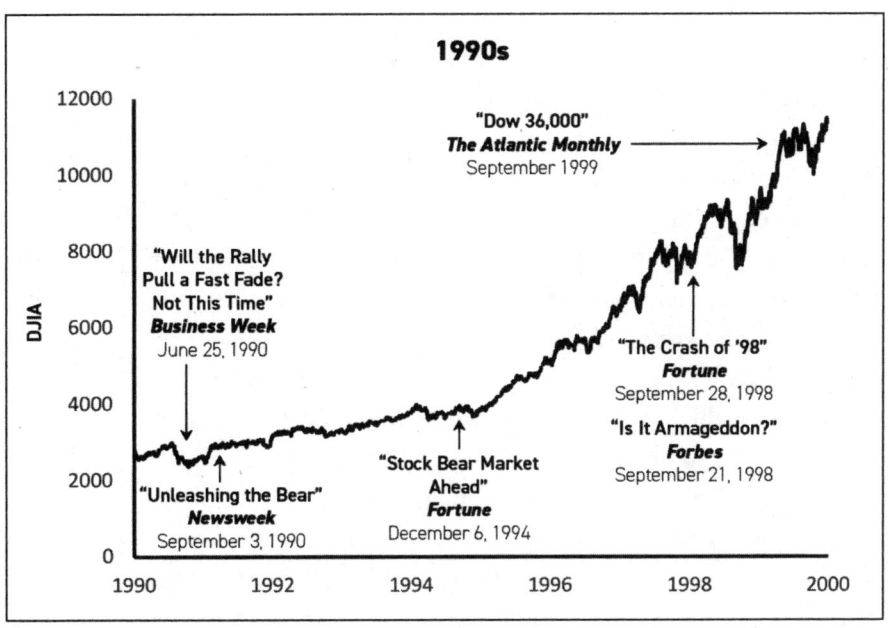

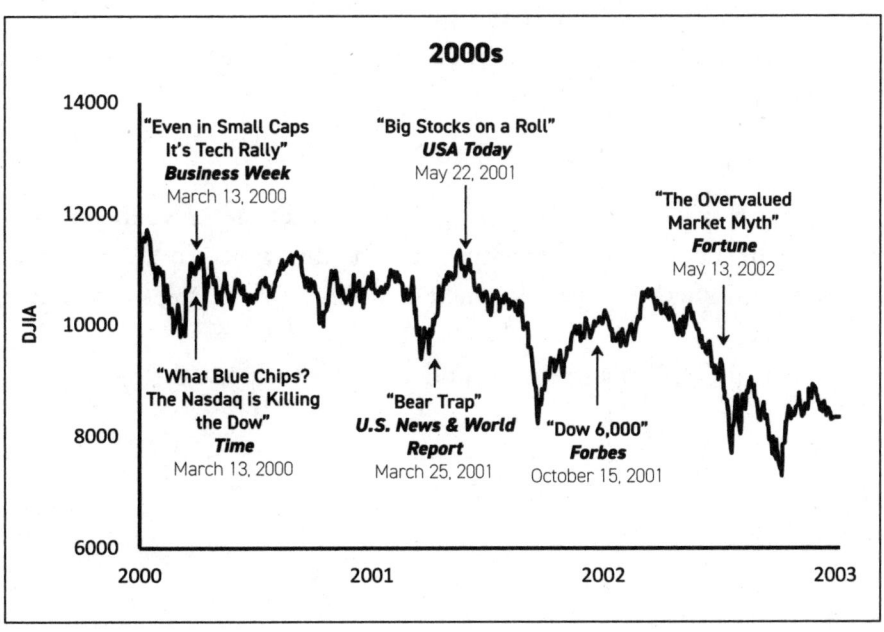

24/7 plus infinite internet leads to a focus on sensationalism. The need to "feed the beast" never ends, and quality suffers. Even subscription-driven publications have a regular schedule to fill, to justify the cost, regardless of if there is nothing new to say. Award-winning *Wall Street Journal* columnist Jason Zweig (a member of my All-Star team) brilliantly defined what he actually did: "My job is to write the exact same thing between 50 and 100 times a year in such a way that neither my editors nor my readers will ever think I am repeating myself."

I love that.

The most valuable thing I get from media is surfacing people (and their ideas) who I might not know about. I particularly like those who do not need the publicity and have no agenda, and nothing to sell.

This is where wisdom is found. Any investment giant with a spectacular track record over the long term (meaning it's skill, not luck-based) is worth hearing. I especially am interested in what I can learn from their thoughts about improving my investment process. As for the rest, savvy investors know it's just noise and entertainment.

Rethinking your news consumption and re-engineering your media diet is a worthy goal.

You might think *lose the news* is hyperbolic, but let me prove to you why listening to media recommendations can be disastrous. In the next few chapters, I'll share my favorite media stories of companies, executives, and stocks.

I suspect this will change your mind about how you use the news…

TIKTOKINVESTORS

NESTLED IN BETWEEN lip-sync dancers and fashion influencers, financial fraud lurks on TikTok.

At least one person has noticed.[74] Since August 2020, @TikTokInvestors has been curating the most outrageous money-losing videos culled from the "financial experts" on the (at the time of writing) ByteDance-owned social network.

The advice ranges from foolish to risky to criminal:

- 401ks? Dumb idea!
- Want to earn more money? Day trade at home!
- Want to turn $100 into a million? Follow my strategy earning 2% a day!
- Pay taxes? Not if you spend tax season on a boat!

No, no, no and Hell, no!

It is the Dunning-Kruger effect writ large: Inexperienced, overly confident *Finfluencers* reduce financial complexity into misleading sales pitches. No audited returns, mathematically impossible claims, and zero accountability.[75]

Sure, the mainstream media is bad, but social media is so much worse. No editors or gatekeepers, just a Wild West of grifters mixed in with everybody else. Bad financial advice reaches naïve, impressionable consumers without any guardrails or controls.

@TikTokInvestors (TTI) pointed out a few of their favorite idiotic videos from TikTok:

HOW NOT TO INVEST

That guy who thinks that 401ks are the dumbest idea ever?[76] TTI observes:

> Apart from his misleading arrogance and the inaccurate market statistics mentioned, a 401K is possibly the best investment vehicle for the average American. I doubt he's run the real numbers of being invested in the stock market tax deferred with an additional company match. Always be wary of social media influencers who use engagement bait tactics to sell a course or event.

Then there is the brilliant and simple strategy to turn $100 into a million: All you need to do is make 2% a day![77] TTI notes that:

> Turning $100 into $1mln by earning 2% daily in the market is nearly mathematically impossible. What's dangerous here is that she's well spoken, seems trustworthy, and comes across confident in her ability to do this for her clients. The reality is she can't; the majority of professional investors in the world can't even beat the S&P on an annual basis.

Some of the more absurd claims date back to the pandemic. One of my faves is a handsome couple explaining "How do we maintain our lifestyle?"[78] TTI noted:

> This was at the peak of the bull market during the pandemic and it still makes me laugh. It goes without saying that investing is not this easy; whether you're trading or investing long-term there's a variety of factors and risks to consider before putting capital to work. Assuming every stock goes up and to the right is hilariously ignorant.

There is endless bad tax advice likely to *get-you-sent-to-jail-for-tax evasion*: Live on a boat during tax season![79] (Nope); Spend $400k on a house, and the $189k depreciation offsets your taxable income[80] (LOL). It is so absurd the IRS posted a list of 46 tax avoidance claims[81] that are "frivolous." Oops.

PART I: BAD IDEAS

Two others worth mentioning: It's probably better if you do not teach your home-schooled 10-year-olds to day trade.[82] And, you gotta love this advice: Don't index, just buy the best stocks![83] (Why didn't I think of that?)

This is not remotely close to a comprehensive list, just a flavor of what's happening in the Finfluencer space.

While the government debates whether or not to ban TikTok, investors should consider making some changes on various social media consumption. A good start would be eliminating all of the terrible FinTok advice on taxes, day trading, and investing.

How reliable are the stock picks you see on magazine covers?

Let's find out…

"NO MATTER HOW YOU CUT IT, YOU'VE GOT TO OWN CISCO."

"THE FUTURE IS inherently unknown and unknowable." That is a core philosophical belief I hold dear. The world is filled with endless and often-invisible random events. These unknowns have a huge impact on what comes next, derailing even the most thoughtful predictions.

Which leads me to our first delightful cover story:

"No matter how you cut it, you've got to own Cisco."

On May 15, 2000, *Fortune* published a laudatory cover story about the networking gear maker Cisco Systems and its brilliant CEO, John Chambers.[84] The cover poses these questions about Cisco:

1. "Is John Chambers the best CEO on earth?"
2. "Is it too late to buy his stock?"

© 2000 Fortune Media IP Limited.

PART I: BAD IDEAS

Rather than cherry-picking the most egregious quotes, let's jump to the opening paragraph:

> Suppose you were stranded on a deserted island and could own just one single stock. What would it be? Think about it for a minute. Would it be a stock that's been battered this spring and is down 20% from its high? A stock that trades at more than 100 times earnings? A stock that's already climbed around 100,000% since going public ten years ago, that's already enjoyed one of the greatest rides in stock market history? The stock of a company that now faces unprecedented challenges in tough new markets dominated by the likes of Lucent and Nortel, plus a posse of red-hot upstarts?
>
> Yup, that would be the stock. *No matter how you cut it, you've got to own Cisco.* (emphasis added)

I cannot recall a magazine story more accurate in its assessment of a manager—Chambers really was a good CEO—and less accurate about the prospects for his company's stock.

At the time, Cisco was one of the most successful companies on earth. The 1990s had been good to the company, whose routers were getting snapped up by internet providers and telecoms. By the time this landed on the cover of *Fortune* on May 15, 2000, the price of Cisco was making all-time highs—and it was predicted to be the first trillion-dollar firm in history.

Only, not so much.

Cisco had *already peaked* on March 27, 2000—less than two months before the story was published. Ever since, it has been one of the poorest performers on the Nasdaq. By the time the Nasdaq bottomed in October 2002, Cisco had plummeted 89.3% from its all-time highs. It didn't quite get to a trillion either, peaking a little more than halfway there, at $556.74bn.

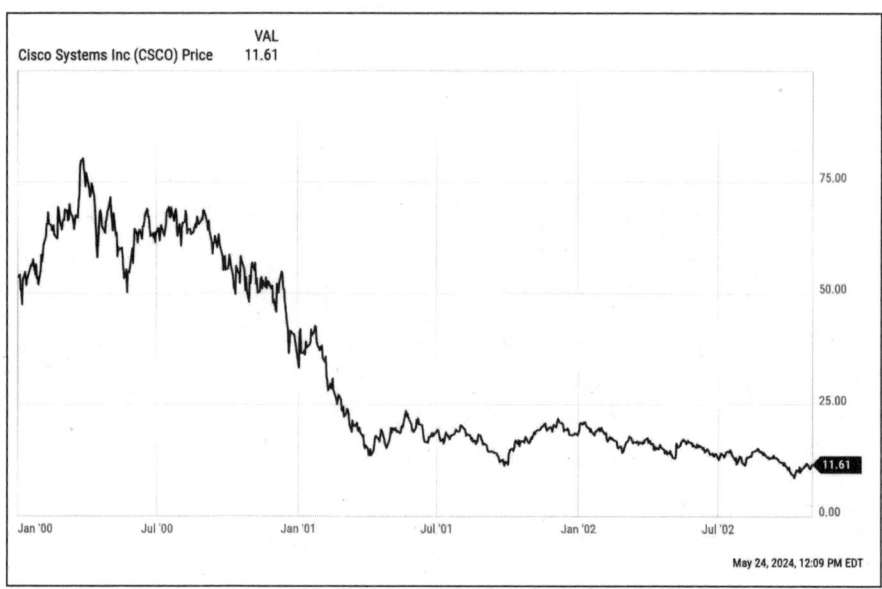

Source: YCharts.

Fortune chose Cisco over Microsoft and GE, and it did the poorest of the three. Microsoft has demolished all comers, gaining nearly 600%. GE is down nearly 30% since then, but way ahead of Cisco.

Since that 2000 cover story, the S&P 500 is up over 300%, the Nasdaq 100 gained more than 500%, and Cisco is still 20% below where it was on that date 25 years ago. It is even more remarkable that the Nasdaq 100 is up that much despite the drag its once biggest component—Cisco—had on the index's returns.

It is a stark reminder: When it comes to stock picking or predicting the future, nobody knows anything. Or to be more precise, a tiny handful of outliers have proven themselves to be consistent stock pickers over time (more on them later), but you can be sure they aren't writing cover stories for magazines.

—

I have no beef with any one stock pick, but rather, the way the media constantly makes these grand pronouncements.

The Apple Store is the most successful retailer on earth today. How do you imagine the media covered it at launch? Read on to see…

WHY THE APPLE STORE WILL FAIL...

"**S**ORRY, STEVE: HERE'S Why Apple Stores Won't Work"

> "Few outsiders think new stores, no matter how well-conceived, will get Apple back on the hot-growth path... Maybe it's time Steve Jobs stopped thinking quite so differently."
> —*BusinessWeek*, May 21, 2001

A year after *Fortune's* Cisco debacle, *BusinessWeek*[85] published a story on Apple's foray into retail stores. Not just *BusinessWeek*, but many naysayers laughed off the *inevitable failure* of Apple's push into retail.[86] Numerous armchair pontificators freely shared their uninformed opinions as to why this concept was destined to fail. "I give [Apple] two years before they're turning out the lights on a very painful and expensive mistake," predicted retail consultant David Goldstein.[87]

After all, established consumer electronics chains were all in decline, and the writing was on the wall. Gateway would soon close its retail stores (2004), and not long after, CompUSA would shutter its physical locations (2007).

Investors should always be on the alert for structural errors in media stories: Authors operating outside of their expertise; people unaware of recent developments; extrapolators extending present trends far into the future. It is an excellent reminder of exactly the kinds of errors investors should avoid. A fallible human being publishing their uninformed opinion in print should never be the basis for making any intelligent investment decision.

There are many genuinely revolutionary products and services that when they come along, change *everything*. Pick your favorite: the iPod and iPhone, Tesla Model S, Netflix streaming, Amazon Prime, AI, perhaps even Bitcoin. Radical products break the mold; their difference and unfamiliarity challenge us. We (mostly) cannot foretell the impact of true innovation. Then once it's a wild success, we have a hard time recalling how life was before that product existed.

The Apple Store was clearly one of those game-changers: By 2020, Apple had opened over 500 stores in 25 countries. They are among top-tier retailers, and the fastest ever to reach a billion dollars per year in sales. They did more in sales per square foot in 2012 than any other retailer.[88] By 2017, they were generating $5,546 per square foot in revenues, twice the dollar amount of Tiffany's, their closest competitor.[89] Apple no longer breaks out the specifics of its stores in its quarterly reports, but estimates of store revenue is about $2.4 billion *per month*.

That guy who wrote, "Sorry, Steve: Here's Why Apple Stores Won't Work," I wonder what the rest of his portfolio looks like...

Finance seems to encourage this kind of future forecasting. We are bad at this, because we often lack awareness of what we do and do not know about the limits of our expertise; we do not truly understand the present, let alone the future. We often wishfully predict what we *want* to be true, rather than what will come to be.

We look at the Dunning-Kruger effect later, but the key takeaway is most of us are not very good at *metacognition*—estimating our own skill sets. Learning what we do and don't know—working within our capabilities—that's challenging enough, without other people's bad forecasts in our heads.

If you think the Apple Store cover story was bad, just wait until you see what the media had to say about BlackBerry...

"FORGET THE IPHONE: BLACKBERRY IS STILL THE ONE TO BEAT"

How little do we know about the future? One way to figure that out is to look to our past, to see how we imagined the future would unfold.

Another example: This *Fortune* cover story,[90] lauding BlackBerry in late summer 2007, is a favorite:

> There's a lot of buzz in the smartphone business lately, with Apple's (AAPL) iPhone turning the mobile world upside down and Nokia's (NOK) upcoming phone announcement providing a new challenge. Despite all the hype, though, *Research in Motion's (RIMM) BlackBerry is still the most formidable force in U.S. smartphones.*
>
> This statement, of course, is gadget heresy. Popular opinion holds that the iPhone is today's must-have device, and none of the others stand a chance. But while the iPhone is revolutionary, it's not yet positioned to truly challenge RIM's foothold in the smartphone market. (Emphasis added.)

HOW *NOT* TO INVEST

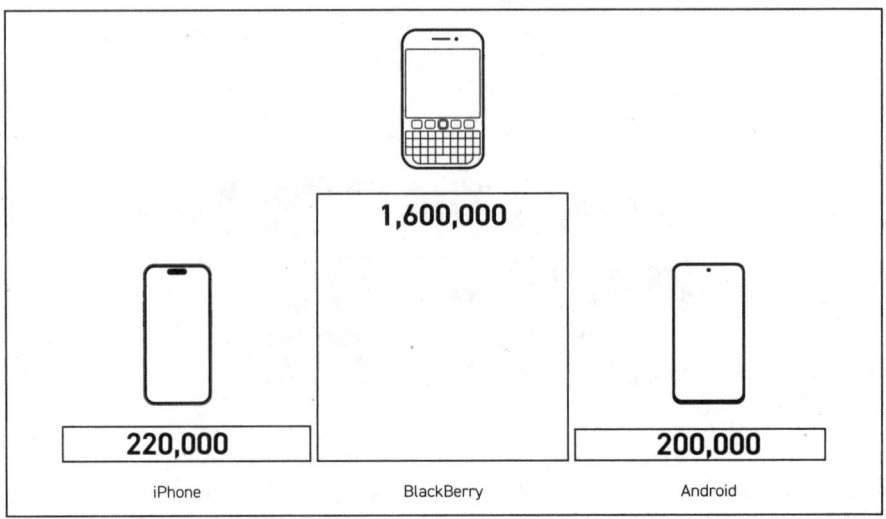

The most formidable force in smartphones?

Around the time of that cover story, RIMM's sales were $20 billion; within five years, they fell 90% to $2 billion.[91] The stock price fell 98.1% from its 2008 peak. Research in Motion changed its name to BlackBerry in 2013.

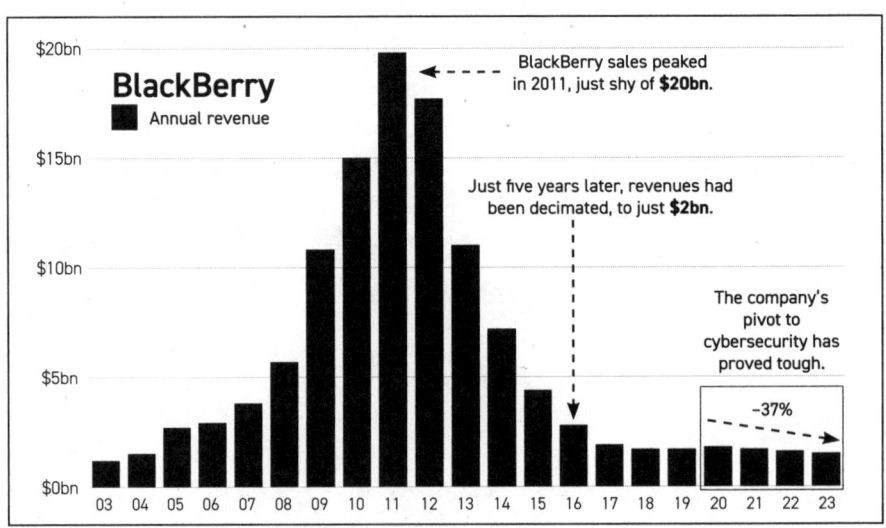

PART I: BAD IDEAS

Even two years later, *Fortune* was on the fence, still rooting for RIMM, while mostly ignoring the massive disruption *already taking place*. This 2009 cover shows how they saw this debate.

The media's tendency to treat issues like a horse race (technology and politics especially) is more than just a poor construct, it is a lazy way to cover *anything*. It lacks insight; it oversimplifies; and as you can see, it ages very poorly.

© 2009 Fortune Media IP Limited.

Investors can be wrong about lots of things, but it's much more than our batting average. Your concern should be that overconfidence will cause you trouble. Studies reveal we believe those exhibiting excess confidence much more than we should. It serves us poorly.

One last case study on magazine cover stories: Nokia. Then, we can move on to the lessons of media stock picking…

CAN ANYONE CATCH NOKIA?

IN OCTOBER 2007, Nokia's CEO Olli-Pekka Kallasvuo landed on the *Forbes* cover.[92] The then still dominant mobile phone maker was lauded with the headline: "Nokia, one billion customers—can anyone catch the cell phone king?"

Are you detecting a pattern yet...?

Apple, who had been working on a touchscreen mobile computing device for several years, would be the dethroner. In 2007, the very same year of the Nokia *Forbes* cover, Apple rolled out the iPhone; not long after, the decline of Nokia's mobile phone business began.

A mere five years later (2013), Nokia sold its entire phone business to Microsoft for about 5 billion euros.[93] What Microsoft wanted were Nokia's patents and intellectual property; Nokia's phone business was arguably worthless.

Nokia suffered the classic innovator's dilemma: Consumers were embracing phones that gave them greater mobile computing capabilities. You can almost hear the boardroom arguments: "But our handset business is so lucrative!" Unwilling to cannibalize those revenues, Nokia missed the shift toward smartphones.

From Forbes. © 2007 Forbes Media LLC. All rights reserved. Used under license. www.forbes.com

PART I: BAD IDEAS

These four stories—Cisco, Apple, BlackBerry, and Nokia—are stark reminders that investors give the media way too much credit for "knowing" the future.

The point is not that a few journalists made incorrect calls about the future of companies. The point isn't even that magazine covers are a contrary investment indicator. There are better, more useful lessons here.

What can we learn from these breathless cover stories that were so expensively incorrect?

This too, shall pass

Throughout history, companies have crashed and burned from great success. Advantages achieved may not be long-lasting; the skills that led to greatness may not be the same as what it takes to maintain those advantages. Sometimes, the world simply changes before a firm recognizes it. It's easy to assume dominant companies will remain that way. Not just BlackBerry and Nokia, but Lucent and Northern Telecom were key players in the 1990s; all soon faded. Think IBM, GE, Sears, K-Mart, GM… the list is endless. Only 12 Dow Industrial components out of 30 from 1996 remain in the average today.

Which of today's dominant companies will eventually suffer the same fate?

We fail to evaluate the content we consume

Everything you read, listen to, or watch must be analyzed for its integrity and accuracy. Every piece of information needs to be seen on its own merits and those of its author and/or publisher. Investors cannot simply accept or reject something because it's in a magazine or on television. *Never assume a source is right or wrong without knowing its track record.*

We underappreciate cycles

Trends feel like they are permanent, especially as they reach crescendos: Nokia looked unbeatable in 2007, but the seeds of its destruction were planted years prior. We have a hard time looking beyond the here and now, and this prevents us from understanding the life cycles of the economy, markets, and companies.

The future is unknowable

People don't know because *they can't know*. Anyone who pretends they know what is coming next is selling something. Instead of predicting, learn to think about the world in terms of probabilities. It is humbling, and it allows you to think more flexibly. Mistakes always occur, but you want them to be smaller and allow for corrections faster.

Change is constant

Flux is a persistent state of affairs, but we can miss incremental change over time. To repeat Paul Graham's astute observation: "We are experts in the way the world used to be."[94] This means we must constantly check our own knowledge base as it ages and decays over time.

This occurs regularly: Grand pronouncements about why a new service or product will be awesome or will fail miserably; forecasts about what companies are destined for greatness, about what will or won't happen. Our own priors are so hard-wired that it's easy to miss when something—or *everything*—has changed.

Recognizing how little you know is a superpower. If we were less certain of ourselves and had more humility, we would all be better investors.

As wrong as the stories about Cisco, Apple, BlackBerry, and Nokia were, magazine covers are actually an inconsistent indicator and you can't always assume they're wrong. Let's look at that now.

WHAT DO MAGAZINE COVERS TELL US?

A 2017 *BARRON'S COVER* story[95] featured Apple's extravagant new $5 billion HQ. The headline: "Apple to Hit $1 Trillion in Market Value in 2018." The knee-jerk response from too many traders was: "That's it, Apple is over," and "Sell!"

Whether through insight or luck, *Barron's* had it right, and by August 2018 Apple crossed the trillion-dollar mark. Five years later, Apple had tripled its market valuation to $3 trillion.

Perhaps those traders learned the wrong lessons from those prior cover stories. You cannot assume every magazine cover is a reliable contrary indicator. I cherry-picked all of the most egregious ones in prior chapters as examples.

Let's delve into the work of Paul Macrae Montgomery. He created the magazine cover indicator, observing that some investment trends reach their crescendos on the covers of print magazines.*

Montgomery had three rules for the classic cover indicator:

1. It must be a mainstream publication, not a business/financial periodical;
2. It should be on a popular investing fad;

---

* Originally called the *Time* Magazine Cover Indicator, it somehow found its way to include any national non-business magazines and newspapers. Long before behavioral economics became popular, Montgomery argued that standard economic theories "overlooked the human factor in markets." Although best known as the Magazine Cover Indicator originator, he was also the creator of the famous Hemline Indicator of the Stock Market, which tracked dress or skirt length. The theory was that skirt lengths get shorter in good economic times (1920s, 1960s) and longer in somber times (1930s depression, the 1970s).

HOW *NOT* TO INVEST

3. A significant run-up in asset price must have led up to the cover.

As his theory goes, by the time some hot investing trend has made its way to the editors of *Time* magazine, it's all over but the crying.

There are lots of examples of how often this was true. In 2005, *Time* gave top billing to housing. Home prices soon topped and what came next was the worst recession since the Great Depression, led by a 32% crash in home prices.

Time named Amazon.com chief Jeff Bezos as Person of the Year in December 1999; that was weeks from the top of the dotcom bubble (Q1 2000). And *Time's* editors did not do Mark Zuckerberg and Facebook shareholders any favors by bestowing the same honorific on him in 2010. Soon after, its IPO was a flop, and the stock did not recover until the firm finally figured out mobile, years later.

From TIME. © 2005 TIME USA LLC. All rights reserved. Used under license. www.time.com

Before you start selling shares of companies that end up on covers, you should know that the indicator isn't applicable to individual firms. Apple is a favorite example—it's been on 100s of magazine covers since 1981. If you used any of those as a sell signal, you left a lot of money on the table...

That is the problem with magazine covers—or TikToks, tweets, YouTube videos, online news, TV segments, or whatever you are using to track investor sentiment. Examples tend to be cherry-picked to agree with what we already believe. Confirmation bias fools us into seeing a signal where there usually is none.

Identifying broad societal changes in sentiment is never easy. It is becoming even harder as national and print media fade. Partisanship and content balkanization means Americans no longer live in one nation—we live in millions of self-created bias bubbles.

PART I: BAD IDEAS

Historically, sentiment readings were useful when they reached extremes. Now, reading sentiment has become even harder to figure out.

———

We too easily overlook the emotions, opinions, and biases in media. Even after readers identify these errors, they often ignore it. Let's look at this issue more closely.

GELL-MANN AMNESIA

MICHAEL CRICHTON EARNED his M.D. from Harvard Medical School—but he never practiced medicine. Instead, he wrote novels and screenplays. His first book was *The Andromeda Strain* in 1969, which became a movie in 1971. He wrote (and occasionally directed) other famous works, notably *Westworld* (1973), *Coma* (1978), *Jurassic Park* (1990), *Rising Sun* (1992), and *The Lost World* (1995). He was also the creator of the long-running television series *ER* (1994–2009).

In addition to being a brilliant writer, Crichton was also an astute observer of the world. His unique place in the entertainment food-chain as an author/director gave him sharp insights into mass media. He was particularly disturbed by the penchant for rank opinion mongering.

In a 2002 speech titled "Why Speculate?"[96] Crichton observed:

> Everybody knows that *Hardball*, *The O'Relly Factor*, and similar shows are nothing but a steady stream of guesses about the future. The Sunday morning talk shows are pure speculation... But speculation is every bit as rampant in the so-called serious media, such as newspapers.

Today's media issues were visible to an insightful observer over two decades ago. Crichton's focus on "totally undeserved media credibility" fits squarely with what investors need to understand about the media they consume.

I find the affect he calls "Gell-Mann Amnesia" disturbing:

> You open the newspaper to an article on some subject you know well. You read the article and see the journalist has absolutely no understanding of either the facts or the issues. Often, the article is

PART I: BAD IDEAS

so wrong it actually presents the story backward—reversing cause and effect. I call these the *wet streets cause rain* stories. Papers are full of them.

In any case, you read with exasperation or amusement the multiple errors in a story—and then turn the page to national or international affairs, and read with renewed interest as if the rest of the newspaper was somehow more accurate about far-off Palestine than it was about the story you just read. You turn the page, and forget what you know.

That is the most damning indictment of speculatory stories, opinion pieces, and general nonsense that passes for journalism you will ever read.

"If somebody consistently exaggerates or lies to you," Crichton continues, you soon stop believing anything they say. Referencing the legal doctrine "*falsus in uno, falsus in omnibus*"—translation: "Untruthful in one part, untruthful in all"—he observes that "we do not apply the same standard to "movies, television, internet, books, newspapers, and magazines."

We obviously should.

—

Next, we apply Crichton's standard to the media, and see how the daily headlines age. Spoiler alert: *Not well.*

HOW NEWS LOOKS WHEN IT'S OLD

EACH YEAR, BIRINYI Associates, the research shop founded by the late Laszlo Birinyi, tracks the most influential media stories and publishes them in a single bound volume.

Scrolling through media stories months later is jarring. Not because the journalists got it wrong—for the most part, they are accurate. But what stands out months or years later is the tone, and how *wildly emotional* it is. With the benefit of time, you see just how *sensationalism* gets embedded in coverage.

Once we know how a story ends—wars, pandemics, takeovers, economic news, legislation, and most of all, market action—the dynamic tension of "What happens next?" is removed. What remains is the panicky zeitgeist of the day.

If you consume news, you must recognize how much infectious sentiment is within the content all along. We learn to our detriment that these passions, overlooked in real time, can be what influences us the most.

Consider Covid-era columns about markets from 2020–21—they have not aged well. Stories you will recall as deeply concerning—back when we all thought washing off our groceries would keep us alive—turn out to be little more than trite speculation. What felt so weighty at the time appears, with the benefit of hindsight, meaningless.

After the zeitgeist passes, all that remains are shrieking headlines. Is it any wonder that investors get distracted or misled?

PART I: BAD IDEAS

Consider these three examples:

Investors Fear the Worst is Yet to Come

On March 23, 2020 the *Wall Street Journal* print edition featured the headline: "Investors Fear the Worst is Yet to Come."[97] The online headline was even better: "The Worst of the Global Selloff Isn't Here Yet, Banks and Investors Warn." That was *chef's kiss* within a day of the exact market bottom, and just as a 69% rally was about to begin.

A Very Contradictory Stock Market Rally

On April 21, 2020 the *New York Times* saw "A Very Contradictory Stock Market Rally" relative to the economy, which meant that lots of people were overlooking a giant opportunity.[98] Once again, the online headline was even more emotional: "Can Investors Trust the Stock Market Rally?"

Global fund managers warn bull run is doomed without coronavirus vaccine

Last, consider the *Financial Times* piece from May 20, 2020: "Global fund managers warn bull run is doomed without coronavirus vaccine."[99] Perhaps the bull market was anticipating a vaccine? This is, as Crichton suggested, "wet streets causing rain."

Note that *none of these stories were factually incorrect*; all of them accurately reported the news of the day. But that does not mean they are not contributing to the angst that so often leads people astray.

Solution: Whenever you read a scary headline, ask yourself these questions:

1. Is this resonating on an emotional or logical level?
2. How might this story look one month from now? A few years from now?
3. How much of this "News" is already reflected in stock prices?

Those questions will hopefully lead you to the appropriate perspective.

———

Next, we discuss ways to reduce the distractions and noise levels, allowing you to focus on what really matters—your investment process. How to separate the media noise from the signal.

SIGNAL-TO-NOISE RATIO

THE SIGNAL-TO-NOISE RATIO is an engineering concept that focuses on the amount of useful information relative to false or useless data. This is an especially important concept for investors.

I constantly seek to reduce noise from my investing process. You should, too. We want less of the annoying nonsense that interferes with our thought process (and our portfolios), and more of the significant information that allows us to make good decisions.

Your goal: Become a less distracted, more purposeful investor.

This is an ongoing refinement process. Finding moments of quiet contemplation that allow me to think things through is an important aspect of my work. Uninterrupted time with no distractions—what some psychologists call "deep work"—is increasingly rare and all the more important for that reason. And I don't mean just quiet time in front of your computer screen—any activity that can get you out of your routine and provides an opening for deep thought (walking, hiking, yoga, even meditation) will help.

As a young trader, I would awaken at dawn when the house was quiet, and sketch out my thoughts on what was happening in the market/economy.* Articulating my perspective by writing was an enormous aid to my understanding. But it's mostly an editing process—I spend much of this quiet time deciding what is *not* worthwhile.

This is... liberating.

We are all distracted by minutiae. Most daily inputs—news, company releases, economic data, punditry—turn out to be distracting irrelevancies

---

* These show up as "Ritholtz Reads" on my site, The Big Picture at ritholtz.com

that do not affect our long-term portfolios. What is left after you remove these is almost all signal, no noise.

It is not an easy thing to do. Removing the noise is a fight against our most ingrained habits.

As a thought experiment, imagine what would happen if you purposefully inverted this idea—what if you tried to assemble a how-to list in pursuit of the exact opposite—getting *more noise* and *less signal?* In other words, what are exactly the *wrong* things to do as a media-consuming investor?

Warning: *You may recognize yourself in a few of these.*

How to get more noise and less signal

1. **Constantly consume mainstream media.** Financial television is an excellent source of actionable trading ideas.
2. **Play down data.** It's overrated. Stick with anecdotes and your own gut instincts.
3. **Pay attention to pundits.** They exist for the sole purpose of helping you reach a comfortable retirement.
4. **Get the inside dope.** All important information about the stock market—especially when it is going to crash or rally—is known only to a handful of secret insiders. Buy the newsletters that promise to share this inside info!
5. **Stress about *this*.** Exert lots of energy, spend lots of time, create lots of tension about the following: Federal Reserve and rates, AI, dollar versus euro, Gaza, Congress, Nvidia, hyperinflation, Ukraine, Tesla, European Sovereign Bank debt, gold, China, deflation, Bitcoin, commodities, and the Hindenburg Omen.
6. **Don't do the math.** Numbers are vastly overrated, and probability analysis is for geeks anyway.
7. **Stay in your bubble.** Focus only on those news sources that are in sync with your politics. Seek out sources that confirm your pre-existing opinions and investment postures. Never read anything that challenges your beliefs.

PART I: BAD IDEAS

8. **Think fast.** Trading is where the big money is made! Don't worry about the long term—it's way off in the future. Measure your success in hours and minutes, not years and decades.

9. **Super Happy Fun Time.** There is no reason that you cannot also have a good time trading meme stocks in your retirement account: It's tax-deferred, so you have no capital gains consequences. Have fun with it—that's what it's there for anyway!

10. **Ask: What have you done for me lately?** Never listen to people with good long-term track records who may have hit a rough patch. When Warren Buffett underperformed in 1999, you should have written him off. Investing performance of the most recent quarter, or even better month, is all that matters!!

Can you recognize any of your own bad behaviors hidden in the sarcasm? These are the recipe for lots of noise and very little signal. Ask yourself: How much noise do I have in my investing process?

Given what we have learned, perhaps it is time we reengineer our media diet. That is what we do in the next chapter.

USE THE NEWS: REENGINEER YOUR MEDIA DIET

LET'S REDUCE THE *noise* in your daily information diet, and help you become a less distracted, more purposeful investor. Or as Ian Cassel phrased it: "The maturation of every investor starts with absorbing almost everything and ends with filtering almost everything."[100]

Addition by subtraction is where we cut out emotional, speculative nonsense. We lose huge swaths of opinion masquerading as analysis, and drop prediction-driven hype.

Media, used intelligently, can add value to your process.

Here's how.

Hold pundits accountable

The lack of accountability in financial media is detestable. All sorts of nonsense gets yelled without penalty. TV guests are rarely called out for their terrible calls or money-losing stock picks. Columnists can (and do) say anything, without fear of readers remembering their worst stuff (except for a few of us geeks).

I use a calendar to hold talking heads accountable. Someone makes a wild claim or prediction, I *diary* it. Any calendar (Google, Apple Cal, MS Outlook) will work. I also like a simple app called FollowUpThen (followupthen.com). Years later, I find out how much (or more likely how little) attention to pay these folk. I continually cull the money losers.

PART I: BAD IDEAS

Create your own media research team

I have a small group of favorites I think of as my personal all-star research team. I subscribe to their Substacks and Twitter feeds, and read most of what they publish.

My shortlist includes **Bill McBride** (Calculated Risk) who reduces economics and housing to its simplest essence; **Sam Ro** understands what drives markets better than most on Wall Street. **Torsten Slok**'s charts are thought-provoking and insightful. Nobody integrates data with investing narrative better than my colleague **Ben Carlson**. I devour all of **Morgan Housel**'s columns for their insight and smarts; **Claudia Sahm** for all things Fed related; few people can help you understand bad investing behavior better than **Jason Zweig** of the *Wall Street Journal*. **Dave Nadig** is my ETF ZenMaster, **Jonathan Miller**, my housing wizard. **Ed Hyman** is the best economist ever. I'll stop at 10, but there are many others.

Create your own list of those whose methods, analytics and track records add value. Remember, this is a process of elimination; and accountability (our *prior* bullet point) keeps your list small.

Focus your financial television consumption

Truth be told, most financial television is boring. People pontificating about *whatever* is not entertaining.

Why is that? FinTV is essentially *televised radio*. It lacks compelling visuals, and so there is massive over-compensation. The lack of visuals also drives manufactured conflict—the pseudo bull/bear debates that a producer told me makes for "compelling TV." (Bleccch.)

YouTube lets me cherry-pick the best of financial television: **Tom Keene** of Bloomberg Surveillance; on CNBC, my colleague **Josh Brown** is so insightful and witty that he makes anything fun to watch. UBS Floor Manager **Art Cashin**'s comments from the NYSE floor is must-see TV.

You will hear more wisdom in 30 seconds from Cashin than any other 10 pundits combined. On Bloomberg TV, **David Rubenstein** hosts amazing conversations. **Consuelo Mack**'s web show, WealthTrack, slows it down with in-depth interviews with investing legends. She is a modern-day **Louis Rukeyser**.

If you must watch TV, make it appointment viewing on YouTube. Focus on those folks worthy of your time, and not hours of sound effects, countdown clocks, and filler.

Learn! Become a better investor

Anything that teaches you how to improve should be on your shortlist of media consumption. Content that focuses on your process, on understanding your behavior, and on creating context is worth considering.

Skip the stock picking, the opinion-mongers, and the forecasters. It's worthless nonsense. Focus on those in the media who are teachers, who can share their experience and hard-won expertise. You are better off being taught how to fish, rather than being given a fish.

I keep my media consumption consistent with my desire to better understand the world I live in. This means saving my limited attention span for the good stuff. You should, too.

So far, we have seen lots of bad advice, and looked at how it spreads. But where does it come from? Read on to find out…

SECTION 3:
SOPHISTRY: THE STUDY OF BAD IDEAS

SOPHISTRY: The use of fallacious arguments, especially with the intention of deceiving; subtly deceptive reasoning or argumentation.

In this section we look at where bad ideas come from, the forms in which they persist, and how good investors think about ideas.

DEFINING INVESTING: THE STUDY OF HUMAN DECISION-MAKING

WHAT IS INVESTING?
This is a subtler question than you might imagine, one that should not be dismissed lightly. Many finance professionals find it to be one of the more challenging problems they encounter.

Over the years, I have refined my own definition to this:

> Investing is the art of using imperfect information to make probabilistic assessments about an inherently unknowable future.

Take apart my definition and you learn there is a lot of nuance packed into those 17 words.

- *"Art"* refers to the fact that this is not a science, and there is no single optimal solution for everybody.
- *"Imperfect information"* refers to the fact that the information we have is dynamic, incomplete, often confusing, and frequently wrong. No one can know all there is to know at any given moment.
- *"Probabilistic"* recognizes there are many possible outcomes; investors need to plan not just for the ones they hope for but other contingencies as well.
- *"Inherently unknowable"* is a humble acknowledgment of how little we know about the future. Most of the time, we do not—and cannot—know what comes next. This should be reflected in how we manage risk and allocate capital.

- *"Future"* demands optimism. Pessimists have been on the losing side of the trade for all of human history. Setbacks like the dotcom implosion, the GFC and the Covid-19 pandemic were temporary. Pessimism is a bet against human ingenuity, and for half a million years, that has been a losing wager.

Rather than define investing as the science of generating a return on capital, I prefer to consider our *behavior* when we interact with money; how financial desire impacts our decision-making abilities; what risks we embrace, how we think about wealth, and what emotional pain we willingly suffer in order to generate a return on capital.

Every study of *behavior* looks at how we solve problems. If this entire endeavor is a problem-solving exercise, then for us to become better investors, we must learn how to make better decisions.

I have learned that the skills needed to be a better investor—to be "less stupid"—are similar to the skills and judgment we need to make better decisions in so many other areas. This affects every aspect of your life—who your spouse is, how successful your career will be, your healthcare outcomes, even how fulfilling your relationships are. Good decision-making leads to increased happiness, greater life satisfaction, and perhaps even becoming the best person you can be.

Too much woo? I am not suggesting that you have to be a great investor in order to have a good life; rather, I want you to think about the skill sets that go into investing and how transferable they are to so much of what you do outside of the world of money.

—

The more you contemplate it, the more you realize investing is a massive problem-solving exercise. The best at it are intellectually flexible; they approach their craft as a discipline, and focus on process. They understand *probability theory* and view mistakes as learning opportunities. They use mental models and engage in second-order thinking; they use counterfactuals; they have good information hygiene. They possess a high level of self-awareness regarding their own psychological states. They know they have blind spots and are aware they *don't know what they don't know*.

PART I: BAD IDEAS

The process by which you make decisions is worth examining. Whether we are thinking about important milestones in life or our asset allocation, we cannot let our decision-making run on its default setting.

—

Our definition of investing depends on recognizing what we do and don't know about the future. We want to make better decisions that will withstand *whatever* might occur. To do that, we need to ask ourselves what we believe and why. That is what we do next.

WHAT DO YOU BELIEVE? WHY?

ONE OF THE most important aspects of becoming a good investor is creating a model of the world around you. To do this, you must have the ability to make sense of incomplete and sometimes contradictory information.

This is not easy. It is often counterintuitive.

What seems like an obvious market-moving data point or piece of news is very often *already* reflected in prices. If I know this thing—because I found it through public sources—doesn't everybody else already know it too? Well-known and widely understood information is almost always already reflected in market prices.

This is the key difference between investing and other pursuits, like politics, sports, or religion: The feedback loop in markets for mistakes is so much faster than anything else. If your fundamental belief system is wrong, if you rely on "facts" that turn out to be false, you typically find out sooner rather than later. These errors are *expensive,* too. If your fundamental beliefs are wrong, it will show up in your portfolio's performance.

If you want to make fewer money mistakes and develop the right thought process for successful investing, ask yourself, "Why do I need to have an opinion on everything?" Why can't we admit where we are ignorant and move on from there?

That is how a good investor thinks about the world.

"I don't know" is a very powerful tool that will help keep you out of trouble a lot, if only you have enough courage to say it. As we see later on, the fear of saying "I don't know" can lead to very costly errors.

Regardless of your hot take on pandemics, or presidential immunity or the Middle East, there is not a whole lot you can do about it. But notice

PART I: BAD IDEAS

how people talk about these topics. Most of the people I see discussing these issues—especially on social media—are not epidemiologists, constitutional scholars, or foreign policy experts. Most have spent less than 30 minutes *boning up* on these topics. The media makes coverage of events like these all-consuming, and so we are fooled into believing we have anything more than a superficial understanding of the subjects. People's thought processes go off the rails when they forget about what they do and don't know. Especially when their process is such that it's likely they *can't* possibly know.

All good investors must constantly ask themselves these questions: *What do I know? What do I believe in, and why? How can I tell when I am wrong? What will I do about it?*

I am constantly trying to refine how I think about investing, and that has evolved over the decades. One of the best things about being the host of Bloomberg's Masters in Business show is every week, I sit down for an hour or two with the most successful investors in history to discuss their thinking processes. It's deeply revealing and informative.

The great public debates over the past few years have been instructive as to how to *think about thinking*: Vaccine skepticism, January 6 attacks, inflation, the debt ceiling, even the flat-earther stuff. Close scrutiny reveals people's thought processes, and where they can go awry.

———

You might be surprised to learn that I believe the three most important words in investing are, "I don't know." *Not saying* those three words has cost investors billions. Read on to see why.

ON THE VALUE OF NOT KNOWING

I WANT TO DISCUSS my ignorance. Or rather, my justifiable pride in saying, "I don't know." I use this phrase frequently, as there is a wealth of subjects I know very, very little about.

Sometimes I am asked things I could not possibly know—particularly about the future. Rather than guess, I believe the best approach is to admit the truth and plan accordingly. The alternative is to do what too many people do: **Make predictions, then marry those forecasts**. This usually leads to catastrophic results. It's a classic avoidable error.

Understanding what it is *I do not know* is a core part of my approach to the world. It's why I focus so much on investor psychology and cognitive issues. I want to understand what I don't know, and when my brain is lying to me. My experience has found this approach to be rewarding.

Unfortunately, this is not a standard operating procedure in many fields. Perhaps we might blame this failure to admit ignorance on an excess of testing in schools. Maybe that's the reason—but maybe not—*I do not know*.

In the world of investing, recognizing what you do not know and therefore should not be betting on is paramount. It is an important trait for any investor to have. Too many people assume they are making decisions based on what they know, but oftentimes their decisions are based on what they think they know but really don't.

I am not trying to be cagey or contrarian for its own sake—although I will admit to a dollop of mischievous joy when a TV anchor asks me where prices will be in the future:

Q: "Where is the Dow going to be one year from now?"
A: "I have no idea."
Q: (*Twitch*)

PART I: BAD IDEAS

Everyone who answers that question with anything other than "I don't know" is lying. They CANNOT know, and even worse, they are often unaware of their own ignorance (more on this in our discussions on the Dunning-Kruger effect later). Perhaps worst of all, they mislead the viewer into thinking that they, the expert, does know, and that you, the home viewer, does not ... and therefore, you should *BUY MY PRODUCT*.

That twitch is not why I answer the way I do (though it is amusing). Rather, it is the proper answer—a reflection of accepting a simple reality denied by most people in finance.

There are tremendous advantages in recognizing what you do not know. Acknowledging shortcomings in your informational intelligence is a form of *situational awareness* that prevents you from being blindsided.

There are other benefits as well. It shifts your focus to *process over outcome*; you can better understand what results come from *skill* versus dumb *luck*. It prevents you from being *fooled by randomness*. And as history constantly informs us, repeatable results that are the result of a process are vastly superior to lucky but random outcomes.

This is a valuable trait, a reflection of a more insightful set of perspectives than you might realize. I once had a branding expert tell me (more or less), "You moved into the niche market of 'Truth' because the larger firms abandoned it for more lucrative fields."

I doubt that—the genesis of my approach was not marketing schtick. It was a simple acknowledgment of reality, which leads to smarter planning and better outcomes. It might be more challenging to sell to people— it ain't slick, does not lend itself to glossy brochures, and is hard to put in a tagline.

But it works. Want to be a better investor? Ask yourself what you don't know.

Knowing what you don't know is important, because salespeople use the nervousness around it to sell their wares. We will soon see how saying "I don't know" can help you save millions by avoiding disastrous financial products.

LEARNING TO SAY "I DON'T KNOW"

I NEVER UNDERSTOOD WHAT was going on at Theranos, the Silicon Valley tech company that was going to do a full set of blood tests without having to draw blood from a vein. I never had a clue.

At the time, very few were willing to admit this. An expensive and recurring problem in the technology and investment communities is the simple inability to say those three words, "I don't know."

Folks who *claimed* to understand the company and its founder—putting lots of capital at risk and giving the start-up a multibillion-dollar valuation—didn't have a clue either. The venture capitalists who funded this unicorn were unable to admit this. Their bravado created a costly blind spot.

The backstory: A biotech start-up whose young founder was afraid of needles drops out of Stanford at age 19 to commercialize a blood test that relies on a finger prick instead of the dreaded needle to draw blood from a vein. Accolades follow, and soon after, Elizabeth Holmes becomes the youngest person ever to win the Horatio Alger Award.[101] Despite her lack of medical or scientific training, she is appointed to the board of fellows at Harvard Medical School(!). *Time* magazine names her one of the world's 100 most influential people. *INC* magazine makes her its October 2015 cover,[102] calling her "The Next Steve Jobs." Theranos is valued, however briefly, at $9 billion, and she becomes the youngest self-made female billionaire in the world.

Given all we know now, how was it possible that so few people and organizations behind these awards, fellowships, and venture capital funding did the due diligence to check out the story? Many were relying on *the next guy's work* when evaluating the start-up and its founder. But how did *everyone* else rely on others' validation?

PART I: BAD IDEAS

It's worse: There was one group of investors who passed on Theranos—the medical and biotech venture firms. But even that didn't dissuade those who believed the story.

How in the post-Madoff era could an entire company built on nonsense so easily slip through the cracks? One theory: Theranos' crash and burn was a function of our own insecurities. The thesis is based on this simple formula:

> new technology + venture-capitalist claims of expertise = no one willing to admit they don't understand what's going on

The unwillingness to admit "I don't know" cost these investors billions of dollars.

Venture capital seeks to invest in the products of tomorrow, services that very often do not yet exist. Skillful VCs have some ideas about where markets and demand could be a few years out, and (*cliché alert*) they skate to where the puck *might* be.

But it is a very different thing to make a wager about one possible future—which by design is highly likely to fail—versus outright fraud. Building out an idea that does not find a market is quite different from lying about a medical product that simply cannot do what you claim (it never could) and, as the medical VCs realized, had no basis in reality.

Modern technology moves so fast that no one can possibly keep up with it all.* This includes professors at Harvard, investors in Silicon Valley, and everyone geographically and technically in between. A venture investor can specialize, but that limits their ability to find and fund deals. Any area can be hot for a while, then cool off, so being a generalist is a preferred strategy.

Successful venture investors cultivate an air of not only understanding new technology, but knowing where it is going in the future. That kind of reputation is handy to have. Whether it reflects reality is almost beside the

---

* Consider all the different tech sectors and subsectors: Biotech, telecom, graphene and nanotech, software, autonomous vehicles, 3-D printing, materials sciences, genomics, robotics, networking, semiconductors, drones, synthetic biology, quantum computing, automation, AI, big data, and cloud computing.

point; what's important is that founders, bankers, employees, and the tech press believe it.

We saw this before with Enron. When the company was riding high, its chief executive officer, Jeffrey Skilling, used to berate analysts who questioned the company's business model, telling them they were "too stupid to get it."[103] That was before we learned it was a giant accounting fraud. The same was true of Bernie Madoff, whose multibillion-dollar Ponzi scheme relied on people not understanding it. Both firms took advantage of our fear of looking stupid in front of our peers.

The lesson here is that when people are too embarrassed to say, "I don't understand this" or "Explain this to me," bad things happen.

Saying "I don't know" is a superpower. It reflects a quiet self-confidence in your own intellect. Anybody who hides their methodology or berates an investor who says, "I don't understand this," is unworthy of your capital.

Unwillingness to admit error is a consistent problem for investors—and everyone else. A simple rule for avoiding mistakes is "If you don't understand it, don't invest in it." That is how "I don't know" could have saved those investors billions.

—

Admitting our own ignorance about investments and technologies is a crucial part of being a good steward of capital. There is a heavy cost to be paid for holding on to false belief systems. Let's look at some of the bad ideas that never seem to go away.

WHEN BAD IDEAS DON'T DIE

WHY DO ZOMBIE ideas exist? These myths, memes, and disproven theories hold sway long after they should have been dead and buried. Why do investors embrace the terrible, fall in love with the wrong, bet money on the fictitious?

Nowhere is this a bigger problem than in the field of economics. A long list of debunked ideas continues to have a vice grip on amateur and professional investors alike.

Here are a few bad ideas that refuse to die.

Gurus, shamans, and prognosticators

People love experts to tell us what is going to happen in the future. Never mind that their forecasting track record is awful, we prefer the mysticism of the television guru to our own actual thinking.

Here is something that should give you pause: The more confident an expert sounds on TV, the more likely he is to be believed by viewers. And the more self-confident they seem, the worse their track record likely is. Forecasters who got one big outlier correct are more likely to make bolder predictions in the future that tend to be wrong.

Shareholder value

This 1970s theory claimed corporate management should concentrate primarily on increasing share prices. We have since learned its problems: Short-term focus on quarterly earnings that leads to a decline in long-term research and development (R&D), typically to the detriment of a company's long-term prospects. Short-termism and stock-option compensation causes management to focus on immediate quarterly returns. It has also led to earnings management, accounting fraud, and a raft of related scandals.

Long-term share owners—not the insiders cashing out—derive much less value than the name "shareholder value" implies.

Homo Economicus

A key principle underlying classical economics states that people are rational, self-interested actors possessing an ability to make objective, intelligent judgments about money. *This is frequently wrong, and occasionally hilariously so.*

We are all too often irrational, emotional creatures who regularly engage in behaviors that work against our self-interest. We evolved to adapt on the savanna, not make smart decisions in the midst of a market sell-off. *Homo Economicus*? More like *Economicus Neanderthal*…

Economics as a science

Economists sure seem to get a lot wrong: They misunderstood the risks of derivatives (mostly because they failed to recognize it was an unreserved insurance product). Heading into the financial crisis, their models stated home prices never fall(!). They missed the worst recession since the Great Depression even as we were in the middle of it. They misunderstood why the recovery from the GFC was so weak. In the 2020s, they misunderstood the inflation surge and subsequent collapse.

All this before we even get to their lack of forecasting acumen.

Markets self-regulate

Another example of an idea that started out reasonably enough but soon after went off the rails. After 30 years of post-war economic growth, there was a credible argument that government regulations had become too costly, time-consuming, and complex. With inefficiencies holding back small businesses, paring the worst of the regulatory burden should prove productive.

A good idea taken to an illogical extreme becomes a bad one. Zealots such as Sen. Phil Gramm (R-Tex.) argued *against all regulations*. Radical deregulation was one of several bad ideas that led to the crash of AIG, Lehman Brothers, Countrywide, Merrill Lynch, and many others.[104] Soon after Lehman collapsed in September 2008, Nobel Prize-winning economist Paul Samuelson observed, "Deregulated capitalism is a fragile flower bound to commit suicide."

Supply-side economics (e.g., tax cuts pay for themselves)

Another bad idea that started well. When tax rates are confiscatory—think of rates at 75% to 90%—reducing them changes behavior for the better. Otherwise, rates that high lead to tax avoidance strategies. We run into trouble when this concept is extrapolated to infinity. The claim that all tax cuts pay for themselves via greater economic activity has been thoroughly debunked.

Austerity

Conceived from Puritanism: We must pay penance for our sins, including a robust economy. The Austerians insist that spending cuts and tax increases will cure a post-bubble economy AND produce a balanced budget. When the United States tried this in 1938, it helped send the nation back into recession. In the 2010s, Greece was forced to adopt austerity measures as part of its financial-rescue terms. It pushed the country into a depression. Austerity measures in Britain and Ireland and Spain—indeed, everywhere they were imposed in Europe—all led to recessions. Despite the wealth of evidence showing that this is a terrible idea, it refuses to die.

These zombie ideas are a staple of academia, economics, and investing, and continue to exist long past their sell-by dates. No matter how outlandish, once these ideas find an audience, it takes a long while for them to go away.

Recall what Max Planck, who won the Nobel Prize in 1918 for originating quantum theory, famously observed: "Truth never triumphs—its opponents just die out. Science advances one funeral at a time."

We are all too easily ensnared by bad ideas. Before we dive deeper into the "why," let's consider how we can shift our perspectives on this sophistry.

SHIFT YOUR PERSPECTIVE

WE RARELY QUESTION our own ideas. We fail to understand from first principles why we think the things we do.

A way to avoid bad ideas is to shift your perspective. Learning to see the world from a slightly different angle is a useful skill for any investor to have. Tilting your perspective can reveal bad ideas for what they are.

Here are a few of my favorites:

Earnings missed estimates

Every earnings season, some high-profile company will have a profit shortfall. "Earnings missed estimates," is intoned by the TV pundits.

Morgan Housel corrects this error: "Earnings did not miss estimates, estimates missed earnings." Earnings are what they are, the profits of corporate America. By definition, they cannot be wrong—only better or worse than expected.

On the other hand, the analyst community are who missed. It was *their* estimates of those earnings that were wrong.

Crash

Eddy Elfenbein manages the AdvisorShares Focused Equity ETF (CWS); it is based on an annual stock list he created which has beaten the S&P 500 by 102% over the last 17 years.

Whenever someone compares the present to some earlier marker crash, he has the perfect perspective shifting rejoinder:

"This market reminds me a lot of 1987."

"Really? You think the market will gain 35-fold over the next 37 years?"[105]

Fair value

Equity valuation confuses many investors. About half the time, markets are above their average valuation, the other half, below. Fair value is somewhere around the middle. Markets trade above or below fair value most of the time.

Fair value is a singular point in a market cycle that equities race by to the upside in a bull market; some years later, those same market prices will plummet past that spot in a bear market. It is a point in time that markets visit only briefly.

Traffic

A friend who was meeting me for dinner called to say, "Sorry, I am gonna be a little late, I am stuck in traffic." He is a stickler for good grammar, so I felt okay correcting him: "You are on the highway during rush hour on a workday near a major urban population center; you are not stuck IN traffic, you ARE traffic."

We imagine life as this thing that happens around us, where we are the narrator of our own stories. In reality, we are merely actors in the midst of a much bigger play.[106]

Consumers suffering from inflation

It is no fun paying more for essential goods and services than we have to. But we overlook the fact that some people *buy these goods regardless of price*—they may be suffering from inflation, but by paying up for those higher prices for discretionary items regardless, they are also creating *more inflation*.[107]

PART I: BAD IDEAS

Commodity traders say: "The cure for high prices is high prices." It discourages some demand, encourages more supply, or both. That helps bring down prices. Consumers that pay up for goods or services do not.

Everything is survivorship bias

Success is deceptive. What you see around you are the winners. This is misleading, as it deceives us into believing success is much easier than it actually is. This leads to some people investing in restaurants and plays.

Survivorship bias rules the world around us. Anything that is successful—products, funds, people—are the result of millions of small and large failures. Success is an iterative process—we often overlook the misses, the almosts, the faceplants, and the failures that precede victory. Behind every winner are hundreds or even thousands of losers, without which success could not have happened.

Counterfactual

"Invert, always invert." So said Charlie Munger, channeling the great 19th-century Prussian mathematician Carl Gustav Jacob Jacobi.[108] Counterfactuals are a worthwhile intellectual exercise for looking at the world from a different perspective.

Simply put, imagine the world if a specific decision never happened. A new corporate initiative is undertaken or government policy is rolled out—and they are declared ineffective. How do we know? How much worse might it have been had "X" not happened? We don't have a lab where we can run a control group to see what happens if this decision never occurred.

The counterfactual allows us to consider the alternative universe where variations of choices are put into effect.

Time

A friend announced out of nowhere that he wanted to learn to speak fluent Italian.

"How long do you think that will take?" I asked.

Him: "Five years."

Me: "Gee, sounds like a long time."

Him: "The five years are going to go by whether I am learning a new language or not."

That insight has stayed with me ever since. Oliver Burkeman observes: "The average human lifespan is absurdly, insultingly brief. Assuming you live to be eighty, you have just over four thousand weeks."[109]

Everybody gets 24 hours a day. The clock is ticking, get busy using your 4,000 weeks in a way that you won't regret in week 3,999.

We have defined what investing is, considered thinking in terms of probabilities, reviewed some bad ideas, and looked at ways to avoid them. Now let's look at some good ideas that will help how you think about money.

THE GOOD IDEAS THAT SHAPED MY INVESTMENT PHILOSOPHY

BAD IDEAS ARE everywhere. The antidote is vigilance—and good ideas. In physics and mathematics, philosophy and investing, we can "see further," to paraphrase Isaac Newton, "by standing on the shoulders of giants."

In mostly chronological order, these concepts have helped shape my worldview, including how I think about the economy, markets, and investing.

1. "I write to discover what I think. (After all, the bars aren't open that early.)" —Daniel J. Boorstin

As librarian of the United States Congress, Boorstin understood the power of the written word. It's a crucial aspect of how I formed my own belief system.

Writing helps me organize my thoughts. It creates a record of what I believed at a specific date—and (hopefully) shows my evolution over time. Sharing my thoughts in public invites comments, criticism, and debate from others who have thought through similar issues. This forces me to sharpen my views about markets, the economy and money.

2. "Ninety percent of everything is crap."
—Ted Sturgeon

Weary of defending science fiction against attacks from those who used the worst examples in the field, Sturgeon pointed out that most human endeavors are filled with garbage. It's not just sci-fi, but 90% of *everything* is worthless junk.

Since you are reading a book: In the United States, about 300,000 new books come out annually via traditional publishers.[110] Sturgeon's law suggest 30,000 of them are not crap—and that number seems generous.

Now think about what this means if we run the same exercise for mutual funds, ETFs, private equity, hedge funds, venture capital, annuities, etc. The vast majority of financial products aren't worth your time or money. Even most publicly traded stocks are filler, as market returns are driven by a tiny percentage of equities.

3. "To make better, more informed decisions about the future, we advise people to have 'strong opinions, which are weakly held.'"
—Bob Johansen, Palo Alto Institute for the Future[111]

The future is subject to random and unexpected events, which change the short-term course of history. We learn our information is incomplete or wrong. Sometimes, a very low-probability event occurs, dashing our expectations.

Whatever my views are about the economy, markets, my portfolio, etc., I am always ready to discard them as I amass sufficient evidence my beliefs are wrong. "Strong opinions weakly held" means reversing your priors when necessary, cutting losses quickly, and never marrying any holding or belief system—ever.

PART I: BAD IDEAS

4. "All models are wrong, but some are useful."
—George E. P. Box

We don't live in objective reality, we function in a model of our own construction. Our brains generate mental outlines, continually filling in missing information to create a 360-degree world within which we operate. This useful evolutionary trait has allowed the human species to thrive in a world that is hostile to us soft, chewy creatures lacking claws, fangs, or armor.

We model the economy and markets; we create Monte Carlo simulations of how our portfolios will perform over time. We interact with artificial constructs of our own making, sometimes ignoring they are at best inauthentic representations.

It's easy to get lost in the usefulness of models, forgetting their wrongness. Understanding this helps us better manage the never-ending stream of model-generated data on consumer spending, employment situation, wages, inflation, earnings, etc.

5. "Nobody knows anything"
—William Goldman

We spent time with Goldman in our chat on *Bad Advice*. Whenever you hear an expert confidently explaining what's going to happen in the future, it's worth your time to recall his brilliant, humble, and counterintuitive insight.

Once you recognize how little the experts (and the rest of us) know, you come to recognize how much humility investing requires. Accept the wisdom of recognizing our collective ignorance, and you will soon see how much better off you will be then if you were both wrong and unaware of it.

**6. "The whole problem with the world is that fools and fanatics are always so certain of themselves, and wiser people so full of doubts."
—Bertrand Russell**

Those who are the least knowledgeable are often the most cocksure about their own skills, abilities, and beliefs. This is an especially expensive error to make in trading and investing. Recall the attitudes of meme stock traders during the pandemic lockdown, or meme coins before that, or dotcoms before that. This is the Dunning-Kruger effect writ large.

It takes skills to understand the risks and challenges of any endeavor. No wonder wise people harbor doubts—they can better see the entirety of a challenge. Or as Charles Darwin wrote, "Ignorance more frequently begets confidence than does knowledge."[112]

**7. "I have approximate answers, and possible beliefs, and different degrees of uncertainty about different things. But I am not absolutely sure of anything and there are many things I don't know anything about. I don't feel frightened not knowing things."
—Professor Richard Feynman**

One of the greatest minds in physics was also one of the wisest thinkers about thinking. His willingness to admit "I don't know" was unusual. Knowing what you know helps, but awareness of what you do not know means fewer blind spots, and reduced likelihood of surprise.

Decision-making is a two-step process: First we make a decision, then we have to decide how much weight or confidence to have in that decision. We often forget the second step.

PART I: BAD IDEAS

8. "Being right may be a necessary condition for investment success, but it won't be sufficient. You must be more right than others… which by definition means your thinking has to be different."
—Howard Marks, Oaktree Capital

Marks is referring to "second-level thinking," which means thinking beyond the news to how market participants will *react* to that news.

Jane Street Trading managed to figure out state-by-state results in the 2016 Presidential election minutes before the major cable channels did.* This allowed them to trade ahead of everybody, making $300 million overnight shorting equity futures. But they failed to fully think through the results of the election—tax cuts and stimulus spending!—and when the markets reversed, their giant win turned into the firm's biggest loss ever.

Second-level thinking requires going past the first recognition, beyond what is obvious. Merely figuring out what happens is not enough; markets are a hall of mirrors, and each new piece of information sets off a cascade of reflexivity, actions and reactions that are nearly impossible to predict. Those who can think of the second- and third-order effects stand to make a fortune.

9. "Never attempt to teach a pig to sing; it wastes your time and annoys the pig."
—Robert A. Heinlein,
The Notebooks of Lazarus Long

I have been writing in public for 25 years. I often get pushback to what I publish. In response, I correct factual errors or share new data. But I will never be able to change a person's deeply held, fundamental belief system.

---

* As detailed in Michael Lewis's book, *Going Infinite: The Rise and Fall of a New Tycoon* (Norton & Company, 2023).

They have invested too much time and energy in their worldview, and it would be way too cognitively expensive for them to reverse that.

David McRaney explains the challenges of persuading people to change beliefs or opinions: It is very difficult to do, especially where their self-identity is involved.[113]

Or as Heinlein observed: "Man is not a rational animal; he is a rationalizing animal."

10. "Memento Mori"
(Latin for "remember that you will die")

At the end of the day, we all shuffle off this mortal coil to our infinite repose.

The Stoic philosopher Marcus Aurelius urged us to "consider how ephemeral and mean all mortal things are." He used the example of a triumphant Roman general: He had a companion stand behind him during his victory procession and whisper *"Memento Mori"* to remind him of his own mortality.[114]

On a long enough timescale, everything is transitory. As we work our way through the detritus and minutia of life, we should not lose sight of that.

These ideas have influenced me the most. Despite the bad advice out there, there is also much wisdom in the world (I could expand this list to 100). But these are the ones that created that *Aha!* moment, and have stood the test of time.

Ask yourself: What fundamental ideas are driving your philosophy? How does this inform and shape your investing?

How can we navigate all of these bad ideas that keep coming our way? You need a few tools to help you through the poor predictions, conflicted advice, and marketing nonsense. That's what the first part of the book was about.

In Part 2, we dive into the numbers that drive the markets.

PART 2: BAD NUMBERS

In Part 2, we dive into the numbers that drive the economy, markets, and your investments.

Misleading math is everywhere. A few tools will help you counter its pernicious impact.

SECTION 1: ECONOMIC INNUMERACY

Economic innumeracy prevents investors from understanding the economy.

In this section, we discuss five key ideas: denominator blindness, survivorship bias, asymmetry, compounding, and framing. These concepts are much simpler than their fancy-sounding names suggest.

Understanding them will help you to avoid costly mistakes.

(MIS)UNDERSTANDING NUMBERS

THERE IS AN old joke about a senior partner interviewing Certified Public Accountants for a junior position. The interview consists of a single question: "How much is 2 + 2?" The CPA who gets hired? The one who responds, "How much do you want it to be?"

Numbers can be precise, and numbers can mislead. Like any tool, the result they produce is in the hands of the craftsman wielding them. Their apparent precision can easily fool us.

To avoid math trickery and abuse that befalls too many investors, you need to understand a few simple concepts. We can do this with some familiarity of basic mathematics. Just high school level basics, including a tiny bit about probabilities and even less about statistics.

You do not need a lot of math to be a good investor. The kinds of things that most investors need to do are look at the relative performance of a fund, or the after-tax equivalent yield on municipal bonds, earnings, or dividends yield for individual companies. There are online calculators that make this fast and easy to do.

The bigger and more challenging task is to avoid being fooled by malicious actors who are facile with math. They abuse numbers to scare you out of markets, to make you fearful about the future, to mislead you about stocks, bonds, economics, politics, just about anything. They can create doubt in your mind about your plan.

The same is true with economic data: Models used to determine nonfarm payrolls or changes in the Consumer Price Index mean that these data series are very noisy, with a wide margin of error. A few insights will prevent you from being fooled by the endless fire hose of economic news. On a long-term trend line, most of it is meaningless noise.

I'll share multiple examples of how we can be deceived with numbers: They are used out of context, with misleading framing, cherry-picked data, and emotional claims that can lead investors to make bad decisions. I will address all of these.

Joan Robinson was a trailblazing economist who taught at Cambridge from 1931 to 1971—she was one of the few women who did so in that era.* She shared this piece of wisdom about the discipline: "The purpose of studying economics is not to acquire a set of ready-made answers to economic questions, but to learn how to avoid being deceived by economists." Her insight was not just about economics, but markets, too.

This entire "Bad Numbers" discussion will give you the tools to identify when bad actors are trying to impact your behavior in ways that are detrimental to your wealth. Sometimes they are selling you crappy products, other times they are affecting your emotions. I want you to understand enough about how math gets abused to get your Spidey-sense tingling whenever someone uses it to mislead you.

The concepts we discuss are easy to grasp. They will help you not get misled by those who do not have your best interests at heart.

Like everything else in life, numbers need context. Let's take a look at what happens when we forget that…

---

* Barkley Rosser, "The Legacy of Joan Robinson," EconoSpeak (May 2, 2016).

DENOMINATOR BLINDNESS

DENOMINATOR BLINDNESS IS the failure to put any number—especially big, scary ones—into context. Examples of this occur every time you see headlines like: Stocks Drop 300 Points; ABC Fund Loses $879 million; XYZ Corp Cuts 3,000 Jobs.

The top number in any fraction is called the "numerator," and it tells you what change took place; the bottom number in a fraction is the "denominator," and it indicates what data set we are discussing (could be markets, or employees, or an investment fund). As we shall see, sharing just the numerator, but not revealing the denominator, is inherently misleading.

Headlines that provide only a numerator are giving a partial picture that is essentially useless.

Let's use the examples above but instead of only sharing the numerator we will show the full context: The fund that lost $879 million—were its total assets $1 billion or $100 billion? Asked in terms of percentages, did they lose 90%—a rout that demolished its investors? Or was it less than a 1% drop, no more than daily trading noise? Based on the headline, you don't know, and without that context, all you see is a big scary number. You cannot tell if it is meaningful without information about the denominator.

A company that fired 3,000 people sounds like a huge downsizing. But is it? We don't know how significant it is to the company until we know their total workforce. Was it a small, regional company that employed 30,000 people? That's a 10% reduction in its workforce, and very substantial. What if it's retail giant Walmart, with 10,500 stores in 19 countries employing 2.1 million employees? It means they fired less than one person at every third store—not meaningful at all...

The 300-point market drop is perhaps my favorite example: If that's referring to the Dow Jones Industrial Average, trading at ~40,000 as I write this, that decline is meaningless, a move of about 0.75%; if it is the Standard & Poor's 500 Index, now over 5,000, that's an unnerving 6% decline.

This lack of context can lead you to misunderstand risk. For investors, it means fearing the wrong things.

Worried about market crashes? Exactly how many market crashes have there been relative to the number of trading days during your lifetime? That's a subtle case of denominator blindness. Crashes are rare, and relative to your portfolio's returns, you would be better off focusing on the everyday things that hurt investors most: Costs, (over)trading, commissions, and taxes.

Market crashes are great—if you have capital handy, are not near retirement age, and can manage your emotions and behavior. Its counterintuitive, and not how most people think about wrenching dislocations.

Concerned about terrorism? The September 11 attacks made many Americans fearful of flying, even though this was a rare event.[115] A study of the years following revealed a decrease in air travel and an increase in driving, resulting in more than 2,000 additional driving deaths than would have been expected.[116]

We may fear terror attacks, but we should be more concerned (at least statistically) with the 43,000 annual automobile fatalities in the United States.[117] We should worry less about terrorist attacks, and instead wear our seat belts and stop texting while driving.

None of those risks is as great as the odds that you will die of heart disease. According to the Centers for Disease Control and Prevention (CDC), one person dies every 33 seconds in the United States from cardiovascular disease; that's one in every five deaths annually in America.[118]

We spend too much time worrying about big, rare events, while ignoring the mundane everyday factors that are far more dangerous.

Much of this was laid out in a 2002 paper called "The Denominator Blindness Effect: Accident Frequencies and the Misjudgment of Recklessness."[119] Lacking the proper context led to disproportionate judgments.

Dan Gardner, in his book *Risk: Why We Fear the Things We Shouldn't*—

PART 2: BAD NUMBERS

and Put Ourselves in Greater Danger,[120] calls this practice "Fear, Inc." There are many industries that thrive on unfounded fears and are only too happy to sell you things you don't need to keep you safe from criminals, terrorists, germs, the end-of-times, hyperinflation, and other outlier calamities.

When we fear things because they seem scary, but in fact they are highly unlikely, that can lead to poor decisions relating to how much risk we should assume. In Darwinian evolution, those who ignore existential risk don't get to pass their genes along. Perhaps that's the reason why we are so instinctually influenced by scary events and large numbers. More than simple innumeracy, it is insidious because we are often unaware of its subtle impact on our psychology.

Denominator blindness is the scourge of anyone who has even the most rudimentary understanding of mathematics in the real world. Anytime someone trots out a big number, make sure you understand the context—and always look for the denominator.[121]

Next up, a few examples of how people take advantage of our denominator blindness.

DEATH, TAXES, AND LAYOFFS

I GOT AN EMAIL from a former co-worker offering "overwhelming evidence" that global warming was a hoax. The proof? A letter signed by 49 former NASA scientists.[122]

That numerator all by itself sent my Spidey-sense atwitchin.

What's the denominator? That's the first question you should ask yourself. How many scientists have worked at NASA? Not just climatologists or meteorologists, but anyone with an advanced technical degree in hard sciences or engineering that was similar to those 49 climate hoaxers listed.

NASA currently employs about 18,000 people. Since NASA began in 1958 with 8,000 workers, they have had many tens of thousands of employees.[123] During the Apollo program, NASA's workforce peaked at over 400,000 employees, contractors, and support personnel. And across its history, about half of its employees had professional degrees. Conservative guess as to how many scientists and engineers worked for NASA? More than 100,000 people at the least.

Of all these people, living and dead, 49 got together and wrote a letter.

Now that we have some context, that letter touting only 49 people looks silly. This handful—only one of whom works as a meteorologist—are an extremely tiny percentage of current (or former) NASA employees. If you invert the math, it proves the opposite: Out of hundreds of thousands of NASA scientists and engineers, you could only find 49 that endorse your debunked hoax theory?

Always be suspicious when you see a single number out of context—too often, it is a tool of deception.

PART 2: BAD NUMBERS

Tech layoffs

Following a massive hiring spree in 2021, 2022, and 2023, many of the bigger technology companies began cutting back on staff late in 2023. For those who had been erroneously forecasting an imminent recession, this was manna from heaven. The long-awaited contraction was finally here!

Only, not so much.

The details reveal this spate of layoffs is yet another example of denominator blindness.

Let's start by looking at the actual layoffs relative to the recent hires of the prior two years:

Company	Layoffs	Recent Hires (2021–23)
Amazon	18,000	746,000
Google	12,000	67,800
Meta	11,000	42,372
Microsoft	10,000	77,000
Salesforce	7,000	30.824
Spotify	590	5,403
Apple	0	95,102

Note these layoffs are small relative to recent hires (our first denominator). Out of over a million recent hires, about 5.5% were being laid off. It's reasonable to assume that one out of every 20 new hires do not work out.

But this is not the total employee headcount for these companies—just recent hires. If we consider the total employment of these seven companies, you get about 2.25 million employees. That puts this spate of layoffs closer to 2.6%.

Last, consider one more denominator: The entire US workforce of 160 million workers.[124] Sam Ro[125] points out technology employment is barely 3% of that group, or about 4.8 million employees. Why are we focusing our attention on 60,000 layoffs out of 4.8 million tech employees out of 160 million workers? From the macro perspective, it seems like a rounding error. It's a classic case of context-free data.

During the GFC, there were massive firings. Shotgun weddings led to redundancies and entire departments were cut. My daily email notes were generating a bounce rate (dead emails) of 20% or worse every month (and I removed bad addresses weekly). Unemployment spiked to 10%; layoffs were ubiquitous. It was a very ugly period, especially so close to the dotcom debacle a few years earlier. Even that implosion sent unemployment to 6.3%, almost double current levels.

You can see the psychological damage created by the financial crisis. People had a form of economic-PTSD. The 2023–25 era—even with higher interest rates and slowing growth—was not remotely comparable to those earlier eras.

The Death Tax

Denominator blindness is so prevalent, it even sneaks into our language.

A perfect example is the Federal Estate Tax, which as of 2024 levied a 40% tax on any estate over $13.61 million for a single individual, or $27.22 million for a married couple.

In the 1940s, attempts to rename estate taxes the "Death Tax" met with only limited success. Frank Luntz, the Republican communication wizard, was more successful in the 1990s, and drove widespread adoption of the phrase.[126]

The most recent data is the calendar year 2023, when about three million Americans died, according to the Centers for Disease Control and Prevention.[127] Only 5,000 of these people left an estate that owed any federal taxes. Said differently, 2,995,000 Americans died in 2023 without owing a penny in estate taxes.

Why name something for the 0.167% outcome? When 99.82% of deaths don't create a taxable event, calling it a death tax is mathematically nonsensical.

Boo-hoo if your estate owes taxes on everything over $27 million. First, it means you had more money than you knew what to do with. And second,

PART 2: BAD NUMBERS

as I discuss in later chapters, if you had done a little bit of planning, you wouldn't even need to pay that.

Why would someone use the phrase "death tax" when more than 99% of deaths don't result in a tax? Always ask yourself, "What are they selling?" Someone is deceiving you in their attempts at persuasion.

—

Since we are already discussing death, let's look at an especially silly example of denominator blindness.

AN EPIDEMIC OF SELFIE DEATHS

OUTSIDE MAGAZINE PUBLISHED a discussion on the "epidemic of selfie deaths."[128] This "epidemic"—a loss of 259 lives between 2011 and 2017—is another example of denominator blindness.

In 2015, there were 12 "selfie deaths"; there were also 737 Americans who died falling out of bed.[129] Selfie deaths got all of the media coverage.

The epidemic described by *Outside* magazine over those eight years averaged 43 deaths annually. That's the numerator. What of the denominator? To figure that out, we need to come up with a credible estimate for the number of selfies taken each year.

Google's I/O developer conference in 2014 gave us a partial answer: Android users take an average of 93 million selfies *every day*.[130] That was a decade and a few billion smartphone sales ago. Now add in iPhone users, and we get about 200 million daily selfies. Each year, that's about 75 billion selfies versus 43 deaths. The odds of a selfie death are about 1.7 billion to one.

This is another example of ignoring the mundane while focusing on the exciting. Common deaths like heart disease or cancer are high-probability eventualities, but they generate far less emotional response than the extremely rare low-probability events like terrorism.

In 2023, not a single person died in a commercial flight in the US, but there were more than 36,000 traffic fatalities. Whether you are flying for business or pleasure, the cab ride to the airport is likely to be the most dangerous part of your trip.

Statistically speaking, you should be far more concerned with your LDL cholesterol and high blood pressure than you should with shark attacks, selfie deaths, or terrorism. Cancer and heart disease account for nearly half of annual deaths in the United States. Not that you could tell by media coverage, but the grim reality is that you are 50,000 times more likely to meet your maker due to that deadly duo than these other rarities.[131]

The parallels to investing are obvious: We fear rare events like stock market crashes, the collapse of the US dollar, and hyperinflation, when we should be focused instead on the mundane. Our attention is captivated by black swan events like the 1987 market crash, when the Dow Jones Industrial Average plunged a record 22.8% in a day. Broad diversification and keeping your costs and taxes low are much more important than worrying about a crash. Metaphorically speaking, crashes are closer to terrorist attacks, while high costs that erode long-term returns are more akin to high cholesterol or blood pressure.

We are all susceptible to these kinds of cognitive and behavioral errors. As *Outside* magazine correctly observed, "Our species evolved as hyper-social creatures uniquely concerned about how others perceive us." We are obsessed with what everyone else is doing—whether it's taking a selfie that leaves others in awe, or a fear of missing out on the next hot investment, be it Nvidia, Bitcoin, house flipping, or whatever comes next. FOMO—fear of missing out—is simply fear & greed by another name.

Selfie deaths are an example of how silly it was to focus on the numerator without considering the denominator. It is revealing of both our innumeracy and psychology; understanding each better is one of the keys to successful investing.

Since we are already discussing death and taxes, let's move to our next example of bad math: Survivorship bias.

THE HIDDEN WORLD OF FAILURE: WHAT IF EVERYTHING IS SURVIVORSHIP BIAS?

YOU MAY RECOGNIZE this image. It is a World War Two bomber, showing a composite of where American planes returning to base had taken fire during their bombing runs.

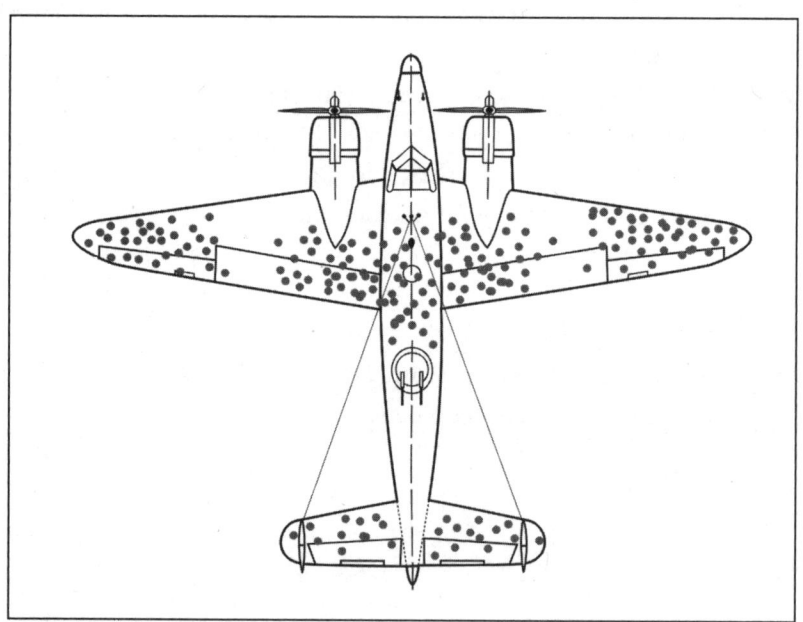

PART 2: BAD NUMBERS

This was of concern to the US military. Senior brass went to the Statistical Research Group (SRG), "a classified program that yoked the assembled might of American statisticians to the war effort—something like the Manhattan Project, except the weapons being developed were equations not explosives."[132] The generals wanted to improve the survivability of their bombers by adding more armor. The trade-off was greater fuel consumption, and reduced range, speed, and maneuverability. Exactly how much armor got added (and where) was crucial to the success of the war effort.

Abraham Wald was an Austrian mathematician and a Jew who had been chased out of Europe by the Nazis. Wald was a senior member of the SRG, and his advice to the military: "Put the armor where the bullet holes aren't" had a huge impact on the war.

It's counterintuitive, but it makes sense when you think about it: Shot-up planes that returned meant the areas they were hit were not critical to the plane's survivability. Wald's great insight—"Where were the holes on the bombers that *weren't* coming back from their missions?"—was crucial to understanding the problem.

Looking only at where returning aircraft had been shot has become one of history's most famous example of **survivorship bias**. Wald taught us to always consider the full data set—including set members *you cannot see*.

This tendency to give too much weight to the survivors while excluding the deceased has a long and storied history in the mutual fund industry. Investors first learned what survivorship bias was in the 1990s, after research revealed that fund returns were being significantly overstated.[133] Ignore the funds that closed due to poor performance, leave in only the surviving winners, and the data will look a whole lot better! Add back those dead or retired funds (otherwise removed from the dataset), and the touted investment outperformance disappeared.

Investing giant Vanguard Group found that 62% of surviving large-capitalization value funds outperformed their specific benchmark. But that was ignoring funds that were closed. Adding them back into the dataset lowers the performance metric to less than half—just 46% after five years.

Dimensional Funds Advisors (DFA) found about half of all mutual funds close within 15 years. The non-surviving funds—closed, merged into a more successful fund, otherwise retired—were usually killed off due to poor performance. DFA's analysis found that by only looking at the surviving strategies, the data suffers from a substantial upward bias that overstates the median fund outperformance (alpha) by 50%.[134] Killing off the bad performers in a data set makes the average fund look that much better.

As we shall see, the same is true for collectible artwork, fine wine, automobiles, toys or other alternative asset classes.[135] Which raises a fascinating question:

What if everything is survivorship bias?

Survivorship bias colors nearly *everything* we do.

The successful products we use every day are the result of many trials and errors; initial attempts that failed and subsequent improvements that were made. The iterative process consists of repeated efforts hidden from view. You don't think about all the little widgets that make up your favorite products, or how each has gotten better over time. Your mobile phone, refrigerator, car, house, sneakers, pencil—every product you use goes through this process. The fascinating aspect of this is how truly hidden it is.

Book publishing is instructive: Each year, the *New York Times* bestsellers list totals about 100 books. But consider the long odds each book faced: US publishers release almost 300,000 books per year. Add in self-published books and you triple that number (900,000 total). That is just in the US. Expand your geography to include the entire world and the number rises to 2.1 million books. This is to say nothing of rejected manuscripts, unpublished works, and endless half-finished books that never see the light of day. The probability that an attempt at writing a book that will make it to the bestseller list is incredibly daunting.

Rerun this exercise for apps, Broadway plays, tech start-ups, restaurants, video games—anything people create. Successful products are all built upon two distinct unseen failures: A hidden graveyard of competitive products that didn't make it, and another containing all of the earlier drafts, edits, iterations, and versions of products *before* they succeeded.

Our frame of reference is *success*: That hot restaurant, an Academy Award-winning movie, this bestselling book, that successful small business, a trendy new retailer. As consumers, just about everything we buy is a winner, having beaten out the lesser products whose producers have left the marketplace.

The challenge is that this *hidden world of failure* creates a deeply flawed understanding of the world. By not recognizing failure, we underestimate how challenging success is.

The other side of Survivorship Bias: *Success is a rare and delicate thing*. As a percentage, failure is far more common. Our constant exposure to winners—the things we buy, use, or consume—disguise just how rare they are. Failure is far more present than most of us realize.

The result: Our faulty mental models misperceive how difficult it is to be successful in any given sphere. As we shall see, our models are unusually bad at understanding probabilities. They do an excellent job of keeping us alive long enough to procreate and pass genes on to the next generation. But when it comes to calculating odds on the fly, we just were not built for that. The foundation of the entire gaming and casino industry rests on this flaw in our wetware.

Some fund managers will outperform this year; *someone* is gonna win the lottery; sports leagues crown a champion every year (when might it be the NY Knicks again?). We underestimate how rare these occurrences are, and how difficult it is to achieve them. Why would anyone ever open a new restaurant or invest in a Broadway play if they truly understood how much the odds were stacked against them? This is why we sometimes make low-probability investments in long shots that are much less likely to pay off than we imagine.

Everything we see is the result of survivorship bias. It is hidden and easily overlooked. That is why success is so much rarer, more difficult and fragile than it appears to be.

It's not just mutual funds where survivorship bias lurks. We see it in the art world as well. Let's visit that space to see what we can learn.

SURVIVORSHIP BIAS IN FRAMES AND ON WHEELS

WHAT HAPPENS WHEN we ignore failures, and only consider the big winners? It distorts our sense of how challenging it is to identify where to put our capital today, before we know what asset classes are going to be the biggest winners and losers over the next few decades. Failing to understand that makes us susceptible to sexy pitches for our money.

It's not just mutual funds: There are sexy pitches for collectibles markets, from art to cars to toys.

To make a fortune, all you need is an eye for important, beautiful works, some capital—and a time machine. Go back a few decades and buy the Monets and Ferraris that have appreciated the most. But knowing what will bring huge prices in the future in these markets is very, very hard.[136]

In 2019, one of Claude Monet's haystacks paintings, "Meules" (1890), was auctioned at Sotheby's for $110.7 million. It was a record sum for a work by an impressionist. That price, including auctioneer fees, was 44 times more than the $2.5 million the painting fetched when last sold at auction in 1986.[137] This works out to an annual rate of return of 12.2% over 33 years.

The estate of former Condé Nast chairman S.I. Newhouse Jr. auctioned off Jeff Koons's stainless-steel "Rabbit" at Christie's in New York in 2019. At $91 million, it set a record for a sale of a sculpture by a living artist.[138] Newhouse bought the sculpture in 1992 for $1 million. At 91 times more than the sculpture cost 27 years ago, the annual rate of return was 18.2%.[139]

Giant winners, to be sure, but what about the millions of other works of art that fail to appreciate in value? Think about millions of originals

PART 2: BAD NUMBERS

hanging in homes from La Jolla to East Hampton to London. The vast majority of these "investments" have returns that are nothing like Monet or Koons. Many—indeed, most—lose value.

To say nothing of museums' back catalogs. Curators have amassed a massive set of holdings, most in storage. The permanent collection at the Met in New York City is over 1.5 million artworks (about 50× what is on display). Not far away, the Museum of Modern Art has almost 200,000 modern works in storage. Most of these won't fetch nine (or eight or even seven) figures at auction.

Other luxury items attract similar attention from time to time. Watches, fine wine, and classic automobiles all vie for investor attention. It is human nature to look at big winners after the fact, while failing to think about the impact of the losers.

What we see matters less than what is not visible to us.

The media deserves some blame for this. A weak fourth quarter in 2018 (off ~20%) led *The Wall Street Journal* to claim wine, art, classic cars, and exotic-colored diamonds did better than stocks that year.[140]

Not exactly.

By only including the big splashy auctions while ignoring the rest of the wine, jewelry, art, and car markets, we get a distorted sense of performance.

Author and investment advisor William J. Bernstein makes the point that much of the appreciation in art and other collectibles is really just a lesson in the magic of compounding.[141] He calculated that a painting of one of the Old Masters bought from the artist for the equivalent of $100 and sold 350 years later for hundreds of millions of dollars returned just 3.3% annually. "If you save and you have even a modest rate of return over hundreds of years, then you'll have a fabulous amount of money" he said on our Masters in Business podcast in April 2019.

Selecting those appreciated artworks *after the fact* is easy. But consider this challenge: What work of art are you willing to buy today and hold for the next 50 years?

Tough question! It reveals just how difficult investing in collectible assets really is.

HOW NOT TO INVEST

I love beautiful automobiles. What is more delightful than a cruise in a gorgeous rolling sculpture of steel and glass, plenty of horsepower, and an open top for those sunny spring days? Kids of my generation grew up lusting after joyful toys like Corvettes and Porsche 911s and Ferraris.

Finding the cars that have appreciated wildly *after the fact* is easy, but it proves nothing about how well that asset class has performed. The bigger question for investors is how well the overall investment class (e.g., all collectible automobiles) has done, not just a handful of limited production rarities.

Owning these cars can be tremendously rewarding. They are fun projects,* you meet other people interested in them, you get to *drive them*.

But my experience is they cost money to maintain, store, and insure. To keep them in concourse show condition is expensive. The market for these vehicles is small, if you ever *need* liquidity. The rarest and most valuable collectible cars that go for eight figures have a very modest pool of potential buyers. Turning any passing fancy into a successful investment is very difficult.

To remove the survivorship bias, look at Hagerty's Price Guide Index.[142] It tracks 1400 vehicles in four different conditions. Since 2006, Ferrari (+500%) and Post-War German (+300%) and what they call Blue Chip (+300%) collectibles have all seen significant price gains. "Affordable Classics" have doubled over those 18 years, and American Muscle, British, 1950s classics are up marginally. In this period, the S&P 500 was up 340%, the Nasdaq gained 1110%, all without the need for insurance, maintenance, gas, and storage.

---

* I've rebuilt a few older cars that were a lot of fun to drive. In 2021, I redid a 1978 Toyota FJ40 in Colombia for my wife (she hated it, and it's since been sold); in 2022, a 1988 Porsche 911 Cabrio (M491) that the prior owner had tracked—I restored it to original stock condition. In 2023–24, I converted a 300,000-mile 1987 Porsche 911 Coupe into an EV. I believe it is the first one in New York, and I get lots of offers to buy it. It's fast as hell, unlike anything else on the road; license plate: EV 911.

PART 2: BAD NUMBERS

Selecting investments after the fact is easy, but ask yourself this question: *What car do you want to buy as an investment to hold for the next 50 years to be sold in 2075?*

OK, we now understand survivorship bias, but what else do we need to know regarding economic models and data series? That's what our next chapter is all about.

WHAT MODELS DON'T KNOW

MATHEMATICAL MODELS CAN help us make sense of the world. They depict versions of just about any area you can think of, from real estate sales to Covid deaths. But if you follow any modeled data series, you must always keep in mind statistician George E. P. Box's warning: "All models are wrong, but some are useful."

That is if your assumptions are valid and that we are not feeding bad data into them.

Most models have a fundamental flaw: They are based on the idea that the future will look a lot like the past. Nothing throws a model off more than when an event we failed to anticipate destroys its fundamental premise. Box's admonition serves as a reminder that models create a false shadow of reality. The universe is more complicated than what our mathematics suggest.

Yet, we place a great deal of faith in models. The problem occurs when, as journalist Jonathan V. Last[143] observes, we forget that models are "not a report sent back from the future." He observes the three types of inputs that go into models:

1. Stuff we know;
2. Stuff we think we know;
3. Stuff we have no idea about.

Sometimes, the errors that models produce are not that important. Netflix has built its business modeling what you are likely to enjoy streaming, based on your viewing habits relative to what the rest of its

PART 2: BAD NUMBERS

167 million subscribers enjoy. If the algorithms get it wrong, the downside is the service suggests a movie you end up not liking.

Where modeling errors become more costly is when we forget they are imperfect depictions of economic reality. In 2008, economists' models failed to see the financial crisis that was already unfolding.[144] None of their models anticipated the rise of nonbank lending and mortgages that eschewed traditional standards like credit checks, employment verification, and loan-to-value ratios. They did not even consider the possibility that *housing prices might go down*! These models were in part why there was such significant delay in recognizing and responding to the GFC—the worst recession since the Great Depression.

Our faith in financial models should already have been tempered by events a decade earlier, when the hedge fund Long-term Capital Management collapsed. Their complex models[145]—created by two brilliant Nobel laureates—never anticipated that Russia would default on its debt.

When the world changes, but our models don't, we run into trouble:

- Models for securitized mortgages and related derivatives (CDOs, CMOs, CLOs, etc.) never anticipated housing prices going down. This was a major factor leading up to the GFC.
- Value investing models, championed by Benjamin Graham and Warren Buffett, ran into trouble in the 2010s because they failed to anticipate low inflation, quantitative easing (QE), and zero interest rate policy (ZIRP) by the Federal Reserve.
- In 2020, models went mad due to the pandemic lockdowns. With demand for crude oil crashing, and storage space for oil completely filled up, oil futures briefly traded at a negative $40 a barrel—meaning those holding oil had to pay to have it taken off their hands.
- Before 2020, the Bureau of Labor Statistics never had to cope with 20% of the workforce filing for unemployment claims in a single month. You can be sure that those models did not anticipate that.
- Negative interest rates around the world in the 2010s blew up a lot of models of inflation and yield, including those used by the

Federal Reserve. The old bond trader joke turned out to be true: If the Fed can't model something, it assumes it doesn't exist.

We don't live in objective reality; in truth, we function in a model of our own construction. Our brains generate mental outlines, continually filling in missing information to form a picture that we can discern and identify. It is a useful evolutionary trait. We are delicious, easy-to-catch prey, and to survive in a hungry, hostile world, we rely on the mental models of the world our big brains create.

What happens when we fail to recognize how error prone economic models can be? We pay way too much attention to them. We dig into the recession forecasting problem next…

THERE IS ALWAYS A RECESSION COMING...

YOU HAVE TO hand it to economists; they always seem to see a recession right around the corner.

Let's just look at the recent history here.

In 2016, *The Wall Street Journal*[146] surveyed a group of economists who "put the odds of the next downturn happening within the next four years at nearly 60%." There was no recession in 2016. Or 2017, '18, or '19. The primary reason we had a short, sharp recession in 2020 was the COVID-19 pandemic. After the lockdowns ended—and fiscal spigots opened up—the recession came to an abrupt halt. It had begun in February 2020 and by April 2020 it was over.

The CARES Act I was passed by a freaked-out congress—only weeks before they were stalemated over renaming a DC-area library—and signed into law by then President Trump. It was huge, the largest ever fiscal stimulus as a percentage of GDP; at over 10% of GDP, the only fiscal stimulus comparable was the mobilization for World War Two and the Marshall Plan that followed afterwards. Stock markets took off, consumer spending exploded, and a surge of inflation followed closely behind.

After the Covid recession, economists continued forecasting a recession that never came. The closest the US economy came was due to a statistical quirk in how we measure GDP in real (inflation-adjusted) terms. To oversimplify, when the surge of economic activity sent prices higher, those price increases are subtracted from GDP. This made GDP slightly negative for two quarters,* even as the economy was overheating. Despite this, the steady drumbeat of recession calls continued throughout 2021 and 2022.

---

* Subsequent revisions made only one of the quarters negative.

Strong consumer demand for goods sent the consumer price index (CPI) surging in the latter half of 2021 and the first half of 2022. By June 2022, inflation had peaked, and it collapsed down to about 3% (year over year), where it has mostly stayed (or fell) for the following 24 months.

Yet the calls for a recession continued. They intensified in 2023, even as the S&P 500 added 25% and the Nasdaq gained 55%. This is yet another entry in a long series of predictions that continually reveal economists' long-term forecasts as uniquely useless.

———

Let's start with the math: That *WSJ* survey of economists stating a recession might occur within the next four years is a statement that contains almost *no information*. During the 20th century, there were 20 recessions, or one every five years on average.[147] If you predict a recession over the next four years you will be on average right 80% of the time. How much usable information is contained in a weather forecaster that predicts temperatures will fall this winter (in the northern hemisphere) and rise next summer? This prediction is, of course, absolutely true and of no value whatsoever.

Why do economists have a penchant for extrapolating current data series while ignoring the broader—and more important—context about economic cycles? Perhaps it is because they don't like admitting that they don't have any idea when the next recession will come. Almost without exception, economists failed to "anticipate the three most recent recessions of 1990, 2001, and 2007—*even after they had begun*."[148] Do not expect any improvement on that track record any time soon.

Economists tend to use models that "reduce a complex economy to a rigid set of largely backward-looking relationships."[149] Extrapolating from the recent past is a sure-fire recipe for being surprised by the next cycle turn.

This has not escaped the data analysts at various Federal Reserve banks. The Federal Reserve Bank of Cleveland looked at statistical models that estimate 12-month-ahead recession probabilities. The Federal Reserve Bank of New York has developed its own model.[150] Both found the limits of the forecasting models drop off dramatically when using time horizons of 12 months or more. The reason for this is that the standard economic measures used to predict recessions—the yield curve, corporate profits, credit spreads, and consumer confidence surveys—change so much from month to month and quarter to quarter that they become useless more than a few quarters out.

It's hard to believe, but in 2025, we are *still* dealing with the fallout from the GFC of 2007–09. That *Wall Street Journal* article warned that in 2016, the expansion has "continued for 88 months, making it the fourth-longest period of growth in records stretching to 1854." Had you paid heed to those recession warnings, you would have missed another eight years of robust GDP expansion and ongoing new market highs. That includes the 34% sell-off into the start of Covid, and a weak 2022 that saw equities fall about 20%.

The economy doesn't just get old and die; something fundamental must occur to halt progress.

Media types love to toss around the word "unprecedented," but unprecedented things happen all the time. In 2020, there were 32 new highs in the market. *Unprecedented!* A global pandemic? *Unprecedented!* As Bridgewater founder Ray Dalio points out, "unprecedented usually means you haven't seen it in your lifetime, but it very likely has happened before." Records get broken all the time.

Forecasts of a recession arriving during the next four years are just a waste of print and pixels. The only thing these predictions do accomplish is to remind us that yes, there is always a storm somewhere off in the future. But you can never tell very far in advance when it will strike.

A risk of relying on modeled data is that we can too easily forget how things like money are supposed to work. We tackle one of the most deceptive data crimes involving cash in our next chapter.

DOLLARS ARE FOR SPENDING AND INVESTING, NOT SAVING

"**T**HE DOLLAR HAS lost 96% of its purchasing power over the last century."

This statement is the most misleading claim in all of finance. Full stop.

The *collapse of purchasing power of the US dollar* is used to scare investors, sell dubious products, and fool people into believing nonsense. I see this misleading meme all the time; we will unpack the many reasons it is so deceptive.

Let's begin with the biggest issue: The US dollar (USD) is not a long-term **Store of Value**. That was never its intended purpose. Rather, the USD is a **Medium of Exchange**. There is an enormous difference between these two use cases, and those who seek to mislead people rely on their not understanding the difference.

People get paid in dollars. As a currency, it is widely accepted. I need the USD to be a store of value between the time I earn it, up until the moment I spend it, invest it, pay my taxes with it, or give it away. It manages that use case splendidly.

You work 40+ hours a week, and you get paid for your time, efforts, and expertise. Your compensation likely gets deposited directly into your bank account, where it is available for purchasing necessities (food, housing, clothing, medicine, transportation, etc.), discretionary spending (entertainment, travel, etc.), and for paying your taxes. The money you spend in 2025 is money you earned in 2025, not 1925.

PART 2: BAD NUMBERS

So far so good.

But that's not all. You also have the opportunity to *invest those dollars*: You can buy a broad market index, and patiently wait for it to appreciate. You can buy bonds, and enjoy the income they yield. You could purchase real estate, which gives you a place to live, or to rent out for income. You could also use that money to start or build a business.

Whether it's a few decades or a century, the math works the same.

Let's consider a real-life scenario for that dollar which *supposedly* has lost 96% of its purchasing power. Imagine two young men, each with $1,000 cash, getting ready to go off to war. The US declared war against Germany in April 1917, thus entering World War One. In 1917, $1,000 was a fortune, and our two soldiers each took very different approaches to dealing with their cash.

One decides to bury the cash in mason jars in the backyard, while the other buys a broad set of stocks in the market (held in a trust just in case). Their descendants take possession of these in July 2023.[151]

If your ancestor was the soldier who put that $1,000 into equities over that same period, well congratulations. Since then, markets have returned about 10.23% a year, and that small fortune has grown to an enormous one, now worth over $30 million.[152]

Returns over a century are exponential, and therefore very counterintuitive. We have a hard time wrapping our heads around $1,000 growing that large. An easy way to understand how this works is to use the Rule of 72. This is a useful formula that calculates how long it takes for invested money to double. Simply divide 72 by 10.23% (the annual rate of return) and we find your investment will double every 7.03 years.

HOW *NOT* TO INVEST

Here is what that looks like since 1917, doubling 15 times:

Year	Dollar amount
1917	$1,000
1924	$2,000
1931	$4,000
1938	$8,000
1945	$16,000
1952	$32,000
1959	$64,000
1966	$128,000
1973	$256,000
1980	$512,000
1987	$1,024,000
1994	$2,048,000
2001	$4,096,000
2008	$8,192,000
2015	$16,384,000
2022	$32,768,000

Pretty incredible, huh?

All you had to do was patiently invest this money for a little over a century, and instead of losing 96% of its purchasing power, it gained 3,112,292%.

———

You get paid in dollars, and you can and should use them for exchange. If you have to hold them for a few months, try a money market fund—they yield over 5% today. For a year or two, I prefer an actively managed investment-grade bond fund. For more than a few years, it is best treated by equity, preferably a broad, cheap, passive index.

PART 2: BAD NUMBERS

I always dislike these one-sided arguments—*Come see how much the dollar has depreciated over a century!* At best, it's denominator blindness; at worst, it's purposefully misleading, ignorant, or full-blown Russia's Internet Research Agency propaganda. These junk arguments reveal little other than their authors' fundamental misunderstanding of finance.

If it was your ancestor who buried the cash in the mason jar, then yes, technically its buying power is 96% less today than when he stuck it in the ground in April 1917. But that's not the dollar's fault, it's your great-grandpappy's. You would be much wealthier today if your ancestors were not innumerate investing neophytes.

Currency like the USD is primarily a medium of exchange, not a store of value. That's why you don't leave it doing nothing for a century…

———

Holding cash for a century may be foolish, but what about holding cash for a few years or decades? Let's take a closer look.

HOME ALONE WITH INFLATION (BUT NO WAGES)

TIKTOK INVESTORS ARE pretty bad, but so too are the economic grifters on Instagram.

One of my favorite bits of stupidity is about the movie *Home Alone*. It's a Christmas favorite, and gets heavy play during the holiday season. Kevin McCallister, played by Macaulay Culkin, accidentally gets left home alone by his parents in the mad holiday rush to the airport. At one point, he goes to the supermarket to buy a bag of assorted goods.

"*Home Alone* fans are shocked by a 264% increase in grocery prices since the movie was released," screamed an Instagram channel mistitled "Wealth."[153] That data is both accurate and misleading. It has no context, and purposefully leaves out the other half of the spending equation: Wages.

Someone had to earn that money for Kevin to spend, right? The McCallister's 1990 grocery list was $19.83 and by 2023, these exact items cost $72.28. So let's do the math on this: *Home Alone* was released in November 1990, and this Instagram post appeared in December 2023. Over that period, that basket of goods rose 264%, but over the same period, wages[154] increased 274%. Meaning, it was *cheaper* to go to the supermarket in 2023 than in 1990.

The asymmetry of showing rising prices while remaining silent on rising wages is another form of denominator blindness.

If *Home Alone* fans were shocked that grocery prices rose 264% since 1990, I imagine they would also be surprised to learn wages rose even more, 274%. But can you imagine their amazement to find out that the S&P 500 was up 2670% over the same period! That is 10x the price increases of these goods.

PART 2: BAD NUMBERS

The people who make these arguments are either financially incompetent (innumerate), or purposefully misleading. There is nothing in between.

How far would $1 from 1999 go today?

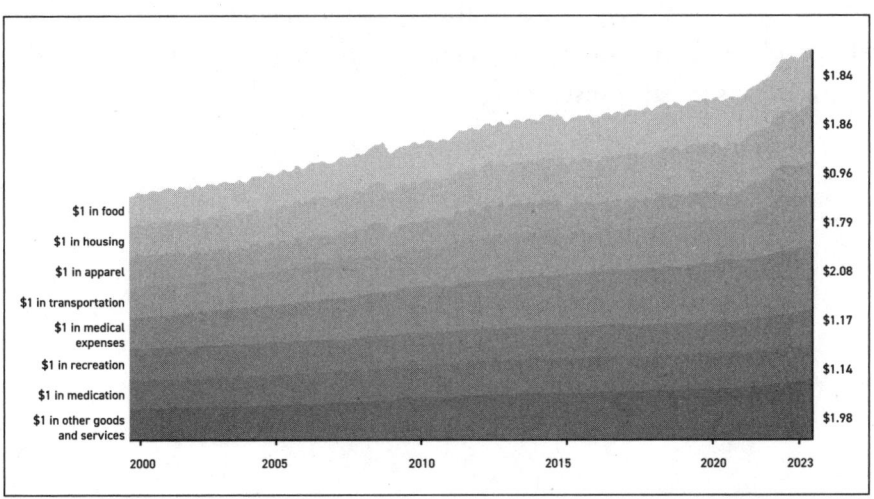

Take a look at the chart. It asks the question "How far would $1 from 1999 go today?"[155]

Same sort of foolishness, showing half of the ledger while ignoring the other half. If you want to compare how prices have risen for the things we buy, then you should also show people's salaries used to buy those goods over the same period. Without it, you only see half of the spending equation. By itself, it is a big scary context-free number designed to frighten you.

The Bureau of Labor Statistics (BLS) tracks all of the individual prices shown in that chart, which runs from December 1999 to July 2023. The BLS also tracks wages, which have also risen over that period, from $573 a week to $1145. That's a 275% gain, much greater than the various products' price increases shown. And again, you buy goods today with 2025 dollars, not 1999 dollars.

What if that 1999 dollar was put into a simple investment like the S&P 500? It would have grown at an annual rate of 6.94% and be worth about $5 dollars.¹⁵⁶ For each 1999 dollar you could buy those 2023 groceries and still have $3.16 left over.¹⁵⁷

Hey, that's a very different outcome—if you understand money and math, *you have actually gained purchasing power.*

Every month, traders, TV, investors, and the media eagerly anticipate "the single most important economic data point for your portfolio." The problem? It's mostly noise...

DENOMINATOR BLINDNESS: MONTHLY NONFARM PAYROLL REPORTS EDITION

EVERY MONTH, WE see what some people believe is the most important data point of our lives: The Employment Situation, or more informally, nonfarm payrolls (NFP).

On a good month, NFP is up a few hundred thousand—about +250,000 or so. Bad months are under +100k to flat. *Really bad* months are down -100,000 to 300,000 or so.

But that monthly NFP number is the numerator; the denominator is the number of people employed full-time in the United States.[158]

That is about 160 million people. This might make you ask yourself, "Why place so much emphasis on a number that is so small?" The monthly NFP is a little more than one- or two-tenths of 1% of the labor force.

It gets worse: Consider that each month, about 3.6 million people quit their jobs in the US. Some are job switchers, leaving for another firm; some leave to launch their own company. Some retire, some take time off for a sabbatical, or go on parental leave. And some folks, to quote Monty Python, "join the choir invisible." [159]

Then there is the flip side: Each month, about 3.6 million start a new job; they begin working after graduating school, or return to the labor force after an absence, or leave one job for a new one.

The monthly employment report is the difference between those two groups of leavers and starters. Not quite 4 million people in motion out of 160 million people.

Said differently, NFP is the net difference between 4 millionish job enders and 4 millionish job starters. That's it! And that is before we get to how noisy this data series is, subject to subsequent revisions and updates.

The NFP obsession is a classic case of recency bias, where we pay way too much attention to what just happened while ignoring both the context and the longer-term trend.

A solution for those who do not want to be distracted with this is to consider a moving average. Rather than focus on any one report, what is the three- (or six-) month average of payrolls? Is it expanding, contracting or just staying steadily on course?

The ongoing trend matters—are we creating jobs or losing jobs each month?—and at key turning points in the economic cycle, the shift is meaningful. But the other 98 out of 100 months? The specific number is more or less a rounding error.

———

Next, we consider how recency bias can prevent us from seeing the impact of gradual but consistent improvements, and why we fail to grasp the power of compounding.

GRADUALLY, THEN SUDDENLY

INCREMENTAL CHANGES OCCUR at a very deliberate pace.

Winter snow melts, the runoff water follows gravity downhill, washing away soil, then clay, and eventually, cutting into the bedrock itself. Winter, spring, summer, fall, snow, melt, year after year. Hardly visible over decades or even over centuries; after a few millennia, barely the smallest of changes are noticeable.

Five million years later, it becomes the Grand Canyon.

Geologic timescales are very different than our usual frames of reference. It's unlike the pace that humans experience.

This is how the world changes, slowly, a little bit at a time—but it adds up.

In Ernest Hemingway's *The Sun Also Rises*,[160] a character is asked how he went bankrupt: "Two ways. Gradually, then suddenly." That has become a favorite phrase of mine, the closest in wisdom per word to William Goldman's "Nobody knows anything."

Sometimes, big changes can be obvious to spot: When the internet first came along, it was apparent to even Luddites that it was going to change a lot of things. But even when massive change occurs, we can underestimate its impact. This is because of all the smaller, incremental changes that occur without our awareness, beneath our collective notice.

Fire, the wheel, the printing press, electricity, flight, internet, and now AI were all big technological advances. We may recognize a game-changing technology, but we have no idea what the game is going to look like a few decades into the future. The iPhone put an immense amount of computing power in everybody's pocket, but I doubt Steve Jobs ever imagined how mobile telephony would combine with social media to wreak so much havoc on teenagers' lives.

I drive a lot of different automobiles, and recently spent some time behind the wheel of a 1967 Corvette. I know cars; I have been driving (or at least steering while standing on my father's lap) for more than half a century. It's easy to forget incremental changes in automotive technologies that have occurred over that time. *This* new feature, *that* improved function, a new safety design, a better engineering solution.

The change from year to year is hardly noticeable, but they add up over the years.

Spend some time in a car without power steering, ABS brakes, 360 view cameras, traction control, lane departure warnings, three-point safety belts. You quickly realize how spectacular new cars have become.

Gradually, then suddenly. Perhaps that helps to explain why "Nobody knows anything."

The C2 Corvette from the years 1963–67 is a gorgeous design, a sleek, sexy, and surprisingly modern-looking car. It's (arguably) the best-looking American car—ever. But old brakes are not great, the manual steering is a beast to use, even the clutch is a bear. It has a lap belt—no shoulder belt. *The car was not even made with a passenger-side mirror!* It looks great, and sounds fantastic, but driving a 1967 *anything* makes you realize just how far automotive technology has progressed over the past half a century.

Today's cars are safe, fast, reliable, and efficient.

The same thing happened with investing. Former Federal Reserve Chairman Paul Volcker once quipped "The only thing useful banks have invented in 20 years is the ATM,"[161] but I am forced to disagree with Tall Paul.

We live in a golden age of innovation for investors, banking, and financial transactions. Financial technologies have made things so much better today than they were 50 years ago. Hell, it's ten times better than it was just a decade ago.

PART 2: BAD NUMBERS

A few examples:

Investing

1. Index funds allow purchases of entire markets or sectors cheaply.
2. ETFs allow funds to be purchased intraday, and operate without unintentional capital gains taxes.
3. Expense ratios have plummeted; costs are much lower.
4. Investor behavior has become much better understood.
5. More market data is broadly available than ever before.
6. Factors that drive returns are well catalogued.
7. Digital platforms allow professional management regardless of account size.
8. Tax-loss harvesting increases net returns for investors.
9. Portfolios can be tailored to reflect an investor's personal values.
10. Direct indexing gives investors enormous flexibility.

Trading

1. Costs have dropped to zero.
2. Trades clear and settle much faster, with next-day settlement (T+1).
3. Apps allow access to markets via mobile devices.
4. Analytic tools are ubiquitous.
5. Market and company information is available instantaneously.

Banking

1. Apps (Venmo) allow individuals to send cash as easily as texting.
2. Square allows vendors of any size to process credit card transactions.
3. Deposit checks into your bank account via your phone camera.
4. Sending money internationally is easy (GlobalRemit and Remitly).
5. Oh, and yes, ATMs are convenient for those who still use cash.

I'll stop there.

If you have yet to recognize this is the golden age of innovation for investors and financial transactions, it's because this remains an outlier opinion. But even that short list above makes it clear how much we have progressed. Gradually, then suddenly.

You might not have noticed these gradual improvements, but to your grandparents they are so futuristic as to seem alien.

Changes compound, just as surely as dollars do. This mathematical sleight of hand occurs slightly faster than a geologic pace. This is how the world changes.

"Gradually, then suddenly." Perhaps that should be the mantra of investors.

People tend to overuse anecdotes and narratives to argue points better analyzed using data. But some anecdotes can lead us to ideas we might have overlooked. That is where we go next.

THE PLURAL OF ANECDOTE *IS* DATA

ONE OF THE key lessons of behavioral economics is the danger of not examining your own beliefs. Failing to consider the reasons that underlie our decision-making increases the risk of error. Although it's fine to operate much of our daily lives on autopilot, not every situation is so forgiving. When we put capital at risk, the danger of not understanding what influences our decisions can be monetary losses, career risk, or even bankruptcy.

In this context, let's consider the aphorism, "the plural of anecdote is not data." This is the idea that a single example should never be used to extrapolate a broader rule about, well, *anything*. This applies to stocks, the economy, politics—just about any situation where a compelling narrative might influence your views despite a dearth of evidence.

The truth of this statement is so self-evident that there seems to be little reason to have to investigate whether the quote is accurate or not. We tend to use it almost reflexively, usually in an attempt to refute a conclusion that cites a personal story. Anecdotal evidence is not mathematically or scientifically sound. When our sample set consists of a single example (N = 1), our conclusion will have a margin of error of plus or minus 100%.

Anecdotes are statistically insignificant.

We have learned the problem with extrapolating from single examples thanks to the work of Amos Tversky and Daniel Kahneman.[162] In 1973, they were studying various mental shortcuts people rely on when making decisions with incomplete information. How easily an example might come to mind—including anecdotes or random examples—might not be representative of the real world. Thus, they discovered the availability bias.[163]

Perhaps the best real-life example of the availability bias is shark attacks.

Most of the time, interactions between humans and sharks occur without harm to the humans, but in the rare cases where there is an attack, lots of media coverage tends to follow.[164]

In reality, the risk is very low. More people were killed by mosquitoes last year than have been killed by sharks in the past 100 years. Indeed, annual deaths from selfies exceed yearly shark fatalities. As we discuss later, you are much more likely to die from a medical error—the third largest cause of death in the US—than from a shark attack. What else is more deadly than sharks? Try armed toddlers—young children who happen to get their hands on a firearm.[165] But shark attacks are more memorable and dramatic, and therefore readily and easily recalled.

Which brings us back to anecdotes: As it turns out, the original quote about anecdotes had a very different context, and a much more nuanced meaning. It is attributed to Ray Wolfinger, who was a political scientist at the University of California, Berkeley.[166]

Wolfinger's original statement was quite literally the very opposite of the quote we all have been using. He had actually said "the plural of anecdote is data." This might affect how we should think about and use narratives and data.

The earliest discussion I could track down of the original quote was via the American Dialect Society. Fred Shapiro, former editor of the *Yale Dictionary of Quotations*, had an email exchange with the professor about the statement's origins.[167] Wolfinger recalled responding to a student's dismissal of a factual statement as a mere anecdote, and told Shapiro: "It was meant to suggest that data does not have an immaculate birth, and that anecdotes lead to deeper research and then data."

The professor's take was not a warning against extrapolation or anecdotal evidence. If anything, he was encouraging data scientists to delve deeper into their experiences to discover fertile new areas for research and exploration. To the alert observer, a compelling anecdote should start the process of digging into the data to determine if something is merely an intriguing one-off, or emblematic of a nascent trend. A good story should be considered preliminary evidence, the start of a more serious inquiry.

In other words, the plural of anecdote, to be more precise, *might be* valid data leading to a potentially significant conclusion. For that reason,

PART 2: BAD NUMBERS

when an unusual anecdote captures one's attention, it shouldn't be casually dismissed, lest a deeper truth be missed.

Consider the ramifications of this for how analysts, economists, fund managers do their jobs. Algorithms are increasingly replacing repetitive tasks, and for people who work in finance, this is potentially an existential risk to their careers. The ability to identify something via an anecdotal observation, then use data to discover a new idea or concept, might be relatively immune from the machines coming to replace you. So take heart: It might be a while—if ever—before AI and big data are sophisticated enough to do just that.

—

The past ten chapters are a good start to understand economic innumeracy. In our next section, we are going to look at some shocking truths about the markets.

SECTION 2: MARKET MAYHEM

What do we mean when we discuss bull or bear markets?

In this section, we are going to dive deeply into what bull and bear markets are (and are not). We will take apart the bad definitions of both, and discuss a more useful and powerful definition.

I will explain why corrections are normal and the massive opportunities crashes create.

We will also delve into the numbers behind markets: How long they run, how far they go, and why market timing (as much fun as it may be) is so terribly difficult.

Let's jump in.

(RE)DEFINING BULL AND BEAR MARKETS

WHAT IS A *bear market?*
The popular definition is a 20% drop from peak to trough in multiple broad market indexes. There are other "round" number definitions—for example, a 5% drop is a "dip," a 10% decline is a "correction," and a crash is a fall of 30% or more.

These are made up numbers; media/pundit creations with no basis in any history or statistical analysis. Other than the fact that these are base 10 numerals—a coincidence of us primates having 10 fingers and 10 toes—there is no rational basis for these percentiles. There certainly isn't any hard data supporting the significance of these percentages.

What is a bull market?

The popular definition is a 20% rally from the lows.

Why 20? Why not 25%, 30%, or perhaps 21.759%?

There is no historical origin of these numbers. The more important question for investors is this: *Are they useful?* Do these definitions assist in managing risk, deploying capital or even in thinking about market cycles?[168]

No.

That's definitively my answer.

Defining a bull or bear market by a percentage change doesn't offer the insight needed to make investment decisions.

Just consider the depth of the 2015 correction peak to trough: The S&P 500 fell 15%, while the Russell 2000 Index lost 27%. Was it helpful to know the S&P 500 wasn't in a bear market, but the small-cap Russell was? In May–October 2011, the S&P 500 suffered a 22% peak-to-trough decline, while the Russell 2000 fell 31%.

The strongest example of why 20% is a meaningless framework was the Covid-19 panic. From February 19 to March 23, 2020 the S&P 500 crashed 34%. From that February peak to March 11, it was down 19%; the next day, it was down 27%. What should you have done? March 13, the SPX was down 19.94%—now what?

In all of those instances, knowing a bear market had begun based on faux percentage definition was utterly useless. In every instance, markets were appreciably higher a year later (in 2020, a few weeks later) and much higher three to five years later. Sellers who dumped equities into the so-called bear market were punished.

And what about other terms we have for downs and ups in the market; are these helpful and how do we measure them? Here is a list of other names we put to these events. Best of luck putting percentages on these terms.

Corrections, retracements, crashes, and dips

Terminologies used to describe negative market action:

Sell-off	Bear
Crash	Collapse
Pullback	Dip
Retracement	Bubble
Reversal	Profit-taking
Wealth destruction	Crisis
Volatility	Panic

Terminologies used to describe positive market action:

Recovery	Counter-trend
BTFD	Bull market
Rally	Bargain-hunting
Snap back	Calm
Priced in	Surge
Bull	Gains
Bounce	Trend
Wealth creation	Greed

PART 2: BAD NUMBERS

These descriptive phrases are colorful, but they lack any precise meaning. The US NBER has a formal definition of *recession*, but there are no similar definitions for any of the above phrases for market action. That entire list is squishy and imprecise. What information do they provide to an investor? *None.*

Consider this to be a truism whenever you flip on the news and become frightened by the first draft of history. The odds are very much against decisions made under those circumstances working out well for your long-term portfolio.

Why do I claim definitions are pointless and unable to help investors in any meaningful way? They don't assist in managing risk; they don't inform as to when or how to deploy capital. They lead to bad decision-making and worse outcomes. What they reveal at most is what some other investors, relying on similarly meaningless numbers, may believe. It seems to be one of those trading myths that get passed along from generation to generation, with no one ever considering whether it has any actual validity.

I have been refining a better way to define markets for over 20 years.[169] In the early 2000s, I began to consider a different set of definitions for bull and bear markets. The idea was to create something useful that I could use as an investor, reflecting what was actually occurring during longer market trends. I found it practical to start with the market gains or losses, then add equal parts long-term economic trends and investor psychology—specifically regarding valuations—to the equation.

Thus, my definitions of bull and bear markets are as follows:

- **Secular bull market**: An extended period of time, typically 10 to 20 years, driven by broad economic shifts that create an environment conducive to rising corporate revenues and earnings. Market volatility tends to decrease. The most dominant feature is an increasing willingness from investors to pay more and more for a dollar of earnings as the bull market progresses.

- **Secular bear market**: After an extended secular bull run, a period marked by rising volatility, frequent cyclical counter-trend rallies and retreats in an economically challenging environment. The dominant feature is that investors become less and less willing to pay the same amount for that dollar of earnings.

Two factors are missing from the percentage-only definition: The broader secular underpinnings, and the psychological concept of earnings multiple expansion or contraction.

Societies change over time: Waves of industrial, technological, and economic progress make their way into employees' wages, consumers' pockets, and corporate profits. Improving standards of living are reflected in the psychology of an era. Not surprisingly, markets do well as investors become willing to pay more for a dollar of earnings as the cycle progresses. Multiple expansion, in the form of rising price-to-earnings ratios, drives returns even more than rising profits. These are not short-lived or modest phenomena. They represent significant change affecting all of society.[170]

When we look at the sources of market gains, earnings improvements are often a much smaller factor than multiple expansion. Three-quarters of the gains of the 1982–2000 bull market were attributable to rising price-to-earnings ratios. At the start of that bull market, in December 1982, S&P 500 earnings in dollars for the year were $31.72; 18 years later, at the end of the bull market, they had more than doubled to $70.39.[171]

But during the same period of time, the broad indexes gained 1,000%. The P/E ratio for the index was about 7 at the start of that cycle and ended at about 34.[172] Most of the market's gains were attributable to the psychology of paying more for the same dollar of earnings; actual increasing corporate earnings only accounted for a fraction of the gains (about a quarter by my estimates).

This is why I have (repeatedly) argued that it isn't the valuation of markets that is so important, but rather, which direction that valuation is moving.[173]

People who are perplexed by a market that keeps rising—despite the usual wall of worry—should look at the psychology underlying this expansion. Bear markets don't begin until this psychology eventually shifts.

PART 2: BAD NUMBERS

Pay attention to what is actually driving markets in this period, and not the pundits.

—

How significant is the idea of a *secular* bull market? As we see in the coming chapter, it should never be underestimated.

THE SIGNIFICANCE OF SECULAR MARKETS

PEOPLE WHO WORK in specialized fields seem to have their own language. Jargon has a storied history of creating the appearance of complexity that, of course, requires expensive expertise. Finance is filled with colorful jargon, too: "Spoos," "Vol," "Monte Carlo simulation," "Gaussian Copula," etc.

I try to eschew the usual Wall Street jargon, but occasionally lapse. I use the phrase "secular cycles," and so before I am called out on it, let's discuss what a secular—vs. cyclical—market is, its significance, and what it might mean to your portfolios.

Based upon my study of market and economic history, I have come to understand that societies, beliefs, even fashions move in long arcs of time. We call these eras by different names: cycles, periods, phases, stages. They vary in length and intensity, but they are typically characterized by an idiosyncratic set of qualities that set them apart from each other as unique.

Regardless of the name we affix to them, we intuitively understand what defines a specific period of time. In any era, there will be a series of dominant economic and societal themes. Ultimately, these themes find their way to equities and bonds.

Let me give you a definition, and then a few specific examples:

Secular cycles are the long periods—as long as decades—that define each market era. These cycles alternate between long-term bull and bear markets. Societal elements affect these markets. These cycles are driven by specific and dominant economic ideas.

Each secular market cycle reflects the key issues of an era. These can include geo politics, economics, resource consumption, technology, or any one of a number of other elements. Over time, each of these factors comes to define the dominant economic theme of a generation. Consider the post-World War II boom, the inflationary malaise of the 1970s, or even the roaring 1980s–90s. Each of these three can be defined as a secular cycle.

With each secular period, a dominant market trend emerges. Historically, these trends have been extremely powerful and, once established, are very difficult to break. They can last 10 to 20 years.

As an example, let's use the post-World War II boom. This long expansion lasted from 1946 to 1966 (with a few mild recessions along the way). The economy was driven by a broad assortment of factors that all aligned at once: 12 million troops (nearly 10% of the US population in 1945) returned home from the war and about two-thirds of them took advantage of the GI Bill, which provided a $110 per month stipend (that's $1,937 per month in today's dollars) to obtain a college education.

A well-educated workforce *always* powers the economy higher.

After being on a wartime footing for so long, civilian manufacturing responded to years of pent-up consumer demand. Commercial aviation expanded dramatically, and soon became an ordinary part of life. The electronics industry also grew rapidly; the seeds for the semiconductor and software revolution were planted. The post-war period also saw the suburbanization of America, the rise of the homeowner, the build-out of the interstate highway system, the rise of automobile culture, as credit availability expanded dramatically.

The top dozen factors all drove a broad economic expansion that was the envy of the world, helping to turn the US into an economic superpower. It's no surprise that the stock market had a fantastic run from 1946 to 1966. The long economic boom led to a long market rally. During that period, the secular bull produced outstanding returns. The DJIA was well under 200 in 1946. By 1963, it was trading five times higher at a level of 1,000.

Of course, there is always a flip side: That post-war expansion was followed by another secular cycle—the ugly secular bear market of 1966–1982.

The 1970s era conjures a vivid memory of disco, polyester, gas lines, stagflation, and recession. It was an era of socio-political upheaval and a general economic malaise, defined by spikes in inflation, the Watergate scandal, the oil embargo, and the Vietnam War. The market experienced a lot of rallies and sell-offs, but stocks failed to make much forward progress overall. The Dow kissed 1,000 in 1966 but did not manage to get over it on a permanent basis until 1982—16 frustrating years later. On an inflation-adjusted basis, stocks lost 75% of their value over this period.

The period from 2000 to 2013 was similar. Defined by the bursting of the dotcom bubble, the September 11 terror attacks, massive corporate accounting frauds, and the wars in Iraq and Afghanistan, and of course the GFC, it too featured an inflationary spike and high oil prices. But the GFC killed inflation, making deflation the greater threat. Big rallies and sell-offs also defined this era. The S&P 500 hit 1,500 in 2000, but did not permanently climb above that until some 13 years later in March 2013.[174]

That is the yin and yang of long cycles. The underlying factors that drive each era come to dominate them. Sometimes it's war, or inflation, or technology, or some combination of these. But they are extremely powerful, and they can drive global economies for decades at a time.

The takeaway is that secular bull markets lead to secular bear markets which, in turn, lead to new secular bull markets, and the cycle repeats into the future.

I was in the new secular bull market camp in 2013. It may be obvious in retrospect, but the great secular bear market of 2000–13 ended in March 2013, when the market notched new highs. That is the big signal after a long bear market—when prices beat the prior highs from the previous bull markets.[175]

If you were paying attention in the spring of 2013, you would have noticed most major US stock markets and indices had broken above their previous 13-year trading range. All-time highs soon followed, including for the Dow Jones, the Russell 2000, and the S&P 500. Eventually, the Nasdaq caught up. Having collapsed 81% from its March 2000 peak, it soon recovered to its prior highs, and blew past other indices. A new secular cycle had begun.

No two cycles are identical. The first half of the 2010s expansion was a typical post-credit crisis recovery. Historically, these have been weaker than the usual recession recoveries.[176] The 2010 cycle was subpar GDP, weak job growth, and poor retail sales. Despite this, the markets powered higher. The connection between the economy and what is reflected in the earnings of publicly traded companies is much looser than many people realize.

PART 2: BAD NUMBERS

The folks I know who worked on The Street in the 1970s and 1980s—people like Jeff Saut, former chief strategist at Raymond James, or Ralph Acampora, the former director of technical analysis for Prudential Securities and founder of the Market Technicians Association—all commented about how similar the sentiment was in the early 2010s to the environment in the early 1980s. No one back then seemed to be willing to accept that the 1970s bear market was over. The pain was still too fresh, the muscle memory too strong, and so the same skepticism prevailed.

The big difference was how aggressive the post-GFC Federal Reserve was. The era of quantitative easing (QE) and zero interest rate policy (ZIRP) was conducted on a scale that never happened before.

I recall discussing this in a canoe at Camp Kotok with my friend Jim Bianco of the highly regarded Bianco Research. Bianco pointed out that with rates at zero, money had nowhere else to go but into equity markets. I reach a similar conclusion, but from a different angle: I *always* want to be an aggressive buyer anytime US markets are cut in half—and from the October 9 highs in 2007 to the March 9 lows in 2009, the S&P 500 fell 56.8%.[177]

In the summer of 2009, when Jim and I were fishing in Maine, both of these positions were outliers. The psychology of the moment did not allow many people to see the rationality of these views.

Research in 2013 from Fidelity[178] noted the specifics of secular markets:

- **Average secular bull market** lasted 21.2 years and produced a total (annual) return of 17.2% in nominal terms and 15.9% in real terms. The market's P/E more or less doubled, from 10.1 at the start to 20.5 at the end.
- **Average secular bear market** lasted 14.5 years and had a nominal total return of +1.0% and a real return of −2.3%. The market's P/E compressed by an average of 9 points, from 20.5 at the start to 11.3 at the end.

Those are great guidelines, even if every bull or bear market is somewhat different.

In 2014, I explained that if historical patterns hold true, the new secular bull market could last much longer—another decade or more.[179] A decade later, that proved prescient, but the same logic still holds: Underestimate secular cycles at your peril.

Now that you understand secular markets, let's consider cyclical ones—the shorter counter-trend moves that confound so many investors.

SECULAR VS. CYCLICAL MARKETS

LET'S TALK *CYCLICAL* markets.

As noted last chapter, a **secular market** is defined as a broad expansion in the economy, with rising corporate profits and revenues. It typically includes a bevy of new types of employment, with many new products and services offered, and increased consumer spending. A secular expansion touches upon just about every element of society. Secular bull markets tend to last anywhere from ~15 to 20 years (or longer), and secular bear markets about half to three-quarters as long.

A **cyclical market**, on the other hand, can be thought of as a counter-trend move—either up or down. Cyclical markets tend to be much shorter in duration and depth; very often, they are confined to a narrower segment of the economy. They include both recessions and expansions, and specific booms and busts of single sectors.

This is more than just a technical distinction followed by a handful of market historians, but rather an explanation as to why markets can move in ways that perplex so many.

Why are these distinctions so important?

They have a substantial impact on the probabilities underlying any portfolio's expected returns. Understanding this can be a driver of how you set your risk posture and positioning. Emotionally, it is the key to getting through either type of market intact.

Consider the chart, courtesy of Stephen Suttmeier of Bank of America Merrill Lynch. It shows three distinct secular bull markets (arrows) including the post-war era (1950–1966); the late 20th-century era (1982–2000); and the current expansion (2013–?). All three of those periods can be defined by the dramatic technological and economic growth of each.

Note the many drawdowns, pullbacks, and market drops within each of these longer-term uptrends. These counter-trend moves are cyclical bears within a broader secular bull.

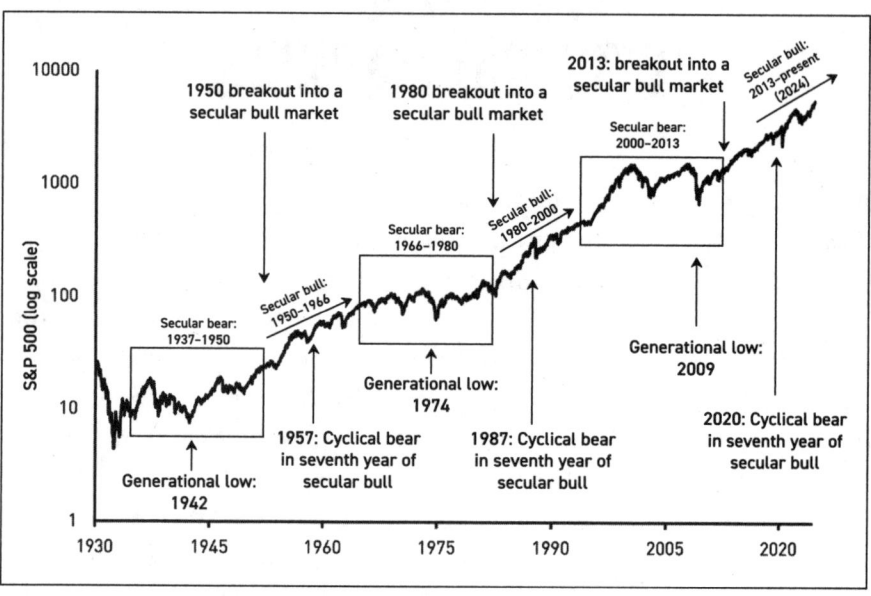

Consider too the three secular bear markets (boxes): 1937–1950; 1966–1982; and 2000–2013. Each involved economic weakness, geopolitical and/or social unrest, with little to no gains in corporate profitability. Again, allow me to point out the many rallies, surges, and market pops within each of these longer-term downtrends.

I have looked at dozens of other cycles, and do not find much value in them as an investor. The 10.8-year sunspot cycle[180] matters to farmers, as does the El Niño and La Niña. But to muni bond or index investors? Not so much.

Human lifespans are not long enough to put much stock in the theories such as Balenthiran's 17.6-year cycle, or Benner's 56-year cycle. We simply don't have enough data—or solid rational explanations—to put any weight on either.

Our current era has been driven by new technologies, ranging from

PART 2: BAD NUMBERS

mobile computing apps to fracking to materials science to mRNA, to say nothing of what AI will do. These are every bit as significant as some prior cycles (e.g., commercial aviation or electronics) with just as large ramifications. Any one of these could have an outsized impact that changes the secular environment.

Instead of hard and fast rules, you should think of market cycles in terms of broad ranges, with no two eras exactly alike. But generally, you should recognize some commonalities as to what drives economies and the markets across various eras. And since we never know exactly what the future holds, it is useful to lean toward probabilities instead of specific binary (bull/bear) forecasts.

Now that we understand the difference between secular and cyclical markets, let's consider how valuations of stocks affect markets. The answer might surprise you.

HOW MUCH SHOULD FAIR VALUE MATTER TO INVESTORS?

How cheap or expensive are stocks *today*? This is always one of the more interesting investing debates. It is a confusing question for everybody, at any point in the market cycle. It often leads to fear, paralysis, bad decision-making, or some combination of the three.

In reality, it is a *trick* question. Most of the time, it is not especially relevant. The better and more important question to ask is, "Should valuation matter to long-term investors? Is it a meaningful input to your decision-making?" The answer is likely to surprise you.

A perfect example of this debate was a 2018 New Year's Day *Wall Street Journal* article, "What to Buy When Nothing Is Cheap?"[181] The dilemma facing large institutions and individuals alike was that nagging question: "Are stocks too expensive to buy?" This implies valuation is the singular factor investors should use.

As it turns out, avoiding US equities because they were over fair value was a terrible, money-losing strategy. That is especially true if you dollar cost average (DCA), putting a fixed amount into the stock market via a 401(k) or any regular savings plan each paycheck.

Since January 1, 2018, the S&P 500 (SPX) has doubled in price. Investors had to endure a near 20% drawdown in Q4 2018, a 34% crash at the start of the pandemic in 2020, and another near 20% drawdown in 2022. A major market event every other year was the price you paid for gains; endure that, and by mid-2024, you were up 103%.

PART 2: BAD NUMBERS

And that was the more *reasonably valued* SPX index; if you owned the *wildly overvalued* Nasdaq 100 (NDX), you gained over 200% in the six years from 2018 to 2024.

What about the even more reasonably priced Russell 2000? Less than 33% in gains. Even cheaper were European and Asian stocks, but the performance was lacking here too—for example, the MSCI ACWI Ex-US was up about the same as the Russell, a touch less than 32%.[182]

That was 2018. My colleague Nick Maggiulli[183] pointed out that if in 2012, you did a Google search for "stock market overvalued," lots of media stories were discussing how pricey stocks were and how far the markets had climbed since the March 2009 GFC lows.[184] If you listened to Nick and ignored that bad advice, you were rewarded over the next five years, as the S&P 500 more than doubled (131%), and the Nasdaq more than tripled (236%).

Name a decade or year, and I can show you a bevy of terrible advice from pundits and the media followed by substantial gains in the markets. Even in a secular bear market, the negativity peaks as markets bottom. In fact, crash bottoms are not made until we have a capitulation—*surrender*—by market participants.

My takeaway is that you cannot allow valuations to affect your regular equity purchases in your 401(k) or any other dollar-cost averaging (DCA) into equities. Maggiulli sums this up in his delightfully titled book, *Just Keep Buying*. He smartly argues this is especially true if you are a youngish person. In your 20s or 30s, you have an investing time horizon of 40–60 years. Even *if* valuations are high and prices are expensive, sell-offs are not something to fear; they are opportunities to buy stocks when they go on sale at reduced prices.

Understanding valuation as a point along a continuum, changing as investor appetite for equities grows with the underlying bull market, is a very different idea than traditionally presented. Rather than think of value as one specific moment in time, a freeze frame, instead consider the full moving picture.[185]

Allow me to sum up with a few broad observations about market valuations:

- Valuation cycles are driven primarily by psychology, making *fair value* a point along a chronological continuum, starting out with investor indifference and ending with investor overenthusiasm.
- Cheap stocks are not always good buys, and pricey stocks don't always disappoint.
- Expensive stocks should lower your future return expectations, while cheap stocks should raise them—but only over longer periods of time, when mean reversion can eventually assert itself.
- There are rare moments when valuations become so distorted—either radically cheap or wildly expensive—that making adjustments to your equity exposure is tempting. These occur less than 2% of the time in my estimation.
- As tempting as it is to sell into the highs and buy into the lows, most people are terrible at doing this. As we see later, they usually make the opposite choice from what they should.
- Rebalancing your portfolios on a regular basis—selling a little of what is up a lot and buying a little of what is down a lot—is the best valuation strategy we know of that works.

Overall, valuation matters less than we tend to believe, and even when it does matter, we tend to make the wrong decisions.

—

Rising earnings are good for stock prices, but what turns out to be even better are rising multiples. Let's explore how that works next.

EARNINGS OR MULTIPLE EXPANSION?

THE 1980S-90S BULL market was one of the most fascinating eras in US market history. So much that is important to our understanding was evident during that era. Not only does valuation *not* drive equity gains, but earnings—a core part of valuation—is a much smaller part of what moves equity prices higher than commonly understood.

Keith Wibel of Foothills Asset Management observed that:

> Over 10-year periods, the major determinant of stock-price returns isn't growth in corporate profits, but rather *changes in price-earnings multiples*. The bull market of the 1980s represented a period when multiples in the stock market doubled, then they doubled again in the 1990s. Though earnings of the underlying businesses climbed about 6% per year, stock prices appreciated nearly 14% annually.[186]

That's comparable to my own estimates of equity price drivers. About 75–80% of the gains of that 1982–2000 bull market are attributable not to rising profits, but to P/E multiple expansion. This is very counterintuitive, and the opposite of what is taught in business schools. But the data is very persuasive that the conventional analysis is wrong.[187]

To test the conventional wisdom, Wibel examined the growth in earnings in each decade, beginning with the 1950s. Here is his historical data:[188]

HOW *NOT* TO INVEST

S&P 500

Decade	Annual change		P/E Ratio	
	EPS	Index	Beginning	Ending
1950s	3.9%	13.6%	7.2	17.7
1960s	5.5	5.1	17.7	15.9
1970s	9.9	1.6	15.9	7.3
1980s	4.4	12.6	7.3	15.4
1990s	7.7	15.3	15.4	30.5
2000s*	4.1	−3.8	30.5	20.7
Average	6.1%	8.1%	7.2	16.4

*Through Dec. 31, 2004
**Compound rate
***From S&P 500's level of 1234.18 on July 31, 2005

The conclusion about earnings:

> There is very little correlation between earnings growth and share-price appreciation. During the 1950s, earnings grew less than 4% a year, yet that was one of the best decades for stock-price performance. The 1970s saw the fastest earnings growth in the past 55 years, but that was the worst decade for investors in the stock market.

If there is so little correlation between rising profitability and stock prices, why do we focus so much on earnings? They are singular measures, and easy to understand. But we put way too much emphasis on corporate earnings, while ignoring numerous other factors that matter a great deal as well.

When we reduce an incredibly complex ecosystem that includes much more than simply prices and profits, we get a distorted picture of the universe.

―

Earnings may matter less than we think, but Mr. Market is more rational than we give him credit for. Let's explore why next.

MR. MARKET IS RATIONAL AFTER ALL

O R, WHY MARKETS don't care as much about the economy as you think.

Recall the Covid-19 pandemic that ramped up in 2020 (we'll discuss why this was a unique externality in later chapters). After the March 25 lows, the stock market took off—and went pretty much straight up for the rest of the year, gaining about 69%.

This was so despite the worst US economic collapse since the Great Depression. It was an *Off the Charts* economy,[189] with data series like GDP, unemployment rate, and initial jobless claims so bad they had to be rescaled just to fit on charts. There has never been an economic contraction of the depth and speed of the Covid-19 pandemic in American history.

The single biggest question of spring 2020 was, "How did the market become so unmoored from reality?" I was asked this by clients, colleagues, journalists, friends, and family members. With the economy in the dumps—unemployment was 10%, GDP had collapsed, and business closings seemed to be everywhere—it perplexed people that the stock market had decoupled from reality.

As is so often the case, the answer is found in the data.

The economy we each experience—local, personal, and (for the most part) not publicly traded—was awful. But *that* economy was only a small part of the stock market. To explain why these subjective experiences did not weigh down equity markets, we must look at the weakest industry sectors in 2020 and their impact on market indices.

The surprising conclusion:

> The most visible and economically significant market sectors are also among the smallest weight by market capitalization.

Let's start with some of 2020's worst-performing industries' stock prices: The first half of 2020 through July saw department stores down 63%; airlines off 55%; travel services down 51%; oil and gas equipment and services down 51%; resorts and casinos down 45%; and hotel and motel real estate investment trusts off 42%. The next 15 industry sectors in the index were down between 31% and 42%. And that's four months after the market rebounded from the lows of late March. The table shows performance for various sectors for January 2020 to July 2020.

Sector performance, January 2020 to July 2020

Sector	Performance	Sector	Performance
Department Stores	−63%	Banks – Regional	−33%
Airlines	−55%	Insurance – Life	−32%
Travel Services	−51%	Leisure	−31%
Oil & Gas Equipment & Services	−51%	Pharmaceutical Retailers	−31%
Resorts & Casinos	−45%	Auto Manufacturers	−30%
Oil & Gas E&P	−43%	Beverages – Brewers	−30%
REIT – Hotel & Motel	−42%	REIT – Healthcare Facilities	−30%
Oil & Gas Refining & Marketing	−42%	Real Estate Services	−29%
Apparel Manufacturing	−40%	Luxury Goods	−28%
REIT – Retail	−40%	Advertising Agencies	−28%
Oil & Gas Midstream	−39%	Insurance – Diversified	−26%
Lodging	−39%	Steel	−25%
Food Distribution	−38%	REIT – Residential	−24%
Banks – Diversified	−38%	Aerospace & Defense	−23%
Oil & Gas Integrated	−35%	Building Materials	−22%

These are highly visible industries, with companies that are well-covered by the news media—all household names well-known to consumers. Retailers are everywhere we go. Gas stations, chain restaurants and hotels are ubiquitous in cities and suburbs across the country. Even though most Americans only fly a few times a year, we plan family trips and vacation travel to places with theme parks, resorts, hotels, and casinos.

A reasonable person might have argued that GDP fell by about a third in the second quarter and the S&P 500 should have been in sync with that. What's more, of the 500 companies in the S&P 500, about 450 of them were doing terribly. Retail, travel, energy, entertainment, dining saw sales evaporate. Bankruptcies were piling up—legendary retailer Lord & Taylor was one of many. Yet, the S&P 500, after a huge plunge in March, rallied the rest of the year.

Although high-visibility industries may be of considerable significance to the economy, they are not very significant to the capitalization-weighted stock market indexes.

Consider how little these beaten-up sectors affect market indices: Department stores may have fallen 63%, but on a market-cap basis they were a mere 0.01% of the S&P 500. Airlines were larger, but still weighed in at only 0.18% of the index. The story is the same for travel services, hotel and motel REITs, and resorts and casinos. The table shows the cap weightings of sectors in July 2020.

Sector capitalization weighting in S&P 500, July 2020

Department Stores	0.01%	Luxury Goods	0.06%
Insurance – Specialty	0.02%	Personal Services	0.07%
REIT – Hotel & Motel	0.03%	Health Information Services	0.07%
Beverages – Brewers	0.03%	Trucking	0.07%
Utilities – Independent Power Producers	0.03%	Utilities – Regulated Water	0.09%
Insurance – Reinsurance	0.03%	Food Distribution	0.09%
Security & Protection Services	0.03%	Grocery Stores	0.09%
Business Equipment & Supplies	0.03%	Building Materials	0.10%
Leisure	0.03%	Tools & Accessories	0.11%
Rental & Leasing Services	0.04%	Furnishings, Fixtures & Appliances	0.11%
Steel	0.04%	Utilities – Regulated Gas	0.11%
Real Estate Services	0.05%	Pharmaceutical Retailers	0.12%
Auto & Truck Dealerships	0.05%	Auto Parts	0.12%
Advertising Agencies	0.06%	Building Products & Equipment	0.13%
Copper	0.06%	Engineering & Construction	0.15%

If in mid-2020, the 30 most economically damaged industry categories were delisted, it would have shaved off just a few percentage points from the S&P 500. Markets, it turns out, are not especially vulnerable to highly visible but relatively tiny industries.

The most battered industries didn't matter much because of the way stock indexes are structured. Market capitalization is the reason why.

The US economy is not the stock market and vice versa.

The sectors that do matter? Consider just four industry groups: Internet content, software infrastructure, consumer electronics, and internet retailers. Those accounted for more than $8 trillion in market value, or almost a quarter of total US stock market value of about $35 trillion in mid-2020. Take the 10 biggest technology companies in the S&P 500 and weight them equally, and they would have been up more than 37% for the

PART 2: BAD NUMBERS

year. Do the same for the next 490 names in the index, and they were down about 8%. That shows just how much a few giants matter to the index.

The giant FAANMGs* derive about half—and in some cases even more—of their revenues from abroad. Beyond that, the pandemic lockdown in the US benefited these giant tech companies' sales and profits.[190] Despite the big first-quarter sell-off, the Nasdaq, dominated by those big tech companies, was up 17% by mid-year. From the lows, the NDX was up 84%; for the full calendar year, it rose 47%.

When terrible economic data does not yield a correspondingly bad market reaction, it leads to yet another form of investor denominator blindness. Everyone sees the numerator—the economy's impact on these sectors—but most miss the denominator, namely, the weightings of these sectors in broad market indices. The 50 worst-performing industry sectors in the first half of 2020 were less than 6% of the S&P 500's capitalization. Not to be blasé, but Mr. Market is informing investors that these tiny sectors do not matter all that much to index performance.

On one level, it's completely understandable that people believe markets are not tethered to reality because market performance doesn't correspond to their personal experiences of job losses, economic hardship, and personal despair. But what's important to understand is that indexes based on market-cap weighting are often driven by the gains of just a handful of companies.

The one thing the market isn't irrationally disconnected from is the reality of market capitalization and its impact on stock indexes. Mr. Market, as it turns out, is far more rational than your personal experiences may have led you to believe.

Next, we look at how externalities—non-financial events like pandemics, war, terror attacks, and assassinations—affect markets.

---

* "FAANMGs" was the acronym for Facebook, Amazon, Apple, Netflix, Microsoft, and Google—the big tech companies that boomed during the pandemic lockdowns.

HOW EXTERNALITIES AFFECT SYSTEMS

It took about a billion years for life—single cell organisms—to develop on planet earth. Another 500 million years led to simple organisms that used photosynthesis; another 1–2 billion years later, multi-cellular life appeared. The next ~billion years led to plants, dinosaurs, birds, and mammals.

Evolution was the driving force of these changes. Suitability and adaptation was a key to competitive success. Life evolved so it could adapt to changing conditions. But every now and again, fate intervened, in the form of five mass extinctions.[191]

The most recent: About 66 million years ago, a 7.5-mile-wide asteroid traveling about 50,000 mph slammed into the earth in the ocean near Chicxulub, Mexico. The collision resulted in an explosion estimated at over 100 trillion tons of TNT. That's a billion times more energy than the Hiroshima atomic bomb. The impact gouged the earth's crust several miles deep and more than 115 miles long.

It was not a good day to be a dinosaur.

Everything within 1,000 miles was killed by a giant fireball. That was followed by a 1,000-foot-high tsunami, extinguishing the fires, and drowning anything that survived. Just in case a few creatures were still standing, a 600-mile an hour wind blast tore through the region. And that was just day one. Nuclear winter followed, chilling the planet by a global average of 14 to 18 degrees. Eventually, the critters that could adapt to these circumstances did. The demise of the dinosaurs created an opportunity for the mammals.

PART 2: BAD NUMBERS

What does any of this have to do with markets, economics, and investing? More than you might imagine.

The impact of externalities on economic systems is too often ignored. Typically, familiar variables affect the secular cycles. The ebb and flow of the economy, inflation, consumer spending, employment, fiscal and monetary policy, sentiment, interest rates, etc., all impact the longer cycle of price.

What happens when an externality hits the markets like that asteroid from space?* What happens when a non-economic event crashes into stocks and bonds, and derails their prior path? Consider some of history's externalities that have impacted markets:

1914: Assassination of Archduke Franz Ferdinand, sparking WW1.
1941: Attack on Pearl Harbor, bringing the US into WW2.
1963: Assassination of President JFK.
2001: September 11 terror attacks.
2011: Tōhoku earthquake and tsunami, causing a system failure at the Fukushima Daiichi nuclear plant.
2020: Covid-19 pandemic, leading to a global lockdown.

These are just six of the more obvious examples out of many.

When externalities hit, the initial emotional reaction causes markets to wobble. A spike in fear leads to a sell-off that is fast and hard. The next reaction is the assertion of rationality that follows the emotions. The initial panic is seen to be overwrought, the impact on economies and revenues less than initially feared. Then, markets normalize, and resume their prior trend.

Panic, rationality, and resumption of prior trend as markets reflect new information into expectations. Market historians[192] have seen this over and over again throughout history.

Covid-19 is a textbook example. It led to the fastest bear market in history, and the fastest snapback to prior highs.

---

* Throughout the book, I use the term "externality" to refer to any shock or event that originates outside the financial system and/or the economy. This is different from the way academic economists employ the term, which refers to costs (or benefits) that are dumped on third parties not directly involved in an economic transaction.

We should never assume that an externality is sufficient to derail whatever prior trend was in place.

—

What do we do when these meteors from outer space come from outside the economic or market system and blow things up? We find out in the next chapter.

DO EXTERNALITIES END SECULAR BULL OR BEAR MARKETS?

OF ALL THE things I have ever written or said about the markets over the past three decades, none have generated as vociferous a response as the Bloomberg column published on April 1, 2020.[193] Seeing this five years later provides a glimpse of what panic and emotionality looked like in real time. It is a harsh reminder why investors must *always* manage their emotions.

The column was titled "Maybe Coronavirus Didn't End the Bull Market." The immediate response, often in ALL CAPS or festooned with R-rated language or both, was that I was an idiot or a fraud or some kind of a clueless incompetent. And those were the nicer emails.

The frightened angry tone made it obvious that people were in full-blown panic mode. The 34% drop in the S&P 500 was *obviously* only the first leg down of a worsening sell-off. Rather than look at the historical record of externalities, people instead looked at the GFC crash, still fresh in their minds. I suspect some combination of recency bias and PTSD were at play.

The first quarter of 2020 saw a sudden collapse in equity markets into late March. Widespread assumptions were that the long bull market was over, and a new secular bear market had begun.

As discussed earlier, that 20% yardstick for determining the beginning or end of market cycles is simplistic and blindly mechanical. This 20% measure doesn't help you figure out where—or more importantly when—to put investment capital to work.

Instead, consider what markets typically look like when things go awry:

On average, it takes 255 days for indexes to fall 20% from their peaks.[194] The Covid plunge was the fastest on record, taking just 17 trading days.

With so many unknown factors at play—how fast will the spread of Covid-19 be brought under control, when will a treatment become available, when will a vaccine be ready and, most critically, when can the economy open up for business again?—it's no surprise so many were panicky. But demand related to people working from home drove technology spending; and pent-up demand for entertainment and home modifications was another source of consumer spending. It just was not obvious from driving around your neighborhood.

A market externality such as a pandemic isn't the same as a recession driven by falling consumer spending, rising unemployment, or tighter monetary policy. Nor is it anything like a financial crisis caused by a loss of confidence in bank-asset quality. Instead, it was an exogenous shock that *spilled over* into the broader economy and equity markets. The Japanese attack on Pearl Harbor or the September 11 terror attacks were the better comparison than the GFC.

All of this underscores the need to keep the following in mind: Regular sell-offs in the midst of long-term bull markets, sometimes of a shocking magnitude, are more common than believed. The same can be said about vicious rallies in longer bear markets.

Just consider each of the past three secular markets: 1966–1982 (bear), 1982–2000 (bull), and 2000–2013 (bear) in terms of the above.

A 20-year post-World War II market rally eventually hit a wall in 1966, with the Dow approaching what seemed like an astronomical 1,000 early in that year. It didn't last, and the deficit spending to fund the Vietnam War followed by the Arab oil embargo and the Watergate scandal dragged down the economy and the market. It took the Dow 16 years to finally clear 1,000; in the meantime, it had several brief rallies of about 27%, 19%, 67%, 75%, and 38%. None of these heralded the end of the bear market or the start of a new bull market.[195]

The inverse occurred during past bull markets: The 1982–2000 bull market saw declines in the S&P 500 of about 33% during 1987, including a one-day fall of 22%, the near-20% drop during the 1990 recession, the 14%

PART 2: BAD NUMBERS

stumble during the Asian currency crisis of 1997, and the 20% fall during the collapse of hedge fund Long-Term Capital Management in 1998.

Sell-offs of 20% or more can and do occur during a bull market without disrupting the underlying strength of the expanding economy.

March 23, 2020 turned out to be the bottom, although at the time, very few people could even conceive of such a thing, much less believe it. The long-term factors that drove the US economic expansion after the GFC were still in effect: Low interest rates, technological innovation, and the continuing shift to services.

The average investor should be working from a long-term plan that won't blow up because of a short-term disruption caused by issues like a pandemic or the assassination of a politician. It is always important to remain disciplined and stick with your goals.

—

Despite the pandemic-induced crash, in 2020 the market bottomed and then rallied strongly, quickly making up the drawdown, and then moving on to all-time highs. Let's see what lessons can be learned from that experience.

LESSONS FROM THE 2022 POST-COVID BEAR

WHAT HAPPENS DURING market sell-offs and crashes? It's worth examining when, how, and why they happen, as they present lessons to any investor who was paying attention.

We can take any significant bear market as an example, but let's use the one from the first quarter of 2020, as Covid-19 gripped the world. It barely took a month for markets to crash 34%—from February 19 to March 23, 2020. People dumped stocks in a panic, and then just as quickly panic-bought them back. Most lost money on the transaction, both selling and buying late, but at least they incurred giant capital gains tax bills for all their troubles.

Source: YCharts.

PART 2: BAD NUMBERS

After a monstrous 68% recovery from the March 2020 pandemic low, and another nearly 30% gain in 2021, markets decided to have one of their all-too-regular spasms. Blame whatever you want—Too far, too fast? End of ZIRP? Rapid interest-rate increases?—but the giveback off the highs was substantial: In 2022, the S&P 500 was down 19%, the Russell 2000 was off 22%, and the Nasdaq 100 came down 33%.

A year later, the indices were just about back to all-time highs. Thirteen months after the June 2022 lows, and nine months after the October bottom, markets returned all the way back to where they were pre-Covid.

Let's take a look at this round trip, to see where it led so many astray.

The crowd

Did the crowd's YOLO enthusiasm infect you on the way up? Were you a late FOMO buyer in 2021? Did the palpable panic in June/October 2022 lead to ill-advised sell(s)?

The wisdom of the crowd is why the efficient markets work *most of the time*; at the extremes, you must recognize when the rational crowd turns into an unthinking mob.

Framing and context matters

Major indices had an enormous run in the prior decade of 2010s. It is useful to put drawdowns of 20% or 30% into proper context when they follow gains of 100% (SPX) and 200% (NDX).

Markets go up and down; it is easier to ride out a drawdown when you realize the giveback is but a small percentage of the prior gains.

Forecasting folly

Did you get sucked into the endless predictions of doom and gloom? Were you convinced by the people who *saw the recession coming*? Never forget that forecasts are marketing. Or as John Kenneth Galbraith observed: "The only function of economic forecasting is to make astrology look respectable."

HOW *NOT* TO INVEST

Tech concentration

Yes, a handful of giant tech stocks are driving market gains. But these are not the profitless ideas of the dotcom era. Companies like Apple, Microsoft, Google, Amazon, etc., are fast-growing, highly profitable key players in the modern economy.

Take Apple as an example: Nearly $400 billion in 2023 revenues, $101 billion in profits, five-year revenue growth at 11.5%, and five-year profit growth of over 20%. The Magnificent 7 (Apple, Amazon, Facebook, Google, Microsoft, Nvidia, Tesla) have about $2 trillion in revenue and over $300 billion in profits. No wonder they are called Magnificent—I keep wondering why technology is not more than 29% of the S&P 500.

Expensive markets

There is a fantasy that markets should always revert back to fair value. As we discussed, that is a poor framework for conceptualizing equities. Instead, think of fair value as a point on the spectrum from cheap to dear that markets wave hello and goodbye to as they blow past in either direction.

Overvalued markets can stay overvalued for much of a bull market cycle.

Yield curve inversion

Cam Harvey, the creator of the inverted yield curve recession indicator, points out that it is eight for eight in terms of recession forecasts.[196] That is a good track record, but also a very tiny sample set. And it never has operated in an era where rates were at or near zero for more than a decade.

Some people have argued that instead of predicting recessions, an inverted yield curve actually predicts the FOMC (Federal Open Market Committee) response to falling inflation, which can be—but isn't always—associated with economic contractions.

The lesson is there are no holy grails, and no indicators that are perfectly reliable.

PART 2: BAD NUMBERS

Narratives and holding periods

Traders have very short holding periods, and are concerned with catalysts that drive prices day to day and even minute to minute. Investors hold asset classes, to benefit from long-term value creation and compounding.

Damage occurs when narratives of traders are used to justify the actions of investors, and vice versa. Understand your investment horizon, be it minutes or decades. Never use someone else's narrative to justify your investment behavior.

Oaktree Capital's Howard Marks is fond of saying, "Experience is what you get when you don't get what you want."[197] If you did not get what you wanted from markets since those 2022 lows, then perhaps the silver lining is you gained experience.

Those were a few of the lessons learned from a short-lived bear market caused by an externality. What lessons do full-on market bubble crashes teach us? Read on to find out.

LIVING THROUGH A BUBBLE CRASH

BEAR MARKETS TYPICALLY wipe out years' worth of gains. Think back to the 2000–02 crash. The dotcom implosion saw the Nasdaq fall 81% peak to trough. By October 2002, the NDX had fallen to 815—levels not previously seen since early 1997 or late 1996!

It is worthwhile to delve deeper into various crash scenarios for those of you who have not been paying attention (or were not yet alive) during the unwind of the last few bubbles.

Understanding it intellectually is easy, but truly grokking the forces at work on people's psyches during a crash is challenging. Some have said it is similar to warfare: You can try to imagine what it's like, but only those who have lived through the terror truly understand its intensity and magnitude.

Our frame of reference is the Nasdaq-100, traded as the QQQs. Nasdaq was where all the action was in the 1990s. I won't bore you with war stories from trading that era; but being a trader or a strategist or a portfolio manager through that boom and crash is supposed to have been a once-in-a-lifetime experience (if only!). You could not help but learn about psychology, risk management, human behavior, and more—so long as you were not hiding underneath your desk.

I have lived through several other 30%+ crashes besides the dotcom implosion. There was the GFC in 2008–09, and the Covid 2020 crash. Prior to that, the 1973–74 inflation/stagflation/oil embargo/malaise led to a 56% crash (I was distracted prepping for my bar mitzvah); and the 1987 crash (also distracted, this time in my second year of law school). But none of those examples were stock market bubbles. The 1990s was a singular experience. Here is what stood out to me from those years:

- **Skill and experience**: Good traders use many strategies to their advantage: They could pyramid, for example add to successful positions as they rose in price. Some averaged down (sometimes a lucky strategy, other times a disastrous one). The strategies that paid off handsomely when they were used during a bull market up 5X over four years were less successful during the ensuing decade of lower returns.
- **Capital is crucial**: Successful, experienced traders were rewarded with more capital and greater risk tolerances by their firms and clients. They could hold positions longer (enormously beneficial in a bull). In the days before full computerization, they could exceed their capital limits intraday. Those who were proven moneymakers got more ammunition to trade with, and much longer leashes. This worked wonderfully during the 1990s phase, but led to mixed results once the peak was behind us. Managing these kinds of risks is what sets apart the best trading shops (Citadel, Renaissance, Millennium, Jane Street) from everyone else that had trading disasters befall them.
- **Leverage is deadly**: Some folks try to make up for a lack of capital by using leverage or options to magnify the results of their trading. That merely creates an enhanced two-sided bet—more upside, more downside. It is a risk that I suspect newbie traders on apps like Robinhood and Reddit did not fully understand; they (eventually) figured it out, often painfully.
- **Muscle memory persists**: Investors who were rewarded for buying every 1990s dip take a long time to unlearn what has worked for the decade prior. The 1997 Asian financial crisis and the Long-Term Capital Management collapse in 1998 each led to robust recoveries and further gains. Those experiences make dip buying a difficult habit to break once the market cycle has ended. One of the things that made the March 2000–October 2002 period so pernicious was that the recoveries that followed every single drop subsequently failed. Starting in December 1999, there were drops of 16%, 11%, 32%, 21%, 14%, 27%, another 27%, 28%, 49%, 45%, and 50%. Each one of these moves lower led to buyers jumping in to take advantage of discounts, only to see the

subsequent rally fail. New lower lows occurred, with fewer dip buyers each time. This is how we eventually work our way toward what technicians call a "sellers' exhaustion."

- **Volatility is a two-way street**: Risk and reward are two sides of the same coin. Very often some of the biggest gainers give back more than average. In the 1990s, the Nasdaq outperformed the S&P 500, which regularly beat the Dow Industrials. The crash saw the NDX 100 fall 83%, the S&P was down 49%, while the DJIA fell only 38%. As my friend J.C. Parets, a technical trader, likes to say, "The bigger the top, the harder the drop."

- **Regret minimization**: I'll share the details in a later chapter, but when you are sitting on immense gains, especially in your employer's stock or your own start-up, taking something off of the table can be a smart move. You still have lots more stock, so if the market continues to rally you participate; if it doesn't at least you have something to show for it.

- **Other asset classes lessen the pain**: A popular mid-1990s trade was to sell some stock to buy real estate: I vividly recall clients rolling out of equity to buy vacation properties, bigger homes, shorter commutes, or nicer neighborhoods. Some rationalized the swap as stocks continued to rise as a fair exchange, but they were delighted after the crash. Not everyone was so lucky.

Bull markets have a tendency to run much further and longer than even the most optimistic investors expect. What most people imagine as the last at bats of a game is often only the 5th or 6th inning of a secular bull market that continues for years.

All these bubble and crash forecasts! Let's look at the excuses for when these predictions fail to happen.

EXCUSES FOR BAD CRASH PREDICTIONS

WHY ARE MARKETS *so difficult to forecast?* I have spilled a lot of words[198] researching this question. The bottom line seems to be that the factors that drive markets do not lend themselves to predictability: They are a volatile mixture of rational and irrational beliefs, unmet expectations, and wholly unknowable events. The resulting potpourri looks a lot like the randomness that Burton Malkiel and Nassim Taleb describe.

The halfway point is the fascinating research by University of Pennsylvania professor Philip Tetlock. He first showed that most professional forecasters are pretty terrible at what they do;[199] then, he explained what the more successful forecasters do to make better predictions.[200] It's a brilliant one-two punch.

Tetlock labels the excuses used when predictions don't come to pass (via Ben Carlson[201]). See if you can spot what they all seem to have in common:

1. If only this one thing would have gone my way, I would have been right.
2. Something completely unexpected happened so it's not my fault.
3. It didn't happen but I was close.
4. I'm not wrong, I'm just early.
5. It's just one prediction.

The commonality is this: *The future is both unknown and unknowable.* That your forecast was derailed by an unanticipated event is not an excuse for it not coming true—it is what happens all the time, and why nearly all forecasts are worthless. Forecasting assets, time, and price at once is felled by this mortal wound.

The bane of all forecasts is the assumption that the future will be like the past. What gets missed is how much of what actually happened was not anticipated, unforeseeable, and therefore not in the models. We make forecasts *a priori* (before) but we experience the world *a posterior* (after). The result is that we believe we knew more than we actually did.

Hindsight bias is only the start of this erroneous process. This is how we are wired.

I have personally made some brilliant market calls (let's just forget the really dumb ones); I cannot tell you how much of these were hard work, genius, or luck. It's some of the former, much of the latter, and none of the middle. It is certainly *not* how I manage client money.

But the world wants to hear that someone has a secret formula, and they are willing to share that secret to fabulous wealth with you (for the low, low price of…).

Unfortunately, that is not how the future works.

Up next, I reveal the secret to making perfect forecasts. You are not gonna like it…

THE SECRET TO PERFECT MARKET FORECASTS

When was the last time anyone got good investing advice from the front page of a newspaper or magazine? Ask yourself the following questions:

- When has the mainstream media made a timely warning about an imminent recession?
- Has the punditocracy ever correctly identified a bubble in real time?
- When have the public's perspectives on market valuation and future market direction been right?

Look no further than mutual fund flows to see how wrong individuals are. Aside from the obvious utility to contrarians at the extremes, sentiment from the public, media, and pundits is simply of no use to me as an investor. I can make a strong case that the commentariat has cost those who listen to them far more money than they have ever saved.

What about you, Ritholtz? How can you impugn the media and well-intentioned pundits when you yourself are a member of the chattering classes?

I plead, "Guilty with an explanation." You will note a consistent theme in my columns and TV and radio appearances:

- I don't offer opinions about things I don't know anything about.
- The use of data from credible sources is always the underlying basis for discussions.

- I recognize my own cognitive foibles and consistently attempt to be self-aware of the limitations and failures of the human wetware.
- I never make predictions.

On that last bullet point, I must admit to engaging in that sort of tomfoolery in the past. At one time, I was happy to make wild speculative guesses, but it always surprised me when people actually took them seriously. The tell was a column I wrote in 2005 titled "The Folly of Forecasting."[202] But lots of other folks do take forecasts seriously, and make investments based on these silly prognostications.

So I just stopped. I am not in the forecasting business.[203] My preference is to try to identify some aspect of markets or the economy that is overlooked—a "variant perspective"—and expound on that. It's more productive and useful than pointlessly speculating about the future.

The reality is that expert forecasts are statistically indistinguishable from random guesses. Here is what makes them so dangerous: The more specific and confident the forecaster is, the more likely the viewing public will believe them. And even more amazing, the more self-confident a pundit is, the worse their track record is likely to be. As we saw in "Bad Ideas," the least-accurate guesses come from those who got lucky with one big outlier call.

Consider what you would have had to do over the past few decades to successfully predict the market. The dotcom top, the double bottom in October 2002–March 2003; the highs in 2007, the lows of 2009. The Flash Crash in May 2010. The Q4 2018 20% drop. Sidestepping the 34% drop during the 2020 pandemic; calling the March 2020 lows. Then there was foreseeing the impact of the 2022 rate hiking cycle on stocks AND bonds. Calling those lows in October 2022 for the next bull leg upwards, still in progress as of this writing.

My own track record at making big calls is pretty good, but none of our clients wants me slinging around their retirement monies based on my gut instinct. I sure as hell don't want to either.

PART 2: BAD NUMBERS

Somebody always nails tops and bottoms by sheer luck. The right call for all the wrong reasons is of no help to investors. What they need is a rational, repeatable process.

—

I was surprised to realize that the bear markets that matter the least were those where I had the most money on the line. We find out why that is next.

HOW MANY BEAR MARKETS HAVE YOU LIVED THROUGH?

THIS IS ONE of my favorite charts, but for reasons that might not be readily apparent at first glance.

The chart shows the peak-to-trough declines of all the bear markets with the popular definition of a 20% decline, measured up until the start of the first 20% rally.* The move from 2022 highs is shown in **bold**.

---

* By now you know I hate the 20% definition but let's work with it for this exercise.

PART 2: BAD NUMBERS

My colleague Michael Batnick[204] likes to point out that all of these horrendous periods of market pain are already factored into long-term returns of equities. Meaning, you do not get the 8–10% long-term gains without living through a significant number of market events, ranging from cyclical drawdowns to longer secular bears to full-on market crashes. It is all part of the dynamics of risk markets, where we obtain our returns in exchange for tolerating that risk.

"If you want to be there for the good times, you must also suffer through the bad times."

This led me to an insight from my own experiences:

The bear markets that mattered the least felt like they mattered the most, and vice versa.

Allow me to unpack this.

Since I began on a trading desk in the mid-1990s, I have lived through multiple cyclical (short-term) and secular (long-term) bear markets:

1990: Recession: Markets fell 20%.
1998: Russian ruble: Markets fell 19%.
2000–03: Dotcom implosion: 81% Nasdaq crash.
2007–09: GFC: S&P 500 falls 57% as credit markets froze.
2000–13: Secular bear market: 13 years between all-time highs (March 2000 to March 2013).
2018: 19.8% pullback as the economy slowed, FOMC hiked.
2020: Pandemic crash: 34%, fastest fall ever.
2022: Stocks & bonds both down >10%, first time since 1981.

All of these meet that silly definition of a bear of a ~20% move off of the peak.

I graduated from law school in 1989 into the oncoming recession (data suggests this negatively impacts your lifetime earnings). I had zero dollars in the market and was deep in student loan debt. The first bear I experienced was utterly meaningless to me portfolio-wise, but felt bad economically. By the mid-1990s, I switched careers from law to finance.

My economic future was uncertain, but I felt confident I could make a go of it. My portfolio was tiny; I had no 401k, and my wife's 403(b), with less than a decade's worth of contributions, was barely five figures.

1997 was a little scary, as was 1998. The 2000 crash was the worst of all of these: The Nasdaq plummeted >80% from peak to trough.

From a purely economic perspective, these crashes were meaningless to me. I had almost no capital at stake; I had lots of decades of savings compounding ahead. If anything, meaningful price decreases created genuine buying opportunities to accumulate more investments (not that I was smart enough to take advantage of them).

But at the time, that was not how it felt. In a new job where market levels affected salary, bonuses, economic stability, and even financial survival, it did not feel good. In fact, *it felt horrible*. People all around me freaked out, stress levels went through the roof.

These early bear markets mattered very little to me financially, but that was not how it felt at the time.

Where things begin to get interesting is in the latter years of my career. By then, we began to have substantial assets in our savings/retirement accounts. Bear markets would meaningfully impact those finances. The GFC and the pandemic were global phenomena; the 2022 market was the worst since 1981 for a 60/40 portfolio. Not only is my portfolio substantially larger, but my entire business—about $5 billion dollars of client assets managed at Ritholtz Wealth Management—is tied to markets. As is my 401k, my salary, my quarterly profit distributions, and my annual bonus. And, the value of the firm!

Downturns literally cost millions and should hurt a lot... but they don't, and in fact, they have the exact opposite effect. *These recent bear markets mattered a great deal to me economically but did not feel that way.* This was curious. The more you think about it, the more it makes sense.

Reframe the idea of bear markets by putting them into a broader context of life experiences. You get older, you've lived through these things before; you know *everything* is cyclical. "This too shall pass" is attributed to King Solomon, an adage to remind the sovereign to be humble in the face of good times and optimistic in periods of despair.

Markets are the same: They go up, they go down, and all of it is out of your control. We are reminded by Stoic philosophers like Marcus Aurelius that the only thing we can control is how we respond to the challenges and opportunities that present themselves.

The biggest single factor that determines your success or failure when these events occur—or as an investor entirely for that matter—is the way you behave due to how you psychologically contextualize what is occurring.

And as it turns out, that is (somewhat) in your control.

SECTION 3: STOCK SHOCKS

It's so much fun talking individual stocks! Watching as they rise and fall and rise again in the markets. As investments, they are *collectively* great.

In this section, we will focus on the numbers behind the individual companies. In particular, why finding the right stock to buy and figuring out how long to hold on to it is tough, and why recognizing when it is time to sell is so challenging.

Let's jump in.

WINNER TAKES ALL APPLIES TO STOCKS, TOO

THE WINNER-TAKE-ALL PHENOMENON is well-documented among sports stars, pop singers, fiction authors, actors, and hedge fund managers—those at the top reap fabulous rewards while everyone else scrapes to get by.

It turns out the same holds true in the market for stocks: Just 1.3% of the public companies in the United States account for *all the market gains during the last three decades*. Outside the US, the gains are even more concentrated, with less than 1% of all equities driving all net appreciation in share prices.

Those numbers come from a ground-breaking study on equities analyzing how gains are distributed.[205] Ardent stock pickers reading the paper might find themselves turned into indexers as a result of what they learn.

The lead author of the paper, Hendrik Bessembinder, is a professor of finance at the Arizona State University Carey School of Business.[206] He and his research team looked at 62,000 global common stocks from 1990 to 2018, and ranked them on a compounded, total-return basis. That period includes two decade-long market expansions, from 1990 to 2000 and 2009 through 2018, as well as two major market crashes in 2000 and 2008. These periods, encompassing bear and bull cycles, make it unlikely the findings are due to anomalies or one-off events.

Their data analysis reveals that net gains for equities can be found in a small group of outliers—and much fewer in number than is commonly thought of by market participants.

Just five companies—Apple, Microsoft, Amazon, Alphabet (Google), and ExxonMobil—accounted for 8% of global net wealth creation. It is hard to imagine a greater example of the winner-take-all distribution—these five companies account for just 0.01% of the total sample set of 62,000 publicly traded companies. Expand that to the top 0.50%, or 306 companies, and they account for 73% of global net wealth creation.

The best-performing 811 companies (1.33% of the total) accounted for ALL net global wealth creation. During that 1990–2018 period, those companies accounted for the entire net stock market appreciation of $44.7 trillion, in excess of Treasury (e.g., riskless) returns. Outside the US, less than 1% of international equities generated $16 trillion in capital appreciation, also in excess of Treasury returns.

Fewer than half of the stocks in the study—23,905—had cumulative positive returns. When added to the top gainers, these stocks generated $66.6 trillion of wealth. However, a majority of stocks—37,195, or 60.90%—were net money losers, subtracting a $21.83 trillion from the total. The total gains of winners minus losers netted out to that $44.7 trillion figure.

Concentration of stock returns was not the original focus of the research; ironically, the study sought to determine how many stocks managed to outperform bonds over shorter time frames. The discovery of the intense market concentration seems to be a happy accident. The researchers found during shorter periods of time, about 56% of US stocks and 61% of international stocks underperform one-month US Treasury bills. In any given month, only 44% of US stocks and 39% of non-US stocks outperformed the accumulated returns of one-month Treasury bills over the full sample period of 29 years.[207]

We can shrug at that data point: After all, stocks are long-term investments and we really shouldn't care very much about any given month's returns. It's the compounding, especially with dividends reinvested, that investors and savers should be thinking about. The obvious data point: The longer buy-and-hold investors retained their equities, the greater the outperformance relative to Treasury bills. It is about 1% for any one month on average, about 14% for a year, 95% for a decade, and a giant 260% for the 29-year sample period.

This isn't necessarily all bad news for active investors; some of the data could be encouraging or even useful to stock pickers. One revelation might

PART 2: BAD NUMBERS

be that active managers should consider focusing less on being stock pickers, and more on being "stock-unpickers"—in other words, avoiding the dogs.

This is very consistent with our core themes: Charley Ellis's "fewer unforced errors" and Charlie Munger's "be less stupid."

Identifying the characteristics of those 37,195 long-term money losers—the quantitative characteristics they share that could be screened out—might be useful. That negative screening strategy works very well in the world of fixed income. It is a common practice for quants, but the sheer number of money-losing stocks makes one wonder if that approach is being fully exploited. If screens could eliminate some of the long-term losers, it might not only improve returns, but could help to justify fees higher than simple indexing. Nearly all active managers today are not earning their keep relative to a cheap simple index strategy.

My interpretation of this study is it reveals another advantage of indexing: Not only are low costs and beta (market-matching performance) of indexing a given, but the research suggests that investors who index broadly may be more likely to hold the rare and outsized winners that drive much of the market gains over time.

What would you think if I told you there was a *guaranteed* way to own all of those outsized winners—that 1% of all equities? Read on to find out how...

FIND THE BEST-PERFORMING STOCKS BY BUYING THEM ALL

"IN THE HISTORY of the markets since 1926, Apple has generated more profit for investors than any other American company."

Jeff Sommers wrote that in the *New York Times* in September 2017. Up until 2016, the leader of all public stocks since 1926 had been ExxonMobil.* The oil giant has been publicly traded three times as long as Apple.

Amazon.com annualized stock price returns were the highest, at 37%, but it hasn't been in existence long enough to create as much investor wealth; it ranked 14th on a list created by Hendrik Bessembinder, the finance professor we met last chapter. Other notable companies on the list include Meta (Facebook), Visa, Alphabet (Google), Microsoft, and Berkshire Hathaway.

We discussed that three-decade-long period where very few stocks were responsible for all net wealth creation. Sommers pointed out even more provocative data from Bessembinder's research: 4% of publicly traded stocks account for *all of the net wealth* created by the stock market since 1926. Within that 4%, 30 stocks account for 30% of that net wealth; 50 stocks account for 40%.

Let that sink in a moment: Only one in 25 companies are responsible for

---

* Exxon and Mobil, along with Chevron, are among the descendants of the Standard Oil trust, which was broken up years ago. The Center for Research in Security Prices database handles this in a method that might understate Exxon's total value creation.

PART 2: BAD NUMBERS

all stock market gains over nearly a century. The other 24 of 25 stocks—that's 96%—are essentially ballast.

Buried within that data point is the implied question all of investment management has been wrestling with since, well, forever: "How can investors find the top-performing stocks like Apple, Amazon, and ExxonMobil?"

Many investors have been following up that question with their own answer: "Why should we even bother trying?"

As it turns out, there are only two ways an investor can own these enormous winners: Through *inclusivity* or *exclusivity*.

The exclusive approach is to carefully screen and research every company that is publicly traded to home in on those rare, outsized winners. Exclude everything else, own what you hope are the best of the best. Patiently wait a few years or decades to find out.

The inclusive approach is the opposite: *Buy every stock*, thereby ensuring that you will own the big winners, as well as lots of mediocre performers and plenty of outright losers.* This keeps your costs low, and time works in your favor. Eventually, winners push aside the losers, as they accumulate market capitalization-weighted size.

"Don't look for the needle in the haystack. Just buy the haystack," advised Jack Bogle, founder of investing giant Vanguard Group, which today manages $9.5 trillion in client assets.

Each approach has advantages and disadvantages. The exclusive approach requires that a high number of low-probability events break your way. First, your methodology must allow you to identify rare companies that will generate outsized returns over time, in advance. At the same time, you must be able to avoid the various value traps and other false starts. This is not impossible, but it is very, very difficult. It has worked wonders at separating investors from their money.

---

* The losers can be useful. We will meet them again in a later chapter on tax-loss harvesting.

There is a second implied question here: Once you find the rare companies in that fortunate 4%, you have to hold on to them. This too is much more challenging than most realize. The stellar stocks tend to have regular, gut-wrenching price slumps; name any big winner of the past few decades and all have suffered retreats of 50, 60, even 90% on the way to creating great wealth. The typical stock picking investor lacks the fortitude and discipline to manage the pain of these severe price fluctuations, especially when they become a very sizable proportion of their net wealth.

Once you get through those two challenges, next you must decide when to jettison the winners. Even the best performers eventually lose their luster. After decades of great performance, General Motors declared bankruptcy in 2009. AT&T was broken into many smaller parts, some of which have done very well (Verizon), while others not so much (Lucent). International Paper, Sears, US Steel, Bethlehem Steel, and Woolworth were all once Dow stocks, and now are worth fractions of their peak values. It was not that long ago that General Electric was a beloved Dow stock; today, it is a shell of its former self. This is to say nothing of the endless parade of frauds that took down companies like Enron, WorldCom, Lehman Brothers, and all the rest.

Finding the very best companies to own is very difficult to do. Figuring out which ones to hold on to is even harder.

The inclusive approach also has challenges. Indexing is boring, and it gives you nothing to talk about at parties. It is considered a lazy way of investing, even un-American[208] and antithetical to capitalism[209]—or worse.[210]

But it does have two undeniable advantages for those hunting for the market's biggest winners: First, it's much less expensive, with lower costs and less taxes. Second, it is all but guaranteed to work.

Think about that the next time you wistfully look at Nvidia's stock price.

If you think *buying* the best stocks is hard, wait until you see the degree of difficulty involved in selling those winners. That's our next chapter.

FUND MANAGERS ARE GOOD BUYERS BUT TERRIBLE SELLERS

MONEY MANAGERS KNOW how to buy. What they need to do is to learn how to sell. Most of them are terrible at it.

That is the stunning conclusion of a research paper published in 2019.[211] If you manage money—or have your own money invested in managed accounts—its findings are essential. It goes far beyond the usual underperformance critiques of active management in an attempt to decipher why fund managers are so bad at this critical aspect of investing.

The paper's authors make numerous observations about institutional managers, but the most profound and alarming is this: Fund managers would be better off, and in some cases much better off, *selling holdings completely at random.*

The study did find money managers exhibited skill in picking which stocks to buy, but:

> While investors display clear skill in buying, their selling decisions *underperform substantially*—even relative to strategies involving no skill such as randomly selling existing positions—in terms of both benchmark-adjusted and risk-adjusted returns.

There is an asymmetry between buying and selling. Purchase decisions are forward-looking, conducive to an analytical process that seem to be consistent and quantifiable. Where problems arise is in the decisions about what to sell and when.

Selling stock in a portfolio is backward-looking; the retrospective nature seems to be susceptible to the kinds of behavioral biases and cognitive errors we typically think of as common among non-professional investors. The study found that professionals were just as likely to suffer from these behavioral errors as the amateurs.[212]

You might think that selling stock, so important to the total return of any portfolio, was a well-understood science. *You would be wrong.* Instead, asset managers often lack a sound analytical framework for selling, using crude rules of thumb or gut instinct, neither of which has a good record for creating outperformance. Indeed, the most common reason to sell is to free up capital to buy the next great investment idea. This effort to chase stocks or other assets that look hot has been a recipe for disaster, both for returns and the active-management business model in general.

Of course, simply selling holdings at random is a methodology that seems unlikely to be accepted by institutions or paid for by investors.

This study is intriguing because the methodology used is both robust and clever: The data set contained the daily holdings and trades of 783 portfolios, with an average value of about $573 million. The researchers then evaluated more than 89 million trading data points and 4.4 million trades. The study encompassed the years between 2000 and 2016—a period that included at least two major market crashes, and two recoveries, one modest and the other significant for its duration. That avoids the common issue of a cherry-picked era. Overall, the research looked at 2 million sells and 2.4 million buys made by veteran institutional portfolio managers.

The clever part comes in how the researchers evaluated performance. Rather than comparing the portfolio returns to a benchmark, the study created what the authors call a counterfactual sell portfolio. Whenever the actual portfolio manager would sell a security, the counterfactual portfolio would sell a different, randomly selected security.

The result was rather astonishing: A random sale of other holdings *consistently outperformed* the one selected for sale by the manager—and by a fairly wide amount.

The counterfactual portfolio with the random sells outperformed the portfolio with managed sells by 50 to 100 basis points over the course of the following year. In other words, the random selection did a better job of keeping winners and tossing losers than the fund manager did.

Just as fascinating: When the researchers created a similar counterfactual portfolio, only randomizing the buys, it underperformed the active strategy. When compared with randomized buys or sells of existing portfolio holdings, managers demonstrated genuine skills—but only when making their buys; they showed little or no skill when making their sells.

This has profound ramifications for active managers, but also shows a path toward improvement. If this group hopes to regain market share and fee-generating assets versus the uninterrupted trend toward low-cost indexing, they must become as skilled and disciplined at selling as they are at buying. Given the results of this study, they have a lot of work to do.

———

What would your portfolio look like if you were the world's greatest trader? How well do you think you will have done versus those low-cost indexers? I promise you the answer to these questions is stunning.

WORLD'S GREATEST STOCK TRADER®?

IMAGINE THE FOLLOWING: You, the investor, believe you have an uncanny skill at picking stocks. You set up an online trading account and begin to buy and sell.

As it turns out, you are quite good. In fact, you're the world's greatest.

You pour more money into your brokerage account and up your trading volume. After the first year, you look at your results: You have trounced the indexes. You snicker at your friends who invest passively in low-cost, low-turnover indexes.

You keep at it, year after year trouncing the S&P 500. Over the long haul, you beat that benchmark substantially—in some years, you gain 30, 40, even 50% more than the S&P 500. You track your returns in a spreadsheet to see just how well you have done.

Over 24 years, you tally up gains and losses. The markets are up, on average, about 9% annually. You, the World's Greatest Trader®, do much better, averaging over 12%. That's better than most hedge funds over that stretch, and better than most average mom-and-pop investors.

How did you do vs. your friends who put their money into broad low-cost indexes?

About the same.

Wait, how on earth is that possible? You trounced the indexes, you crushed the benchmarks, you are the greatest! How could this possibly happen?

In a word, taxes. Depending upon the length of your holding, your tax bracket, and which state you live in, the government could end up capturing a lot of your gains. The long-term federal tax rate on capital gains is 24%; short-term rates are 30%. And then add in state taxes of as

PART 2: BAD NUMBERS

much as 13%, and then city taxes—the government may end up taking almost half of your winnings.

Meanwhile, the buy-and-hold indexers have the benefits of compounding on all of their gains. Over time, the tax disadvantage has a tremendous impact on your net returns. This is a hefty price to pay for the small chance of getting the stock picks right.

This is a huge bogie to overcome. You don't only have to get your stock picks, and your entries and exits right, but you must exceed a "vig" of anywhere from ~24% to ~45% on the transaction due to realized gains caused by the exit *just to break even*.

———

Imagine, around the turn of the century, your best friend invested $10,000 in the S&P 500 and held on through last year. They would have amassed $76,266. That number includes taxes paid annually on whatever dividends came their way at the highest taxable bracket.

Compare that with you, the World's Greatest Trader®. Had you put that $10,000 into a trading account that same year and annually crushed the S&P 500 by 400 basis points, you would have amassed an after-tax return of only $69,197.

In other words, your passive-index buddy would have beaten you, the World's Greatest Trader®, by about 10%. (Note that I am ignoring all of your trading costs.)

The number-crunching for this analysis comes from my colleague Michael Batnick. When he first ran the numbers, he spent a few hours rubbing his head in astonishment. We tried hard to pick holes in it. Sure, it's well established that passive beats active most of the time before taxes. Once we added in the big slice of the pie to Uncle Sam, active trading began to look downright silly. Makes you wonder why anyone would engage in such a ridiculous hobby!

What if you were the World's Greatest Market Timer®?

Same scenario, different skillset: You, the individual investor, have an uncanny ability to sell high and buy low. Your prescience allows you to buy near the bottom of every major crash. Anytime the market has a substantial drop, you manage to make a purchase of broad indexes at advantageous prices. Similar to the World's Greatest Trader®, you set up an online account, and then you are off to the races, timing markets with the best of them.

How would you imagine a trader with these skills would do?

This idea came from a thought experiment run by my colleague Ben Carlson: What if you were the world's *worst* market timer, and you only bought stocks just before major crashes?[213]

Carlson's terrible timer made purchases at the highs before huge drops. Starting in 1970, his unlucky investor saved $2,000 per year to be invested at market peaks. He raised his annual savings by $2,000 per decade (that is, $4,000 a year in the 1980s, $6,000 in the 1990s, etc.) as his salary increased over time. He planned on retiring at age 65 at the end of 2013.

By contrast, the World's Greatest Market Timer only buys when indexes are trading at 52-week lows (assuming they are 17% below the last purchase).

The results of these two thought experiments might surprise you. The World's Greatest Market Timer did very well, as you would imagine someone buying near lows would. But when we compare the trader trying to bottom-tick markets against someone who was dollar-cost averaging into the same broad indexes, the results were fairly close on a percentage basis. In much of the world, the timer edges out the dollar-cost average (DCA). In the US markets and Greece (?!), our diligent averager actually comes out slightly ahead.

Surprisingly, Carlson's top-ticking worst timer of all time did pretty much okay. The results will vary somewhat based on which global index is used, but overall they were comparable.

One would imagine that only catching the lows (World's Greatest Market Timer) would create a huge performance advantage versus the ordinary dollar-cost indexer. And I bet most of you assumed buying only at the all-time highs (World's Worst Market Timer) would create losses.

As it turns out, that is not what occurs.

The reason? In a word: Compounding. It's what happens when gains accumulate on top of gains. It is an urban legend that Albert Einstein ever said, "Compound interest is the most powerful force in the universe,"[214] but it remains true regardless of authorship.

For proof of the power of compounding, consider your mortgage. A

PART 2: BAD NUMBERS

30-year, fixed-rate $500,000 mortgage at 5% gets paid down over time. Despite the fact that your total debt is less each year, it still costs you nearly double the amount you borrowed ($966,279.60) over those three decades. Now consider the average 8% market returns over 30 years—that adds up to over $5 million! (That's assuming a one-time investment and no additional contributions or dollar-cost averaging.) That is the power of compounding returns.

The world's best timer misses out on those advantages (as does the world's best trader). Buying only at the lows means that there are going to be long stretches when either is not making buys. Consider the post-GFC era: Buys were made in March 2009, followed by subsequent purchases in July 2010 and October 2011, but not again for years.

And then, just as we saw for the World's Greatest Stock Trader®, the World's Greatest Market Timer® will also be affected by taxes.

———

How can the pros do this? Mutual firms and hedge funds have a huge advantage that you, the individual investor, do not. They are a business. As such, they pay taxes on their total net gains. Losing trades offset winning trades dollar for dollar each year.

And, they *get paid* to engage in active stock selection and/or market timing. They can get away with active trading because for better or worse (and its usually worse), it's their jobs.

As an individual investor, when you have a losing year, you only get to carry forward a grand total of $3,000 a year in losses to offset against ordinary income. Sizable portfolios in the 2008–2009 crash lost millions of dollars. Folks who sold at the bottom in 2009 lost anywhere from 40 to 60%. Even if they watch their blood pressure and cholesterol, they may not live long enough to write off those losses at $3,000 per year for the next century.

Long-term investors who use an asset-allocation model have another advantage over active traders: Tax-loss harvesting. It's even more productive today via the latest software innovations.

Tax-loss harvesting used to be an inefficient act of guesswork, as well as a commission-generating sales tool. Today, it's a precise process to efficiently capture tax losses at the touch of a button.

HOW *NOT* TO INVEST

How it works: Any asset allocation portfolio will see various asset classes gain and lose relative to their model weighting (e.g., 60/40 stocks and bonds). It's a good idea to rebalance regularly. Rebalancing back to your original weightings has been shown to add 75 to 150 basis points of additional returns over the long term, at no additional cost or risk. It is the closest thing to a free lunch that Wall Street has to offer.

Thanks to new software, investors can harvest some of their paper losses to offset capital gains tax during the rebalancing process. My firm uses Canvas, created by Patrick and Jim O'Shaughnessy (OSAM) and now owned by Franklin Templeton. RWM was the first shop to experiment with Canvas after we introduced the product at our annual conference in 2019, and we now have over $1.5 billion (out of $5 billion in client assets) on the Canvas platform. I find it to be both powerful and flexible. There are lots of other tools on the market, and if you use an online broker, you probably have access to one for little or no cost.

What about the World's Greatest Trader®? Two choices: Quit the day job to open a hedge fund, or invest in an asset-allocation model using broad indexes, rebalancing regularly.

What of an ordinary investor who is a dollar-cost averager into broad indexes? They have a huge advantage over the world's best market timer, in that it's possible to actually do this! The perfect market timer does not and cannot exist. There is no crystal ball or a magic formula that allows for perfect market timing. Instead, our dollar-cost averager simply makes regular contributions to their portfolio. It is a simple, powerful strategy that requires no special prescience into the future, and uses a formula that really exists.

People who sit out of markets for long stretches while waiting for the perfect entry point into the markets are giving up their single most precious asset: *Time*.

The demographic group with the longest investing time horizon are the millennials and Gen Zs now in their 20s and 30s. The aforementioned Patrick O'Shaughnessy also wrote the book *Millennial Money: How Young Investors Can Build a Fortune*. In it, he observes that despite their

PART 2: BAD NUMBERS

long timeline, members of that generation have been missing out. They were significantly underinvested relative to how much time they have until retirement—at least until the 2020 pandemic. Then many took their stimulus checks and began day trading on Robinhood. That worked out exactly as well as you would expect it would: *Disastrously.*

Following the many Wall Street scandals of the 1990s and 2000s, culminating in the dramatic GFC, O'Shaughnessy writes it is no surprise that millennials as a group "don't trust Wall Street." They also rank "major banks among most hated brands."[215]

"The most basic (and important) decision you make as an investor is your allocation between major asset classes—primarily stocks, bonds and cash." O'Shaughnessy observed in 2014 this cohort was significantly underweighted in equities at 28% and overweighted in cash at an astounding 52%. The group with the longest potential runway for absorbing market volatility seems to be the least interested in investing in stocks.

Time, not timing, is key to investing success.

———

What makes market timing so difficult? Those of you who fantasize about being able to sidestep the downturns but still participate in the recoveries must ask yourself three simple questions:

1. What repeatable (not chance-based) process would have had you selling equities near the last 10 market highs?
2. What process would you have followed to buy back in after a 30+% panic collapse?
3. Most importantly, have you demonstrated the necessary discipline to ignore every instinct in each fiber of your being to make a timely repurchase at the lows?

Both ends of those trades are hard to time, emotionally challenging to execute, and much more costly than many realize.

In July of 2020, my Bloomberg colleague Farnoosh Torabi announced she was reducing her equity exposure from 81% of her portfolio to 60%, and tripling fixed-income holdings to 27% in her retirement accounts.[216]

For a variety of reasons, not least of which was age—she was 40 at the time and had decades before she retired—I thought those actions were inadvisable.

Why? Consider all that has to go right when timing the market, including the emotional challenges and financial costs. Here we are five years later, and markets are appreciably higher.

The exit

What motivates people to exit equities, in whole or in part? Most of the time, it is emotion. You never hear investors say, "Everything is going great, the market and the economy look fantastic. Liquidate all of my holdings immediately!" But that is pretty much what you would need to do to catch the market at a top. It is rarely cool, contemplative analysis about a high-probability event that no one else sees coming. Those are incredibly rare, as is having the disciplined personality to manage that process.

What tends to happen is that as markets fall, the drumbeat of bad news feeds upon itself. Eventually, that leads to panic. Too often, the exit is part of what technical-types call "capitulation." The word means total surrender, and it usually means doing whatever it takes to make the pain stop. There are endless studies showing that strategy is never the recipe for strong portfolio returns.

The re-entry

Getting back in when everyone else wants out is even harder to do. We have evolved as social primates, and your skills in cooperation and group dynamics create a distinct survival advantage as a member of the group. Doing the exact opposite of what your peers are doing requires fighting your most basic instincts.

Buying into a panic sell-off is much easier said than done. There are a variety of indicators—technical, quantitative, sentiment, momentum, economic—but none has shown much reliability in nailing the lows.

Catching the bottom requires three things: First, you must have a subjective feel for when stocks have reached their nadir and that the

PART 2: BAD NUMBERS

selling has reached its conclusion. Second, you must have conviction in your ability to do what nearly all investors cannot. And last, you must have the discipline to act on your beliefs, following your trading plan despite the sheer mayhem that always accompanies market bottoms.

None of this is easy.

It turns out that most people are much better off merely riding it out than trying to time the market. Unless you have developed a secret formula that none of the PhDs roaming Wall Street have been able to replicate that ensures being able to successfully move in and out of equities, do your future self a favor and stay away from market timing.

———

Funny thing about traders: All but the best of them tend to resemble Pinocchio. Let's find out why...

WHAT DO TRADERS LIE TO THEMSELVES ABOUT?

Michael: I don't know anyone who could get through the day without two or three juicy rationalizations. They're more important than sex.
Sam: Ah, come on. Nothing's more important than sex.
Michael: Oh yeah? Ever gone a week without a rationalization?

—*The Big Chill* (1983)

ONE OF MY annual habits is a mea culpa. That's where I look back at the prior year to evaluate what I got wrong and why. It is a humbling experience designed to make me a better investor, and I have been doing it—in public—for several years. I am told this is a rarity in the world of finance.

But every year, I hear from a small segment of active traders who misread what the discussion is about, seeing it as an invitation to brag about their best trades. Astonishingly, these e-mailers have all significantly outperformed the markets over the years, putting up fantastic return numbers. They never seem to have a losing trade. They sold Tesla at exactly $409.97 and bought gold precisely at the bottom. Even more amazingly, they got out at the market top in October 2007 and bought in at the exact lows in March 2009.

The technical term for these people is "bullshit artists."

Mathematical probabilities make these claims of uniformly spectacular track records extremely unlikely. And what I find most intriguing is that these Pinocchio traders are not really lying to you or me, but, rather, to themselves.

Little white lies are told by humans all the time. Indeed, lying is often how we get through each day in a happy little bubble. We spend time and energy rationalizing our own behaviors, beliefs, and decision-making processes.

As investors, we want to believe we are smart, insightful, and uniquely talented—even though we often fail to do the heavy lifting, put in the long hours, and make the uncomfortable but necessary decisions to achieve success.

But self-deception is especially costly when it comes to investing. Let's consider some of the lies that a lot of you may be telling yourselves and the impact they may have on your portfolios.

You know what your investment returns are

You would be surprised at how few people actually know what their returns are. Even fewer understand their performance relative to a benchmark.

According to a study of online investors by Markus Glaser and Martin Weber, "The correlation coefficient between return estimates and realized returns is not distinguishable from zero."[217] In other words, what we think our investment returns are, and what they actually are, have literally nothing to do with each other.

It is not that complicated to correct this. Set up a simple spreadsheet using Microsoft Excel or Google Sheets or any of the available online tools. Keep careful records of your portfolios, cumulative and YTD returns, and you will avoid the performance delusion.

You can predict the future

You may not say you believe you can forecast what will happen next year, but you certainly behave that way.

Whenever you try to pick market tops and bottoms, you are making a prediction. Guessing what stock is going to outperform the market is forecasting, as is selling a stock for no apparent reason. Indeed, nearly all capital decisions made by most people are unconscious predictions.

I've discussed this many times, but it bears repeating: No one can consistently predict the future with any degree of accuracy. If your investing approach requires that you become Nostradamus to succeed, then you are destined to fail.

You know how costs, fees, and taxes impact your returns

Not too long ago, an acquaintance was bragging about what a great year he was having. And truth be told, his gross returns were impressive.

Then I had him calculate his net returns. Once he figured in his turnover, commissions, and especially taxes, he realized he had an enormous cost structure that ate into his P&L. After all costs, his great gross returns turned into below-market returns.

At the time, I informed him, "My 75-year-old mom bought an S&P 500 tracker last January, paid an $8 commission (today it would be zero) and forgot about it for the year. She kicked your professional butt." He was not happy about that.

Perhaps we need a corollary rule about active trading: Gross returns don't count, only net returns do.

You can pick fund managers

Yes, we all know who the great fund managers of the past 20 years were, but that's after the fact. What makes you think you have the skill set to evaluate the best ones of the *next 20 years*—their methodology, discipline, character, and ability to express their thesis in investment assets?

Only 1% of fund managers actually earn their fees: Why do you believe that you can pick them out?

PART 2: BAD NUMBERS

You understand mean reversion

Every year, it seems, some fund manager gets the hot hand and becomes a media darling. They attract lots of assets as investors chase past performance. The size of their fund balloons. Then the disappointments come.

Here's why: Outperformance is often random among the 20% who manage to do much better than their benchmark each year. But it's always a different 20%. Following that run of good fortune, they typically follow with a subpar year, as their chosen style or sector cools off—it reverts to the mean, or average. (Math is a cruel mistress.)

You have a plan

I am constantly astonished at how few people actually have any sort of long-term plan other than throwing some money into a 401(k) or IRA and hoping for the best.

You can pick stocks

Let's be brutally honest about this: Discussing specific stocks during a bull market is loads of fun. Chatting about new products, management, and exciting new technologies makes for great cocktail party chatter.

The problem is that most of us lack the specific skill set to do this well. This includes understanding valuations, recognizing problems early and, perhaps most of all, following your discipline to limit losses when things don't work out.

You are saving enough for retirement

I'll spare you the lecture, but for most of you this is not true.

The average retirement account held by 60% of Americans is less than $25,000, according to the Employee Benefit Research Institute (EBRI). The average 401(k) is $77,300, according to Fidelity. EBRI states only 14% of American workers are very confident they will have enough money to live comfortably in retirement.

As Mark Twain wrote: "Everybody lies—every day; every hour; awake; asleep; in his dreams; in his joy; in his mourning."

What are you lying to yourself about?

———

Let's take a look at a few bad trades, including some of my own, to see what we can learn from these errors.

MY WORST TRADES

I WAS ON BLOOMBERG TV one day, when anchor Tom Keene surprised me with this question: "What is your best Apple story?"[218]

I said that in the early 2000s I managed to snag a pre-release loaner iPod. It was obviously a new, digital version of the ubiquitous 1980s Sony Walkman. At the time, Apple's shares were trading at $15, with $13 a share in cash on the balance sheet. I did not see a lot of risk in the shares. I pitched it to my firm's 800 or so brokers, many of whom bought big blocks of shares for their clients.

Soon after the shares had shot up to $20 and the brokers began to sell. "Up big, 33%, gotta ring the bell," is what I was told. I held on, and finally sold when my rising stop loss was triggered on a pullback after the shares reached $45, leaving me with a 300% gain.

"A triple!" I smugly chided the brokers, in what was the **worst sale I ever made**.

In a career filled with other bad trades, missed opportunities, and judgment errors, some fails stand out. Not just for the lost money, but for the lessons learned:

Apple at $15

I may have paid $15 a share, but that was numerous splits ago,[219] which means that had I held on to that Apple stock through last year, my post-split cost basis would have been 26.78 cents per share. That was about $2.4 trillion dollars ago in Apple's market capitalization.

From this I learned two lessons: The first and obvious one was to avoid too tight stop losses. I was raising my stop with each $10 gain; a $13 stop on a $15 purchase became $23 once the price crossed $25. Volatility guaranteed that such a tight stop would eventually get executed.

But the more important lesson was on *how to think long term*. I was behaving like the former trader I was, and not the investor I had become. Trade management is important, but mine did not properly align with my time horizon or risk tolerances. They eventually fell into sync, but it—expensively—took time.

Robinhood's 2014 seed round

"That is the dumbest investment idea I have ever heard."

That was what I told Howard Lindzon, who runs a successful venture fund in San Diego and was an early investor in too many tech winners to list (Facebook, Twitter, etc.). We were sitting outside the Ferry Building in San Francisco and Howard was pitching me on putting money into the seed round of Robinhood Markets Inc., a new app that allowed people to trade stocks for free.

"Howard, the world is moving from active to passive, from stock trading to ETFs. Why in the world do I want to own an app that gives trades away for free to young people with no capital? How are they ever going to generate revenue, let alone profits?" I smugly asked.

I do have a defense, weak though it may be: Robinhood was totally "off brand" from how we were investing at my firm and what I was writing for Bloomberg. I could argue that Robinhood's success was due to bored millennials looking for something to do during the pandemic lockdowns, but what good would that do?

Still, it would have been a fantastic hedge, and the returns from the seed round have been nothing short of eye-popping. It was a nine-figure winner for Lindzon; one that I missed. My mea culpa to Howard was, *"Wow, I really suck!"*

I learned several things:

1. Stay in your lane. My expertise was not in the venture space, so I should have deferred to the pro.
2. Beware of recency bias. An earlier start-up Howard and I invested in never found an exit. That sample set of one colored my view.

3. Do not assume that any start-up, or even mature company, will look the same in six months, let alone five years later. Failing to recognize these truisms meant that I left a lot of money on the table.

In the price

When I was pitching Apple to retail brokers to buy for clients, I could not help but notice the certainty of some people's conclusions about the company's attempted turnaround. Even my mother, a former real estate agent and stock dabbler, sounded like everyone else when she said to me: "Apple? They are going out of business!" (Note my own *smugness* in the above examples.)

When any trading idea creates a knee-jerk reaction of disgust, *pay attention*. This reaction reflects all of the bad news that is already priced in, not the good news that may come later. The lesson to be learned is in recognizing emotional reactions as revealing widespread, backwards-looking sentiment.

Short the market

On Wall Street today, short sellers are an endangered species, and that is too bad. The firm I worked for during the GFC was short several key stocks heading into 2008: American International, Lehman Brothers, and CIT. And the year before, we were short Bear Stearns.

But even getting those trades rights turned out to be missed opportunities. First, there was a constant threat of a short squeeze and our positions could be called away at any moment. Second, we did not size the positions correctly. These shorts were high-conviction trades, and we should have had much more of each.*

The gains from these positions failed to offset the losses (in dollar, not

---

* Note this is not hindsight bias, but actual arguments made in real time. A classic problem with managing a portfolio by committee instead of a single person making the final decision. Years after my departure, that firm went out of business for lots of other reasons.

percentage terms) of other portfolio managers. One such trader had tried to catch the falling knife in banks like Wells Fargo that got crushed during the GFC. The firm would have been in the green in 2008 but for his money-losing long positions. He was such a terrible trader that I tended to ask, "What would MC do?" and then take the opposite position. It was easy money.[220]

Last, and most important, was the limited upside. Short sellers can only double their money—make a 100% return—if a stock goes to zero. I lamented the modest returns of what looked like great trades to the well-regarded short seller, Seabreeze Partners' Doug Kass. His simple suggestion: Always marry a put option (a bet a stock will fall) to your short positions. It's painfully obvious in hindsight, but it was how Doug traded from the short side. I have not put on any high-conviction shorts since then,* but next time, I would marry a 20% put position to any equity short—meaning, for each $100 of equity I wanted to short, I would buy $20 of put options and short $80 of the common stock.

The lesson is that you must have the courage of your conviction. If you really believe in a trade, it should be meaningful enough to affect your profits. Otherwise, why bother?

My bad trades cost me a few million dollars in missed opportunities. Let's take a look at someone else's bad trade that cost them about one-third of a trillion dollars…

---

* I desperately wanted to short Tesla in late 2021 but since RWM owned it through index holdings, and clients owned it individually through Direct Indexing, it was a non-starter. ETF wizard Dave Nadig and I spent hours watching it top out, lamenting the opportunity the whole way down…

SOLD 10% OF APPLE IN 1976

EVERYBODY KNOWS WHO Steve Jobs is. If you follow technology, you also know who Steve Wozniak is.

Do you have any idea who Ronald Wayne is?

In April 1976, Wayne was the third co-founder and 10% shareholder of Apple Computer. For reasons that are both interesting and relevant to our discussion here, he sold his stake for a mere $800.[221] Had he held on to it, that 10% stake of Apple stock was worth $329 billion 40 years later in 2016.

I'll let that seep into your brain for a minute... $800 into $329 billion.

This may possibly be the worst stock trade—ever.

There are lessons for all of us in this. Before we get to those, a brief digression.

Apple was born almost 50 years ago, on April Fools' Day 1976. The story of Jobs, the marketing genius/visionary, and Wozniak, the brilliant engineer/hacker, toiling away in a garage is well-known Silicon Valley lore. But less well-known history is that of Wayne, the third partner, who was there from day one.

His contributions were not insignificant: He designed the company's logo, wrote the Apple 1 computer user's manual, and drafted the company's original partnership agreement. But after less than two weeks with Apple, he'd had enough of the Steves, and on April 12, Wayne sold his stake for $800. In Wozniak's autobiography,[222] he described Wayne's contribution: "Ron ended up playing a huge role in those very early days at Apple."

Wayne's departure sets us up to learn some lessons from this incredible but true story.

HOW *NOT* TO INVEST

No one knows what the future will bring

The future is inherently unknown and unknowable (pardon the repetition, but it bears repeating). Occasionally, some people get small glimpses of it. Jobs gets credit for recognizing the value of the graphic user interface, of making complex technology easy to use, of putting all of the power of a desktop computer into a touch screen on a mobile device. Woz, to a lesser degree, gets credit for reducing the impossible to an engineering problem. But in 1976, nobody but nobody thought Apple would become the world's largest company a few decades later, and completely change the world.

Make sure your risk tolerance aligns with your actions

Wayne was in his 40s when he joined the Steves; he had other life experience, including prior businesses that had gone belly-up. He understood the legal risks of a partnership—including joint and several liability, which holds each partner personally responsible for debt incurred by the partnership.

His risk tolerance was not a good match for this venture.

Wayne had become friendly with Jobs when they were working at Atari. Given the youthful inexperience of his partners—and recognizing that Jobs embraced risk with reckless abandon—Wayne ultimately thought the better of having to deal with the fallout if the venture crashed and burned, which is so often the outcome for any start-up.

He was also the *adult supervision*. Whether it was the risk of the partnership structure or concern about simply trying to keep up with two 20-somethings, this was not the right fit for him.

A good lawyer is worth his weight in gold

Setting up Apple as a partnership—and not Apple Inc.—was the fastest and cheapest way to create a legal structure.

PART 2: BAD NUMBERS

It was also one of the worst ways to do this.

Any good lawyer will tell you that a partnership structure does not protect the founders if the venture fails. The better way to do this is to set up a limited liability corporation (LLC). Different state regulations and tax rates affect different planning needs, and these might lead savvy founders to another structure—an S Corp. or C Corp.—that best fit their specific needs.

All these variables should be understood and discussed in terms of tax consequences and personal liabilities. A good attorney who can explain this—and draw up proper incorporation documents—is invaluable.

Who you work with and what you do is important to your happiness and life satisfaction

Not to get all Zen on you, but starting a new firm means you are going to be spending a lot of time working with the same people day in, day out. After your spouse, it's the most intimate relationship most people have. I am fortunate to work with a brilliant group of "crazy ones, who think different," are fun to be around and keep things moving forward in fascinating ways.

Making sure you are compatible with your fellow workers makes a big difference in your life satisfaction. Had Wayne stayed, he very well could have ended up rich but miserable.

Have a plan

Have a well-thought-out (business/financial/investing) plan. Failing to plan pretty much guarantees future failure.

The early days of Apple were pretty ad hoc. It seems as if little planning was done and that the partners were not on the same page in terms of priorities and focus. Of course the initial partnership did not survive.

Too many financial writers love to quote boxer Mike Tyson: "Everyone has a plan till they get punched in the mouth." But with a plan (and a contingency plan), at least you have options that were decided when you were coolly rational—not when you are bloodied and emotional. Quoting Tyson is the laziest of dodges versus thinking about what might happen in the future.

Compounding is a miraculous thing

When you are forming a new venture, the very last thing you are thinking about is how gains reinvested on top of prior gains compound over decades. Yet that is exactly what occurs with companies that succeed.

Now reinvest those gains again and again for 50 years, and you end up with a substantial sum of money. Obviously, $329 billion is a huge outlier. In 99.999% of instances, gains won't be anything like that. But they do add up over time, and after four decades, even a modestly successful company (or portfolio) can amount to many millions of dollars.

That's the miracle of compounding.

Understand valuation

Not understanding what a company's potential could be decades hence is a mistake anyone could make. After all, the world can change dramatically in a few years. Recall the infamous one-word cover of the June 1997 *Wired* magazine: "Pray." [223] That was when Apple was thought to be on the verge of bankruptcy. Anything can happen.

Three years before that, Wayne wasn't done making bad trades regarding Apple. He sold the original partnership document in 1994—the one he, Jobs and Wozniak all signed—for a mere $500. This was 14 years after Apple went public, and the company had already developed a cult following.

In 2011, the same document sold at auction for $1.6 million.[224] Not understanding the intrinsic and market value of things is an expensive error to keep making.

PART 2: BAD NUMBERS

Wayne is 90 years old as of this writing and occupies himself "a couple of days a week to try his luck on the video poker machine."[225] He was once sitting on the biggest lottery ticket in corporate history. Some people never see what is right in front of their own eyes.

We've spent a couple of chapters looking at bad trades. But what can we learn when a single trade goes bad? As it turns out, a whole lot…

LEARNING FROM A BAD TRADE

WHAT DO YOU do when a trade goes awry? That was the subtext of a *Wall Street Journal* column on Christmas Day, "Eleven Years in the Making: Breaking Even on JPMorgan's Purchase of Bear Stearns."[226]

"It only took 4,209 days, but I am finally even!!!"

So declared Stephen Bearce, then a broker at Wells Fargo. He had taken a flier on 100 Bear Stearns shares amid its epic collapse from $171.51—its all-time record closing price on January 12, 2007—to where Bearce bought it at $30 a share on Friday, March 14, 2008. Over the weekend, it was sold in a pre-bankruptcy fire sale to JPMorgan Chase & Co. at $2 a share in stock. (Eventually, JPMorgan raised its bid to $10.) It took 4,209 days—more than a decade—for gains in JPM shares to bring Bearce's investment back to break even.

Why did Bearce buy stock in Bear Stearns? It was a speculation on the chance the investment bank would be taken over at a premium, making him a quick buck. The lesson offered in the column—"Money is made slowly and lost quickly"—doesn't truly do the trade much justice.

On a hunch there might be other more useful insights for investors, I reached out to some of the savviest traders and portfolio managers I know. What follows are some of their takeaways from our email exchanges about trades gone bad.

PART 2: BAD NUMBERS

Avoid rationalizing errors

John Roque, former analyst and strategist at Soros Fund Management, and now a managing director at Wolfe Research, urges analysts:

> Admit you're wrong immediately. If you're on the sell side and publishing research, your (buy-side) clients will have more respect for you if you admit you made a mistake when you are wrong. Continuing to justify your thesis while your thesis fails is a serious mistake.

Roque also points out that "the cost of being emotionally burdened by a losing position" is substantial. Traders must consider how much of "your time and efforts are being monopolized by your losing position" including the time you spend "rationalizing the holding."

Beware of the sunk cost fallacy

Howard Marks is co-chairman of Oaktree Capital Management, which oversees $192 billion in institutional assets. He is also the author of the classic investing book, *The Most Important Thing*.[227] He points out that the original sunk cost of the purchase price is irrelevant: "The money is gone from your wallet, and that fact cannot be reversed. The question is what you should do today." Marks notes that in the Bear Stearns trade, the JPMorgan purchase price means $28 is gone, and what you have is an asset worth $2. "The question isn't whether you should hold it from a cost of $30. The question is whether you would buy it today for $2."

Past actions should not determine present ones.

Skip the mental accounting

Eddy Elfenbein, manager of the AdvisorShares Focused Equity ETF (CWS) and writer at Crossing Wall Street, points out: "The worst investor in the world is the person who bought a stock, then realized it wasn't the company they thought it was and they're now sitting on a loss." The investor who refuses to sell because they don't want to take the loss has not realized yet that the loss of capital has already occurred. Waiting to break even is a form of mental accounting and a poor use of capital. As Elfenbein says, "The stock is completely unaware of your purchase price."

Consider opportunity costs

Peter Mallouk, CEO of Creative Planning, a $345 billion registered investment advisor, observes: "I look at each position I own regularly and ask 'Would I buy this today?' If the answer is no, I sell." He adds, "Investors should not forget their goal is to see capital grow, not merely return to break even."

Listen to what the market is telling you

Nicholas Colas, co-founder of DataTrek Research, advises against fighting the tape: "Never buy a new low or short a new high." Stepping in front of that momentum can become an expensive error—a lesson he learned as a portfolio manager at SAC Capital. "When a stock is in free fall you wait days (if not weeks) for it to stabilize. And when it makes a new high every day, if you must short, short small."

Counterintuitively, Colas notes the trade in Bear Stearns was, "LUCKY to get back to flat. This is a cautionary story, not one of success."

Always have an exit strategy

J.C. Parets, the well-regarded market technician and founder of the All Star Charts, says all portfolio holdings should be treated as capital: "If this was a trade sitting in cash, would you buy this stock, or is there something else you would do with it?"

Parets observes what he describes as an obvious but overlooked strategy: "Always know where you're getting out before you even get in." This includes having a sell discipline for both winning and losing trades. The

PART 2: BAD NUMBERS

key to successful trading is managing your exits regardless of how the trade turns out. "Markets don't care what your cost basis is," he says.

Own your errors

When you make a trade that turns out to be a loser, admit it, own it, and learn from it. Not admitting an error sets up your portfolio for more losses in the future. Ray Dalio's *Principles*[228] is based on the concept that when mistakes happen, they present an opportunity to learn. Those who fail to accept this not only don't improve, they become more likely to fail again.

Holding an investment until it breaks even is merely a way to refuse to acknowledge an error. A sale won't happen unless and until you admit your thesis was wrong.

As I read the *WSJ* article about the Bear Stearns trade gone bad, I immediately thought of the questions the head of my trading desk would ask a newbie trader in a losing position:

1. What is your edge in this trade?
2. Can you catch the proverbial falling knife?
3. Should you let a trade turn into an investment?
4. What is the opportunity cost of sitting in a bad holding?
5. What should you do when you realize a trade is a mistake?
6. What plans do you have if the position works out? What if it goes against you?
7. What should you do when your original reason for owning something is no longer valid?

I haven't been a trader for a long time. Still, the instincts honed over years in trading are never too far away.

Selecting where to put your capital—stocks, fund managers, or advisors—is much harder than it looks. Let's see exactly how hard it is.

HOW TO SUCCEED IN ACTIVE MANAGEMENT

DESPITE MY ADMONITIONS in the prior chapters, some of you will *still* want to actively manage your assets. To succeed, you are either going to be selecting individual stocks or fund managers. You may want to own bonds for yield; perhaps you will allocate capital to an alternative manager, either a hedge fund, VC, or private credit/equity shop, or a fund of funds.

The data on these investments reveal two important things: First, the odds are against you succeeding at any of these things. Not impossible, just a very slim chance at success. And second, there is a very small percentage of people who manage to do just that, outperforming their benchmark and/or the S&P 500 in any given year. Because these birds are so rare, most of us working in financial services know who they are when they beat the index. Few can do it for more than a couple of years, and the ones who do it consistently over time—the Warren Buffetts and the Peter Lynches—are such rarities they become household names.

Active management is a difficult but not impossible task, and that possibility, no matter how slim, is what keeps people coming back again and again.

Meir Statman, professor of finance at Santa Clara University, studies how people make financial decisions and he sheds further light on the appeal of active management and trying to beat the market. Statman's book *What Investors Really Want*[229] set the standard for analyzing the true motivations of investors. He found that investors seek more than capital appreciation—

PART 2: BAD NUMBERS

they also want well-being, security, alignment with personal values, and fairness. Many seek to show off their intelligence, thereby gaining recognition and status. Setting out to beat the market clearly ties into various of these motivations of investors, especially intelligence and status.

If you still think you can do this, let's look at what you must do in any of the above areas—stocks, bonds, mutual funds, private equity, hedge funds, and fund of funds—to actively beat the market. In increasing order of difficulty:

> Stocks: You must pick the stocks that beat the market.
> Mutual funds: You must pick the guy that picks the stocks that beat the market.
> Hedge funds: You must pick the guy that picks the trader that picks the stocks that beat the market.
> Fund of funds: You must pick the guy that picks the guys that pick the traders that pick the stocks that beat the market.

And so on.*

This is cheeky, but true. Each of these active-management strategies requires an increasingly rare skill set and rising degree of luck higher than the preceding investment vehicles on our list.

We can apply this logic to other asset classes. It is a little easier for bond pickers, as simply eliminating the least attractive credit risks in fixed income allows an active bond manager to beat their index. There are 3,500 US equities, but almost 4 million different bonds, so a negative screen works well here. Picking the bonds that perform better than the fixed income benchmark—the Bloomberg Aggregate Bond Index ("the Agg")—has the best odds in all of active management.

It gets more complicated when we get into the alternatives space. Instead of a known set of data for each potential investment, private companies share what they wish to—or not. There are no SEC regulations for timeliness of disclosures or financial reporting, short of "No fraud,

---

* I use "guy" or "they" as gender-neutral pronouns.

please." This creates information inefficiencies, which means that *someone* is likely to identify a market-beating strategy. But figuring out who that is in advance is difficult; finding a manager whose strategy is durable and long-lasting after you identify them is even harder.

Technical digression: Much of the value in private equity and credit comes from the "illiquidity premium." When investors agree to lock up their capital for five to seven years—something many find unattractive—it creates inefficiencies. Meaning, there may be less available capital than opportunities, which can lead to outperformance.

At least, that was the case *before* the US Federal Reserve kept rates near zero for almost 20 years. Private equity and private credit both boomed, becoming multi-trillion-dollar asset classes. Time will tell if those inefficiencies still exist and whether all that PE capital can capture any of it.

Finally, venture capital involves a unique approach to finding winners. Rather than picking stocks or even companies, venture investing means selecting founders (and management teams). These founders create (pick) ideas that become new technologies. Do a seed or angel round (aka friends and family), and you are picking the guys that pick the ideas that hopefully become successful. If you elect to give your capital to professional venture capitalists, then you are picking the guys that pick the founders that pick the ideas that may become successful.

Stock selection is hard. These other areas are even harder.

Up next, we look at a simple solution to all of these challenges. There are no sure things in investing, but this one is as close as it gets.

FINDING THE NEEDLE IN THE HAYSTACK

THERE HAVE BEEN a series of attacks on indexing over the years. All have failed—at least in terms of how investors vote with their dollars. So far, both legislative and regulatory attempts to restrict indexing have similarly failed to persuade investors of the *evils* of indexing.

We shouldn't be surprised by gaslighting by the anti-indexing community. As Upton Sinclair explained a century ago, "It is difficult to get a man to understand something when his salary depends upon his not understanding it."[230] Sinclair had a clear bead on the financial industry, especially the high-cost, active-investing side of it, even though he was writing about politics and the meatpacking industry.

Regardless, we can channel Vanguard founder Jack Bogle to remind ourselves why indexing has succeeded. As Eric Balchunas, Senior ETF Analyst for Bloomberg, noted, low-cost indexing has saved investors about a trillion dollars in Wall Street fees.[231] The two largest indexing managers—Vanguard at $9.5 trillion and BlackRock at $11.5 trillion—make it self-evident why active managers are terrified of low-cost indexing.

Alas, the war against misinformation is never-ending series of skirmishes.

To understand why indexing should be a core part of your investment strategy, consider the following five issues.

Costs

Investors can own an array of broad indexes, ranging from the 30-stock DJIA to the S&P 500 to the MSCI Global for just a few basis points (a basis point is 1/100 of a percent). Active management is no longer as pricey as it once was (e.g., 200 basis points); it has come down in cost to the 50 to 100 bps neighborhood.

Hence, the people making various claims (absurd or otherwise) against indexing always seemed to overlook this simple issue. Somehow indexing is riskier than buying a single stock, or it can lead to industrial conspiracy to fix prices driven by the indexers (?!?), or the perennial favorite, "Just wait until the next downturn, you will clearly see the value of (higher cost) active management." Yet each time, that value fails to manifest.

Stock selection

Throughout the history of investing, there have been a group of savants who have proven themselves to be brilliant stock pickers: Peter Lynch, Warren Buffett, Benjamin Graham, John Templeton, Thomas Rowe Price Jr., John Neff, Julian Robertson, and Will Danoff round out the list. Their numbers are few—they are the exception that proves the rule.

The challenge in selecting stocks is that the vast majority of stocks don't move the needle. As we saw in earlier chapters, the academic research is clear: Most stocks don't really matter; the typical stock may be up a bit or down a bit, while quite a few disasters crash and burn. But the big drivers of market returns are the 1-ish% of publicly traded companies that put up giant performance numbers over an extended period of time. To succeed as investors, YOU MUST OWN THEM.

The odds are worse than 50 to 1 against you picking those big winners, and are near impossible that you pick *only* those big winners.

Market-cap-weighted indexing, on the other hand, guarantees not only that you will own them but that as these companies get bigger, you will own more of them. Over time, this has proven to be tough to beat. Add in low costs and low taxes, and this formula is nearly impossible to beat.

PART 2: BAD NUMBERS

Behavior

When investors index they make a series of decisions: How much equity, how much bonds, how globally diversified, how much will I add each paycheck, and how often do I rebalance? But that's pretty much it. Once you get past those five decisions when you set up your accounts, it's pretty much *set and forget* for the next few decades.*

Therein lies the true genius of indexing: Everything else involves cognitive errors common to human decision-making. Whether it's stock selection or market timing or when to sell, these decisions invariably are suboptimal. Avoid behavioral problems and eliminate the vast majority of mistakes, and once again you are guaranteed to do better than almost everybody else.

Average becomes outperformance

Howard Marks astutely observes the long-term advantage of being average: You avoid the bad years that negatively impact compounding. By finishing in the middle among managers year after year and avoiding common mistakes, you will gradually work your way into the top quartile of all performers. Average performance turns into outperformance over time.

The counterintuitive reason is that it's not the excellent years that lead to this outcome, but rather the avoidance of disastrous down years. It's not that you need to be smart; as Ellis and Munger inform us, fewer unforced errors and being less stupid leads to enormous wins. Take what the market gives you year after year while others occasionally beat the market, often fail to do so, and occasionally blow up. Over time, merely earning market returns (beta) bubbles to the top of the performance ranks.

---

* We will discuss in later chapters when you *should* make changes to these five decisions.

Simplicity

All other things being equal, simplicity beats complexity every time. A portfolio of passive low-cost indexes should make up the core of your holdings. If you want to do something more complicated, you need a compelling reason.

There are lots of things we do at my firm that go beyond this core philosophy, but only when the upsides outweigh the downsides *significantly*. We will discuss various approaches beyond indexing as your core later in the book. You may need to offset large capital gains; manage emotions, incentivize good behavior, create income. Each of these goals has a degree of complexity, but it is outweighed by the positive results they create.

The bottom line: Indexing has moved from an abstract theoretical approach to investing widely ignored by investors to a key methodology for millions of people, despite—or perhaps because of—the disdain Wall Street has shown.

PART 3: BAD BEHAVIOR

The challenge in writing about behavioral finance is that there is so much wonderful work already in circulation. For those who want to better understand the subject, a few books stand out:

- Danny Kahneman: *Thinking, Fast and Slow*.
- Richard Thaler: *Misbehaving*.
- Jason Zweig: *Your Money and Your Brain*.
- Morgan Housel: *The Psychology of Money*.

I don't want to duplicate the content of these marvelous books, so I focus on the errors I have personally observed in money management over the past three decades.

To make these easier to follow, they are organized into three sections:

1. Avoidable mistakes
2. Emotional decision-making
3. Cognitive deficits

Let's examine how our brains lead us to bad behaviors that harm our wealth and learn what we can do to stop outsmarting ourselves.

SECTION 1: AVOIDABLE MISTAKES

THE BIGGEST MISTAKES THE WEALTHY (AND NOT SO WEALTHY) MAKE

OUR DISCUSSION OF behavioral errors begins with "Avoidable mistakes." As we shall see, these differ from emotional decision-making and cognitive errors in how they manifest in people's portfolios.

Financial mistakes can come from different sources; identifying them might help you spot and avoid them. Self-awareness and humility are enormously valuable traits for any investor. Being aware of when your emotions are driving your decisions helps you manage your choices more rationally. A little enlightenment can go a long way.

It is important to understand that the investing mistakes you have made in the past—and will likely make in the future—are not your fault. It is simply our wetware trying to do its job of keeping us alive. Give yourself a break from the self-recriminations. When it comes to investing, we just weren't built for it.

None of this means we cannot use our big, energy-hungry brains to find solutions to this problem. If fact, we already have. As discussed earlier, "Investing is a problem that has been solved." The problem of human behavior is what remains unsolved.

Bad behavior leads to bad investing outcomes. For simplicity's sake, let's categorize this into ten areas:

1. Planning failures.
2. (Mis)understanding your own needs.
3. Active versus passive management.
4. Improper asset allocation between stocks and other asset classes.

5. Excess concentration (lack of diversification).
6. Excess fees (not getting what you pay for).
7. Not managing or recognizing risk.
8. Trusting the wrong people.
9. Capital gains taxes management.
10. Arrogance and a lack of humility.

The behaviors that fall into this rubric cover nearly every error I have witnessed in three decades working with investors, traders, brokers, fund managers, and clients. In the next few chapters, we will use real-life examples. See how many of the above examples of behavior you can spot.

What if I told you a family of billionaires hit such an unlucky streak of nearly all of the above mistakes that it almost wiped them out? Read on to learn about the trifecta from hell.

THE UNLUCKY BILLIONAIRES' TRIFECTA FROM HELL

Have you ever heard of the Belfers? They are a great American immigrant success story. But contained within this family narrative are a few examples of how easily things can go off the rails. This is true even for the most financially successful people.

After learning of the Belfers' amazing story—a generous family who despite all of their setbacks, are doing just fine today*—you will have a much better understanding of why avoiding mistakes is so much more important than actively chasing the nonsense Wall Street is selling. It is also a reminder that it is not just you or me, but *everyone*—including billionaires—who make money mistakes.

If only we made better decisions, we would all be so much better off.

—

Arthur Belfer and his family lived in Kraków, Poland, where he worked as a dealer in feathers and down. He came to the United States over the summer of 1939, with a few *zlotys* in his pockets. Between the time his ship left Europe and arrived in America, Germany invaded Poland. As the Blitzkrieg advanced toward Warsaw, Belfer's wife and children escaped, joining him in New York City months later.

The *zloty* had been the official Polish currency since 1528, giving Poland four centuries of stable money. But once the Nazis rolled over the border, the Polish currency Belfer held in his pockets became suddenly worthless. Penniless, he set about rebuilding his life in New York City, while waiting for his family to arrive. He did what he did best: Selling down and feathers.

---

* You'll see...

Despite being broke, he found a New York broker to import feathers from Europe for him, which he then resold at a profit.

Thus was born the Belfer Corporation.

Arthur Belfer was so good at selling down feathers that he won the United States Army contract to supply down sleeping bags to the military during the Korean War. He expanded into foam rubber, and then in 1953 founded the Belco Petroleum Corporation. His son Robert joined the company in 1958.[232]

Belco Petroleum grew rapidly over the next decade. In 1962, it became a Fortune 500 company, and soon after, Belco Petroleum went public on the NYSE. Arthur's son Robert was named president in 1965.

The firm continued to grow. With the price of oil rising in the 1970s and 1980s, Robert successfully navigated the firm through several M&A transactions. In 1983, Belco merged with InterNorth Inc., forming BelNorth Petroleum Corporation. Two years later, InterNorth (including its BelCo assets) merged with Houston Natural Gas Corporation.

The Belfer family had become wealthy as their stock compounded over the decades. By 1993, when Arthur Belfer passed away at 86, he had quietly become a billionaire.

That 1985 merger would prove fateful: If the name "Houston Natural Gas Corporation" sounds somewhat familiar, perhaps you might recognize it by its modern name: **Enron Corporation**.

We think of Enron today as a debacle that went bankrupt in 2001 due to its accounting fraud. But for much of the 15 years prior, it was a fast-growing natural gas and commodities firm.

Robert Belfer sat on its board of directors for much of that period. He had graduated Columbia with a bachelor's degree before getting his JD at Harvard Law School. Despite his education, he was just as bamboozled by the bullshit Enron's founder, chairman, and CEO Ken Lay and President Jeff Skilling was spreading as the rest of us.[233]

The *New York Times* reported, "In a disaster the size of the Enron collapse, it can be hard to choose the biggest loser, but a leading candidate has to be the Belfer family of New York City."[234] Thinking it was a bad look for

PART 3: BAD BEHAVIOR

a director to sell in the face of these accusations, Robert Belfer rode the family's Enron shares down to zero, losing about $2 billion dollars.

It was a fortunate twist of fate that the family's philanthropic pursuits led them to avoid an even greater catastrophe. The Belfer Family Foundation, established in 1990, had been extremely generous to New York City arts and culture, to higher education, especially medical research, and to Jewish philanthropic causes (some of that cash likely came from the sale of Enron stock). They funded the enormous Metropolitan Museum of Art's north wing, which is today known as the "Robert and Renée Belfer Court for early Greek art."

The list of beneficiaries goes on and on: Lincoln Center for Performing Arts, MoMA, Guggenheim, Carnegie Hall, the Whitney Museum, the Anti-Defamation League, American Jewish Committee, Central Synagogue, Israel Policy Forum, the UJA, and the Federation of the Arts. They established the Belfer Center for Science and International Affairs at the Harvard Kennedy School, and the Belfer Research Building at the Cornell Medical College. Robert Belfer became chairman of the Yeshiva University's Albert Einstein College of Medicine, where the family funded Belfer Hall, as well as many other endowments.

To fund all of these donations, the family had done some modest diversifying. They sold enough stock in the 1990s to have "big holdings in real estate" as the *Times* described it. Robert Belfer also took their 1992-formed Belco Oil and Gas public in 1996, raising $100 million.

The family had not diversified enough by what we would consider best practices today, but they were still wealthy holders of many assets. Regardless, two billion of losses in 2001 was enormous (and still is today!). Friends described Robert as "sad and self-conscious" and "depressed and he felt stupid."

If managing the family's billions yourself wasn't working out, perhaps some professional advice might help?

The Belfer family was well-connected in the New York art, philanthropy, and financial worlds, and had been very generous to Jewish causes. It was inevitable that they would eventually be introduced to Bernie Madoff.

Following Enron, the Belfers placed their trust in a highly regarded market professional. Whatever due diligence the family did into Bernie Madoff was obviously incomplete, as there were plenty of warning signs that he was not what he appeared to be.

A 2001 article in *Barron's* discussed the excessive penchant for secrecy.[235] Others had looked into Madoff's operation and steered clear. The returns were too consistently good, with zero volatility and no drawdowns. The conclusion was Madoff was either trading on inside information, front-running other clients, or engaging in fraud.

Harry Markopolos was a quant at a derivatives trading shop in Boston. His boss asked him to replicate Madoff's returns. Markopolos said: "It took me five minutes to know that it was a fraud. It took me another four hours of mathematical modeling to *prove* that it was a fraud."[236] Others had reached similar conclusions.

Madoff's claimed strategy was to own blue-chip stocks and buy an option collar ("split-strike conversion") on them. He wasn't actually doing that, just saying it. His entire operation had been a Ponzi scheme since at least 1993, perhaps even longer. But options collars are a well-known hedging strategy, a derivative that protects against loss costing a few percent a year—like fire insurance on your home. Ironically, had the Belfers had an options collar on their Enron stock, they would have avoided that $2 billion disaster.

Maybe this is why the Belfers thought of Madoff as a better alternative than trying to manage their holdings themselves. One could imagine them thinking post-Enron: "If only we were with Bernie, we would have avoided those losses."

If only…

The early 2000s pressured Madoff's fraud. Decimalization—the move away from stock prices quoted in fractions—had reduced the profitable spread between buying and selling prices captured by his legitimate market-making business. That loss of profitability for the firm took a toll, but Madoff was able to ride it out; as it turns out, stealing billions from clients gives you some wiggle room. But once the 2008 financial crisis hit, the full extent of Madoff's crimes could no longer be hidden. There was a sudden and urgent demand for liquidity across nearly all of Wall Street's

PART 3: BAD BEHAVIOR

clients—including Madoff's. The firm's inability to liquidate supposedly liquid assets revealed Madoff's Ponzi scheme for what it was.

What we know about the Belfers' relationship with Madoff is this: They "withdrew more than $28 million from Madoff's scheme before it collapsed."[237] Madoff court documents cite "The Arthur and Rochelle Belfer Foundation" as a potential creditor as well as "Belfer Two Corporation, Unknown."[238] We have no idea how much additional wealth they had tied up with the fraudster; we don't know who referred them to Madoff, or if they referred anyone else.

What we *do know* is that this billionaire family's unlucky streak was about to get much worse.

Managing their own portfolio of stocks and bonds did not work out very well for the Belfers, neither did entrusting it to somebody else. Maybe this entire publicly traded *thingy* is an unlucky mess for us! To hell with all this public stock stuff—we need something new and different that isn't filled with low-life thieves and incompetent weasels.

Enter Sam Bankman-Fried and FTX.

Alameda Research was the wildly successful crypto trading firm SBF (as he was known) launched in 2017. Two years later, SBF launched FTX as a cryptocurrency exchange. The money and profits rolled in, along with accolades and political influence. He became the first self-made billionaire under 30, the fastest to $26 billion, and a crypto wunderkind.

The Belfers rolled a pile of cash into FTX as investors in the underlying company, and perhaps in crypto itself. According to the *Financial Times*: "Belfer Investment Partners held shares from FTX's equity fundraisings in 2021 and early 2022, as well as investing in the crypto exchange's US business… Another firm linked to the family, Lime Partners LLC, also held shares in FTX and FTX US."[239]

Given the Belfers' streak, you might guess what comes next: $8 billion in capital went missing, and FTX was forced to declare bankruptcy. The comingled funds between Alameda and FTX caught the attention of US SEC attorneys; SBF was extradited from the Bahamas to stand trial in America. He was convicted and sentenced to 25 years in jail.

HOW *NOT* TO INVEST

Enron, **Madoff**, and then **FTX**: Has there ever been a greater, more unholy trifecta than this?

I said up front that the Belfers were going to be okay, and they are. The most recent report of the Madoff Victim Fund shows a recovery of 91% of fraud losses.[240] And the FTX recovery—coincidentally special mastered by John J. Ray III,[241] who helped oversee the Enron recovery—is now at 118%.[242]

The way fraud recovery works is this: Victims get a percentage of their investment back, depending upon how successful the bankruptcy special master is at locating the stolen funds. When it is a few million in stolen funds, the percentage losses tend to be larger but the actual lost number of dollars are smaller. Those minor thieves spend money on real estate, travel, watches, cars, and other luxury items. Between depreciation and transaction costs, there is a large amount of slippage.

For larger thefts—the $5ish billion Madoff stole and the $8 or so missing billions from FTX—recoveries are often much higher. It's easy to recklessly blow a few million, but spending billions in a "Brewster's Millions" way that is unrecoverable is more difficult.*

But the recovered losses are what the defrauded clients had invested—not the make-believe returns the fraudster told you about. For many long-time Madoff clients, the damage was not the stolen 9%, but decades of missed opportunity.

It was not so much money that Madoff stole as it was time.

If you gave Bernie a million dollars in 1985, you got ~$910,000 back by 2015. Over the same period, a million dollars in the S&P 500 would have grown at an annualized rate of 11%, appreciating 2,257%. The $90,000 Madoff stole is nothing compared to the 30 years of missed compounding. By the time you got that 91% of your million dollars back, it *should have* been worth $23,567,689.[243]

Hence, stolen opportunity costs were the true Madoff losses.

If only Madoff was as good at understanding compounding as he was at

---

* In the 1985 film *Brewster's Millions*, Richard Pryor must blow $30 million in 30 days, and learns it is quite a challenge.

PART 3: BAD BEHAVIOR

lying and stealing. His math failure screwed his clients out of billions of dollars of ordinary market appreciation.

According to Dante's *Inferno*, fraud sends you to Malebolge, the eighth circle of hell. It is a complex area of ten pits leading to even deeper levels of torture and damnation. That seems about right for Madoff.

The Belfers weren't the only billionaires who made terrible financial decisions—lots of ultra-wealthy people do. Up next, we look at another way to lose billions of dollars, just by pouring half of your total wealth into one single concentrated investment...

DON'T PUT HALF OF YOUR NET WORTH INTO ANYTHING

BILLIONAIRES DO NOT need my unsolicited advice. They seem to be doing just fine without me. Besides, nobody likes to hear from the cheap seats, especially when they just made a terrible, horrible, reckless, investing error that poses unnecessary risk and could cost quite literally billions of dollars.

After I read this May 3, 2018 headline, "This Billionaire Has Put Half His Net Worth Into Gold,"[244] I could not help myself. "Egyptian billionaire Naguib Sawiris is taking action," wrote Bloomberg's Billionaire Index.[245] He's put half of his $5.7 billion net worth into gold. Regardless of the outcome of this investing bet, it is very concentrated and full of unnecessary risk. At the time, $4.75 billion of his wealth was cash.

The billionaire in question, who is buying gold directly and investing in gold miners, is No. 338 on the Bloomberg Billionaires Index and comes from the wealthiest family in Egypt. His father, Onsi Sawiris, is also a billionaire who established Orascom Group. Naguib's youngest brother is the richest man in Egypt.

But our discussion isn't for the benefit of the Sawiris—they can take care of themselves. Rather, it provides an opportunity for us to discuss portfolio construction, concentration, risk, and (of course!) gold. The risk to ordinary investors is that they imitate billionaire investors who have very different risk profiles than themselves.

This gold trade was full of unforced errors. Here is what we should learn from it:

- **Concentrated positions**: As we see in a later chapter regarding General Electric, employees often have too much exposure to one stock. It is no different for *any* asset class: Concentrated positions hold lots of upside potential as well as lots of downside risk. The question you must always consider is: "Toward what end am I adding additional risk to my portfolio?"
- **Investment by forecasting**: Inherent in *any* concentrated bet is a forecast: At some point in the not-too-distant future, THIS asset will be higher than THAT asset. Whether that comes to pass or not, it is what any concentrated position represents. Market history teaches us that making bets based on forecasts is an unrewarding way to deploy capital. We as a species simply lack the ability to see what the future will hold. Humans are terrible at making these sorts of guesses, as we know little about today and even less about tomorrow.
- **Overvalued stock markets crash**: Again, a forecast, and a fairly extreme one. Hardly the basis for making a multibillion-dollar capital allocation. It also reflects a misunderstanding of one's own abilities to time the market based on valuations. Markets have spent most of the past 30 years, except for immediately after the huge crashes of 2000 and 2008, as overvalued. There is little in the market data to suggest people can effectively time their investments, using valuation or any other basis.
- **Forecasting track record**: Always ask yourself: Has the forecaster generated above-average market returns based on their predictions? If they have, is it because of their skill, or was it merely random luck? Most forecasts reflect emotions and wishful thinking. They are *not* the stuff of a good investing process.
- **Already in the price**: People seem to misunderstand what is already known and therefore reflected in market prices. A perfect example is the gold bug[246] tendency to cite the cultural significances of gold in societies like China and India. They are absolutely correct: In those countries, gold acts as a status symbol, a store of wealth, and a wedding dowry. But here is the thing: It has done this since time immemorial. That is why it is *already reflected* in gold's price. The key for asset price movement is not the historical buyer already

reflected in the market, but rather, the *next marginal* buyer that is not yet incorporated in prices.
- **Why invest?** An important yet overlooked part of the investing process is this simple question: Toward what aims and goals are you deploying your capital? Excuse my Financial Planning 101 talk, but depending upon the answer, there is a specific and appropriate level of risk commensurate with your goals. It is challenging to imagine having 50% of your net worth in any single investment. Note that founders such as Bill Gates, Steve Jobs, Jeff Bezos, Elon Musk, and Warren Buffett let their sweat equity ride while they spent decades building the companies for which they are known. Is that what is happening here? Could be. Or maybe he is just:
- **Talking his book**: Be skeptical when anyone is out promoting an investment they already made. We don't know if Sawiris was merely hyping the extensive holdings in gold and gold miners he already owned. In 2017, he launched a "new investment vehicle to acquire gold-mining assets across the world, expanding on the nearly $1.5bn of assets he owns in the sector," according to the *Financial Times*.[247]

This sort of investment leads to an obvious question: Why? Why do this, when you already have $6 billion: *You have already won*! Why put so much of that at risk with a hyper-concentrated bet? Because you have a feeling THIS asset class might do better than THAT one?

Ignore the outcome of this bet for a moment and consider the process. It is intensely concentrated, unnecessarily risky, and serves no understandable purpose. Even if he is correct in the forecast, so what? The risk outweighs any potential reward.

I like to ask billionaire clients this question: "What is the difference between one billion and two billion dollars?" The answer is not one billion dollars, the answer is NOTHING! There is nothing more you can do with two billion than you cannot accomplish with one billion. To put that at risk is to put the next few generations of your family's wealth, philanthropy, lifestyle, and security at risk. Why bother?

PART 3: BAD BEHAVIOR

About that outcome: In 2018, Sawiris said he thought gold prices would rally further, and hit $1,800 per ounce from just above $1,300 while "overvalued" stock markets would crash. By late summer 2024, gold was over ~$2500, up 92%. But the stock market as measured by the S&P 500 was up even more: 94%.

But that's just the theoretical returns, not the actual ones. Had Sawiris merely bought the ETFs representing gold and the markets, he would have fallen further behind—GLD was up 85.5%, while SPY had gained 105.8%. Blame higher costs of the gold ETF and the advantage of reinvested dividends.

But that is not what this billionaire did: He bought bullion (physical gold), as well as the gold miners. When you own bullion, you must pay for storage, shipping, and insurance. Then you have to hire people to make sure nobody steals any of the billions in metal you have. It seems much more complicated to own gold that way than, say, the GLD ETF.

Next consider the gold miners as a class. Since inception in 1993, the NYSE Arca Gold Miners Index has returned about 40%.[248] Not per year, but in total over the past three decades. During the same time period, gold has returned 650%, while the S&P 500 has gained roughly 1150%. The gold miners are lagging the metal for obvious reasons—execution risk, management and company costs, and so on. Even worse, since the SPDR Gold Shares ETF was introduced in 2004, investors buy it rather than shares of the miners as a proxy for the metal.[249]

Sawiris's forecasts were wrong. But as I explained in 2018,[250] his portfolio was a concentrated and risky bet. That's not the best way to manage personal wealth, even when it's measured in billions.

Not that it matters, but since then, Sawiris has dropped from number 338 on the billionaires index to number 405. He'll be just fine, but the investing errors he made are instructive for the rest of us.

Let's consider another classic investing error: Hyper-concentrated holdings.

AVOIDING A CLASSIC INVESTMENT ERROR

IT'S NOT JUST gold that creates a problem when it's half of your net worth—it's *any* concentrated position.

It is even worse when your biggest single asset is also the stock of your employer. Tying your financial health to the fortunes of just one company can create a risk to both your income and assets. History teaches us this is a recipe for disaster.

It's not just frauds like Enron or Lehman Brothers—even the bluest of the blue chips eventually fade away. Consider one of the best performing stocks of the 1980–90s bull market, the mighty General Electric.

Or should I say *once mighty*.

GE was one of the original 12 companies listed on the Dow Jones Industrial Average in 1896. It was more than a blue chip; it was a bellwether for the entire US economy. Today, GE is a shadow of its former self, split in 2024 into three parts—aerospace, medical equipment, and energy.

That's not how it looked a few decades ago, when GE was an unstoppable industrial giant. The company encouraged its employees to buy GE shares directly, making an incredibly generous 50% match of their purchases (taken directly from their paychecks). Considering most firms match only 0–6% of their employees' 401k contributions, for too many employees, this misaligned incentive was too good to pass up.

How did the employees who chose to take their matching 401k contributions in GE stock do? Not so well.

Reading the *Wall Street Journal* one morning in 2018, I spied an article discussing the $140 billion drop in the value of General Electric Co.'s

PART 3: BAD BEHAVIOR

stock price during the prior 12 months: "The stock value lost by GE [in] 12 months is twice the amount that vanished when Enron Corp. collapsed in 2001—and more than the combined market capitalization erased by the bankruptcies of Lehman Brothers and General Motors during the financial crisis."[251]

That sounds like a lot of money lost in a year, but the full story is much worse. At its peak market cap in August of 2000, GE was worth $594 billion. Today, its three surviving parts are valued at about half of that, at ~$300 billion. When that *WSJ* article was published, GE's market capitalization had fallen nearly half a trillion dollars since its 2000 peak. It has since partly recovered—down *only* 50%—small comfort to those retirees who needed that money in the 2000s or 2010s.[252]

Since GE's 2000 peak, markets have done what they usually do over time—gone higher. Had you been in the S&P 500, your returns over the same 25 years when GE was cut in half were 473%, or 8% annualized; a basic 60/40 stock and bond portfolio would have returned 356%, or 7% annualized.[253]

GE's crash was not caused by scandal, catastrophic economic conditions, or a market meltdown. It was, like so many companies before it, simply that GE's time had passed. Professor Aswath Damodaran teaches corporate finance at the Stern School of Business at New York University. His book *The Corporate Life Cycle*[254] describes the normal lifespan of all companies: They are born, they grow, they mature, they decline, and they die.

The list of once-dominant, household-name companies that faded from glory to obscurity is legion: Woolworths (1879–1997), Sears (1886–2024), IBM (1911–present), Kodak (1889–2012), General Motors (1908–2009), Blockbuster (1985–2010), Nokia (1864–2013), Toys "R" Us (1948–2017), BlackBerry (1984–2013), Polaroid (1937–2001), Pan Am (1927–1991), Borders (1971–2011), Compaq (1982–2002), Atari (1976–1993), Oldsmobile (1897–2004), Tower Records (1960–2004), Boeing (1916–?)—on and on the list goes.

What is noteworthy about GE's collapse wasn't that it was unique or special, but that it was so ordinary.

The fall in GE's shares caused many people a lot of pain. It could easily have been avoided. What keeps people making these same mistakes? Why do so many overconcentrate in a single stock?

Recognizing the reasons why is crucial to avoiding them.

Survivorship bias

We tend to evaluate our world based on what we see and remember. That can lead to a somewhat distorted view of how individual companies behave over the long run.[255]

A favorite example of this is the lost or forgotten stock certificate;[256] it resurfaces every few years. A classic example is the person who in 2000 discovered they owned shares of EMC, purchased in 1987 for about $16,000, that were worth about $5 million; today's version is the forgotten and rediscovered purchase of Bitcoins.[257]

The wrong lesson is that if you buy a good stock and forget about it for decades, you will become rich. Employees of GE were thinking the same thing when they overweighted their retirement accounts with company stock.

The survivorship bias is in all of the stories that *aren't* published. Newsworthy stories happen when great wealth is created by accident. Dusty old shares of Enron or Lehman Brothers or Blockbuster or Sears do not warrant the same sort of attention. "Local man finds worthless paper in attic" is an article nobody would write, no website would publish, and no one would read.

Risk and reward are closely related

The flip side of all high expected returns is *increased risk of lower returns*. This is the single most important rule of investing. To get better than average returns you must be willing to accept higher—sometimes much higher—levels of risk. This means that sometimes, you will receive lower returns or even losses.

This is how investing works. The inverse is that if you want safety you must accept the inevitability of *lower returns*. Failing to understand the

PART 3: BAD BEHAVIOR

simple trade-off between risk and reward is one of the biggest errors most individual investors make.

Not having a financial plan

Why are you investing in the stock market in the first place? Toward what end? For most savers and 401k investors, it is to a specific goal: Saving to buy a home, paying for the kids' college, or securing a comfortable retirement. If those GE employees had a long-term financial plan, they might have realized they were taking on much more risk than was necessary to achieve those goals.

Failing to appreciate diversification

Why didn't these people have a broadly diversified portfolio? Maybe they are afraid it shows a lack of loyalty to their corporate employer; perhaps it reflects a bit of a lottery-ticket mentality that your employer might be the next Apple, Amazon, or Alphabet.

Wishful thinking suggests diversification is giving up a potential fortune. But every worker who gets company stock also gets a salary from that same employer. Diversifying their company stock into broad indexes is a prudent approach. You won't become the next Jeff Bezos or Elon Musk, but you will have a happy, well-funded retirement.

The sort of heady gains and fall from grace that GE suffered is typical—it has happened many times at many different companies and will surely happen again. It may be hard to imagine today, but your great-grandkids would probably laugh at the reverence once showed for Starbucks, Facebook, Nvidia, Amazon, Google, and even Apple.

Up next, we look at the impact of fees and misaligned incentives. You won't believe what happened to these people…

THEIR. ADVISORS. BECAME. BILLIONAIRES.

Throughout this book, I have shared many of my favorite war stories. What they all have in common is that they teach us how to manage our money better. From reviewers disliking the Beatles to the hellish trifecta a couple of chapters back, the stories range from amusing to amazing. It's a subtle psychological trick: If you find the narrative compelling, the lesson will sneak through.

This chapter tells two astonishing tales. The title hints at what happened, but the details are spectacular. They both snuck by in the summer of 2024, so you might have missed them.

The first shocker was when Bloomberg published this headline: "Secretive Dynasty Missed Out on Billions While Advisers Got Rich."[258]

Two managers of a single-family office managed to siphon off so much money that each of them became billionaires. These managers, Peter Harf and Olivier Goudet, serviced the Reimanns, a family "whose wealth stems from the 19th-century founding of German industrial-chemical maker Benckiser."

The advisors' "audacious" strategy was to build a portfolio of coffee investments in order to take on industry giant Nestlé. They spent $30 billion of the Reimann's capital, buying K-cup maker Keurig, Peet's Coffee, Krispy Kreme, Panera Bread, and Pret A Manger, along with other acquisitions. And, they paid huge premiums for each of those brands.

Bloomberg reported: "That big bet, along with other gutsy consumer wagers, has been a flop relative to their own benchmark index for success. If the Reimanns had instead invested in a low-cost fund tracking that index, they would be worth more than $50 billion."

And yet, those consumer bets "have proven highly lucrative for Harf, 78,

PART 3: BAD BEHAVIOR

who has advised the family for 43 years, and Goudet, 59." It likely cost the family somewhere between $13 to 17 billion in missed gains.

Unimpressive performance leading to an accumulation of more than $1 billion? "It's a rare example of executives who've made 10-figure fortunes by managing another family's riches." Bloomberg's writers emphasize that there's no indication of wrongdoing by either advisor.

I would phrase it differently: Any advisor who manages to siphon off a billion dollars in personal compensation while wildly underperforming their benchmarks is more interested in their own financial well-being than that of their clients.

A Latin phrase comes to mind: *Res ipsa loquitur*, or the thing speaks for itself.

———

You don't need to be a billionaire to trust the wrong people.

In the spring of 2008, Paul and Sue Rosenau of Waseca, Minneapolis, won a $59.6 million (after-tax) Powerball jackpot. With their winnings, the devout Lutherans—Paul was the son of a pastor—created a nonprofit organization, now known as the Rosenau Family Research Foundation, to treat and support children with Krabbe disease. Their granddaughter Makayla had died five years earlier of the disease. Putting nearly half of their windfall—$26.4 million—into the nonprofit was an easy decision.

They were inexperienced investors, so they hired John Priebe, a local insurance agent who worked for Principal Securities, to help manage the family's and the foundation's money.

The red flags began to show up almost immediately. As Jason Zweig reported in the *WSJ*,[259] "Only weeks after their Powerball score, the Rosenaus were flown on a private plane[!?!] with Priebe to Principal's headquarters, where they met with senior management and 'everybody but the janitor.'"

As was revealed at the arbitration hearings years later, Priebe purchased $18.9 million in variable annuities for the foundation, earning himself $1.2 million in commissions. The size of that commission check alone should make you sit up and pay attention, but even more egregious is the variable annuity vehicle.

HOW NOT TO INVEST

The biggest advantage of annuities is their tax-deferred status. Similar to IRAs and 401(k)s, annuity holders don't have to pay taxes until they withdraw their money, decades down the road. This is useful for investors in high tax brackets who maxed out all of their other qualified tax deferred alternatives.

But a nonprofit foundation funded with after-tax dollars? It's the worst possible vehicle—expensive and underperforming on an after-tax basis, with no advantages other than that enormous commission check. Matthew Wright is the former chief investment officer of Vanderbilt University and president of Disciplina Group, specializing in asset management for nonprofits. "I've never heard of a nonprofit entity purchasing variable annuities as part of an investment strategy," he told the *WSJ*.

And those commission checks kept getting larger. The insurance broker Priebe charged the foundation annual fees of 2% and carried commissions that could exceed 6%. The *WSJ* reported total commissions were $3.3 million, or even higher.

Not only that, but the performance was abysmal. Priebe's investments over six years had lost $2 million of the foundation's assets, even as the stock market had more than doubled.

The Rosenau Family Research Foundation won an arbitration that ordered Principal Securities to repay $7.3 million in compensatory damages; that's a fraction of what the Foundation's assets would have been worth had they been invested properly.

Are you detecting a pattern yet?

Entrusting your money to anyone who is not a fiduciary is a recipe for excessive fees and poor performance.

Jason Zweig, the author of the article on the Rosenaus, is one of *The Wall Street Journal's* experts on investor behavior (he wrote the book *Your Money and Your Brain*[260]). He observed: "I think investors should welcome regulations that require advisers, brokers and insurance agents to act in their customers' best interests." The industry has vociferously argued against such standards, fearing they will negatively impact profits.

In an interview for a 2011 Harvard Business School profile, the Reimanns'

PART 3: BAD BEHAVIOR

advisor Peter Harf said, "I'm not afraid of taking risks. I'm not afraid of losing. I'm not afraid of buying something."

Only someone who is not a fiduciary would say something like that. If your charge is your clients' best interest, you would be asking, "What is the least amount of risk and volatility my clients must endure to reach their financial goals?"

If you squint, perhaps you can see the difference…

—

Up next, we dive deeper into the risks of sudden windfalls…

THE DANGERS OF SUDDEN CASH WINDFALLS

MICHAEL SAM MADE sports history when the St. Louis Rams made him the first openly gay player to be drafted into the National Football League. If he is smart, he can join an even more elite fraternity: The small fraction of professional athletes who don't eventually go broke.

This used to be a dirty little secret of the sports industry: Professional athletes have been going bankrupt with alarming regularity for decades. In the early days of sports, the dollar amounts involved were relatively modest. But giant television contracts and endorsement deals brought bigger and bigger paydays. Rookie minimum salaries today are at levels that yesteryear's all-stars could only dream of.

Despite all of this increased cash—or, in some instances, because of it—more and more athletes are filing for bankruptcy. A 2009 article in *Sports Illustrated*, "How (and Why) Athletes Go Broke,"[261] detailed the ugly truth: "Many NFL, NBA and Major League Baseball players have a penchant for losing most or all of their money. It doesn't matter how much they make. And the ways they blow it are strikingly similar."

The data on professional athletes are startling: Shortly after they retire, nearly four of five NFL players are bankrupt or under financial stress, according to *Sports Illustrated*. Joblessness and divorce are the main reasons. It's marginally better in the National Basketball Association, where after retirement nearly two of three players are broke within five years.

It doesn't matter if you won the lottery or just signed a $325 million Major League Baseball contract.[262] As hard as it is for the uber wealthy, even with years of experience and (good) professional advice, to manage their assets, it is much harder for those who receive a sudden windfall. The

PART 3: BAD BEHAVIOR

combination of little or no prior experience managing money and more wealth than you know what to do with can lead to financial disasters.[263]

Let's see another example that illustrates the problem.

Life changed radically during the pandemic—our normal routines were disrupted, we had to live, work, and play at home. A number of companies benefitted from this remote work: Apple, Microsoft, Google, Docusign, Instacart, Target, Walmart, and of course Amazon.

Few companies saw their stocks soar in value as much as interactive exercise bike company Peloton. On March 13, 2020—the day the president declared a national emergency concerning Covid-19—Peloton's stock price was just under $20. Nine months later, in January 2021, it had soared 750% to over $167. Once Covid ended, so too did Peloton's stock run. By the end of 2021, it had crashed all the way back down to $35—a 79% fall. Today, it's 97% off of its pandemic highs.

Peloton's co-founder and former CEO John Foley was once worth $1.9 billion in Peloton stock, but nearly all of his wealth was wiped out.[264] "You know, at one point I had a lot of money on paper," he told the *New York Post*.[265] He was forced to liquidate his holdings, including selling a $55 million East Hampton waterfront home and other properties.

How was someone worth ~$2 billion forced into selling assets?

All the usual ways: Too much leverage, living beyond your means, and too little patience to get rich slowly. That killer combination makes anyone vulnerable to sudden price drops in the assets they hold.

My partner Josh Brown discussed this in his book, *You Weren't Supposed to See That*. Securities-based lending had become the hot new product that (non-fiduciary) Wall Street loved:

> The banks were more than happy to arrange a loan against any stock in their clients' portfolio and why not? This way no one had to sell and pay taxes while the money under management remained *sticky* and eligible for fees forever. You could be rich, stay rich, borrow at will, never come out of pocket, never give up your piece of the pie and yet still be able to pay for whatever you wanted.[266]

What do increased fees and higher retention rates do for the client? Very little. But they allow the brokerage firm to fully monetize you and your assets by selling products and services that are both riskier and not always in your best interest.

I have never seen the Peloton founder's portfolio, but I can guess what it did and did not have: Lots of securities lending against that PTON stock, with no collars or hedges to protect against a fall in price. A highly concentrated position (aka, single stock risk), and little or no diversification.

These things keep happening for the same reasons. Inexperienced recipients of a sudden cash windfall make many of the same errors. And it's not just lottery winners and athletes that deal with this—anyone who sold a business or enjoyed their company's stock surging, or had an increase in wealth due to an IPO, has faced these issues.

A sudden influx of cash is about to become a generational problem. Why? Due to what some are calling the "Great Wealth Transfer."[267] Some estimates are as high as $84.4 trillion in assets will be passed down by 2045.[268] Millennials and Gen Z are the generations that will inherit that cash; trading meme stocks on Robinhood is a suboptimal way to manage those trillions.

There are lessons here for anyone who gets a windfall. It doesn't matter if you are the beneficiary of a modest inheritance, or if the NY Mets signed you to a 15-year, $765 million contract: You can better manage sudden wealth with a few simple guidelines.

Be involved

It is important that any investor is involved with financial planning from the beginning of their involvement with capital. Don't just assume the person you hired is looking out for you. You must completely understand what goes into your portfolio, what you will owe in taxes, and what fees you will be paying.

Be aware of the other numbers involved: How long you plan to work for and what your life expectancy is. How much will it cost to live whatever lifestyle you choose?

Keep your investments simple

What most people think is the hardest aspect of finance is in reality the simplest: A simple asset allocation model of broad indices (US equities, international stocks, corporate bonds, and Treasuries). Your age and risk tolerance will determine the ratio of stocks to bonds.

Once you become wealthy, you can *afford to take less risk*: Don't waste your time stock-picking or timing, just let the markets work for you. Avoid the complex investments, expensive funds, and alts. Build a portfolio of high-quality, tax-free municipal bonds (especially if you live in a high-tax US state). These will pay you an income as long as you hold them.

Have a plan

A financial plan gives you three things: An understanding of how much money you have today; what you likely will have in the future; and a goal for that capital.

Avoid debt and leverage

Living within your means is a crucial financial skill for anyone. It is especially valuable for someone who just fell into big bucks.

The latest snare waiting to trip up the unwary and impatient young athlete is the payday loan. For a very large fee, professional athletes can get huge advances on their salaries. These loans can be usurious, with fees and interest adding up to annual rates of 25% or higher. These are to be avoided at all costs.

Watch your costs

Investors must recognize that costs, taxes, and excess fees are a killer of portfolios over the long term.

So too are ill-advised investments or loans. DO NOT give loans or investments to friends or family. Distant relatives suddenly appear after a windfall, with business plans or sad stories (e.g., requests for money). Tell them your advisor/business manager handles those requests (don't tell them the answer will always be "No!").

And for God's sake, whatever you do, don't put money into a restaurant, play, or movie.

Athletes, lottery winners, IPO stock, employee stock ownership plans—many of these folks end up in rough financial shape after blowing through their windfall. There is no big secret to avoiding this fate. Some planning, a little supervision, and patience always lead to better outcomes. I hope the trillions that will soon be in new hands get managed better than what we have seen in these pages.

The lure of high profits is catnip to greedy investors. In the next chapter, we learn that when an investment looks too good to be true, it probably is…

RISK-FREE ANNUAL RETURNS OF 50%

THROUGHOUT HISTORY, GREED has been humanity's constant companion. Avarice is one of the seven deadly sins in Christianity.[269] The Buddha taught craving for material wealth is the root cause of unhappiness—Buddhism teaches greed is one of the three poisons leading to suffering. Judaism condemns greed and selfishness, as does Hinduism. Islam warns greed leads to spiritual poverty, and the Quran explicitly describes greed as a disgrace and an evil characteristic.

Too many people lack the patience to get rich slowly. Over the course of my three-decade career on Wall Street, I have seen lots of people thrown out of the securities business. Nearly every instance involved taking a short cut to get rich quickly, rather than building their wealth slowly, patiently—and legally—over time.

Investors, being human, are subject to the same foibles. Greed is a huge source of unforced error to them. Let's take a closer look at how this manifests.

In 2022, an investigative reporter was looking into a Ponzi scheme in Las Vegas. It's a riveting and terrible story, and the *Washington Post*[270] shares all the details of lost monies, Mormons, FBI investigations, guns, and murder.

I was preparing a presentation on "Navigating Financial Disasters"[271]—you know it as the chapter on the Belfers—when I read this sordid Vegas tale:

> Authorities had long suspected Beasley of running a massive Ponzi scheme with his business partner, Jeffrey Judd, that mainly targeted Mormons, as members of the Church of Jesus Christ of Latter-day Saints are often called. The investment was pitched as a

nearly risk-free opportunity to earn annual returns of 50 percent by lending money to slip-and-fall victims awaiting checks after the settlement of their lawsuits.

The red flags were there for anyone who could put their greed aside and focus on the math. When this Ponzi scheme began in the 2010s, the risk-free yield—also known as the 10-year US Treasury bond—was between 2% and 3%.

The red flag screaming to potential investors: "How could anything yielding 20 times what US Government Treasuries were yielding be remotely risk-free?" Even sub-prime mortgage-backed securities (MBS) in the 2000s pre-GFC were *only* promising to deliver a few hundred basis points above the 10-year without taking on additional risk. That difference—between Treasuries' 4% and subprime's 6%—is almost quaint compared to this example's *"near risk-free returns"* of 50% versus the 10-year's average of 2.5%.

When your Spidey-sense begins to tingle, pay attention and ask questions:

- In a 2.5% environment, why can't YOU borrow at less than a 50% rate?
- Why would anyone be willing to give up half of their winnings rather than wait only a few months?
- What other borrowing facilities have you investigated?
- Which institutions, banks, VCs have you presented this to? Have any institutional firms considered this deal? (And what did they decide?)
- What other *safe* opportunities are you aware of that are currently yielding 50%, 25%, 10%?

It doesn't take much analysis to recognize that this is a terrible deal for the people who are paying 50%. It's so bad for them, and so good for the investors, that it makes no sense. It's a giant red flag from top to bottom.

PART 3: BAD BEHAVIOR

There are many different ways to say this, but here are a few of my favorites:

> If it sounds too good to be true, it probably is.
> There Ain't No Such Thing as a Free Lunch (TANSTAAFL).
> Reward is a function of assumed risk.

It's one thing to recognize how greatly the odds are stacked against you when buying a lottery ticket; it is something else entirely to think that a risk-free investment is going to generate lottery-like gains.

Compare this Ponzi scheme to those 2000s-era MBSs—they were a legitimate investment, but one where the risk was hidden by aggressive sales and discounted by buyers in the then new era of ultralow rates. Securitized junk mortgages were legal but awful investments, a poor alignment of risks relative to reward. Some of us knew they would eventually blow up, but *good luck* convincing people with dollar signs in their eyes that the risk/reward ratio was stacked against them.

Greed makes people confuse *risk-free returns* with *return-free risks*.

One day, we might implant computer chips in people's heads that will alert them to obvious indicia of fraud. But until that day, human nature will remain forever vulnerable to those who would manipulate you for monetary advantage. If you are aware of what these things look like, you stand a fair chance of avoiding the worst of them.

―

How well do top-ranked college endowments, with their brilliant finance professors and insightful investment research, perform as investors? (Not very well.) You will be surprised which schools earned an "F."

NOT WELL ENDOWED...

SINCE 1985, YALE'S endowment has been academia's gold standard. Long before it was fashionable, the Yale Model was rich with alternative investments, including private equity, commodities, and real estate—assets that weren't plain vanilla stocks and bonds. Developed by David Swensen and his colleague Dean Takahashi, the Yale Model was the envy of the Ivies.

The success of the Yale Model led to lots of copycats. Without Swensen's unique talents, other schools could duplicate the look but not quite the feel of Yale's endowment investments.[272]

Yale's success long frustrated long-time rival Harvard Management Company and led them to seek a successful rival strategy. They found one in Jack Meyer, who, over his 15-year run at HMC, completely transformed how Harvard managed its assets. Meyer grew the endowment from $4.8 billion in 1990 to $25.9 billion in 2005.[273] His annualized return was 16% over ten years and he consistently beat his benchmark using an active strategy that took advantage of the endowment's nonprofit status and long-term perspective.

Long before high-frequency trading became popular on Wall Street, HMC, under Meyer, had mastered it. In 2005, *Fortune* reported, "120 or so people who work there are masters of short-term trading, initiating as many as 250,000 transactions a year. Their bets have often focused on undervalued situations and arbitrage opportunities in global stock and bond markets."[274]

However, Harvard's endowment then went on to become a problem student. What went wrong? It was once one of the best in not just the Ivies but *all* colleges. The problems were caused by a combination of academic hubris and political correctness; this led to a series of terrible—and expensive—decisions.[275]

PART 3: BAD BEHAVIOR

Meyer was paid more than $7 million a year—seven times what Swensen was making. Meritocratic results-based pay for successful managers was common on Wall Street, but it ran counter to certain notions of Ivy League decorum.

Start with Terry M. Bennett and other alums like him. Bennett was Harvard Medical School, class of 1964*—and previously a regular and generous donor to the medical school.[276] He was quoted in a 2004 *New York Times* article threatening to withhold future gifts if Harvard didn't cut the compensation for money managers (despite their above-benchmark returns). "The managers of the endowment took home enough money last year to send more than 4,000 students to Harvard for a year," Bennett told the *Times*.[277] Harvard eventually acceded to its alums' and faculty wishes over management-company pay levels.

HMC's investment performance has never recovered in the decades that followed.[278]

At the time, the high-earning Harvard endowment management team was delivering 13% annual returns, beating lower-paying arch-rival Yale's 9%. The roughly 400 basis point differential was worth almost a billion dollars per year in excess returns to HMC.

Also problematic: Then Harvard President Lawrence Summers bigfooted his way in. As the *Boston Globe* reported, Summers ignored Meyer's warnings that the university was "mismanaging its basic operating funds" and putting too much capital in risky stocks, bonds, and alternative investments.[279] That overinvested posture suffered giant, painful losses during the GFC.

The negative perception of a richly compensated managerial team led to the sort of touchy-feely academic posturing most of us in the real world find silly. Institutions are made up of people, and those people make the same mistakes everyone else does. Offended by the high cost of this talented team of managers, the brain trust that is the Harvard professorial class, with encouragement from uninformed but smug alumni, demanded changes, forcing the Meyer team out.

---

* For reasons we discuss later, many doctors have characteristics that can make them terrible investors; Bennett was worse than most...

At this point in the story, you may be wondering why you should care about an Ivy League school and its $50 billion endowment. The answer is a surprising lesson in this section of unforced errors.

We have discussed already just how rare and delicate outsized success in investing is. You know the names of people like Warren Buffett, Peter Lynch, and Jim Simons *because* they are such outliers.

Since Meyer's departure in 2005, HMC has suffered a stunning fall from grace. It lost money in the financial crisis, failed to participate in the subsequent recovery of the 2010s, and was one of the worst-performing college endowments. All of these investing catastrophes were avoidable, self-inflicted wounds. Worse still, the losses occurred in ways Meyer's approach would have avoided. During the financial crisis, Harvard's endowment lost as much as a third of its value. Even five years later, its annualized returns were only 2%. And in 2016, HMC's annual report was grim reading: Despite markets being up ~12%, the fund lost $2 billion.[280]

After the 2016 debacle, Harvard Management Co. changed the way it oversees the world's largest university endowment. It fired half of its 230 employees and began outsourcing most of its money management.

When an investment management team consistently outperforms its benchmarks, as Harvard's was, *don't do anything to ruin it.* In a world where so much can go wrong, great investment success is both rare and delicate. Do nothing to upset that fragile balance.

Yes, Harvard saved about $50 million in money manager bonuses. Those savings led to the departure of a team that was creating billions of dollars in excess annual investment returns—and was likely to continue creating those fabulous returns over time.

Giving up billions to save $50 million in costs is a trade you should never make.

Next chapter, we consider the dangers of focusing on outcomes over process.

OUTCOMES VERSUS PROCESS

SPORTS FANS AND investors tend to make similar errors. Perhaps the biggest is focusing on outcomes rather than process. Sports fanatics are all Monday morning quarterbacks; they can read you chapter and verse—after the fact—what should have been done late in the game on 4th and goal from the two-yard line.[281]

It's called hindsight bias, and it afflicts investors, too. They can tell you what asset classes you should have owned last year, which hedge fund manager you should have invested with 20 years ago, and why you should have bought Netflix, Tesla, and Apple about 5,000% ago.

Thanks for nothing, Danny!

So, what is process, and how does it differ from outcome?

Process is the methodology used to accomplish an undertaking. It could be a simple checklist or a complex systematic approach. Process focuses on the specific actions that must be taken, *regardless of the results*.

Outcome is the result; it could be due to skill, luck, and intelligence, plus numerous other random factors. At the end of the day, outcome is who won or lost the game, how many planes landed safely, what stocks went up or down, and what surgical patients lived or died.

In sports terms, think of process as your playbook and outcome as the final score. In investing, process is your approach, investment style, discipline, and consistency, while outcome is your return or performance.

Imagine you are watching two people in a coin-flipping contest. One of them flips 10 heads in a row; the other's flips are more random—heads, tails, tails, heads, tails, etc. Are you willing to bet a substantial sum that the first flipper's next toss will be heads? If you said yes, you are outcome focused.

It seems brazen, yet that is exactly what many investors do. They chase the hottest coin flipper of the moment. In finance, that is the person with a *hot hand*—the mutual fund whose manager just finished a great streak, someone who ended up on the cover of a magazine, or any recent award winner.

If you have not analyzed and understood a manager's methodology, how can you possibly know whether the results are due to skill or chance? We are, to channel Nassim Taleb, all too often *fooled by randomness*.

Successful results in investing could very well be a mere coincidence—a result without any underlying causation on the manager's part. Meaning, the outcome was not the result of process, but rather, dumb luck.

Perhaps that manager's investing style (momentum, value, trend following, etc.) came (temporarily) back in vogue. Maybe their sector became red hot, or the part of the world they focus on is seeing a (temporary) boom. What looks like personal greatness very often is not (and vice versa).

This is not to say you should always ignore bad outcomes. A series of poor results may indicate an issue with process.

Ironically, investors as a group have a tendency to attribute their own successes to the skill and insight they possess; at the same time, any losing investments are blamed on bad luck. That's outcome-focus married to ego, and it's not how you make money in the markets over the long term.

Why are we so easily fooled by random outcomes? The pattern recognition subroutine in your brain evolved to identify threats. That shadow in the tall grass might be a predator waiting to make you its lunch. Hence, generating false positives means that you might be wrong 99 of 100 times, but on the savanna, that 100th event saves your life and passes your genes on to future generations.

We all tend to be outcome-focused, often to the detriment of choosing a good process.

Perhaps an example from outside of the world of finance might be helpful. Imagine you have a medical condition that requires surgery. It's a bit tricky, but the procedure has a good chance of success. You interview a few doctors, looking at their academic history, published papers, experience, and reputations. You narrow the list to two surgeons and get access to their surgical records, including patient survival rates.

Both surgeons have very good reputations; one works primarily for

PART 3: BAD BEHAVIOR

private patients covered by insurance, the other is at a top medical school. The private doctor runs a success/survival rate of 86%, while the medical school doc runs at 61%.

Which doctor do you choose?

If you immediately said the 86% doctor, you are outcome focused. You saw the better results and that was all you needed to know. World Series of Poker Tournament Champion Annie Duke, in her 2018 book *Thinking in Bets*, calls this "resulting."[282] This is the cognitive error of evaluating decisions based solely on their outcomes, rather than on the quality of the decision-making process behind them.

Instead of "resulting," you might have wondered why a cutter with a great reputation at a top-ranked medical school had a much worse survival ratio. You do a little more research into her process. You find that she invented this procedure 30 years ago. She did all of the early experimental surgeries, including lots of clinical failures (meaning bad surgical outcomes and low survival rates). But over time, she refined the surgery, where through trial and error she developed what is now a life-saving technique. Indeed, her methodology has become the standard, thanks to her research. Every doctor and patient who followed afterward benefited from her groundbreaking clinical work.*

Because of her background in this area, this doc gets all of the "impossible" surgical cases. When other surgeons don't think they can do the operation—or don't want to negatively impact their batting average—they refer it to her medical school. Hopeless and complicated surgeries make up a big part of her practice. People travel from around the world just to have this surgeon do this procedure on them. She has seen every variation of patient, and because of this, she has done more of these operations than anyone in the world.

Based on this new information, which surgeon would you choose? The first doctor was pretty good, but the second doctor is outstanding! If you

---

* The only surgery I ever had was performed on me by Dr. Claudette Lajam; she replaced my right hip on July 15, 2024 as I was editing this manuscript. The new hip is titanium, cobalt, chromium, and ceramic. Making the doc a female was a reflection of my personal experience.

suddenly are thinking about the medical school doctor with the lower success rate, well, congratulations—you have just become process-focused.

The key to focusing more on process is to understand that good outcomes follow good processes. Without understanding the underlying process, good outcomes could just as likely be due to dumb luck as to skill.

You should be reminded of this every time you read the disclaimer "past performance is no guarantee of future results." What you are actually seeing is an admission of random outcomes. When past performance is the result of luck, then it provides zero insight into what future results might look like.

All too often, Luck = Outcome, and Skill = Process.

We rarely know precisely what the sources of good outcomes are; however, we have a high degree of confidence what the probabilities are for a good process. A strong process is a guarantee—not of outcome or results, but of a higher probability of obtaining your desired results.

That's why process is so important to investors.

Up next, the dozen biggest unforced errors all investors make—and how to avoid them.

YOUR BIGGEST UNFORCED ERRORS

WHENEVER THERE IS turmoil in the markets, my phone and email light up with calls from journalists, investors, and potential clients. They typically are excited about the turmoil of the moment and want my hot take. I disappoint them by channeling King Solomon: "This too shall pass."

Decades as an investor and analyst on Wall Street have taught me that panics come and go. Drawdowns, corrections, crashes are not the problem—investor behavior *in response to market turmoil* is what causes so much harm.

In this book I have used the most extreme examples of unforced errors I could find to illustrate these behavioral problems. But don't think it takes an enormous screw-up to cost you—even moderate mistakes lead to bad outcomes.

Let's sum up a dozen or so lessons we have learned from the mistakes billionaires and the rest of us make.

Common unforced investor errors

1. Have a plan
2. Excess fees
3. Be tax aware
4. Your behavior
5. Asset allocation
6. Passive vs. active management
7. Reaching for yield
8. Understand cycles

9. Get what you pay for
10. Be a long-term thinker
11. Misunderstanding the nature of risk
12. Emotional decision-making and cognitive errors.

Have a plan

The best time to make an investment plan is before a crisis, not during it. If you have a strategy, goals, and an understanding of your own risk tolerances, once trouble comes along, you are prepared. Consider the kind of financial planning you need, then find a competent fiduciary to assist you.

Many people with simple, straight-forward financial needs—who learned the lessons in these pages—can do it themselves. (You have to be able to manage your own behavior!) Those with more complex circumstances should find a good advisor to help with creating a plan.

Excess fees

Any cost will impact your returns, but the high or excess fees we have seen examples of in the prior chapters take an enormous toll on long-term performance. At least, that is according to every academic study that has ever looked at the issue.

Fees of 2% to 3% may not sound like much, but compound that over decades, and it adds up to a lot.

The typical alternative fee structure of 2% carrying charges plus 20% of the profit is an even bigger drag on returns. Other than a handful of superstar managers (whose funds you cannot get into), the vast majority of these managers simply do not justify their costs. The same is true for most of the retail stockbrokers and for many of the so-called investment advisors (who are not fiduciaries) on Wall Street.

Be tax aware

Your goal is to follow the IRS guidelines while keeping the maximum amount of your returns after taxes. This is easier to accomplish than it sounds.

PART 3: BAD BEHAVIOR

Substitute low-cost, tax-efficient ETFs for more expensive mutual funds in any taxable account. Max out your tax-deferred accounts (especially those with matching company funds). Use software to increase your tax loss harvesting. Be aware of where you locate your holdings, and what goes into taxable and qualified accounts. Reducing fees is a sure-fire way to improve long-term results.

Your behavior

Unforced errors are avoidable mistakes. None of these terrible outcomes you have been reading about were inevitable. They were all the result of someone making bad or even catastrophic decisions. The purpose of this book is to help you avoid these mistakes.

Many investors are their own worst enemies, but they don't have to be…

Asset allocation

Of all the positive steps you take, your mix of how much stocks, bonds, and cash you have matters a lot. The decisions you make about the mix of your assets have a far greater impact on your success than your stock picking or market timing. This too has been proved repeatedly in academic studies and the real world.

If your allocation mix contained too much cash or too few equities, you probably missed out on the giant rally in stocks since March 2009 or March 2020. And now that bonds are yielding something, you may want to rethink your mix and duration.

Stock picking may be fun, but asset allocation is where you make your money over the long haul.

Passive vs. active management

Hard to believe I am still saying this in 2025, but active fund management—when managers try to outperform their benchmarks through superior stock picking and/or market timing—is exceedingly difficult. It has been shown repeatedly that 60–80% of active managers underperform their benchmarks each year. We know the names of the dozen or so managers who have outperformed over time—they are the exceptions that prove the rule.

Your portfolio will be better served replacing most of the actively managed funds with passive indices.

Reaching for yield

Few mistakes are more costly than chasing yield. Just ask the folks who loaded up on subprime-mortgage-backed securities for the extra yield how that worked out.

The three most common ways to chase yields are: 1) Buying longer-duration bonds, 2) Buying lower-rated, riskier paper, or 3) Using leverage to amplify your gains (which also amplifies your losses). All three of these strategies have been big money losers over the past few decades.

Understand cycles

Societies, economies, and markets all move in long (secular) eras. Sometimes they are positive (1946 to 1966; 1982 to 2000; 2013 to…?) and we call these secular bull markets. Sometimes they are negative (1966 to 1982; 2000 to 2013) and we call them secular bear markets.

Enjoy your gains during the long bull market—that's the easy part. You have to be willing to ride out the hard parts—and that includes recessions and bear markets. That is where advisors earn their keep and investors set up their futures.

Get what you pay for

For many people, hiring a professional makes sense. If you have complex tax issues, if your financial situation is complicated with ex-spouses and children, if you are concerned with generational wealth transfer, the sale of a business, or have questions about philanthropy and gifts, then you probably need help.

But don't pay me or anyone else for services unless you make full use of them. After you complete your financial plan, go through it regularly (at least once a year, more often when things change). Consult with us on taxes, estate planning, insurance coverage, security, and anything with a financial element. If you are having an issue, the odds are that we have seen something similar, if not identical, before.

It surprises me how often people fail to take full advantage of the services they pay for.

Be a long-term thinker

Bull markets tend to pull gains forward from the decade ahead. It is during secular bear markets (e.g., 2000–2013) where the real money is made. Anyone who upped their stock purchases during that period and rode out the long bear made out like a bandit in the 2010s. It will feel terrible for a decade, but it is worth it.

Start thinking in terms of decades, not months or minutes.

Misunderstanding the nature of risk

A good definition of risk is the probability of not getting your expected returns.

This is because returns are always a function of the risk you assume. They are two sides of the same coin, and you cannot have one without the other. Anytime you are looking at an investment with high potential returns, you should translate that as high risk. Anytime you are shown an investment described as "safe" or "low-risk," it means low returns.

Emotional decision-making and cognitive errors

Both of these types of errors are hardwired into our nervous systems. We cannot avoid these built-in shortfalls, but if we are aware of them, we might avoid their most pernicious effects.

In the next two sections, we are going to look deeply into where these various investor errors come from. Cognitive errors are a big source of the mistakes we make, as is emotional decision-making.

Strap yourself in for some wild insights as to what makes you tick!

SECTION 2:
EMOTIONAL DECISION-MAKING

BLAME YOUR LIMBIC SYSTEM

THE HUMAN LIMBIC system controls emotions, behaviors, and long-term memory (among other functions). The amygdala is the part of the limbic system that processes emotions. Small, almond-shaped, and deep inside your brain, it also links emotions to memories, learning, and your senses.

When a threat is detected, it directs your hypothalamus to produce hormones, including cortisol and adrenaline. You are more familiar with it by its informal name: fight or flight.

This is enormously important to investors. "To the extent you succeed in finance, you succeed by suppressing the limbic system, your system 1, the very fast-moving emotional system. If you cannot suppress that, you are going to die poor."[283]

So says Dr. William J. Bernstein, PhD, MD, a retired neurologist, principal in the money management firm Efficient Frontier Advisors, and author of several bestselling books on finance.[284]

In *The Delusions of Crowds*, he explains why the human brain's evolutionary development leads us astray in modern capital markets.[285] In his view, "Humans are the Apes that tell stories, imitate others, and seek status." This combination ultimately leads to group dynamics where entire populations become deeply entrenched in a belief system that, before revealed as false, runs amuck.

Nowhere in the modern world do we see the effects of our emotional behavior more clearly than in markets. Our emotions lead us to be overconfident when we should be humble, panicked when we should be circumspect, and deeply engaged in seeking information that confirms (rather than disconfirms) our preexisting beliefs.

The consequences range from witch burnings to financial ruin. In the modern era, this tribal behavior can lead to belief in false narratives, the rise of meme stocks, and, eventually, bubbles and market crashes.

Why is this so?

According to Bernstein, humans are "cognitive misers," relying on simple narratives instead of using complex analytical thinking. The more compelling a narrative is, the more corrosive it becomes to our analytical abilities. The two most compelling tales are the Apocalyptic "End of Days" stories and the "effortless riches" meme. These are rife in both social media and religious narratives because they are such effective emotional triggers. They create frequent and substantial crowd delusions.

From an evolutionary perspective, there is little cost to our *patternization*—seeing patterns where none exist (amateur chartists are notorious for this). Jumping out of the way at the sight of a vine that looks like a venomous snake is a false positive that is mildly embarrassing at worst. But false negatives—ignoring the vine that is actually a deadly viper—carries the ultimate evolutionary cost. Perhaps this explains why we pay so much attention to bad news while ignoring positive developments.

Existential threats matter deeply to our limbic systems. Investors need to understand why these same evolutionary traits—the ones that helped us survive and adapt on the savanna—can lead to expensive errors today.

———

This evolutionary baggage we all carry—why does it still have so much sway in the modern world? Haven't we evolved past this?

Put simply, we just ain't built for it.

The best explanation why comes from Michael J. Mauboussin, adjunct professor of finance at Columbia Business School, and head of consilient research at Morgan Stanley's Counterpoint Global. He explains why we aren't hardwired to undertake risk and reward analysis in modern capital markets: "The mind is better suited for 'hunting and gathering' than it is for understanding Bayesian analysis."*

Mauboussin reaches a similar conclusion to Bernstein: Most people lack the emotional detachment and discipline required for good, long-term performance in the markets.

The primate species we know as *Homo sapiens* has been around for about two million years. Modern finance has been around for a handful of decades. If all of human existence was a 24-hour clock, then investing as we understand it today has been around for merely 2 seconds.

Mauboussin asks the human species this question: "What have you learned in the past 2 seconds?"[286]

The answer, unfortunately, is "Not enough…"

Been round here long?

Timeline of *Homo sapiens*

Event	When (years ago)	Time of Day
Homo sapiens appear	2,000,000	12:00 AM
Mitochondrial Eve ("mother of all humans")	180,000	9:50 PM
Domesticated *Homo sapiens*	20,000	11:46 PM
Hindu/Arabic numbering system introduced in the West	800	11:59:25 PM
Modern Finance Theory	40	11:59:58 PM

Up next, we look at how and why we panic at exactly the right time to stay alive, but precisely the wrong time to be good investors.

---

* When you see the term "*Bayesian*," think of it as meaning "Probabilities;" for any given theory, what probability best expresses the degree of belief you have that the hypothesis is true?

RISK IS UNAVOIDABLE. PANIC IS OPTIONAL.

LAST CHAPTER, WE discussed how and why we respond to threats: Our limbic system's immediate surge of adrenaline urges us to take action. This has been built into us slightly cleverer primates over millions of years, an evolutionary development that has helped make our species one of the most successful on the planet.*

At least, when it comes to adaptation and survival. Our species has been much less clever in terms of allocating capital in markets than we have been in dominating the planet.

Douglas Adams' charmingly witty absurdity *The Hitchhiker's Guide to the Galaxy* begins with this reveal: Arthur Dent discovers his friend Ford Prefect is not human—he is a Betelgeusian.** Oh, and the Earth is about to be destroyed by the Vogons, who are building a hyperspatial express route straight through our solar system.

Ford lends Arthur his copy of *The Hitchhiker's Guide to the Galaxy*, which is the galaxy's bestselling book:

> It is said that despite its many glaring (and occasionally fatal) inaccuracies, the *Hitchhiker's Guide to the Galaxy* itself has outsold the *Encyclopedia Galactica* because it is slightly cheaper, and because it has the words 'DON'T PANIC' in large, friendly letters on the cover.

"Don't Panic" turns out to be excellent advice when your wetware urges

---

* We are in the top 10, somewhere behind fungus, bacteria, mosquitoes, crabs, and viruses.
** From a planet in the Betelgeuse star system.

PART 3: BAD BEHAVIOR

you to have an immediate reaction to perceived threats (real or otherwise). Unfortunately, most of the time, this advice is useless. No one responds well to being told to "calm down!" when they are in their fight or flight mode.

To ensure you understand why "Don't Panic" is such good advice—now, while you are sitting on the couch reading, or listening to this book in your car—let's quantify the damage it can do.

Panic selling quantified

The easiest button to press is the one marked "**Sell**." It's a salve for your emotional distress, especially when facing volatile, disruptive stock markets. Panic selling might ease your upset stomach or help you sleep better, but it wreaks havoc on your portfolio.

The single biggest challenge of panic selling equities: *How do you get back in? When? What determines your repurchase decision? What metrics do you base this **Buy** upon?*[287]

My experience with panic selling was deeply influenced by the investor behavior I observed firsthand during the 2008–09 financial crisis, the 2000 dotcom implosion, and the 2020 pandemic sell-off. (Other asset managers have had similar experiences.)

It's more than mere anecdotal—we have hard evidence to back up what makes panic selling so bad.

A very interesting study[288] examined what happened when freaked-out investors panic-sold. The study was based on "the financial activity of 653,455 anonymous accounts corresponding to 298,556 households from one of the largest brokerage firms in the United States."

An amusing finding: "Investors who are male, or above the age of 45, or married, or have more dependents, or who self-identify as having excellent investment experience or knowledge tend to freak out with greater frequency."[289]

But that buries the lede. The more important issue is what those investors who panic-dumped their equity portfolios did subsequently. The most important takeaway from this research: "We find that 30.9% of the investors who panic sell never return to reinvest in risky assets."

That is an astonishing data point: Nearly a third of investors who panic sell ***never buy equities again***—ever! The rest of the panic-sellers repurchase equities at higher—often MUCH higher—prices than they sold for. These buys tend to be later in the recovery once the news flow improves—markets bottom when the headlines are horrific, leading to this emotional capitulation.

This is very consistent with my experience following the GFC. I cannot count how many times I was told: "I followed you out of the market in 2008, but when you flipped bullish in March 2009 I thought you were crazy." I was getting those emails in 2010, 2011, and 2012; the big surprise was after we launched RWM in 2013, they continued, even into 2014 and, shockingly, 2015.

Panic-selling is easy, getting back in at the lows is hard, not ever getting back in is ruinous.

"Don't Panic" is the best advice you can get when you are calm and contemplative; it is applicable in every situation you will be familiar with, whether its Vogons about to demolish your planet or the S&P futures market set to open lock limit down.

In markets, panic does not make anything better and often makes things worse—and occasionally much worse.

Coming up, we consider emotional decisions based on politics. As you might surmise, this does not mix well with investing.

WHY POLITICS AND INVESTING DON'T MIX

I THREW A HAND grenade with the very first column I wrote for the *Washington Post* back on February 6, 2011:

> Washington, I'm here to tell you, politics and investing don't mix. Yep, I thought I'd begin our conversation about investing by rocking your most cherished beliefs. Many of you are active in party politics, work for government or are involved in related fields. Well, I have some bad news: Your politics are killing you in the markets.[290]

By this point, you should be somewhat familiar with my mix of behavioral psychology, data analytics, statistics, and market history. I use all of these to help me make better investing decisions. As I told D.C. 15 years ago, "these are the key to learning precisely *what not to do*. While making good decisions can help your portfolio, avoiding bad ones is even more important."

We all make the same mistakes over and over. That flight-or-fight response might have helped your ancestors deal with hungry saber-toothed tigers and territorial Cro-Magnons, but it drives investors to make costly emotional decisions.

To the neuro-physiologists who research cognitive functions, when people are emotionally driven they appear to suffer from cognitive deficits that mimic certain types of brain injuries.[291] Not just partisan political junkies, but ardent sports fans, the devout, even hobbyists. Anyone with an intense emotional interest in a subject loses the ability to observe it objectively: You selectively perceive events; you ignore data and facts that disagree with your main philosophy. Even your memory works to fool you, as you selectively retain what you believe and mask memories in conflict with those beliefs.

Studies have shown that we are actually biased in our visual perception—literally, how we see the world—because of our belief systems.[292]

How does this play out in the world of investing? Let me share two examples. I don't pick favorites: Both Democrats and Republicans are implicated.

Back in 2003, the dotcom crash had about run its course. From the peak of the market in March 2000 to the October 2002 trough, the Nasdaq had gotten crushed, losing 83% of its value.

As Federal Reserve chief Alan Greenspan took rates down to 1%, the George W. Bush administration passed $1 trillion in tax cuts. As someone once said about the stock market, "Give me a trillion dollars, and I'll throw you one hell of a party."

Yet many of my Democrat friends on Wall Street—fund managers, traders, and analysts—were highly critical of the tax cuts. At the time, I heard all the reasons why they were so bad: They were deficit-busters, unlikely to create jobs, giveaways to the wealthy.

While those critiques may have been true, they were also irrelevant to equities. As armchair policy wonks obsessed over these issues, they missed the bigger picture: Liquidity is a major factor in how the economy and stock markets perform. Trillions of dollars in fresh cash were very likely to goose equities higher. (Sound familiar to the Covid-19 response?) Indeed, the impact of the tax cuts did just that. Combined with Greenspan's ultra-low rates, you had the makings of a cyclical bull market rally. From 2003 to 2007, the S&P 500 nearly doubled.

And my politically active friends on the left missed most of it.

Fast-forward six years to the GFC. Since the October peak in 2007, the S&P 500 had fallen 57%. On March 6, 2009, an op-ed by Michael J. Boskin in *The Wall Street Journal* found the apparent reason: "Obama's Radicalism Is Killing the Dow."[293]

Never mind that the crash had begun years earlier, driven by many factors, including real estate losing a third of its value and a collapse in securitized mortgages. To Boskin, a hard right economist at Stanford University's

PART 3: BAD BEHAVIOR

Hoover Institution and former chair of the Council of Economic Advisers under President George H.W. Bush, it was the month and a half of the Obama presidency that was at fault.

This was one of many misguided attempts by partisan economists to use their *art* as a political cudgel. Woe to those investors who confused their biased political braying for legitimate economic analysis.[294]

I explained this to clients, the news media, and co-workers. But the greatest pushback this time around came from the right side of the political spectrum. My Republican pals were lamenting the new occupant of the White House: "Obama is a Kenyan, a Muslim, a Socialist. He is going to kill business."

When stock markets in the US are cut in half, it has historically been a damned good entry point into equities.[295] On March 9, three days after Boskin's op-ed, the market bottomed and would go practically straight up for both of Obama's terms, with the S&P 500 gaining 375%.

And many of my politically active friends on the right missed it.

Remember, the cycle of booms and busts is a surprisingly regular occurrence. What some people call a "100-year flood" actually happens far more frequently—since 1929, there have been 18 crashes. Even since the turn of the 21st century, we have had three *once in a generation* market events.

As the next chart by my colleague Callie Cox[296] shows, it is not the party in the White House that drives returns, it's market compounding over time.

Growth of $1 invested in the S&P 500 under different political regimes (1950–2024)

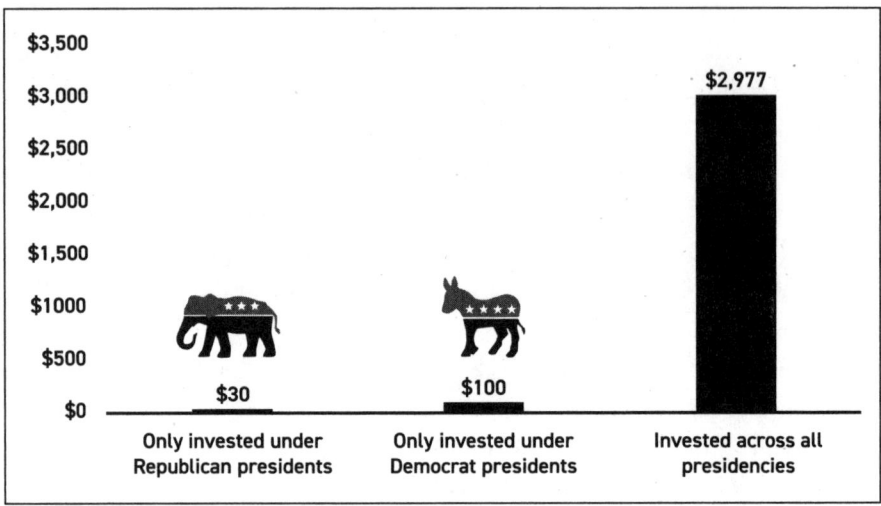

The conclusion should be obvious: When you are in the polling booth, vote your conscience, but when you are reviewing your investing options, it is best to do so with a cold, dispassionate eye.

Understanding how your own biases impact your investing process is a key step. If you want to avoid making certain errors, you must at least be aware of them.

—

Boskin's poorly timed, politically motivated op-ed cost his readers untold billions in market appreciation. But it's only the second worst-timed editorial in market history.[297]

The very worst op-ed in history? That's up next.

QUIT DOLING OUT THAT BAD-ECONOMY LINE

IN THE LAST chapter, we examined politically tinged market commentaries that were neither objective nor helpful to investors. These commentaries hurt Democrats during the Bush presidency and Republicans when Obama was in the White House.

But to truly show you the damage partisan-motivated commentary can wreak, we need to go to Donald Luskin, the commentator with the world's worst timing. No one is a more reliable ideological contrary indicator than he. His track record as an investment writer is unmatched on either the left or the right. It's not just that his hot takes on the market were so bad—yes, they were awful—but rather, it is his impeccable timing that brings him to our attention.

He is a one-man instruction manual on how *not to allow* your partisan leanings to influence your investment portfolio.

September 14, 2008 was the day the single dumbest column ever published in the *Washington Post* appeared: "Quit Doling Out That Bad-Economy Line," by Don Luskin.[298] In it, he explained that the economy was great and all the worrying was like "a virus."

Breathtaking in its ignorance, shocking in its fallibility, astonishing in its author's perversely misperceived worldview, it stands as a monument to the degree of sheer cluelessness any single person could possibly possess:

> There have been 11 recessions since the Great Depression. And we're nowhere close to being in the 12th one now. This isn't just a matter of opinion. Words—even words as seemingly subjective as "recession"—have meaning.
>
> —September 14, 2008

It is almost cruel to criticize this wretched piece of writing. Every thought was wrong, every paragraph contained multiple errors, and each word somehow made the one before it worse.[299] Even the subheading—"A Nation of Exaggerators"—remains offensive to this day.

As it turned out, the United States was already in month nine of the worst recession since the Great Depression. The Sunday when *The Washington Post* edition with this column landed on doorsteps throughout Washington D.C., things were about to get a whole lot worse. That very day, Lehman Brothers blew up; it filed for bankruptcy the very next day (September 15, 2008); insurance giant American International Group also blew up that day, but AIG, unlike LEH, was deemed "systemically important" and was bailed out.

You need to read the entire column to get a full measure of how awful it was. It denied the housing slump, misread the debt markets, stated that bank capital was more than sufficient, looked at employment trends as proof there was no recession, applauded economic growth levels, decried the use of the terms "crisis" and "meltdown"—and gets every single one of these issues exactly wrong. If you had a time machine, knew the future, and purposefully tried to write something as wrong as possible, you could not have done a better job.

Had you listened to his advice—things aren't that bad, just relax—and bought equities, you were about to suffer a 46% collapse. A year after the column came out, markets were still off by almost 20%.

Hey, anyone can have unlucky timing for any one column. But what makes Luskin stand out among all of the other terrible market commentators is his consistency. Readers who followed his columns regularly lost money with his terrible, mistimed advice.

Almost a year prior to the "Quit Doling" column, Luskin told us there were "11 Reasons to Buy Stocks Now."[300] That was November 2007, a month after the market peak and the start of a nauseating 18-month, 57% slide in equities. If you followed his advice, it would have taken you six years *to merely break even*. He even singled out Citigroup as a favorite buy—and the stock subsequently plummeted 97%. If you still own Citi today, you are 87% below when that recommendation was made.

After those two columns set up buyers for getting their portfolios cut in half, he went the other way at the worst possible time: On March 6, 2009, Smart Money published "Even Worse Than the Great Depression," which claimed we were only halfway through the sell-off.[301] Hilariously wrong—the market hit bottom *that very day*, tagging 666, and then launching into a furious 139% rally.

A year later, on May 10, 2010, Luskin wrote "Stocks Slide—It's About Time."[302] He advised readers to "become cautious" on equities, telling them, "I have my bets placed on Gold. Buy Gold." Gold rallied a little, fell back down, and five years later, was off -3%. Meanwhile, the S&P 500—Flash Crash and all—doubled over the same five-year period.

Luskin's partisanship was not done losing his readers money: On May 4, 2012, he exhorted *Wall Street Journal* readers to dump equities because "The 2013 Fiscal Cliff Could Crush Stocks."[303] He advised readers to "Do the math on dividend taxes," warning that dividend yields would be lower, and stock prices would be considerably lower—"maybe by 30%."

Narrator: Not even close.

Over the ensuing year, there was a torrent of dividend increases. And equities? After that May column, the S&P 500 was up modestly for the rest of 2012 and was 35% higher by the end of 2013.

All of these terrible market calls are a classic cognitive error—allowing politics from either side of the partisan aisle to drive your analysis. Bullish when your favored party holds the White House and bearish when not is a recipe for disaster. These epic fails are really just political screeds in the guise of analysis, all of which turned out to be monumental money losers for anyone foolish enough to listen to them.

Also noteworthy: These columns came out years *after* Luskin's mutual fund closed with disastrous losses in 2001.[304] No wonder *Money* magazine went under. If its readers followed Luskin's advice, they could no longer afford the $5 each copy cost.

The lesson for investors is clear: Avoid the *ministers without portfolios*. Those commentators who are on the sidelines, not responsible for client assets—and don't have to answer for their radical underperformance—whose priorities and agendas are not your financial well-being.

People active in party politics—donors, organizers, true believers, and activists—shouldn't be allowed anywhere near your investment portfolio or your psyche. The reverse is also true: Anyone running money should avoid party politics since it leads to a lack of the objectivity and dispassion needed to do the job well. Politics is a huge distraction; it is rarely compartmentalized and typically leads to ill-considered emotional decision-making.

Berkeley professor of economics Brad DeLong called Luskin "the stupidest man alive" in December 2005.[305] I think that might be too harsh. Luskin is actually an intelligent fellow, but his political bias has consistently led him to the wrong conclusions at precisely the wrong moment in time. Nobody has suffered more due to his inability to manage his limbic system than the folks who read his columns and followed his emotional advice. They paid the price for his lack of objectivity.

I keep repeating this, but only because it is so true: *Politics and investing do not mix.*

—

If mixing politics and investing is bad, what do you think occurs when investors change their portfolio allocations based on whether their preferred candidate wins a presidential election (or not)? Let's find out.

LOVE OR HATE TRUMP, IT'S NO WAY TO INVEST

JUST BECAUSE INVESTING based on how you vote is a terrible idea doesn't stop some people from doing it. Consider this Bloomberg article with the headline "Republican Voters Bet on Stocks After Trump's Win. Democrats Didn't."[306]

I suppose we shouldn't be surprised, since it's clear that much human behavior is based on feeling rather than thinking. Still, I'm disappointed that something so well understood *still* elicits bad investor behavior.

The article discussed a study published by the National Bureau of Economic Research, laying out how political party affiliation affected household investment choices. After Donald Trump won the November 2016 presidential election, half the country was elated while the other half was depressed. That is expected in politics. But things soon changed for the better or worse, depending upon how you voted. The research found:

> Republicans increase the exposure of their investments to the U.S. stock market relative to Democrats following the election. Democrats increase their relative holdings of bonds and cash-like securities.

You read that right: For no other reason other than the outcome of the presidential election, Republicans bought more stocks, while Democrats shifted to bonds and cash.

Even worse, this was not a one-time allocation shift. Instead, it was driven by "active trading over a six-month horizon following the election." The study noted that the relative change in equity shares was "twice as large among previously active investors." Not only was there an asset allocation shift, but these investors traded more actively for the two quarters after the election.

To my Republican friends, I say, "Congrats. Good results for the wrong reason—you should remember that you're lucky, not skillful." To my Democratic friends, I say, "Come on. How could you? You missed out on some great gains out of partisan spite."

This is not the first time we have mentioned this phenomenon. As noted earlier, during the presidencies of George W. Bush (2003–07) and Barack Obama (2009–17), partisan affiliation seemed to negatively affect investor performance. Those observations were based on anecdotes; the NBER study now provides hard data on the dangers of mixing politics and investing.

From weeks before an election right up through election day, talking heads yell about how momentous election results will be for the stock market. For example, in 2016 they warned us that "Markets Are Afraid of Donald Trump."[307] (LOL.) When markets ignored that statement and rallied after Trump's victory, a new explanatory narrative was crafted, this one of deregulation, infrastructure stimulus, and tax cuts. Soon after, markets plateaued and went sideways for a while, and the sages blamed high US stock valuations. (LOL again.)

History strongly suggests those pundits should pour themselves a tall glass of *STFU* and be roundly ignored by you, the investor class.[308] There are many reasons why this is so, but between George W. Bush, Barack Obama, and Donald Trump, it's pretty obvious: Acting on partisan political views only increases your odds of making poor investing decisions.

Regardless, this serves as yet another reminder to avoid investing based on emotions. The range of reasons so many of us use to make investment decisions are impulsive, irrational, and often costly. You (and your children) will be grateful 50 years from now if you keep this in mind today.

Next, we consider what happens following a recession. You will be surprised to learn who suddenly becomes the most influential group of people.

AFTER A RECESSION, THE LEAST RATIONAL RISE (TEMPORARILY) TO PROMINENCE. IGNORE THEM.

IF YOU ARE reading this, the previously scheduled end of the world did not occur.

Despite millennia of Armageddon forecasts, betting on the end of the world has always been a money-losing wager. Given this oh-fer batting record of 0.000%, one wonders why people still regularly make this forecast. Wall Street fund strategists, religious zealots, economists—all seem strangely drawn to it. Never mind that if it ever were a winning trade, no one would be left for you to collect from. (This is called counterparty risk.)

Us humans are a hardy breed. No matter how dire the circumstances, our species has prospered.

We survived the Ice Age, the Dark Ages, the Middle Ages, and the Age of Aquarius (as well as Disco and Polyester). Mother Nature has thrown floods, earthquakes, droughts, plagues, pandemics, tornadoes, asteroids, tsunamis, hurricanes, melting glaciers, and global warming at us. Not to mention world wars and nuclear proliferation.

Economically, we've withstood the Panics of 1819, 1825, 1837, 1847, 1857, 1866, 1873, 1884, 1890, 1893, 1896, 1907, 1929, 1933, 1938, 1973, 1987, 1998, 2000, 2007–09, and 2020—and that is just over the past two centuries. We also saw through the Tulip Bubble, the South Sea Bubble, the Great Depression and the Great Recession, the Nifty-Fifty, the Asian Contagion, the Dotcom Bubble, the subprime fiasco, Bernie Madoff, and most recently, the Covid-19 pandemic.

What is it going to take to kill this species off—or at least to bankrupt it?

Given this long and storied history of survival, why does anyone pay attention to the damn fools predicting the end of the world?

There is a very good explanation: We are wired to see danger and negative news. And our recency bias—our unfortunate tendency to greatly overemphasize our most recent experiences—makes it worse. Our memories of recent events are more vivid than those of older events. We tend to concentrate more on what we can see in the rearview mirror than on what we see through the windshield.

This has enormous consequences. It's why we buy so much stock at euphoric tops and sell most heavily at panic bottoms. Traders have a tendency to describe themselves as bullish *after* they buy; they are more likely to describe themselves as bearish *after* they sell. What happened recently is used as part of a broader rationalization process. It is how you justify your own actions.

The recency effect may help explain the rise of the cranks, who have enjoyed undeserved credibility in the aftermath of the past few recessions. (These include the "End of Days" forecasts Dr. Bernstein wrote about.) Following a collapse, these people can only see doom and gloom in the future. They include:

- **Crisis rock stars** who made their reputations in either the dotcom crash, the GFC, the Flash Crash, or the pandemic, and cannot seem to get back to normal footing.
- **Hyperinflationistas** who are convinced we are returning to the days of the Weimar Republic.
- **Goldbugs** who despite the long-term underperformance of the yellow metal (four decades or so), are convinced now is its time.[309]
- **Conspiracy theorists**: From Birthers to Truthers to Anti-Vaxxers to Flat-Earthers, all manner of blithering idiots who would be ignored during normal times draw attention.
- **Austerians**: Those people who believe the only way forward is through painful spending cuts.
- **Thinly veiled partisans** who opportunistically grab the crisis as proof the other guy is unfit to govern.

PART 3: BAD BEHAVIOR

- **Analysts** trying to turn one good call into a new business model.
- **One-sided websites** that never see any positive data in anything; their URLs tend to have "Doom," "Collapse," or "ZeroHedge" in their titles.

It is no coincidence that negative predictions increase after major recessions or market collapses. They are predicting what just occurred, not what is likely to happen. And they are not making their followers any money.

Listening to their advice, their readers miss the greatest market rallies. They pile into commodities in time for a major collapse; they get frightened out of municipal bonds that have no credit issue or default threat. They otherwise miss opportunities and lose capital.

I have never been a perma-bull—not only because that is not my nature but also because throughout most of my career, equities have always felt like market risk was higher recently than it has been in the past.

But that doesn't mean that you start paying attention to cranks with terrible track records who are trying to sell you something.

What affects people's tolerance for risk? It's not their ability to withstand risk, but in fact it's whatever the market just did. Let's find out why.

HERE COMES ANOTHER CRASH!

IN THE EARLY 1980s, markets were on a tear. Paul Volcker, then Chairman of the Federal Reserve, cranked Fed rates up to 11* and broke the back of inflation. That set the stage for a 40-year bull market in bonds and a 20-year bull market in stocks. In 1982, stocks eclipsed their prior highs, set in 1966. They began climbing steadily upwards, and in 1986, they were *much* higher. By August 1987, they were even higher.

Then came the crash: On October 15, 1987, the US stock markets fell 22% *in a single trading session*. This was unprecedented, and it has never been seen again.

How likely is a replay of the '87 crash? It depends on who you ask. But even more importantly, it depends on *when* you ask.

This is due to the recency effect—our tendency to overemphasize the most recent data point in any series. We see this in monthly Non-Farm Payroll reports, quarterly earnings releases, and weekly new unemployment claims. These data series tend to be highly variable and noisy, but we always wildly overemphasize what just happened.

Like so much else in this book, you can blame evolution. We have evolved to survive in a hostile world and to react quickly to any existential threats. What might be a potential danger to us *right now*? The long term is meaningless if you become something else's dinner *tonight*.

A good financial plan requires knowing your tolerance for risk. The problem is that few of us know how much volatility we can withstand or what a large market drawdown will do to our psyche. We don't know our own risk tolerances.

---

* My apologies for the *Spinal Tap* reference.

PART 3: BAD BEHAVIOR

Worse, we are deeply affected by whatever the stock market has done over the past six months. After the market has rallied hard upwards, people will tell you they are okay with risk. You will most commonly hear: "I am a risk-tolerant, aggressive investor."

This is greed speaking.

Ask the same question after six months of relentless selling and lower prices, and you will get a very different answer: "I am a risk-averse, conservative investor."

This is fear speaking.

Neither answer is fully accurate, but both reflect what just happened. That is the recency effect in action.

———

Let's compare two *Wall Street Journal* articles published three years apart. The first was dated October 15, 2007, and the second was on May 17, 2010. The only thing separating the two stories is three years—and a 57% market crash during the worst recession since the Great Depression.

Can you guess how the tone of the articles differs?

The 2007 headline was telling: "Exorcising Ghosts of Octobers Past." Even the subhead was optimistic: "Despite Housing Slump, Crashes Such as in 1987 Likely to Stay Memories."[310] It came exactly 20 years after the 1987 crash and seven years past the dotcom implosion. Those disasters were distant memories, and besides, stock prices had doubled off the 2003 lows. Housing and credit were shaky, but we were told the impact was "contained."[311]

As the Dow passed 14,000 and the dominant psychology was bullish, here is what the *Journal* said about the 1987 crash:

> With the stock market booming lately, many investors are putting aside worries about the housing slump and the summer's credit crunch. At the same time, some are thinking about a looming anniversary... But some of the root causes of the 1987 crash appear to be missing today. A big problem 20 years ago was that stocks had risen too far, too fast. At their August high, the Dow industrials were up more than 43% for 1987 alone, a stunning short-term gain.

Then came the GFC. Housing lost a third of its value, and stocks were cut in half (and then some). They wouldn't bottom until March 2009, and would not eclipse their prior highs until March 2013.

About halfway through this, in 2010, markets experienced the Flash Crash. Caused (arguably) by a combination of the "largest ever toxic order imbalance" and high-frequency trading (HFT), the May 6, 2010 Flash Crash started at 2:32 p.m. EDT and lasted for 36 minutes. It wiped out over a trillion dollars in market value.

With the 2007–09 GFC still fresh in everybody's minds, here is what the *Journal* published in 2010:

> On May 6, "The velocity of the volatility was stunning, beyond anything I had ever seen, with the **exception of October of 1987**, when I was on the trading floor," said Ted Weisberg, president of Seaport Securities in New York.
>
> "There's a strong parallel between the **Black Monday** crash and the flash crash," said Michael Wong, an analyst at Morningstar who tracks stock exchanges.[312]

What was different between 2007 and 2010? Not high-frequency trading—that had been around since 1983. The *New York Times* had a prominent column about it in 2009: "Stock Traders Find Speed Pays, in Milliseconds."[313]

On October 19, 1987, the Dow Jones Industrial Average tumbled more than 22%, and the swoon extended into the following day before rebounding. Floor traders, working by telephone, dominated the action; computer-generated trading was still in its infancy. Dark pools and high-frequency trading were the stuff of science fiction. Trading was about 600 million shares.

Fast forward to May 6, 2010: The lightning descent lasted 10 minutes, and the decline hit 9.8% at its worst. Trades, many executed in milliseconds, reached 19 billion shares.[314]

Despite the same technological factors driving the markets three years earlier, the perspective from the market pros (who are all too human) was

PART 3: BAD BEHAVIOR

very different. That is because the recent past had an outsized impact on their outlook.

Of course people see similarities to 1987 a year after the 2008–09 crash. That is the recency effect at work! This is how we are wired.

Our frame of reference is *what just occurred*. We look backward, not forwards. By over-emphasizing the recent, we believe we can avoid current danger. That strategy evolved to be effective on the savanna, where it has worked great for millions of years. In modern capital markets? Not so much…

—

All this human emotion distracts from good portfolio management. Maybe we would all be better off if *Star Trek's* Mr. Spock managed our portfolios…

THE SPOCK MARKET

I **KNOW MR. MARKET'S** real name:

Mr. Spock.

A short explanation for the non-Trekkie reader: Spock is the science officer and second in command aboard the starship USS *Enterprise*.[315] He was born to a human mother and a Vulcan father.[316] The Star Trek Universe portrays humans as emotional, unpredictable, and irrational (in other words, accurately). Vulcans are an ancient civilization whose history of violence and emotion brought them to the brink of self-destruction, which was avoided only when the entire species embraced a radical control of their emotions.

Raised on planet Vulcan, Spock fully embraces the Vulcan philosophy of logic.[317] But since he is half human, he struggles to balance logic and emotion. Once you accept that Mr. Market *is* Mr. Spock, the raging confusion about markets, the economy, even equity prices, disappears.

Consider the following.

Investors are rational

Much of the time, markets are understandable and make intuitive sense to investors. Profits rise, so too do stocks. The economy tanks and stocks roll over. There are long trending periods when stocks meander upwards, reflecting positive developments in technology, taxes, inflation, etc. This is the Vulcan logic of equities, a reflection of investors' collective rationality.

PART 3: BAD BEHAVIOR

Investors are irrational

At extremes, traders seem to lose their minds. They indulge their emotional halves. It is especially obvious at turning points: Recall the March 2000 dotcom highs, when start-ups went public at 100 times revenues. Or the March 2009 GFC lows, when prices were cut in half and selling was indiscriminate. The points where groupthink takes over the crowd, where emotions run rampant, and greed and fear can overwhelm investors—that's investors indulging their human half. The Nobel Prize committee recognized this in 2013 when they awarded the Sveriges Riksbank Prize in Economic Sciences to both Eugene Fama and Robert Shiller.[318]

In 2020, day traders were buying bankrupt companies because their prices were rising; they sold quality holdings at very low prices because others had done so. What could be more human than FOMO—the fear of missing out on gains? Perhaps only loss aversion, our very real fear when real money disappears into an ugly sell-off. Irrational investors create opportunities for those who recognize this as it happens in real time.

Markets are efficient

The volume of information is so enormous that it can never be fully grasped by one person. Yet prices reflect all of what is publicly known, manifesting when people act on their collective knowledge. This allows markets to effectively communicate all of the known information and data expressed by these information holders through their buying and selling of equities.

Price, in other words, is the most efficient collective probability bet about the future. Very rational, indeed.

Markets are inefficient

They are efficient, yes, except when those efficient expressions turn out to be wildly wrong. Note that this is not when a trade turns out to be a loser, but part of a good probabilistic analysis when the analytical framework underlying the trade turns out to be completely unfounded.

This is when our emotional half makes the rational half go off the rails. Rather than describing markets as efficient, it is more accurate to describe markets as somewhat efficient, much of the time, getting there eventually, with their efficiency rising and falling in opposition to levels of human emotions. Markets are more or less efficient, except when they are not.[319]

Most investors do not know they don't know

Listen to any explanation of market behavior; they are filled with hindsight bias and rationalizations. It is rare to hear someone answer a question about markets and not give a detailed after-the-fact narrative. Few are willing to say, "I don't know," or "It's essentially random."

Spock, however, is far along the Dunning-Kruger curve (more on this next section). He often notes his lack of understanding with a simple, "Fascinating." His logic and ego control allows the admission of not knowing. Investors often get into trouble when they imagine they have an understanding of things they do not. They are much further back on the DK curve.

Spock's mixed human-Vulcan heritage was a great plot device that allowed *Star Trek* to subtly comment on human nature (as well as the Cold War). Long before Amos Tversky and Danny Kahneman started their research into human decision-making, this metaphor of Vulcan duality was an observation of the battle between logic and emotion, between our intellectual capacity and our baser motives.

Investors who understand what the Spock market[320] is will better recognize the impact of their own behavior on their portfolios.

Is there a more abused word in market commentary than "uncertainty?" If we understood what the word actually means, we wouldn't be so easily fooled by its misuse. Let's take a closer look.

KISS YOUR ASSETS GOODBYE WHEN CERTAINTY REIGNS

"*THE MARKETS HATE uncertainty.*"

If you wander anywhere near a television in advance of any election, a Federal Open Market Committee meeting, or the next employment report, it is an unavoidable cliché. It has become the pundits' preferred proverb.

Wall Street has a sweet tooth for such investing maxims. They infect the trading community like influenza in December. Repeat mindless dictums ad nauseam, and soon enough, it becomes accepted wisdom.

The problem with these *truisms* is that they are fabricated and no more useful than the made-up 20% bull or bear market measure. A closer look at this uncertainty meme reveals it to be a *false-ism*—an emotionally appealing phrase that pings around trading desks. The lack of evidence supporting its premise seems to matter very little.

To recognize how meaningless these statements are, consider the opposite: Could markets function without uncertainty? It takes only a little thought to realize that markets actually thrive on doubt, imperfect information, and a lack of consensus.

Uncertainty drives the market's price-discovery mechanism. Investing requires there to be differences of opinion. Without any uncertainty, who would take the opposite side of your trade?

History teaches that whenever the opposite occurs—when certainty overwhelms uncertainty—the herd tends to be wrong. In rare instances, when there is a near-total lack of uncertainty in the market, the outcome is usually a spectacular disaster.

HOW NOT TO INVEST

Recall the dotcom era, when certainty ruled. Everyone knew that profits no longer mattered. Uncertainty seemed to be banished. The Nasdaq doubled over six months, followed by an epic crash.

After that implosion, we saw the opposite extreme: Profitable, debt-free tech companies were being traded for less than book value, and in a few rare instances, they were being sold for *less than cash on hand*. Investors had become certain that a dollar was worth only 75 cents.

There was little uncertainty heading into the March 2009 stock-market lows. Almost everyone was sure the world was falling into the abyss. In that massive and indiscriminate selling, it seemed almost certain that no one was ever going to buy another house or car, send their kids to school, or for that matter, clothe and feed them. How did the consensus work out in that instance? (Not well.)

When we discuss uncertainty, what we are really discussing is the unknown. All unknown outcomes contain risk, and therein lies the possibility of loss. Risk is inherent in the concept of uncertainty. However, anyone looking for performance must embrace risk, for without it, there can be no reward.

―

Michael Mauboussin, the original thinker we met in earlier chapters, points out that people sometimes confuse *risk* with *uncertainty*.

Risk, he observes, occurs when we don't know what is going to happen next, but we do know *what the distribution set looks like*. Uncertainty, on the other hand, occurs when we have no idea what is going to happen next and *we do not know what the possible distribution looks like*.

In other words, the future is always unknown, but that does not make it uncertain. Rather, we should quantify this in the language of *statistical probability*.

When we don't know what a future outcome will be but understand the probability distribution—think of dice or a multiple-choice exam—we have risk, but we do not have uncertainty. We never know what the roll of the die will be in advance, but we do know it will be one of six possibilities.

Is that uncertainty? The answer is no—it is an unknown outcome with well-defined possibilities.

PART 3: BAD BEHAVIOR

Uncertainty is when the possible outcomes are wholly unknown and unknowable. War is a classic example of uncertainty. When the New Horizon's space probe did its flyby of the Pluto system, what we would find was truly uncertain. Actual surprises occurred.

The problem is when pundits conflate *uncertainty* with *unknown*. Consider alternatively what is the true definition of uncertainty: It occurs *when we have no idea of what the possible outcome might be*, when the probability distribution is unknown (or so extremely large as to functionally be the same as unknown).

—

It finally dawned on me what drove the uncertainty trope. It took a nervous chief executive on Bloomberg TV during a big sell-off, but his nervousness revealed the answer.

Most of the time, humans exist in a happy little bubble of self-created delusion. We lie to ourselves constantly. We rationalize everything we do, past and present. We engage in selective perception, seeing only the things that agree with us. Our selective retention retains the good stuff and disregards most of the rest. In our minds, we are all younger, better-looking, slimmer, and with more hair than our selfies reveal.

In short, we create a construct of reality that bears only a passing resemblance to the objective universe.

The uncertainty trope arises during those moments when our delusions fade, in those instances where we recognize our own permanent ignorance of the future. Most of us are not especially happy with the naked truth, preferring the comfortable lie. (This often occurs mid-crash.) It is in these brief instances where the facade fades, the curtain gets pulled back, and the ugly reality becomes known to us. We get a glimmer of understanding of our own *lack of understanding*. That's when the grim reality of the human condition is revealed—and it scares the living hell out of us.

Uncertainty is a state of mind. Certainty is a level of comfort—the unjustified belief that you know what will happen. You have a good sense of the future, so it is easy to plan for what comes next, *because* of the lack of uncertainty.

Of course, this is a false belief, a completely misguided fallacy inherent to the species.

Your lack of uncertainty only means that you feel pretty good—comfortable and unthreatened enough to casually lie to yourself about how much you imagine you know. You can pretend you can see what is coming because there is nothing to make you worry about it otherwise. When the stock market rallies, you are optimistic about the future. You can comfortably extrapolate from today out years or decades ahead.

This is, of course, utter bullshit.

You had no idea what was going to happen this year, and you have no idea what is going to happen next year. If you were comfortable last year, it was because nothing was rubbing your face in how little you actually knew about the future—not the market, not the economy, not geopolitics. Despite this, you keep making forecasts, regardless of overwhelming evidence that you are terrible at it.

You managed to somehow forget how little you knew about the future. When your limbic system is not overly stimulated, when you can relax a bit ... *deep inhale ... hold it ... deep exhale ... let it out ...* you can fool yourself into believing any form of nonsense. This is the normal state of human affairs.

The next time you hear someone mention *uncertainty*, ask yourself this: How much less do they actually know about the future today versus what they knew last week or year? How little do they *realize they don't know*?

The uncertainty trope arises not when things are uncertain—and *they ALWAYS are uncertain*. Rather, it comes up during those all-too-rare instances when we mortals briefly acknowledge reality. When it passes, we all manage to go back to our previously constructed artificial reality.

In the film *The Matrix*, Neo (played by our *John Wick* friend, Keanu Reeves) is faced with the choice of choosing the red pill or the blue pill. Take the blue pill and go back to your little bubble of delusion. *The Matrix* was a Hollywood fantasy where Neo takes the red pill, and all is revealed. In the real world, the blue pill dominates. Most of us prefer the comfortable fantasy that we actually know what is going on. (Narrator: We don't.)

Pundits may hate uncertainty—it tends to make them look foolish—but markets harbor no such bias. In fact, markets thrive on uncertainty. It is their reason for being.

PART 3: BAD BEHAVIOR

Your artificial construct beckons…

Okay, now that we better understand what uncertainty is (and how we lie to ourselves about it), some advice as to what to do during market crashes might be useful. That's next.

DO'S AND DON'TS OF MARKET CRASHES

EVERY FEW QUARTERS, we find ourselves running through the same muster drill. Something happens somewhere in the world, and the markets go a little wild. They sell off a dozen percent or so. The usual suspects panic. Eventually, things stabilize, and everyone wonders what the hell just happened. Post-mortem explanations come along that seem reasonable (after the fact, of course, never before).

Lather, rinse, repeat.

The phones ring with reporters wanting a comment on the volatility. "What's going on in the markets?" they say. My response is always the same: "You won't like my answer: This is what markets do—they go up and down, sometimes violently."

"Thank you," they say as they hurriedly hang up.

I can do the drill in my sleep.

End of 2015? China down 15%, and Europe off the same. Fourth quarter of 2018? S&P 500 off ~20%. Q1 2020? S&P 500 down 34%. 2022, stock markets off 20%, Nasdaq down over 30%, and the bond market off 15%! Summer 2024, Japan falls 9% in two days!

Any given week can have a surprise in store, which then cascades around the world. It's almost as if this is a pattern, a normal part of markets!

My colleague Callie Cox has run the numbers.[321]

On a typical day, the market swings ~0.5%. In fact, Callie observes, "the S&P 500 has gained or lost less than 0.5% on 53% of trading days." Plus or minus 1% days occur about 20% of the time. That averages out to once a week, but "it isn't a predictable, once-every-five-days type deal." Drawdowns of 5–10% happen more than you might realize—there have been 57 sell-offs of that size since 1950 (that's two out of every three years).

There have been 23 sell-offs of more than 10% and less than 20% over that time (once every three years). And over the past 75 years, there have been 11 drops in the S&P 500 of 20% or more.

When the usual occurs, my advice is always the same: Turn off the TV, follow your plan, and start flipping over couch cushions to find spare cash, because a wonderful buying opportunity is coming your way.

Let's get more specific as to the "Do's and Don'ts" of market crashes:

Do notice how cyclical markets are

Markets rise and fall with shocking regularity. They may not stick to schedules as tightly as the solar system does—think seasons, sunrise and sunsets, moon phases, even the appearance of comets—but they do move in semi-regular cycles. As do market corrections and crashes. Between 1950 and 2014, half of all annual periods saw a correction of 10% or more. Bull and bear markets come along on their own timelines, stay for as long as they like, then move on. There is not a whole lot you can do about it, except recognize that it happens.

Don't react emotionally

Do not give in to your gut, which might cause a momentary lapse in reason. Remember, the flight or fight response we discussed earlier—that knot in your stomach, sweaty palms, accelerated breathing, and increased heart rate—are signs of stress. The discomfort is a feature, not a bug. This agitation is supposed to crank up your body and make it ready to react to danger. It did a terrific job keeping your ancestors alive, but works against you in the capital markets. Adrenaline, it turns out, is not the basis of sound judgment or portfolio management.

Do stick with your plan

You made a long-term plan in the first place for money you do not need access to in the next year (or for years after), but rather, decades from now. In 2050, you will not care what the market did in April 2025. The short term always seems to get in the way of the long term. I've heard countless stories from investors who panicked out of the market at the March 2009 lows and never found their way back in. They missed out on a huge climb in value. That's not sticking to a plan, and it's not what good financial planning looks like.

Don't rely on gurus, shamans, or talking heads

They haven't the slightest idea about your financial needs, your risk tolerances, your tax bracket, or anything else about you. I have been doing financial TV and radio for more than 20 years and have met many of these people. Very few have the slightest idea what they are talking about, and their general advice is for entertainment purposes only. Their forecasts are nothing more than marketing. Treat them that way.

Do notice your own state of mind

Are you agitated, freaked, stressed out? Is the market keeping you up at night? Notice the subtle difference between reacting emotionally to external stimuli and that nagging feeling that you forgot something important. At times, your body may be telling you something. Is your portfolio in sync with your own risk tolerance? Are you carrying more exposure to high-risk assets than you are comfortable with? Have your circumstances changed, but your portfolio has not? Try to be perceptive to when your subconscious is trying to get you to notice something. It could be important.

Don't take action while in a state of discomfort

Decisions made to *stop the pain* are the ones you will regret. The time for action is when you are in a thoughtful, calm state of mind. Any significant financial decision you make should be circumspect, carefully considered, and according to plan. If you are merely reacting to the latest market moves, breaking news, or headlines, then what you have is not a plan—you have an instinctual, fear-driven reaction, and that's the makings of a disaster.

Do take notice of the panic around you

Watch the reactions—and overreactions—of the guests on financial television. How emotional and strident are they? Are their voices up an octave? Can you see them sweating? There was a time during the GFC when I could tell how much the market was down that day merely by listening to CNBC anchor Maria Bartiromo's voice. There is a feedback loop from markets to TV anchors and back—see if you can spot it. Just don't let yourself become affected by it.

Don't try to time the markets

You lack the skill, the discipline, and the ability. Even if you get lucky, it's just that—dumb luck—and that serendipity is likely to encourage you to engage in even more reckless and foolish behavior in the future.* The odds of you jumping out on time and getting back in are stacked against you. Add in taxes and other costs, and it becomes a fool's errand.

Do look for signs of capitulation (or surrender)

Market bottoms are made when a critical mass of investors folds, throws in their cards, and panic sells. See if you can spot the moment when everyone finally cries "Uncle."

Don't confuse the short term for the long term

The day-to-day action is noise unless you are an active trader doing this for a living. You will lose money treating investments like trades and vice versa.

---

* We discuss cowboy accounts in Part 4.

Do have a sense of humor about this

My favorite thought on this came from a fund manager who, in the midst of a nasty sell-off, was asked by a fellow trader how he was doing.

"Sleeping like a baby," he calmly replied.

"Really? Given this crazy market, how can you sleep like a baby?"

"It's easy!" he said. "I wake up screaming every two hours, wet myself, and cry for Mommy."

That sort of gallows humor is typical on Wall Street. But if you follow the good advice above, you can sleep soundly, knowing your portfolio is working for you.

—

Up next, we see what happens when people follow the advice above.

WALL STREET PROS PANIC OVER COVID WHILE MOM AND POP BUY

IF YOU'RE ONE of those people—a pundit, investor, or active manager—who's been bracing for passive investing and exchange-traded funds to blow up the stock market, well, I have some bad news for you.

But first, let's recall some warnings about passive investing:

- Index funds are Marxist,[322] or Communist.[323]
- Or socialist.[324]
- Passive investing is "devouring capitalism."[325]
- It has reached a "mania."[326]
- The passive boom is creating "frightening" risk for markets.[327]
- Passive investing is "lobotomized investing."[328]
- Indexing represents a danger to the economy.[329]
- Your love of index funds is terrible for our economy.[330]
- They are a bubble waiting to burst.[331]
- Passive investing poses a systemic risk.[332]

But a funny thing happened on the way to this dangerous, systemic, Marxist bubble:

Nothing.

If ever there was a situation in which the critics told us passive investing was destined to fail, 2020 should have been it: the fastest bear market on record. The market externality caused by the coronavirus pandemic sent volatility spiking wildly, sending markets down the most since the GFC. For anyone younger than 30, March 2020 was probably the worst time of their investing lives. Over the course of four weeks (February 19 to March 20), markets crashed 34% lower.

If ever there was an opportunity for active investing to shine, this was it.

But that's not what happened. The panic emanated from the active money managers on Wall Street, not the plodders on Main Street. Perhaps the most intriguing indicator of this is the difference between the vehicles used by professionals and those preferred by individual investors.

Consider the three largest S&P 500 index funds in the world: State Street's SPDR S&P 500 ETF Trust or Spyder (SPY), Blackrock's iShares Core S&P 500 ETF (IVV), and Vanguard's S&P 500 ETF (VOO). State Street's Spyder is arguably the choice of professionals; it was the first major index ETF and the most liquid. Registered investment advisors and individual investors prefer BlackRock and Vanguard's offerings. Note these funds all invest in the exact same thing; they are simply different ETF wrappers.

During the pandemic sell-off, BlackRock and Vanguard customers were net buyers every single day.[333] At the same time, State Street's customers were sellers.

In other words, during the sell-off, Wall Street pros panicked and sold while moms and pops stayed calm and bought.[334] Some of this is attributable to different timelines between investors and traders, or between short term and long term. But I can't help but think that some of this is explained by psychology: The professionals are the ones whose bonuses and perhaps even their jobs are on the line. Retail investors looked to take advantage of a price drop.

The data from Vanguard Group confirmed this phenomenon. According to the firm's measures of money flows, equities net gained on every day of February and the first week of March 2020.

This is very similar to what former Vanguard chairman and chief executive officer William McNabb observed during the GFC: The pros sold and the amateurs bought.[335]

Retail investors are the dumb money? Maybe a few decades ago, but today? Much less so.

PART 3: BAD BEHAVIOR

Most investment assets today are still managed actively. However, as I noted in 2017, the active part of the money-management industry is still being downsized—or more accurately, right-sized.[336] The active management world still has not yet come to grips with the sea change that followed the financial crisis.[337]

Passive indexing and ETFs have provided a counterweight to the active traders who seem to be panic selling. Remember that the next time someone warns you of the dangers of passive investing.

SECTION 3: COGNITIVE DEFICITS

There are so many different types of cognitive errors that they could fill a book—just not this one! Instead, I want to draw your attention to a few poorly understood mental processes and the ways they work against your best interest. The average investor knows little about some of the fascinating cognitive deficits, including the Dunning-Kruger effect, epistemic trespass, and cognitive dissonance. We will also delve into the relatively young field of neuroeconomics.

BEYOND OUR EMOTIONS and lack of rationality, we have an entirely different set of issues that are hard-wired into our brains: *Cognition-based errors.*

The way our brains have evolved over the past two million years or so has led to issues inherent in our wetware. Decisions about money were not a big issue on the Serengeti plains, but *avoiding being eaten by lions was.*

In medicine, drugs prescribed for purposes other than those they were created for are called "off-label" uses. Similarly, our brains evolved for use in a very different environment than the modern world. As a result, a predictable set of errors affects how we think and act.

The technical term for this is the "evolutionary mismatch hypothesis." This theory states that traits that were once advantageous in the wild become maladaptive in rapidly changing environments. It's what happens when attributes created over millions of years are suddenly thrust into a very different ecosystem. It also perfectly describes today's investors, saddled with biological traits that cannot adapt fast enough to modern capital markets.

This leads to a few unfortunate tendencies that get in our way:

- We see patterns where none exist.
- We have difficulty conceptualizing long arcs of time.
- We do not experience exponential numbers in nature, so compounding presents an instinctive challenge to us intellectually.
- We selectively perceive and recall that which agrees with our preexisting expectations while ignoring things that contradict our beliefs.
- Our ego makes us believe we are much more capable than we really are; we forget our failures while overemphasizing our successes.
- We are also threat-biased—our brains are better at processing bad news than good.

- We get a greater thrill from the anticipation of a reward than the actual reward itself. (Think what this means in terms of *buy the rumor, sell the news.*)
- We seek stimulus for a dopamine high, regardless of how. Whether you are a gambler, alcoholic, sex addict, shopaholic, or hyper-active trader—it's a very similar chemical buzz.
- Storytelling is how we evolved to share information, making us vulnerable to anecdotes that mislead or present false conclusions unsupported by data.

We are simply not wired to perform the risk analysis required for allocating capital and managing investment risk. As a species, we are much better suited to wandering the countryside in small groups of hunter-gatherers than we are at being money managers.

These cognitive foibles affect everyone and significantly impact our decision-making, whether we are aware of them or not. We cannot avoid these inherited shortfalls; it's how we are built. But if we at least become aware of these processing issues, we have some hope of avoiding their most pernicious impact…

―

All of these cognitive errors only prove that you're only human; here's how that hurts your portfolio.

YOU'RE ONLY HUMAN; HERE'S HOW THAT HURTS YOUR PORTFOLIO

MY DAY JOB is Chairman and Chief Investment Officer for Ritholtz Wealth Management. My side hustle is hosting a few shows on Bloomberg radio.* Since 2014, I get to spend two hours a week speaking with many of the world's most fascinating people.

One of those people is Richard Thaler, professor of behavioral science and economics at the University of Chicago. I interviewed him a few times before and after he won the Nobel Prize in economics. Conversations with Thaler are always charming and insightful.

He is also recognized as one of the founding fathers of behavioral economics. His observations about how people behave in the real world are a welcome departure from the false assumptions so endemic to classical economics. What he has learned is eye-opening and of immense importance to investors.

Thaler divides the world into two sorts of people: *Econs*, who are artificial constructs of how people are supposed to behave. They are perfectly rational, have great self-control, calculate like machines, and know exactly what is best for themselves. Classical economics is where the *Econs* reside.

Then there are *Humans* who do the things economic theory suggests they should not. They react emotionally, lack patience, fail to consider consequences, and seem flummoxed by exponential mathematics (especially compounding). They are filled with all manner of biases and

---

* "Masters in Business," launched in 2014, and was the first mainstream long-form finance interview podcast. (It's the most fun I have all week.)

judgment errors. How *Humans* get through each day must appear as a minor miracle to the *Econs*.

In his book *Misbehaving*, Thaler tells the story of how behavioral economics developed.[338] The title references Thaler's great insight: that people do not behave like *Econs*. This has fascinating implications, most notably that human irrationality is both normal and harmful, at least when it comes to our portfolios.

Let's look at a few of Thaler's discoveries and how they manifest in bad investor behaviors.

Endowment effect

In one of Thaler's early experiments, people were given mugs with a school logo—essentially worthless baubles. They were willing to pay far less to buy them than they were willing to sell them for. In other words, they attached a higher value to an asset they already owned than to one they didn't.

This is the *endowment effect*. Its impact is significant for portfolio management. Investors tend to think more highly of the holdings that are sitting in their accounts than the rest of the investable universe. This is true for stocks, mutual funds, alternative investments, and ETFs.

It explains why most people are such bad stock traders. They have a hard time cutting their losers. They believe their own holdings are more valuable than what the market is telling them.

Sunk cost fallacy

Imagine you are in a restaurant and order an expensive dessert. Despite its 1,000 sugary calories, you do not especially like it—but you eat it anyway. After all, you already paid for it!

This is a perfect example of the *sunk cost fallacy*. Thaler suggests what you should be thinking is: "Since I have already paid for this, why should I suffer the caloric consequences of eating something I don't like? It's paid for whether I eat it or not!"

Apply that to any stock or fund you own (endowment effect included). You have paid for it, but more than that, you invested time and energy into it: You researched the company, you know who the senior management is; you have kept up with all the news about the firm, its latest products, quarterly earnings, conference calls, etc.

You have substantial sunk costs, even if the position turns out to be a money-loser. The proper response *should be*: Those costs are already gone, never to be recovered, and you should not stay married to a holding simply because of those already incurred expenses. The same is true for any holding, be it a hedge fund, private equity, or ETF. Of course, this is not how most people behave.

Loss aversion

Perhaps the most important insight is our tendency toward *loss aversion*. As it turns out, people feel the pain of loss about twice as much as they derive pleasure from gains. There are lots of possible reasons for this, but perhaps the simplest is that gains seem temporary—eventually, they are spent or otherwise fade into the background. Losses, on the other hand, are permanent.

Loss aversion is why investors become timid after stock crashes. Look at what happened to so many portfolios (yours included) right after the GFC. Most people had less equity than they should have had. Assets perceived as less risky were overweighted. This reduced the volatility of those investments, but it also reduced their performance.

Hindsight bias

You saw the 2008 collapse coming, right? It was so obvious, you could not miss it. Housing peaked in 2006—you saw that, too. And the dotcom collapse—weren't you warning your friends about the ridiculous valuations?

Sure you were! A tiny number of people were warning about those things—and they were mostly ignored as cranks. But *hindsight bias* is the cognitive error that leads you to believe you were on the right side of those collapses when (statistically speaking) you most certainly were not.

The reason for this: You now KNOW how that event turned out. Your memory combines what you know today and what (you imagine) you knew then. Of course, given what we know in 2025, you were cautious in 2008–09! Once you know what happened, you cannot recall ever *not* knowing!

The key takeaway from Thaler's research is that we cannot trust ourselves to think clearly, plan patiently, or consistently make the right decisions.

Rather than assuming your brain knows what's best for you, you need to make better decisions insulated from your cognitive foibles. That three-pound brain has 200 billion neurons and 125 trillion synapses and is a marvel of biomechanical engineering. It adapted and evolved to keep you alive in the wild. It's less successful at surviving risk/reward decisions in the capital markets.

Thaler teaches us not to let our software interfere with our investment process. By circumventing those instincts, you can outsmart your brain. One way is to own a broad asset allocation of diversified low-cost indexed ETFs, rebalance them regularly, and stay out of your own way.

What goes on in our brains as we make risk/reward decisions? Figuring that out is the purview of the field of neuroeconomics. Let's see what this area can teach us.

NEUROECONOMICS

WHAT'S YOUR LIZARD brain been up to?
All of the behaviors we have discussed are readily observable. We can see people in the world and watch how they spend and invest their dollars.

But what happens as they make decisions about risk and money? What parts of our brains are engaged in this process? How do the bodies we inhabit, filled with hormones, chemicals, drugs, food, etc., impact our thinking?

Neuroeconomics is a natural extension of behavioral economics. It seeks to identify the physiological processes that occur as we make these choices. The field has made numerous discoveries, many of which suggest that our subconscious drives much of our decision-making before we are even aware of it.

Professor Colin Camerer teaches behavioral finance and economics at the California Institute of Technology and is a Distinguished Senior Fellow at Wharton Neuroscience. He is credited with inventing Behavioral Game Theory.[339] His work on risk, self-control, and strategic choice led to his being named a MacArthur Genius Fellow in 2013.

I discussed the concept of *hypothetical bias* with the Cal-Tech professor.[340] When scientists ask hypothetical questions—"Will you vote in this election?"—about 70% of study participants answer affirmatively. However, people's real-life behavior differs dramatically from how they answer: Only around 45% of the people in the study actually voted. In races where a 1%-point swing can determine an election, a 25% difference between intention and behavior is massive. No wonder political pollsters keep getting their projections so wrong.

To circumvent the hypothetical bias issue, Camerer suggests: "Don't ask the person; ask the brain!" Rather than relying on what people *say* they will do, we can examine what occurs in their brains as they make decisions. Technology like fMRI (functional magnetic resonance imaging), EEG (electroencephalogram), eye tracking, blood chemistry analysis, and galvanic skin response all aid in interoception (our ability to identify signals inside the body).

Through a series of clever experiments, Camerer has discovered that some of our decision-making takes place in milliseconds—even before we have any conscious awareness. In response to a threatening image that lasts just 30 milliseconds—the length of a single frame in a movie (films use 24 frames per second)—fMRIs spot increased activity in the amygdala. Even before we are consciously aware of a threat, our brains have already decided upon a course of action.

The brain's frontal cortex distinguishes modern human intellect from that of our ancestors. The fast-responding parts of our deep and midbrain are ancient. These are where we find faults in our wetware.

To paraphrase Daniel Kahneman's book title, our lizard brains think *really fast* and slow.

Dopaminergic neurons, which make up less than 1% of the brain's neurons, are the primary source of dopamine in our nervous system. When we engage in activities like sex, drinking, eating, gambling, etc., these neurotransmitters flood the brain's reward circuitry with dopamine. Feelings of pleasure, satisfaction, and motivation are the result.

Psychiatrist Anna Lembke studies how some indulgences increase dopamine production above a baseline level.[341] Chocolate increases dopamine by 50%; sex causes a 100% increase; nicotine a 150% surge.[342] For smokers, this implies the cigarette after sex is more pleasurable than the sex itself.[343]

Our decision-making process includes much that we are not consciously aware of. If we do not know why we make specific decisions, how can we improve? Understanding that our brains are flooded with hormones when we are excited, fearful, envious, greedy, or scared is only a first step in that process.

PART 3: BAD BEHAVIOR

How good are you at evaluating your own skills? As it turns out, not very. Called "metacognition," the Dunning-Kruger effect is why you *think* you are better at this than you really are. Let's see why...

METACOGNITION

OF ALL THE cognitive errors in human psychology, perhaps the most important to our charge of *be less stupid* is the Dunning-Kruger effect (DKE). Its rise in pop culture is why it may also be the most misunderstood cognitive concern. Dunning-Kruger is an incredibly useful tool that helps me better understand the errors I observe in markets.

David Dunning is a Professor of Psychology at the University of Michigan* who studies human understanding. In 1999, he and Justin Kruger, a graduate student, published an in-depth study of how people, regardless of their expertise, evaluate their own skills. Titled "Unskilled and Unaware of It,"[344] their study found that people with limited competence in a specific area *overestimated* their abilities in that area. Metacognition, it turns out, is a discrete skill unto itself. It tends to increase as your skill in the underlying domain increases. As you improve at a *thing*, your ability to evaluate your skills at that *thing* also improves.

Yes, the least competent suffer from the DKE, but so do those of average competency. Even experts show the effects of DKE, as their deep knowledge and awareness of difficulty may lead them to *underestimate* their own abilities.

Metacognition is tricky.

The DKE is more than mere overconfidence, hubris, or incompetence; it's a very specific way to describe the estimation of skills, and a way to frame an error that helps us understand why it occurs and how it manifests in human decision-making.

---

* Go Blue!

Dunning-Kruger Effect

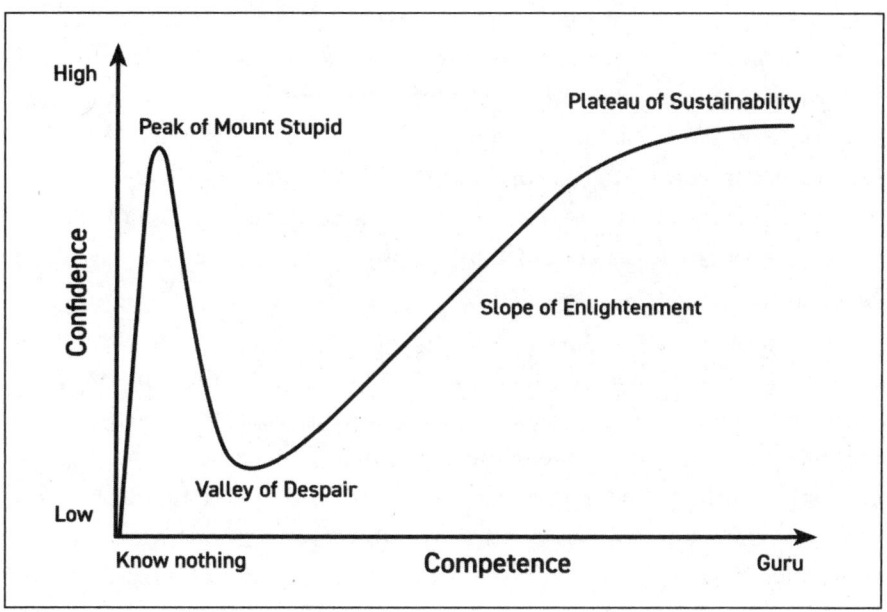

Related to Dunning-Kruger is the DKE curve, which plots confidence against competence.* If the DKE effect were not real, you would expect a gradually rising line from the lower left to the upper right of our metacognition chart. As we gain skills at a given task, our insight into our competence should rise along with our competence.

That's not what we see in real life or in the DKE curve. It shoots straight up to a peak—what some have called *Mount Stupid*—before crashing back to the *Valley of Despair*. It gradually rises slowly over time in a *Slope of Enlightenment*. Much later, it surpasses the initial peak in the *Plateau of Sustainability*.

Think of any task you perform that requires skill and competence. For me, that starts with music, then film, cooking, horology, architecture, cosmology/astronomy, auto-racing, tennis, boating, and investing. These

---

* Ironically, the DKE curve was not created by its authors, but was formed in popular culture as people wrestled with understanding their own lacking skill sets. Years later, Dunning and Kruger researched the curve and discovered it was fairly accurate.

are all things that I find interesting and have tried to do and learn more about.

Tennis might be the most accessible example. I was late to the game, and I only began playing seriously in my 50s. I thought I was pretty good, able to accurately hit the ball with some power and place it where I wanted. Once I began competing against more skilled players, I quickly learned I was on the peak of *Mount Stupid*. I was regularly getting demolished by players I thought I was better than. I spent a lot of time wandering in the *Valley of Despair*.

Out of frustration, I started working with a coach. He put me on the *Slope of Enlightenment* and helped me improve the mechanics of my swing. Previously, my forehands were bouncing up too high, right into the sweet spot of any opponent's swing. A better swing with more topspin cut down on those fat returns. My court positioning and approach to the ball were also poor; my serve was soft, and my backhand (my best swing) was underutilized. I am a much better player today, in large part because I know *just how mediocre I am*. I have learned to play within my own ability and skill level, avoiding unforced errors and letting the other person beat themself. The *Plateau of Sustainability* is a never-ending embrace of improvement and learning.

"Does anyone really know what Dunning-Kruger actually is?" has a recursive character. As you might expect, those who don't study it don't truly understand it. It reminds me of *Fight Club*, the 1999 film starring Brad Pitt and Edward Norton: The first rule of Dunning-Kruger Club is that you do not know you are in Dunning-Kruger Club...[345]

One of the challenges of being knowledgeable about cognitive issues is the Bias Blind Spot. We all have the same biases as everyone else—but we are mostly unaware of them. As I was going through my prior research for this book, I couldn't help but notice—repeatedly—how often I succumbed to the very errors I was writing about.

In discussing his blind spots, Kahneman referenced his own biases, saying "I certainly do not claim to be immune from them. I suffer from all of them."[346]

PART 3: BAD BEHAVIOR

Understanding yourself is crucial to investors. This isn't a Zen discussion of achieving oneness with the universe and self-enlightenment; rather, it explains why knowing what you actually know, understanding what you don't know, and being highly aware of the danger when you think you know (but really don't) is so crucial.

The best question we can ask of an investment manager—or any investor can ask themselves—is not, "How smart are you?" Rather, it's how well do we know ourselves? Can we control our own behavior?

In *The Intelligent Investor*,[347] Benjamin Graham wrote, "investing isn't about beating others at their game. It's about controlling yourself at your own game." His star pupil, Berkshire Hathaway's Warren Buffett, expressed a similar idea in the preface to the revised edition: "To invest successfully does not require a stratospheric IQ, unusual business insights, or inside information. What's needed is a sound intellectual framework for making decisions and the ability to keep emotions from corroding the framework." When speaking in public, Buffett has been known to add, "Any IQ over 125 is wasted."

Self-awareness and control are the keys. Understanding your temperament, skills, and limitations is crucial. Not just amateurs, but many professionals are also stunningly unaware of their inferior knowledge and emotional control. They do not know what they do not know—often fatally so (at least to their portfolios).

Socrates may have been the first person to eloquently write about metacognition: "I only know that I know nothing." It may be counterintuitive, but understanding one's own ignorance is the first step to attaining knowledge. His student Aristotle observed "Knowing yourself is the beginning of all wisdom," about 2,400 years before Professor Dunning delved into the details as to how and why that is.

Or you may prefer Shakespeare's take in *As You Like It*: "The fool doth think he is wise, but the wise man, knows himself to be a fool."

How's your metacognition?

What happens when experts in one field wander to another subject entirely? This version of Dunning-Kruger explains a lot. That's our next topic.

EPISTEMIC TRESPASS

WE HAVE SEEN examples throughout this book that experts are not always right even in their own area of expertise. When they venture outside their field into other areas, the risks of being wrong increase—this is called "epistemic trespass."

Nathan Ballantyne is an associate professor of philosophy, cognition, and culture at Arizona State University. He has observed that experts can drift over "highly visible boundary lines and into domains where they lack the relevant evidence or skills... but they keep talking nonetheless."[348]

Professionals typically possess a hard-won competency that allows them to make good judgments within their area of expertise. All of us should be more skeptical of those who "move into another field where they lack competence and pass judgment anyway."[349] Epistemic trespassers have proved themselves to be unreliable judges in fields where they are outsiders.

One of my favorite examples of this shows up (ironically) in the repeated attempts to debunk Dunning-Kruger, typically by mathematicians arguing the effects are statistically insignificant or just random noise. Those arguments have been contradicted by larger studies that repeatedly confirmed the original, underlying research.[350]

Smart people can suffer from *deformation professionnelle* ("occupational deformity")—a DKE-related tendency to view the world through the lens of one's own profession.[351] It's not surprising that a mathematician looks at a psychological phenomenon and sees only the statistics. Performing statistical analysis on psychology research while unaware of decades of underlying research in psychology sounds a lot like the Dunning-Kruger effect at work.

PART 3: BAD BEHAVIOR

It makes me wonder if Dunning-Kruger explains *everything*—or at least most of the errors newbies make over their first decade as investors.

———

There is a concept I suspect is related to DKE called "The Illusion of Explanatory Depth."[352] It is the intriguing idea that *we think* we actually know much more about things—and can easily explain them—when, in fact, we do not.

Stephen Dubner discussed this idea in an episode of *Freakonomics*: "Think of something you have a really strong opinion about.... Now think about why you have such a strong opinion. How well do you think you could explain your position?"[353]

Could you explain how a toilet or zipper or ballpoint pen or bicycle works? Can you describe how pencils are manufactured? You may imagine you understand these things, but once you try to explain the specifics, you falter.

Steven Sloman is a Professor of Cognitive and Psychological Sciences at Brown University. He is co-author of *The Knowledge Illusion: Why We Never Think Alone*.[354] He told Dubner:

> If you're forced to give an explanation, you have to really understand, and you have to confront the fact that you might not understand. When you give reasons, you do what people do around the Thanksgiving dinner table: They talk about their feelings about it, what they like, what they don't like.

A possible reason for this illusion today is that all of the accumulated knowledge of humanity is but a click away. In an interconnected information environment, we are all *knowledge adjacent*. We may not know exactly how zippers or ballpoint pens work, but we do know how to find out.

Nobel Prize-winning physicist Richard Feynman suggested, "If you want to master something, teach it." (He also observed, "I learned very early the difference between knowing the name of something and *knowing* something.")

The founder of the Institute for Philosophical Research, Dr. Mortimer J. Adler, was even more blunt: "The person who says he knows what he thinks but cannot express it usually does not know what he thinks."

Knowledge is distributed widely in our society. We err when we believe this knowledge is our own understanding.

—

What happens when facts collide with our beliefs? Cognitive dissonance is the result. Let's find out how it hurts our returns.

COGNITIVE DISSONANCE HURTS YOUR RETURNS

OF ALL THE failings of human wetware, cognitive dissonance may be the most intriguing. Social psychologist Leon Festinger[355] coined the phrase in 1956, observing that "human beings strive for internal psychological consistency to function mentally in the real world."[356]

When facts conflict with beliefs, people find ways to ignore the facts, rationalizing them so their disproven theories can survive. Otherwise, the resulting dissonance causes too much cognitive tension.

Economist John Kenneth Galbraith famously referenced cognitive dissonance before that phrase was commonly used, writing, "Faced with the choice between changing one's mind and proving that there is no need to do so, almost everyone gets busy on the proof."[357]

Much of what we think and do is predicated upon our abstract belief systems. In the context of investing, cognitive dissonance occurs in the mind of an individual when a theoretical investment belief is confronted by evidence demonstrating outcomes contrary to what our most cherished theories say should occur. What is important is how we respond to this conflict. We can rationalize the data, or we can accept the facts and change our beliefs.

Or not.

—

Consider the ideological world you inhabit. What you think, what you believe, the ideologies that resonate with you, like politics, religion, and philosophy. Anything that contradicts them is going to be looked at askance, given how cognitively expensive it was to construct your model of the universe.

How expensive? The human brain weighs about 3 pounds—just 2% of our total body weight. But it consumes 20% of our daily calories, 10 times what its size alone suggests it should. That shows you how incredibly costly it is to build and maintain these mental models.

No wonder Bill Bernstein observed, "We are cognitive misers."

Thinking is expensive.

Why is cognitive dissonance so pernicious? Maybe it relates to the sunk cost fallacy. Even when we are shown to be wrong, we defend our costly constructed ideologies. We rationalize, lest all that time and effort be for naught. The energy already expended is gone, regardless of whether we stay with disproven beliefs or not. Rather than discard a belief system that has been shown to be ineffective, we instead choose to double down.

In markets, not updating your beliefs to reflect reality and staying with an ideology that has failed usually proves costly.

Sufferers of cognitive dissonance ignore the facts in front of their eyes, devising rationales for why expected outcomes never occurred. The blame is laid elsewhere, never on their faulty ideology.

There are many examples: Deep value investors who buy depressed stocks regardless of other risk factors, only to see them fall another 50%; Austrian economists warning of imminent hyperinflation and the collapse of the fiat dollar, which never arrives.

Former Federal Reserve Chairman Alan Greenspan was a long-time cheerleader for radical deregulation. After housing, the economy, and the stock market crashed, he *almost* admitted error, saying, "I have found a flaw. I don't know how significant or permanent it is. But I have been very distressed by that fact."[358]

A favorite example comes from the housing market collapse. It wasn't the wildly irresponsible behavior of non-bank lenders and junk-securitized mortgages *somehow* rated AAA that caused the problem. Rather, it was something else, and if we can find a government entity to blame, so much the better. Post-GFC, there were endless attempts to throw manure against the barn door to see what might stick: It was the Community Reinvestment Act! No, wait, it was the FHA's VA loans. No, it was GSE's

PART 3: BAD BEHAVIOR

Fannie and Freddie! A beloved excuse blamed "The Poors" (really), those no-good, low-income borrowers who defaulted on homes when their variable 2/28 mortgages spiked higher![359]

As always, the reality was much more complex. Many factors deserve blame, ranging from ultra-low interest rates and falling real incomes to the mad scramble among fund managers chasing yield. These, combined with a radical deregulation of Wall Street, created a unique set of circumstances that allowed traditional lending standards to fall by the wayside.

You know how *that* ended.

Refusing to acknowledge how complicated reality is once it conflicts with your belief system is a classic example of cognitive dissonance. If you can't face the reality of the boom and bust in housing in the 2000s, just cook up some story that explains what happened consistent with your ideology. That it is easily debunked is beside the point.

When it comes to money, we see the same kinds of errors all the time. There is a fine line between having confidence in your methodologies and living in your own private fantasy world. Like it or not, this is the human condition, the wetware/operating system running the meat sacks we live in.

Recognizing this at least gives us a chance to avoid its grasp. Just because you are human doesn't mean you must always give in to all of our failings.

Everybody loves a good story, a trait that turns out to be deeply problematic. Next, we will find out why.

EVERYBODY LOVES A GOOD STORY

HUMANS HAVE A long and venerable history of narrative storytelling. Our ability to speak emerged 50,000–100,000 years ago, when the only way to share knowledge was verbally, person to person, generation to generation.

Storytelling shared important information: When certain animals were around for hunting, what poisonous snakes to avoid, which mushrooms not to eat, when to plant crops, when seasons changed, how to avoid dangerous weather, and more. Good narratives kept you alive; good stories were easy to remember and share.

It is in our DNA to love a good story: Tales with heroes and villains and conflicts to resolve. A great story is exciting and memorable, pushing our emotional hot buttons and resonating with us.

The idea of narrative fallacy—the term was actually coined by Nassim Taleb in *The Black Swan*—applies to pretty much everything. Danny Kahneman explains it in *Thinking, Fast and Slow*:

> Flawed stories of the past shape our views of the world and our expectations for the future. Narrative fallacies arise inevitably from our continuous attempt to make sense of the world. The explanatory stories that people find compelling are simple; are concrete rather than abstract; assign a larger role to talent, stupidity, and intentions than to luck; and focus on a few striking events that happened rather than on the countless events that failed to happen. Any recent salient event is a candidate to become the kernel of a causal narrative.

PART 3: BAD BEHAVIOR

It should be no surprise that financial types also love a good story. When Wall Street spins a yarn, it is an emotional sales pitch designed to separate you from your money. Brokers *adore* what we once called "story stocks." You've heard the pitch: A new CEO is going to turn a company around; an FDA Phase 3 approval for a miracle drug with a billion-dollar market price is rumored. And everyone's favorite fish tale: An imminent takeover announcement.

People often find these narratives irresistible as the basis for making investment decisions.

It is beside the point that these stories were wrong. As it turns out, it doesn't matter whether a story is true or false. Your natural tendency *wants* an emotionally satisfying story to support your investment thesis despite the many times the data told you something different.

People have been calling for a market crash every year since the GFC ended in March 2009. Cullen Roche of Pragmatic Capital describes perhaps the biggest narrative failure of the 2010s decade: *The Fear Trade*:

> If you've been paying attention over the last few years, you probably remember how many people predicted hyperinflation, surging bond yields, soaring gold prices, a cratering U.S. dollar, and a collapsing stock market. This was the fear trade. You overweight gold, short U.S. government bonds, short the USD, short equities, and laugh all the way to the bank. On the whole, that trade has been a big disaster. In other words, fear lost out—again.[360]

Time proved him right: None of those fearful things came to pass. Worse, anyone who succumbed to the fear trade missed a giant rally to all-time highs in the stock market. Crashes and sell-offs are painful short term, but over the long run, they are temporary. The mathematics of asset class mean reversion is inescapable: Stocks will eventually recover. Failing to participate in the generational bull market from 2009 to 2025 will set back your retirement by a decade or longer.

This is how the narrative fallacy does its worst.

It's clear when emotional storytelling gets in the way of intelligent investing. When strategists come up short in their forecasts, they offer a series of excuses for why. How many times have I witnessed an investor rationalizing their losing position as right—it is the markets that are wrong! Why do so many traders double down on a losing trade, despite the obvious failure of the original thesis, rather than admit the error?

We stick to our favorite stories, no matter what facts present themselves. This is the triumph of the narrative over data, ideology over intelligence, politics over facts, emotion over planning.

It's as if your brain is asking, "Who you gonna believe, me or your lyin' eyes?"

The narrative fallacy takes random, mostly unexplainable market action and provides a storyline that we can make sense of. The primary problem with narratives is that they exist to make us feel better—about a stock purchase, an election, or even ourselves. We are too fond of using narratives to describe the world around us. Depictions of facts and figures were not a compelling form of communication for hunter-gatherers.

People hate randomness, do not like to feel powerless over what occurs, and certainly hate being told life is filled with meaningless coincidences. Investors need to remember this whenever they are told a story. Narratives may be entertaining, but they won't make you money.

What narrative are you following?

How come some people have fundamental models of the universe that are wildly off? That is our next discussion.

THE UNPERSUADABLES: YOUR MENTAL MODELS OF INVESTING

"**WHAT THE HELL** *is wrong with those people?*"

If events of recent years have you asking yourself that question, consider an unexpected answer: *Not very much.*

If you are shocked by what you hear from the more extreme, offensive people on social media, in politics, or in the media, consider that many of these people suffer from a small but *crucial* error in the way their brains create foundational models of the world around them. This is the conclusion of Will Storr's *The Unpersuadables: Adventures with the Enemies of Science.*[361]

Storr embeds himself with people many of us might describe as eccentric if not disturbed. UFO abductees, Holocaust deniers, new earth creationists, medicine-eschewing homeopaths, meditation gurus, extreme yogis, skeptics, and past-life regression therapists are among those whose world views he closely examines.

What is striking about all the people embracing unorthodox views isn't that they are insane, but rather *that they seem normal.* They are high-functioning individuals who, for reasons the book only hints at, have a deep flaw in their psychological understanding of how the world works. The book shows how our models affect not just how we see the world but impact our cognitive processes, too.

Like a rocket sent to Mars, if you are off a few inches at launch, you will miss the planet by millions of miles. So, too, with those people whose models have a large, fatal flaw at its core.

What is *off* with these people? In many ways, they suffer from many of the cognitive failings we all succumb to: They are deeply tribal; they construct storylines to help make sense of the world; when evidence is presented in conflict with their ideologies, they find ways to ignore it. Emotional narratives overwhelm data or evidence-based analyses. They are *Homo sapiens* operating the way *Homo sapiens'* wetware has operated for hundreds of thousands of years.

As Storr writes, "Stories change us first, and then they change the world."

All of our models are imperfect; useful, but wrong. But our mental concepts of the world we live in don't have to be perfect; they need only be good enough to allow us to find food and water, avoid becoming someone else's lunch, locate shelter, and generally survive long enough to procreate and perpetuate the species. Good enough is all we need for those purposes.

That isn't good enough for deciding where and how to risk money in the capital markets.

And yet, this may be counterintuitive: Having an accurate 360-degree view of the world, a model with perfect comprehension of the objective universe, wouldn't aid the purpose of sustaining human life. That sort of mental model would be a huge burden to create and maintain in terms of sensory perceptions and energy consumption.

From an evolutionary perspective, a perfect model of the world would not help the species survive; it might even make perpetuation less likely during times of limited resources or environmental stress.

Storr quotes Jonathan Haidt,[362] the Thomas Cooley Professor of Ethical Leadership at New York University, who notes that the world is "not really one made of rocks, trees, and physical objects; it is a world of insults, opportunities, status symbols, betrayals, saints, and sinners."

In other words, *beliefs*.

You can see this in the investing debates that take place every day. It is how people rationalize their current holdings. They talk their book because portfolios reflect their mental models. Whether you are a value investor or an active trader, you believe you understand how the market or the economy functions, and you deploy your capital accordingly. You can explain your positioning with a quick story, one that is a product of your worldview. But you probably are unaware of how much your inner subjective narrative drives your outer rationalized views.

PART 3: BAD BEHAVIOR

Regardless of where you fall in the Federal Reserve debate, or if you think stocks are cheap or expensive, or if this bull market is too old or has room to run, your mental models are at work. Be aware of how their imperfections might be driving your investing decisions.

—

What comes after the Unpersuadables? Our biases and blind spots lead to the conclusion that investors need to have more humility. Let's discuss why...

REASONS TO BE HUMBLE

WALL STREET SUFFERS from a scarcity of humility. Good money management requires a certain humble quality that is quite rare in the field of finance. I hope at this point in the book, all of the bad behaviors and poor outcomes we have discussed have made that clear.

We know less than we think we do, and we act recklessly despite our ignorance. Those who pretend otherwise are usually selling something.

We do not know what the future will bring. We have only a rough understanding of the past (which occasionally can be useful for extrapolating forward) and little understanding of the present. We assume the future will look like the past, which it often does not.

You must ask yourself, "What don't I know?" Make that self-inquiry frequently.

I do not know what the economy will be like next year; I have no idea what inflation, unemployment, mortgage rates, consumer spending, or GDP will be. I cannot tell you how high or low the markets will be or where the Federal Reserve will set interest rates. I don't know what the endgame is for the Russian invasion of Ukraine, what the next tragedy in the Middle East will be. I have no idea what the next geopolitical blow-up will be (or how it will resolve). I have no idea what corporate profits are going to be next quarter, much less next year. I don't know what the iPhone 20 will be like or when self-driving taxis finally arrive, to say nothing of the flying cars I have been waiting for since childhood.

Recognizing that you don't know these things confers an enormous advantage over those people who *imagine* they do know—and then act on that misbelief.

By now, you are familiar with many of the ways your investments can get derailed by the workings of your brain.

PART 3: BAD BEHAVIOR

As investors we:

- Have an incomplete understanding of the world around us.
- Assume we know the drivers of complex systems such as markets and economies.
- Underestimate the potential for significant random events to occur.
- Believe in numerous myths, false ideas, and incorrect *facts*.
- Misunderstand the degree of complexity that exists.
- Think we are apart from—yet understand—crowd psychology.

Let's put this into the broadest possible terms. Your mental model of the world around you is, at best, incomplete and often inaccurate. The simple truth is that this model works well enough. You can cross the street, catch a ball, or drive a car. It is good enough to allow you to do many things with varying degrees of success. Your model is good enough; wrong but useful.

Consider a professional baseball batter's internal physics engine; that is a model of his world. He needs to have a rough approximation of the speed, direction, spin, and aerodynamic action of a thrown ball to make contact with his bat. If he does that more often than other batters, we call him a good hitter; if he does this a lot, he becomes an All-Star. But his model doesn't need to be perfect, just good enough to understand where the ball will be as he brings his bat around.

Here's the problem: Good enough for a specific task—batting, driving, investing—requires only a narrow understanding of a relatively small subset of factors to achieve success. You don't need to know everything about, well, anything, to be reasonably successful at these tasks.

Investors, similarly, don't need to understand their universe perfectly to be successful. But they need to be humble enough to recognize what they do and don't know to achieve the specific goals they set for themselves via a portfolio.

Morgan Housel writes, "The past wasn't as good as you remember. The present isn't as bad as you think. The future will be better than you anticipate."[363]

Humility is a surprisingly rare trait…

———

Now that we know how much our brains were not designed for the modern world, what can we do about it? That's next.

YOUR BRAIN WASN'T BUILT FOR THIS

OUR BIG, FAT, brilliant brains, which enabled us to dominate the Anthropocene era of this planet, also work against us in the modern world.

We have seen how cognitive issues like Dunning-Kruger, narrative fallacy, recency effect, sunk cost fallacy, loss aversion, endowment effect, and hindsight bias impact our decision-making. They cause us to make bad decisions and engage in poor behavior that ultimately works against our portfolios.

To better manage our behaviors as investors, we need some strategies to outfox our own brains. Here are some ways how.

Disconfirm your beliefs

To counter our inherent confirmation bias, seek information that disproves your prior beliefs. Force yourself to seek out and read opposing points of view. You may find this to be an incredibly frustrating exercise—everyone who disagrees with you is, obviously, an idiot—but ultimately, it will make you a sharper thinker.

Moot Court is one of the more interesting things you do in law school. You are given a case with a set of facts and specific laws to apply. As you prepare your case, you may not even know which side you will be arguing for (or against). You have to truly understand both sides of the case. You can argue pro or con with far more effectiveness if you know what the strengths and weaknesses of the opposing party are. Doing this avoids the confirmation biases that affect most advocates—and investors.

Every forecaster who predicts a stock market top should be able to explain why the rally could go on for years. Every pundit who assures us that economic growth will be robust should be able to spot the immediate recession risks.

Burst your filter bubble

You are a member of a tribe. Whether you are a value or growth investor, a fan of American Muscle or Italian sports cars, a liberal or a conservative, you belong to a tribe. Your group reads the same media sources and hangs around with those who share similar ideas and values.

This creates a filter bubble that reinforces support for your beliefs and holdings. Rather than having an objective view of our investments, this can create blind spots, which, as you might imagine, can lead to expensive errors.

Widen your world. Find other valid sources of information. It takes buyers and sellers for trade to occur; it's not that difficult to find reasonable perspectives that disagree with your own.

Physicist Carl Sagan once observed, "Extraordinary claims require extraordinary evidence."

Be wary of your tribal beliefs.

Choose data over anecdotes

Evaluating data can be challenging. Compelling narratives can easily sway us, even when the math suggests a different course of action. Sports fans and partisans are so deeply invested in a specific outcome that they simply lose the ability to objectively judge reality.

Anecdotes are a single data point; choose the trend over any recent example. Narratives are compelling because they are so neat, with good and bad guys, an obvious conflict, and a satisfying resolution.

We believe what we want to believe, regardless of the evidence. In the capital markets, the costs of such an approach can be quite expensive.

PART 3: BAD BEHAVIOR

Shift perspective

We discussed earlier several ways to conduct perspective-shifting thought experiments. It's worth reiterating that you should occasionally return to first principles and reexamine your belief systems.

In the 1990s and 2000s, I kept track of various real estate data (probably because my mom was a real estate agent). Most of Wall Street was not. By 2005, it became obvious that something was very wrong. Had I not been exploring economic data from a different perspective, I would have missed the coming crisis, just like everyone else.

Seeing the world from a slightly different angle can provide enormous insights.

Emotional awareness

We have seen many ways emotions impact our thinking and our behavior.

When we become aware that we may be looking at things in an excited manner, we have a chance to overcome errors. However much we may seek this sort of self-awareness, emotions can trip us up.

Rudyard Kipling advised his son:

> If you can keep your head when all about you
>   Are losing theirs and blaming it on you,
> If you can trust yourself when all men doubt you,
>   But make allowance for their doubting too;
> Yours is the Earth and everything that's in it!

That's good advice for all of us…

In our first three sections of the book, we reviewed the bad ideas, numbers, and behaviors that hurt all investors.

Our fourth and final section—Good Advice—shows strategies to avoid the mistakes that lead to bad outcomes. Come along.

PART 4: GOOD ADVICE

THE BEST FINANCIAL ADVICE I CAN GIVE YOU

CONGRATULATIONS! You've read 378 pages of cautionary tales explaining how and why we make the same money mistakes over and over. By now, it should be crystal clear that we are uniquely unsuited as a species to making sound risk/reward decisions.

That's the bad news. The good news is that there are many ways to outsmart your instincts and avoid the bad ideas, misleading numbers, and poor behavior that lead to mediocre results.

This last, shortest section of *How Not to Invest* contains 10 steps to achieve better outcomes. I *guarantee* that if you implement these, you will become a better, happier, and less stressed steward of your own capital.

10 STEPS TO BECOMING A BETTER INVESTOR

1. Avoid mistakes (fewer unforced errors, be less stupid).
2. Recognize your advantages (and take advantage of them).
3. Create a financial plan (then stick to it). If you need help, find someone who is a fiduciary to work with.
4. Index (mostly). Own a broad set of low-cost equity indices for the best long-term results.
5. Own bonds for income and to offset stock volatility. Primarily Treasuries, investment-grade corporates, munis, and TIPs.
6. Be tax-aware. Consider direct indexing to reduce capital gains and reduce concentrated positions.
    6B. With outsized single position gains, use a regret minimization strategy.
7. Be skeptical of all but the best alts (VC/PE/HF/PC). If you have access to the top decile, take advantage of it. Otherwise, exercise caution.
8. Spend your money intelligently: Buy time, experiences, and joy. Ignore the scolds.
9. Fail better. Understand what is and is NOT in your control.
10. Get rich: Here are the classic strategies to get rich in the markets, including how difficult each is and their likelihood of success.

Let's consider each of these...

AVOID MISTAKES

A SKETCH OF "FEAR GREED," #1 of 500, hangs on the wall of my office. Carl Richards created the most insightful drawing ever about your biggest investment mistake. When Carl first started out as The Sketch Guy, I gave away print editions #2–50 as holiday gifts.

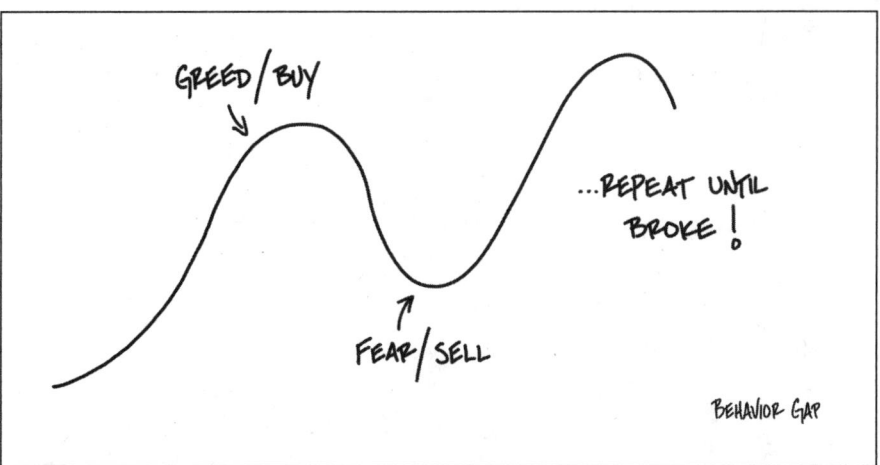

Carl's sketch shows why *most investors underperform their own assets*. That sounds almost impossible, but a quick look at the data shows it is actually a very common result.

In order to obtain returns that mirror your own holdings over an extended period of time, you have to 1) own them for that entire period; 2) make your purchase during normal periods of price, for example not chasing the new hotness upwards and buying near all-time highs; and 3) not sell prematurely when they fall, or otherwise interfere with the power of compounding.

It's *simple, but hard*—simple in the abstract, but difficult to execute in

HOW *NOT* TO INVEST

the real world. Most of us lack the understanding, discipline, and skill to do this effectively.

Each quarter, J.P. Morgan releases its "Guide to the Markets."[364] It's 75 pages of charts and graphs filled with wonderful insights.* One of the most instructive slides shows just how much a lack of discipline costs investors in terms of returns. The behavior gap is the underperformance between what each asset class returns and how investors in those assets did.

Over the decade covering 2012–2021, the S&P 500 generated a total average annual return of 17%; during that same period, the average investor only gained 9% per year—half of what the equity markets generated and a third less than a simple 60/40 portfolio.

10-year annualized returns by asset class (2012–2021)

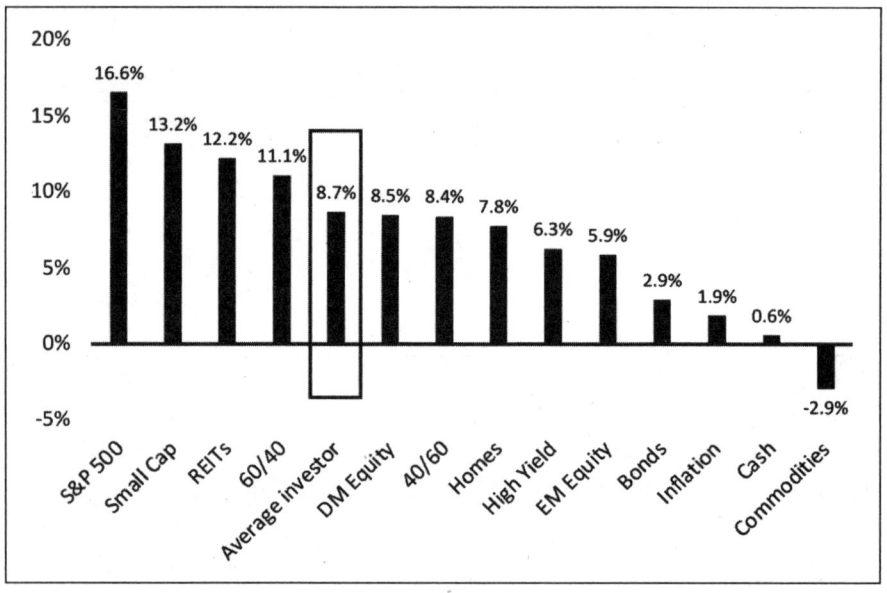

---

* I have been highlighting JPM's "Guide to the Markets" on The Big Picture (Ritholtz.com) since at least 2012, if not before.

It's even worse if you look at the 20 years from 2002–2021. That period covered most of the dotcom implosion and all of the GFC. During that volatile era, the S&P 500 returned 10% annually, while investors garnered about 4% per year—just over a third of the index, and less than half of a 60/40.

20-year annualized returns by asset class (2002–2021)

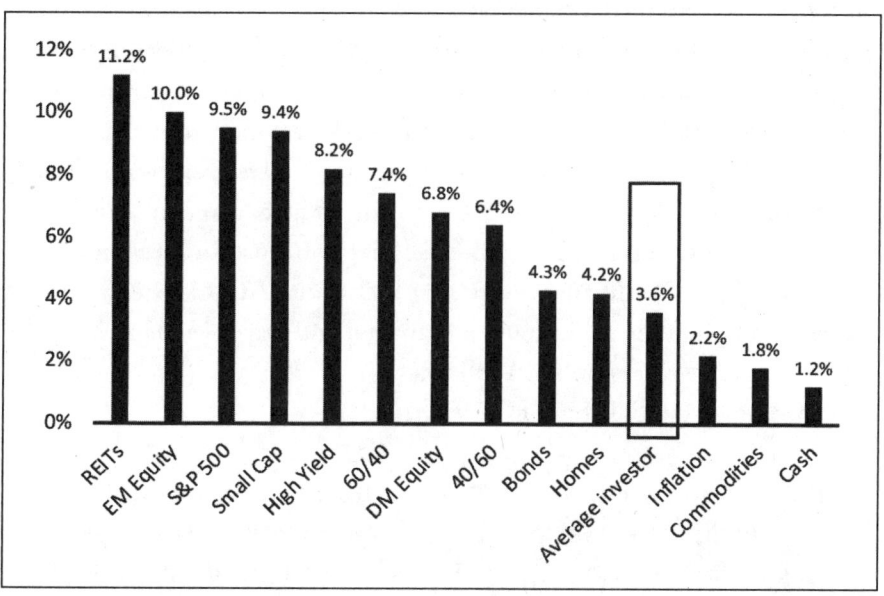

The longer the holding period, the greater the impact of errors that disrupt compounding. This is the cost of the behavior gap.

You can see the same gap between investor returns and the assets they hold across any asset, fund, or ETF you review. Counterintuitive though it may be, this makes sense when you consider our proclivity to greedily chase upwards what's rallying, or to panic sell out of fear what's falling. This has happened every decade since the 1960s.

—

The best example of the behavior gap in the modern era is the ARK Innovation ETF (ARKK), managed by Cathie Woods. In 2020, she had one of the best years *ever* of any mutual fund or ETF. For the calendar year, the fund gained a huge 153%; from the Covid lows in March 2020 to its peak 11 months later, its returns were an eye-popping 359%. Woods was lauded with recognition—and huge inflows. Therein lay the behavior gap: Investors bought ARKK *after* its huge run.

Despite having one of the greatest peak-to-trough runs in ETF history, ARKK has still underperformed the S&P 500 index since its 2014 inception, 247% to 161%.

Chris Bloomstran, the president and chief investment officer of Semper Augustus Investments Group, has been observing ARKK critically. In early 2023, he tweeted a list of 35 ARKK-related facts investors were overlooking.[365] The most devastating: 98% of all ARKK investors were underwater. Nearly all of the buyers of the ARKK ETF got in after its surge, near the 2020 top. This was just before an 81% collapse that bottomed in December 2023.

This is classic performance-chasing behavior. After a huge run of outperformance, the media touts a manager, and buyers pour in late. The inevitable mean-reversion soon follows.

According to Ian Salisbury of *Barron's*:

> The average ARK investor has seen results far worse than the fund itself, according to data from fund research Morningstar. In fact, since its 2014 inception, the fund has returned 9.7% on average per year, according to Morningstar. That's far below the triple-digit returns that investors once dreamed of, but more or less in line with long-term stock returns. For [ARKK] investors, it's even more bleak: Their average annual return, calculated by Morningstar is -17%.[366]

Buy high, sell low, repeat until broke.

―

It turns out that you, the home viewer, have a huge advantage over the professionals. We will find out what that is next.

THE AMATEUR ADVANTAGE

HERE'S SOMETHING COUNTERINTUITIVE: Main Street investors have many advantages over the professionals.

Charles Ellis,[367] when he was overseeing the endowment fund at Yale University (now at $41 billion!), made this observation:

> Watch a pro football game, and it's obvious the guys on the field are far faster, stronger and more willing to bear and inflict pain than you are. Surely you would say, "I don't want to play against those guys!"
>
> Well, 90 percent of stock market volume is done by institutions, and half of that is done by the world's 50 largest investment firms, deeply committed, vastly well prepared—the smartest sons of bitches in the world working their tails off all day long. You know what? I don't want to play against those guys either.[368]

You don't want to get on the same field as investing pros. They have the tools, the manpower, the capital, political connections, inside information—everything goes their way. It's called the *home-field advantage* for a reason. If you try to compete against them in their stadium, playing their game by their rules, the outcome is very likely to be what *they want*: You and your portfolio's losses are their gains.

But here is the thing: People who are not professional investors—the mom-and-pop investors I often refer to—get to play a different game. There are lots of things that you, as an individual investor, don't have to do, deal with, pay for, or worry about.

Let's review the six advantages you have over the pros.

1. Benchmarks

Everyone who manages money for other people is measured against a benchmark. It doesn't matter if you run a portfolio of stocks, bonds, commodities, or crypto. There is an official index against which everything you do is judged, measured, and compared.

If you run *large-cap stocks*, then it's the S&P 500. *Small caps?* The Russell 2000. *Emerging market equities?* MSCI EAFE Market Index. *Bonds?* Bloomberg Barclays US Aggregate Bond Index (US Agg). The list goes on and on. Each is updated in real time so managers literally see how they are performing—or, more often, underperforming—second by second, tick by tick.

You, the individual? You have no benchmark to meet or beat on a quarterly or annual basis; instead, you get to focus on working within your financial plan toward specific goals. Meanwhile, the Street is rife with stories of investors complaining to their fund managers about monthly and even weekly underperformance.

2. Outside investors

That's another thing: You have no outside investors. You don't have to spend a lot of time thinking about how you are going to market yourself or defend your actions when markets get wobbly. You don't need a pitch book or a PowerPoint presentation of any kind. You are responsible only to yourself (and your family).

It's your money! You are the CEO/CIO of You, Inc. Having no one else to answer to allows you to avoid lots of bad (professional) misbehavior. You can skip the quarterly conference calls with angry investors and ignore the withering media glare and cruel criticisms from your peers at other funds.

3. Costs and fees

You can keep your costs cheap, while the pros cannot. Individuals have practically no execution costs—you can buy stocks or ETFs for free today—and pay as little as five basis points for funds. Your cost structure, fees, and even taxes are within your control.

You don't have to fly around the world to meet prospective clients or be seen schmoozing at pricey conferences. You don't need an expensive office (spectacular views required) filled with modern furniture and pricey art. You don't have to build an impressive research department along with legal and compliance personnel. You don't need a multinational accounting team to deal with your global tax headaches.

4. Time

Being able to think long term is a luxury that professionals do not enjoy. You can have a much, much longer time horizon. Daily, weekly, or monthly volatility doesn't matter to you.[369]

That last 15% correction? The pros were pulling their few remaining hairs out, missing the initial drop, and/or not being positioned to take advantage of the recovery. And that happens every time the market moves more than a few percent in either direction.

It is a huge advantage not to worry about every zig and zag. A quarter to an amateur is merely one-fourth of the year, not a measuring stick that will soon lead to your first cardiac event. Time is on your side, and compounding returns are in your favor.

5. Size

If you decide you want to own an ETF or stock, well then, you just buy it. You can enter or exit a position without impacting markets; you don't have to limit yourself to just the largest stocks or worry about position size (this is a huge thing for professionals). High-frequency traders are not trying to pick off your 100 or 1000 share order; you need not worry about dark pools and other such stuff.

And, there is no public scrutiny of your holdings and no disclosures required. You don't have to file with the SEC every time you decide to add or subtract from a position.

6. Career risk

There is a tendency for agents—that's the economist's term for people who operate on behalf of others—to manage risk very conservatively. Take fewer chances.

Don't do anything that might make you look foolish or get you fired. This turns out to be a prudent way to manage your career, but a poor way to run money. Gains require some risk, which is why agents' own interests may not be those of their clients.

You don't have these conflicts. You won't get fired for admitting a mistake. You don't have to stress about temporary drawdowns or buying something that runs into a hiccup soon after. You can do unpopular things that look dumb in the short term but are money-makers in the long term.

The pros have a very specific set of measurements by which their performance gets judged. Unlike the pros, you get to set your own metrics for assessing how well you are doing. That means you first must figure out what your long-term financial goals are and then create a plan to achieve your objectives. You get to measure your success by seeing if you are on track to achieve those goals. This is another enormous advantage you have over the professional stock jockeys.

You *can* beat the pros—but instead of playing their game, with all of the home-field advantages they have, try playing a game of your own choosing.

―――

A good way for investors to avoid all of the mistakes we detail in this book is to create a financial plan and then stick with it. Next, we look at how.

HAVE A PLAN.
STICK TO IT.

HERE IS THE DRILL:
The debacle *du jour* occurs: Klaxon horns sound, lights flash, and suddenly, everyone is urging you to take action—do something! *Anything!*—about these important breaking news items. Pandemic! War! Crash! No matter what occurs, someone is urging you to update your portfolio.

My best advice: Always ignore them.

Maybe it was the Flash Crash, the US fiscal cliff, Brexit (Grexit, too), a 20% drawdown in Q4 2018, a continuing resolution funding bill, the 34% pandemic crash, the Russian invasion of Ukraine, or the Israeli/Hamas/Hezbollah (and Iran?) war. Maybe it was the 18% S&P 500 slide with a 33% crash in the Nasdaq 100 in 2022.

Regardless of the event, you are told to rouse yourself from your slumber and get busy getting busy. Pull on your big-boy pants, and rotate out of this sector and into that sector! Buy this, sell that! And hurry! You must do this NOW!

Sigh

Or not.

My charge is constantly reminding people that the best time to read the safety card on the seatback in front of them is before their jet takes off. At 30,000 feet, with one engine out and the other on fire, you probably missed the best opportunity to think calmly and clearly about your options.

Planning ahead allows you to make decisions rationally and free from emotional distress. Waiting until trouble hits to decide what to do means you are likely deferring to your limbic system, which is the path to panicky decision-making.

HOW NOT TO INVEST

It's the same every time: Something bad happens somewhere, and markets become unhinged. A substantial sell-off ensues, and the usual suspects panic. My email and phone light up, reporters want a comment on the sudden surge in volatility. They don't like my answer: "This is what markets do. They go up and down, sometimes violently."

The noise subsides, markets settle down, and everyone returns to their originally scheduled programming.

One thing the perma-bears never inform you in their never-ending parade of Armageddon forecasts is that there is *always* a reason to sell stocks. The problem with those reasons is they rarely turn out to be smart, or work in the investor's favor.

Have a look at these charts my colleague Michael Batnick[370] created covering all of the reasons you had to get out of equities between the GFC and Covid.

Reasons to sell

Every one of those emotional, ill-advised sales left lots of money on the table.

PART 4: GOOD ADVICE

Or how about this chart, showing how much a dollar invested in the stock market a century ago (1926) has grown, despite myriad reasons to sell along the way.

Growth of $1 (S&P 500)

And that's barely scratching the surface of the endless bad news that can derail investors. *Why, it's almost as if your portfolio compounds over time regardless of the news…*

———

We discussed earlier that markets move less than half a percent on 53% of the trading days; really big moves of 5% to 10% occur in two out of every three years; and sell-offs between 10% and 20% happen once every three years.

This is what normal looks like.

What should investors think about as these events happen? Here is my shortlist:

- Markets surge and sell-off. This is the ordinary course of events.
- Emotional reactions are bad for your portfolios.
- The world is filled with random outcomes. Even more so when humans are involved.
- Gurus and talking heads will fail you. Their forecasts were wrong. Most didn't see THIS coming, whatever THIS is.
- What sounds sexy and looks good in a brochure or website is not what usually makes you money over the long run.
- You need a plan and the discipline to stick with it. EOM.
- "Nobody knows anything" is a truism about the future. It also applies to nearly everything in life. Internalize it.
- Your brain has evolved to keep you alive in changing conditions, not to make capital risk/reward decisions.
- Bull and bear markets have their own timelines. They do not care about your retirement, savings for your kid's college, or the new house you want to buy.
- "Uncertainty" is a misnomer. When you hear people using the word "uncertainty," it is because they are scared enough to briefly acknowledge their own ignorance.
- Neither adrenaline nor dopamine is the basis of sound decision-making.
- All predictions are marketing (not advice).
- Boring, steady portfolios can withstand anything you throw at them.
- The future is inherently unknown and unknowable. Those who claim otherwise are selling something.
- Investing is hard.
- Sometimes, shit happens.

If you learn nothing else, at least learn this: Never confuse day-to-day noise with an actual reason to make a change in your portfolio. If you are merely reacting to the latest market action, then what you have is not a plan—you have instinctual, fear-driven behavior, and it's the makings of a disaster.

PART 4: GOOD ADVICE

Or, as Blaise Pascal, the French mathematician and philosopher, once observed, "All of humanity's problems stem from man's inability to sit quietly in a room alone."

Do you need help managing your assets? Let's determine that and discuss how to find the right person to do so.

GET GOOD ADVICE

ONE OF THE smartest things I ever did was build a team of professionals around me to advise on complex matters beyond my skill set and experience. Unfortunately, I did not figure this out until I was middle-aged. You should not wait as long as I did.

You need a good lawyer and business counselor. They can provide not just legal advice but smart counsel. (They have seen similar problems before.) An experienced accountant and tax professional can save you thousands. Your doctor should be a general practitioner (GP) who can also advise and refer on any medical issue.

And for many people, having a financial planner and advisor can be extremely useful.

Do you need a financial advisor? *Maybe.* Understanding your circumstances will help you decide what sort of financial services you want to pay for. But before we work through this, a pre-emptive counterargument.

Hey Ritholtz, doesn't your firm sell financial services? Are we getting objective advice here?

Fair question: As I buried earlier in a footnote, my firm has an unusual business model. Since the early 2000s, I have been giving away very useful advice to people on how to manage their assets themselves. You only need a little bit of savvy, a few minutes each month, and some self-discipline to be a good investor. That's been my core message, shared at The Big Picture, on my Bloomberg podcasts, and in my *Washington Post* and Bloomberg columns. The rest of the RWM crew does the same—on Substacks and Beehives, in books, on YouTube, TV, radio, and in blog posts.

Our business model—*you don't need to pay us a fee; you can do this on your own*—is not only rare on Wall Street but also very counterintuitive. Despite this (or maybe because of it, I don't know?) people began asking for my help managing their assets right after the GFC. That was back in 2008–09 and $5 billion ago.

Do you need help, and if so, how much? Here are the factors you should consider.

1. How complicated are your financial circumstances?

The simplest financial situation is a young, single working person who is a renter. At the other end of the scale is a successful entrepreneur who owns their own company(s), facing large capital gains reflecting the sale of a business, has children and grandchildren to pass wealth to, has multiple sources of income, and a fairly involved tax filing (including K-1 distributions, loss carryforwards, etc.) to go with it. They own multiple real estate properties in the US and abroad. They work with many attorneys, accountants, and advisors. They have maxed out all of their qualified tax-deferred accounts, own numerous investment portfolios at different firms, have completed wills and trusts, own various insurance policies, and are involved in major philanthropic endeavors.

You are likely in between these endpoints. The more complicated your circumstances, the more likely you would benefit from professional help. Even people who can do this themselves often have better things to do with their time.

2. What are your long-term (five plus years) financial goals?

These are the most common answers, listed here in order of complexity:

- Saving to buy a home.
- Paying for children's college.
- Retirement planning.
- Outpacing inflation.
- Philanthropy.
- Tax management.

- Managing the proceeds from a sale of a business.
- Estate planning.
- Generational wealth transfers.

The simplest investing goals are saving to buy a home, pay for college, or retire.

A good advisor will create a plan that addresses all of these. They are there to assist you when you have life events that change your circumstances. The best of them will talk you off the ledge when markets are going through their regular convulsions.

We all go through our financial life cycles in three phases: *accumulation*, *preservation*, and *distribution*. These phases track with age, income, and assets. Younger people (20s and 30s) have a longer time horizon, less cash flow, and the ability to embrace more risk for potentially greater returns in their accumulation phase. If they can withstand the volatility, they should have an all-equity (100%) portfolio.*

Middle-aged people (40s and 50s) typically have more assets—house(s), investment portfolios, business ownership, 401(k)/IRA, and greater income. However, they also have greater future obligations (paying for college and saving for retirement). They have a moderate time horizon and should embrace a little less risk (80/20 or 70/30).**

People closer to retirement (60s and 70s) have less potential time for markets to work in their favor and should take on less risk. The distribution phase is exactly what you might guess: Drawing down your assets to live on them in retirement, including Social Security distributions and pensions. Life expectancies have increased so much that their portfolios should move from 70/30, shifting to 60/40 and then 50/50 over time.

We often see younger investors fail to take enough risk; they carry way too much cash and bonds for their multi-decade time horizon. We also see the opposite: People who should be in a preservation mode, but are still

---

* Investors' personal risk tolerance is a major factor in deciding how much to hold in bonds. Too much risk can lead to bad behavior during drawdowns, so consider this carefully.

** 60/40 refers to stocks (60%) and bonds (40%). The proportion can change based on your risk tolerance, age, and what bond yields are.

PART 4: GOOD ADVICE

aggressively embracing far more risk than they need to achieve their goals. That increases potential volatility and portfolio drawdowns.

Successful entrepreneurs and businesspeople—hard-working, competitive, and driven—can have difficulty transitioning between these different phases. They are not used to throttling back, and this can show in their portfolios, often more volatile and aggressive than necessary.

Assess your progress on your timeline; determine whether you can adapt to each phase of your financial life cycle yourself. It is not difficult, and with some time and thought, many people can handle it themselves. (Whether you want to or not is a different question.) If you need assistance, find it sooner rather than later.

3. How disciplined are you?

Behavior is the single biggest problem for most investors, and it is the area where financial advisors deliver significant value. Vanguard has studied this and termed the help "Advisor's Alpha."[371] They estimate its impact is as high as 3% annually.

The biggest obstacle to your success is not your lack of stock-picking prowess or inability to time markets, but your inability to manage your own behavior. And unlike whatever the Federal Reserve does at the FOMC meeting next month, this is within your control.

Can you do this yourself? Yes, but you must be a disciplined investor. You should have an investment philosophy that can be expressed in a portfolio. This philosophy should include specific rules that you do not ignore. You want a portfolio with low costs, low turnover, low taxes, and a long holding period. Your success must not depend on news, overhearing tips, or market gossip. Economic data and quarterly earnings should not significantly impact your investments.

Last, you should be able to look back at your own behavior during volatile times without seeing anything embarrassing. Were you a buyer during the sell-offs of 2008–09, 2000–03, Q4 2018, the pandemic in 2020, and October 2022? Did you panic sell during those periods?

Answer these questions honestly to determine whether you have the temperament and discipline to manage your own money or not. If you have the time, interest, and discipline, there is no reason you cannot do it yourself. It is relatively easy: Select an asset allocation model, review it quarterly, rebalance once every few years, wait 30 years, and *voilà*! Retire happy.

If you need more assistance, find a good advisor. Look around. Ask friends and colleagues to recommend someone they have been happy with. Do your homework and talk with a few different advisors. Find somebody whose firm works with people in similar circumstances to yours. This is a very personal, intimate relationship, so make sure both you and your spouse like the person you will be working with.

One last thing: If you do hire a financial advisor, make sure they put your interests first.

The quality of advice varies widely. You already know the quality of *everything* you buy varies widely. You can buy a Chevy or a Mercedes. They may both be automobiles, but their design, build quality, horsepower, and reliability vary dramatically.

Regardless, wherever these cars are sold, the same basic safety regulations, crash-worthiness standards, minimum fuel economy, and consumer warranties apply to both. This is not true of financial advice. Two completely different standards govern advisors: *suitability* and *fiduciary*.

People who operate under the suitability standard are typically called "brokers," but they also go by the name registered representative—or, on their business cards, vice president. (On Wall Street, no one ever has a title below VP.) People who adhere to the fiduciary standard are called "registered investment advisors," or RIAs.*

Fiduciaries have a much stricter duty and legal obligation than do those who operate under suitability rules. The fiduciary standard legally obligates the registered investment advisor to act at all times for the sole benefit and interest of the client. That straightforward, cut-and-dried standard has enormous ramifications. Your financial advisor should be like your lawyer, accountant, and doctor, not like the guy trying to sell you a used car.

---

* My firm, Ritholtz Wealth Management, is an SEC-registered investment advisory and a fiduciary to our clients.

Why do individual investors encounter problems with the suitability standard?

1. It favors the brokerage firm and its employees over the investor.
2. It costs much more than services provided under other standards.
3. It creates an inherent conflict of interest between the advisor and the investor.

Why two standards?

The short answer is that the SEC enforces the standards for fiduciaries, but brokers, aiming to avoid more regulations, created the suitability rules to regulate themselves(!). They did this through self-regulatory organizations called the National Association of Securities Dealers (NASD) and its modern successor, the Financial Industry Regulatory Authority (FINRA).

If you want to see the worst of this, search Google for the history of client NASD arbitrations.[372]

Investors do not do well when a self-regulating entity decides disputes. William D. Cohan's columns on the problems are brilliant, scorched earth criticism; the mergers and acquisitions banker turned investigative journalist reported on the endless systematic abuses at the self-regulatory organizations.[373]

Last, be wary of hybrid firms. These firms embrace the fiduciary standard but are also brokers selling products that may be expensive and not in your best interest. The hybrid model allows them to choose the more convenient standard for each transaction.

In my experience, fiduciary rules protect investors from advisor malfeasance, while suitability rules protect brokers from investor lawsuits.

Do yourself a favor when seeking advice: Find an advisor who is legally obligated to put your interests first. When you are retired and living comfortably off your investments, you will thank me.

What should you own? That's easy! Primarily low-cost index funds. Here's why…

INDEX!

THE CORE OF your investment portfolio should be a low-cost, passive index.

The advantages of indexing have been thoroughly proven, both academically and in actual practice. These include:

1. Lower costs (and taxes).
2. Owning all the winners.
3. Better long-term performance.
4. Simplicity.
5. Less bad behavior.

Indexing should be a core part of your investment strategy. Here is why.

Costs

Investors can own any broad index you can imagine, from the S&P 500 to the MSCI Global, for a mere few basis points. Active management is no longer as crazy pricey as it once was (e.g., 200 basis points); it has come down in cost to the 50 to 100 bps neighborhood. Regardless, those fees compounded over decades will be a return drag between 20% and 30% of the total account value. (This is to say nothing of the 2 & 20 cost structure of alternatives.)

The logic is unassailable: Costs matter, and high costs matter a lot.

In a sea of superlatives, one number stands above all others: $1 trillion.[374] That is the "Vanguard Effect," a phrase coined by my Bloomberg colleague Eric Balchunas in 2016. He calculated how much investors have saved thanks to Jack Bogle and the Vanguard Group's low costs. He also added how much the company has driven down fees in the rest

PART 4: GOOD ADVICE

of the money-management industry. Oh, and that trillion dollars he calculated? That was as of 2016—about a decade ago. It's probably closer to $2 trillion today.

By keeping the annual expense ratio of what you own to a few basis points, your holdings can compound by that much more.

Big winners

As noted earlier, throughout the history of investing, a group of savants has proven themselves to be brilliant stock pickers: Peter Lynch, Warren Buffett, Benjamin Graham, John Templeton, Thomas Rowe Price Jr., John Neff, Julian Robertson, Joel Greenblatt, and Will Danoff round out the list. Their numbers are few, but they are the exception that proves the rule.

The challenge in selecting stocks is that the vast majority of them don't move the needle. We discussed Hendrik Bessembinder's findings earlier—his research showed most stocks don't really matter.[375] But the big drivers of market returns are the *1.3%* of publicly traded companies that put up those giant performance numbers over an extended period of time.[376]

The odds are worse than 50-to-1 against you picking those giant winners, and even worse, you pick *only* those big winners. Market-cap-weighted indexing, on the other hand, guarantees not only that you will own the best-performing stocks, but that as these companies get bigger, you will own *more of them*. Add in the lower costs of indexing and the higher costs of active, and the formula proves nearly impossible to beat.

Outperformance

Each year, S&P Indices Versus Active (SPIVA) publishes its "Institutional Scorecard." The latest SPIVA data (Midyear 2024) shows about 90% of active equity fund managers underperform their benchmark on a 10-year horizon.[377]

Larry Swedroe is the Director of Research at Buckingham Strategic Wealth.[378] He has analyzed the long-term SPIVA data on a 20-year period through 2023 on an after-tax basis, and what he found was pretty damning. Swedroe's research showed:

- 93% of funds underperformed the benchmark S&P Composite 1500.
- 94% of large-cap funds underperformed the benchmark S&P 500.
- 94% of small-cap funds underperformed the benchmark S&P SmallCap 600.
- 95% of mid-cap funds underperformed the benchmark S&P MidCap 400.
- 94% of multi-cap funds underperformed the benchmark S&P Composite 1500.

You can understand why capital inflows have moved away from expensive active management and into cheap indexing.

Some people imagine they can select the 1 in 20 funds that will outperform its benchmark over the decades. Recognize this is a low-probability bet.

Simplicity

All other things being equal, simple beats complex. A portfolio of low-cost indexes is a simple approach. It's easy to manage, execute, and track. You know exactly what you are going to get without any surprises.

If you want to do something more complicated, you need a very compelling reason to do so. Most products and strategies don't meet this test.

Behavior

Indexing has built into it a unique advantage: You avoid most of the opportunities to make silly mistakes. Indexing gives you a better chance to "be less stupid."

PART 4: GOOD ADVICE

The decisions you do make

How much equity and bonds (e.g., 70/30, 60/40), which fund do you want to own (VTI, SPY, VOO, ITOT, etc.),[379] how globally diversified do you want to be (30%, 40%, 50%?), how much will you dollar cost average into your account each paycheck (5–10%), and how often will you rebalance (into deep equity drawdowns, or otherwise every three-ish years)?

Once you make those initial decisions, it's pretty much set and forget for the next few decades.

Therein lies the true genius of indexing: it removes all the human decision-making errors to which we are prone: stock selection, market timing, panic-selling, chasing the new hotness, or knowing when to sell a winning position. Those problems are mostly eliminated from your process. It's a rare investing truism: Miss those errors, avoid the vast majority of expensive mistakes, and you are guaranteed to do better than everybody else.

Indexing has become a key methodology for millions of people, despite—or perhaps because of—the disdain Wall Street has shown.

Your equity portfolio can consist solely of indexes, or you can use a strategy called Core & Satellite. This involves a mix of assets centered around broad market indices but with other strategies added in.

My favorite metaphor is a Christmas Tree as your core index and the rest of your equity positions as the decorations that trim the tree. Figure ~70% core and the rest satellite. There are ETFs for whatever you like—India, momentum, shareholder yield, AI, quality, emerging market, whatever. You can add your own stink to the portfolio in whatever way you fancy, just so long as the key holdings remain that broad low-cost index.

One of my favorite behavioral hacks is for you stock junkies: *The Cowboy Account*.

Are you one of those people who love chatting about stocks at cocktail parties? Do you breathlessly await each new FOMC meeting and

Non-Farm Payroll release? Do you pay attention to famous fund managers' appearances on financial TV or in print?

If so, then you are probably, like me, a dopamine fiend.

You need to take steps to protect yourself from, well, yourself. Set up a mad-money account with 3%–5% of your liquid capital. This will allow you to indulge your inner Jim Cramer. If the investments work out, that's great! You are also more likely to let those winners run because it's for fun and not your 401k. If they turn out to be a debacle, it's a terrific lesson that should remind you that trading in and out of stocks is not your forte. Be thankful you didn't lose most of your retirement assets.

Nobel laureate Paul Samuelson once said, "Investing should be more like watching paint dry or watching grass grow. If you want excitement, take $800 and go to Las Vegas." The cowboy account serves the same function.

In my cowboy account, using 2% of my liquid net worth, I play the dumbest game possible: Market timing with out-of-the-money stock option calls. I have made some fortuitously timed buys, including the Nasdaq 100 (QQQ) into a deep sell-off, and some really bone-headed ones, like buying Silicon Valley Bank (SVB) after it got cut in half—but right before it went to zero. I was up so much on the QQQs trade (purchased during the October 2022 lows) that my trading demons were emboldened. The SVB loss was a reminder of my own arrogance—it served me right.

Regardless of the results, it allows my inner junkie to leave my main portfolio alone. That is the true value of the cowboy account—my real money remains unmolested by me and my big dumb lizard brain.

—

What do you do when you are sitting on a giant winner in an individual stock or holding? One strategy is to avoid doing something you will regret for the rest of your life. We discuss that next.

AVOID REGRET: HOW AND WHEN TO SELL BIG WINNERS

RUNNING A MONEY-MANAGEMENT firm provides a window into the psyches of all kinds of investors: Long-term holders, real estate speculators, institutional traders, tech entrepreneurs, and everyone in between. I speak with all sorts of people who have capital at risk in various asset classes.

Every now and again, I speak with someone suddenly sitting on enormous, life-changing wealth. The sheer size of the windfall has them paralyzed, afraid to make a decision—*any decision*—that might be wrong. It isn't just that they don't know what to do; rather, they have no idea about how to even think about the sell decision.

Let's consider an instructive war story: During the mid-1990s, a good friend took a senior job at a tech startup that came with a good salary—and lots of stock. In late 1996, they were bought by Yahoo! Inc. The shares in the startup were replaced with Yahoo stock options that had a six-year vesting schedule, with 25% vesting after three years and the balance vesting in ~2% monthly increments in years four, five, and six.

These were heady times for those of us trading back then. Tech stocks, especially dotcoms, had galloped higher, doubling and tripling over short periods. It seemed every sale was a source of regret, as stocks simply kept going up, up, up.

My buddy's stock options represented a great deal of wealth. Not merely fun money, but life-altering: Pay off the mortgage and the car loans, pay for the kids' colleges, fully fund retirement accounts, and still have cash left over. He could take any job he wanted for the rest of his life—or none at all.

He was torn about what to do and asked my opinion.

My advice was not based on any belief that the dotcoms were in a bubble, neither did it relate to the (over)valuation of Yahoo's stock specifically or the market generally. It also did not involve optimizing the performance of his equity or competing with a benchmark.

Rather, I suggested employing a *regret minimization framework*.[380]

Although any investment has a range of possible outcomes, I wanted to focus on potential outliers at the far ends of the spectrum. These were:

- **Scenario One**: Hold, and Yahoo's stock tumbles from $300 to $30.
- **Scenario Two**: Sell, and the shares soar to $3,000.

How would you feel if either of these occurred?[381]

For my friend, it was an easy decision. If he sold his 25% vested shares and the stock went higher, he still owned a big proportion of his options. The probability of the second outcome wasn't the issue; what really mattered was the potential future regret if he didn't sell and the stock collapsed.[382]

What happened: He sold the 25%, watched the stock rally for a few months, then saw it collapse. He was happy with his decision, but not everyone at Yahoo was so fortunate. Stories abounded of paper multimillionaires and even billionaires who saw much of their wealth evaporate in the subsequent crash, never to recover.

I have had recent conversations with Apple (AAPL) and Nvidia (NVDA) shareholders, as well as with Bitcoiners—each sitting on massive windfalls. As I write this today, Bitcoin is $97,000; Nvidia's market cap is now $3.6 trillion, just ahead of Apple and Microsoft, making it the most valuable company in the world. Maybe Bitcoin goes to $500,000, maybe it falls to $5,000. Who knows where NVDA goes next? We have to accept the simple truth that a) we have no idea what either price will be in the future, and b) selling *some* can be a life-changing experience for you and your family.

It doesn't have to be an all-or-nothing decision. The middle option is to sell enough—maybe 25% to 50%—to become rich in reality and not just on paper. Then, you can let the rest ride.

Doing this accomplishes several things: First, it locks in sufficient wealth to eliminate a lot of life's money-related worries. Second, it still leaves you with plenty of upside if the best-case scenario turns out to come true. And third, it protects you from a lifelong regret in case of a dotcom-like collapse (I know, that's impossible!).

Note this strategy applies to single stock holdings, not asset classes. (I think of Bitcoin, now a trillion-and-a-halfish market cap, like a huge tech company.) If this sounds a bit conventional, well, it might be, but think about it this way: The goal of life is not always to maximize your returns; sometimes, potential gains must be balanced against the possibility of losses. That's why we need to occasionally consider minimizing regrets.

The fixed-income portion of your portfolio is often overlooked. Let's dive into what you need to know.

DO YOU NEED BONDS?

BONDS PLAY A crucial role in any portfolio. However, allocating to fixed-income assets can be trickier than allocating to stocks. I will skip the basics of interest rates, duration, credit risk, and creating ladders and instead focus on my experiences.

There are two good reasons to own bonds. First, they generate yield. That stream of income is very useful. Second, they can offset the volatility of equities. You can own bonds individually, through mutual funds, money market funds,* or through ETFs.

In the "Get Good Financial Advice" chapter, I suggested that younger people in their 20s and 30s don't need to own bonds. Some find that advice controversial, even with my caveat: *"Only if you could withstand the volatility."*

The same applies to investors in their 40s and 50s. Bonds serve as an emotional relief valve, typically offsetting declining stocks. Owning bonds involves sacrificing some potential gains as equities rise in return for experiencing smaller drawdowns when they fall. This tradeoff was designed to prevent you from freaking out during the all-too-regular market spasms.

During the decade encompassing the 2010s, ultra-low interest rates led many traditional investors to reduce their bond exposure and increase their equity exposure. 70/30 became the new 60/40. Since yields were so low, equity positions would theoretically offset that. Stock gains did offset weaker bond yields, but at the cost of increased risk and portfolio volatility.

The same idea applies to modern longevity: If you are nearing retirement

---

* If you purchase a money market fund, you are a holder of short-term bonds, even though MMFs are effectively cash. They produce income in exchange for taking on a tiny risk of default. As of this writing in late 2024, my Schwab Value Advantage Money Ultra Shares (SNAXX) was yielding 4.74%—down from 5.45% over the summer of 2024.

age, there is a reasonable chance you will live to your 80s or 90s. Therefore, it makes sense to have more stocks in your portfolio than, say, someone who retired in the 1960s or 1970s did.

The year 2022 was unusual in that both stocks and bonds declined by double digits; bonds fell by about 15%, while stocks decreased by around 20% (or more). Some incorrectly declared this the end of the traditional 60/40 stock and bond portfolios, but they had it exactly backward. The last time both stocks and bonds fell simultaneously was way back in 1981. With the exception of one or two years per century, bonds serve as a reliable, non-correlated counterweight to equities.

Depending on your circumstances, you may want a low-risk source of annual income. Treasuries, investment-grade corporates, TIPs, and municipal bonds are excellent for this. You can use the quarterly (or monthly) payments to fund a trust, donate to a charity, guarantee your kids an income for their lifetimes, or live off the interest payments.

If you are in a high-tax state (New York, California, Massachusetts, etc.), the income you receive from municipal bonds is tax free; residents of the 13 states with no state income tax (Florida, Texas, etc.) can purchase a national portfolio of tax-free munis. If you are in the highest tax bracket, munis may make sense for you.

Your specific circumstances will greatly affect the mix of bonds you want to own and the best vehicles for your needs. (Here is where a professional can help.) Whether you are modestly risk-averse and uncomfortable during market drawdowns, or are looking for a steady stream of income, owning some fixed-income securities may make sense for you.

How tax-aware are you when it comes to your portfolio? That is our next topic.

MANAGE YOUR TAXES

OK, I ADMIT that taxes may not be the most exciting subject to read about. But managing them intelligently can have a huge impact on your portfolio and your overall financial well-being. I have seen some amazing errors where people wildly overpaid their taxes. I have also seen sketchy tax decisions that led to big interest and penalties.

With only a bit of planning, you can make sure that your tax bill is as modest as possible. Pay Uncle Sam exactly what he is owed—but follow a few simple steps to make sure that is all he gets.

Tax alpha is real, and it can make a giant difference to your total net after EVERYTHING returns.

We set up a tax practice at RWM because our clients kept asking for it and because my partner Kris Venne insisted that investors needed much more help than they realized. (He was right.) You don't really need us to tell you to keep records and make estimated quarterly payments.* But you may need some help with the more complicated stuff. You want to work with a tax professional or advisor who is doing forward-looking tax planning. Historically, many tax professionals were data-in and data-out, backward-looking only.

From an investor's perspective, these are the most important things I have learned about taxes.

---

* Don't laugh, but this is only true 50% of the time! People need constant reminders to stay on top of their taxes, especially 1099 filers who must make regular payments on their own. (W2 employees have taxes taken out automatically.)

PART 4: GOOD ADVICE

1. Consult a professional

Your tax situation will be specific to factors like income, assets, the city and state you live in, and other personal circumstances. The very first tax advice I'll give you is to consult a tax professional who can best advise you based on those specifics.

This isn't just boilerplate. Most of us (me included) lack the expertise to manage anything beyond the simplest tax filing. The rules change constantly, and the pros understand what is new, what is important, and what is illegal.

Your tax advisor and financial planner will help locate your assets in the right kinds of accounts—ETFs can go anywhere, but you want mutual funds (and their phantom capital gains taxes) ONLY in qualified, tax-deferred accounts. Your tax pro can also discuss whether a Roth conversion makes sense for you or whether Health Savings Accounts (HSAs) are appropriate.

Please don't wait until April 14 to engage them. Good tax planning requires months and sometimes years of advance notice. Staying on the taxman's good side is easy, but it requires some knowledge and effort—the professionals can help.

2. Capital gains taxes

The single biggest area where a skilled advisor and knowledgeable accountant can make a huge difference. Some issues are obvious—make sure your gains are long term (not short term) and avoid wash sales.

But the biggest impact I see is in tax loss harvesting. If you are selling a business or property, have IPO or founders' shares, employee stock options, an inheritance, or just highly appreciated equities, tax loss harvesting is potentially a big money-saver for you. The way this is usually managed is by selling whatever ETFs or mutual funds you hold that are negative for the year and replacing them with similar funds. The loss is booked, and it can offset some of the gains of whatever profitable sales you made. When you own funds, the losses tend to be limited; when you own a portfolio of individual equities, you have more options. (In the next chapter, I go into detail about how direct indexing is beneficial to those fortunate investors sitting on big gains.)

You can use $3,000 of your capital losses against ordinary income each year. The remaining balance carries forward into the next tax year. Don't overlook this.

3. Maximize tax-advantaged accounts

Do you like free money? Then, make sure you max out your 401k, especially if your employer gives you a match. The most you can put into an IRA pre-tax is $7,000 per year; the most for 401(k)s in 2025 is $23,500 if you are under 50, $31,000 if you are 50+ (and more if you are 60+). There are catch-up contributions as well.

You may benefit from converting to a Roth IRA. (*Warning*: This involves paying taxes.) The advantages are that it grows tax free, there are no required minimum distributions (unlike IRAs/401ks), and your beneficiaries can also inherit the Roth IRA tax free.

If you have kids, max out their 529 plans* (in 2025, it's $19,000 per beneficiary per donor). Lifetime limits and ceilings vary by state (there is also a five-year gifting rule without gift tax consequences), so ask the pros what applies to your situation.

4. Estate taxes

The odds are against you owing any estate taxes. The 2025 individual exemption is $13.99 million (double that for married couples). That ceiling expires at the end of 2025, and so it is dependent on what Congress does about it between the start of the new administration and 2026. If the Tax Cuts and Jobs Act (TCJA) expires, then the estate deduction reverts to $7 million per person.

If your estate is under that, well then, you can relax, you won't owe any

---

* The $19,000 is an excludable gift; amounts gifted above that to a child's 529 plan require a gift tax filling, although no tax is generally due.

PART 4: GOOD ADVICE

federal taxes after you join the choir invisible.* But if you are fortunate enough to leave a substantial estate, there are a handful of things you can do now to reduce or eliminate what you owe:

1. Give it away to a qualified charity.
2. Buy enough insurance to cover what will be owed.
3. Create and fund trusts and other vehicles that will transfer your assets to your beneficiaries exempt from estate tax.

There are many more variations, but those three are the major ones. Again, you need to engage an expert to manage these for you.

Lots of famous people die intestate (without a will). Prince died in 2016, leaving his heirs a $300 million estate, six years of legal battles, and a giant tax bill. Pablo Picasso also died intestate (1973), also resulting in years of legal battles and $30 million in legal fees! Howard Hughes, one of the world's wealthiest and most influential people, died in 1976 without a valid will. That led to the most complex and lengthy estate litigation in American history. It took 34 years to resolve, and the legal costs depleted much of the estate's value.

When it comes to estate taxes and having a valid will, a little planning goes a long way. The only excuse for ever paying estate taxes is if you were hit by a bus on the way to see your estate attorney...

Are you lucky enough to be sitting on a giant pile of appreciated assets? The good news is you can legally reduce your capital gains taxes by a substantial amount. In the next chapter, I discuss how.

---

* Note that 16 states levy an estate or inheritance tax, and exemption limits in states like Oregon can be as low as $1 million. Check with a local professional for details on your state.

OFFSETTING BIG CAPITAL GAINS

Tax loss harvesting (TLH) and its operation can be a bit confusing, but it is very worthwhile to understand. Think of these kinds of scenarios:

- Participating in an IPO.
- A huge liquidity event.
- Inheriting a seven or eight-figure portfolio.
- Selling a home for millions more than you paid for it.
- Selling a business for hundreds of millions of dollars.
- Hitting record highs in personal equity holdings.
- Accumulating substantial wealth through an employee stock option plan.

In each case, the person faces a combination of challenges. Concentrated positions come with increased risk—think about how much a single stock can fall compared to a broad asset class. But selling that holding to diversify would lead to a major taxable event.

What's an investor to do?

The latest software technology allows us to manage this today in ways that would have been too expensive and complicated to do on a timely basis in the early 2000s. Direct indexing (DI) gives investors with concentrated positions in appreciated assets a huge advantage in TLH over traditional mutual fund and ETF portfolios. If you are fortunate enough to have enjoyed any of the windfalls mentioned above, you should explore this solution.

Direct indexing has been on my radar since the mid-2010s. Truth be told, I wasn't a fan of the early versions of this technology—they were complex

PART 4: GOOD ADVICE

and kludgy. But Dave Nadig (you met the well-regarded ETF and market structure wizard earlier) made me more open-minded about its potential. Instead of holding a bunch of funds, investors hold most of the individual equities from *within those funds*. My original concern was portfolios with 1,000+ individual stock holdings[383] and statements that were 100s of pages long versus cheap,[384] simple, passive ETF portfolios. If only someone could make it simpler and cleaner to use, I would be interested.

My partner, Michael Batnick, drove Ritholtz Wealth Management's adoption of DI. In 2019, after seeing a demo of O'Shaughnessy Asset Management's software Canvas, he was convinced it would be a giant winner for our clients with concentrated, appreciated positions. Canvas's competitive advantage is that it was built on the OSAM database, continually refined by Jim O'Shaughnessy since his 1996 quant book *What Works on Wall Street*. RMW became one of five beta testers of Canvas, and today, we are its biggest client.

Many other firms built or bought DI technology, including Franklin Templeton, which purchased O'Shaughnessy Asset Management to acquire Canvas. Fidelity launched Solo FidFolios, and Schwab introduced Personalized Indexing. J.P. Morgan purchased 55ip, Eaton Vance (now part of Morgan Stanley) acquired Parametric, BlackRock bought Aperio, Vanguard acquired Just Invest, PGIM bought Green Harvest, and Pershing acquired Optimal.

When this many of the world's biggest investment managers see the potential to save their clients capital gains taxes, you should take notice.

My experience was shaped by the 2020 pandemic swoon when markets fell 34% before hitting bottom and recovering. Those who had taken advantage of DI were able to substantially reduce their capital gains taxes in their concentrated equity holdings. DI performed an order of magnitude better than traditional tax loss harvesting.

Why? Consider traditional portfolios that hold a dozen mutual funds or ETFs. To harvest a loss, you sell the funds in the portfolio that are down for the year. You then replace them with a similar fund. The realized gains in the portfolio can then be offset (in part) by that loss. Done right, it can reduce capital gains tax costs in an average year by 20–30 basis points (100 basis points equals 1%) of the portfolio's value. Some years more, some years less. About 40–50 bps is considered a good year in tax loss harvesting.

DI is vastly superior to mutual fund TLH for several reasons:

- The potential pool of tax loss choices number in the hundreds of individual stocks, not 10–15 funds.
- Market volatility creates numerous opportunities to capture losses.
- Even in years when markets are up big, a substantial percentage of stocks will be down.
- Granularity allows a very targeted approach.[385]
- DI allows investors to "access all the losses" that fund owners cannot.

That last point is the most significant aspect of DI loss harvesting.

Consider these details about equities in general and mutual funds in particular: We discussed previously that most portfolio gains come from a relatively small handful of outsized winners. Depending on your preferred academic study, it can be as much as 4% or as little as 1.3%. In a portfolio of 100 stocks, a handful will account for most of your gains. The rest of your positions average out to flat, that is winners offset by losers.

Herein lies the huge advantage of DI over ETFs and mutual funds: *Accessing losers that would otherwise net out to zero.*

The performance of any fund or index is the sum of its individual holdings' gains and losses. Quarterly or yearly performance is simply the average of the capital invested in the winning positions minus the capital invested in the losing positions (relative to their cost basis). Mutual fund holders who tax loss harvest work with this net average.

Investors who wish to TLH have to treat the mutual fund for what it is—a single security. They don't get to look inside the portfolio and say, "Sell the bottom 10% of my holdings!" to book the losses. They only get to treat the fund as a, well, fund. That vehicle only lets investors access *that average net gain or loss*. Most of the internal losses are inaccessible to the holder. This works against those losers when it comes to tax loss harvesting.

DI grants access to *ALL OF THE LOSERS* without requiring the owner to do anything other than hold on to the winners. This is a massive advantage to anyone selling a concentrated position because it allows for the offset of more of the capital gains tax obligation that sales create.

Sometimes, *a lot more.*

The team at OSAM reviewed clients using Canvas.[386] They saw accounts with tax harvesting in excess of 4.75%. That is a ridiculously good result, an outlier driven by the unique speed and depth of the 2020 crash/recovery (which itself was an *outlier event*). If you direct index, do not expect to capture 475 basis points of losses under most circumstances.

Given how unusual Q_1 2020 was, my guess is offsets of that sort come along quite rarely—maybe once every decade or so? But it does show the proof of concept as to what DI can accomplish when all of the stars line up. I expect DI to show ongoing gains versus traditional TLH of ETFs and mutual funds.*

I am a big believer in the effectiveness of DI. The *tax losses are real*, not a theoretical benefit. They are hard dollars, quantifiable, and specific. Investors see actual dollar savings annually on their personal tax returns. They may not notice a fund that is 50 bps ahead or behind its benchmark, but they certainly see tax savings of hundreds of thousands of dollars.

Another approach can help investors with their appreciated concentrated positions. My pal Meb Faber of Cambria Funds has a new ETF solution based on a mechanism under US tax law, specifically Section 351 of the Internal Revenue Code. (This is similar in theory to Section 1031 real estate transactions.) By the time this book is published, the Cambria Tax Aware Fund (TAX) will be out.**

This new ETF strategy allows anyone to contribute appreciated stocks to seed the formation of a new ETF. In return, they receive a diversified set of holdings in that ETF structure. The fund limits contributions to 25% in any one position and requires a minimum of $100,000 to participate. That's not nothing, but it's a fraction of what is needed in separately managed

---

* I want to emphasize that no one should ever count on 475 basis points in TLH.
** The Stance Sustainable Beta ETF (STSB) is similar, and the ETF they issue is an environmentally and socially conscious fund.

accounts (SMAs). In return, investors receive a diversified set of holdings in that ETF structure without incurring a taxable event and retaining the original tax basis.

Last, Canopy Capital, created by former Fidelity bond manager Eric Golden, aims to do for fixed income what Canvas and other direct indexers did for equities.[387]

Years ago, creating a bond portfolio that could deliver the maximum after-tax returns using software was simply not a viable option. Today, max-after-tax total return in fixed income is a function of smart algorithms and optimization engines.

Hedge funds, private equity, venture funds—let's cautiously consider the world of alternatives.

ALTERNATIVE INVESTMENTS: HF/VC/PE

ALTERNATIVE INVESTMENTS, or alts as they are called, have long been among the sexiest asset classes available. These private partnerships promise better-than-market performance and have the aura of a secret approach known only to a privileged few. Available exclusively to accredited investors and restricted to just 99 limited partners (LPs), with the general partner (GP) as the 100th, these funds create a rarified mystique.

A small handful of fund managers deserve this reputation. Those who consistently beat their benchmarks in excess of the high fees they charge are rewarded with huge capital inflows and massive paydays. For the rest of the alternative investment universe, the hedge funds, venture capital funds, private equity, and private debt, "alpha" has proven to be more elusive.*

Over my career, I have been fascinated by and skeptical of most alternatives. My views have evolved, and I have reached this conclusion: *If you are fortunate enough to have entrée to alternative funds in the top 10% (or so) of each category, you should take advantage of it.* For all the rest, you should be highly skeptical about their claims of outperformance, especially relative to their high costs.

Let's look at the biggest flavors of alts, and their strengths and weaknesses.

---

* If you want to get more granular, we can include impact funds, managed commodity futures, real estate holdings, and nonpublic debt instruments.

Hedge funds

Thanks to rockstar managers who occasionally produce eye-popping returns, hedge funds are probably the best-known of the alt investments. Their biggest challenge, however, is market efficiency—it's incredibly difficult to identify and execute strategies that consistently beat broad indices. That hasn't stopped the global hedge fund industry from scaling up to $5 trillion in assets, with forecasts topping $13 trillion globally by 2032.[388]

Alpha (at least recently) comes mainly from two very different kinds of funds: Quants, who have developed a replicable, mathematical process for identifying winning strategies; and emerging managers, who identify small market inefficiencies that can be captured. No one seems to have cracked the code yet for selecting which emerging managers to give your capital to in advance.

The top decile (or two) of funds is worth the costs. The rest, not so much.[389] Only a small subset of managers outperforms their benchmarks consistently enough to justify the lofty fees they charge—famously 2% of assets under management and 20% of any investment gains (2 & 20).

Jim Chanos of Kynikos Associates, a successful short seller, pointed out that back in the 80s and 90s, there were only about 100 hedge funds, almost all of which created alpha.[390] Today, there are more than 11,000 hedge funds, but as Chanos observes, those 100 hedge funds still capture nearly all of the alpha, generating outperformance net of fees for their investors.

And yet, the lure remains. For too many investors, it's "Come for the high fees, stay for the underperformance."

Venture capital

Wouldn't it be great to invest in the next Nvidia, Google, or Bitcoin *before* it rises 10,000%? VCs offer exposure to early-stage companies and their founders. Most of the start-ups they fund do not amount to very much, but the occasional giant winner more than makes up for it.

Benchmark Capital was an early investor in Uber (2011); their $12 million investment for 11% was worth almost $9.4 billion in 2023. Andreessen

PART 4: GOOD ADVICE

Horowitz (2009) was an early investor in Facebook, Instagram, and Airbnb. More recent investments include Slack, Lyft, and Anthropic AI.

Who *doesn't* want some of that?

The appeal of venture investing is a low correlation to public markets and (on occasion) massive winners. If you have access to the best firms (and their best funds), then *have at it*. But the success of a handful of wildly successful firms attracts lots of imitators who lack the same skills, connections, and track records. You should approach any of these firms with much greater skepticism and caution about tying up your capital.

Private equity and private debt

When interest rates were low during the 2010s, investors sought higher-yielding options. Lending to private companies and private growth was one alternative. This made private equity and private debt the fastest growing alts. BNY Mellon noted that as of 2023, there were 1,080 private debt funds globally, up from 100 in 2011.[391] Assets have scaled up also, from less than a trillion dollars in the early 2000s to nearly $12 trillion today.

There are so many different types of private equity and debt it is difficult to generalize. But the same admonitions go for these funds as any other. Always ask yourself why you are pursuing this structure; be aware of the higher costs. Make sure you are comfortable with long lock-up periods in these illiquid investments—some are 10–12 years! And beware of promises that sound too good to be true.

On my Master in Business podcast, I have interviewed many incredibly successful private equity and debt investors.[392] I wish I had a clue who these people were 20 to 30 years ago. Even better, I wish we knew today which PE funds will put up great numbers over the next 20 to 30 years. But I don't, and probably can't.

Crypto

It's hard to categorize things like Bitcoin or Ethereum. Are they currencies, commodities, or a separate speculative asset class? All three? I don't know.

I think of them like I do an individual company. As of late 2024, Bitcoin has a market cap of $1.8 trillion. That is between the market caps of Facebook (META), which is nearly $1.5 trillion, and Google/Alphabet (GOOG), which is $2.2 trillion; BITC is half of the value of Nvidia or Apple.

For the crypto-curious, there are ETFs that allow you to own these without having to worry about online wallets and 24-digit passwords. Owning a few percent (less than 5%) as a flyer gives you exposure to the space if they continue to rise, but limits your losses the next time there is a crypto winter—as there was in 2013 to 2015, 2018 to 2020, and 2022 to 2023—when coins crashed 50% or more.

One-Offs

Last, in the world of alts, there are many one-of-a-kind investments. These include everything from new restaurants, plays or movies, and hard money lending against assets. Sometimes, I see funding requests for a small strip mall or a 100-unit apartment complex. These things come up all the time.

The challenges here are twofold:* First, you must acknowledge your lack of expertise. You know nothing about what makes a restaurant, play, apartment complex, etc. successful. This is hard enough for the professionals who spend their entire lives toiling in this field. Rank amateurs tend to be a mess of assumptions and blind spots. For these "friends and family" investments, most of you are not well-equipped to make a risk/reward evaluation. (Me neither.)**

The second challenge is doing the proper due diligence on any of these. It is an expensive proposition in both time and money. Do you want to hire analysts, attorneys, and accountants to look into these "opportunities?"

When I see these deals, I do a little *time-traveling*: How will I feel five years from now when this deal goes south? What did I miss? Why did this go wrong? Most of the time, I imagine my future self as recalling all of the

---

* There is also a third issue for me: Scale. When you are investing for thousands of families, a $5 million raise is pointless. I have stopped considering things that can't/won't scale.

** Restaurants, for example, are a difficult, low-margin business. But a great restaurant is a rare moneymaker, and its success makes us forget all the failed establishments that came before it.

PART 4: GOOD ADVICE

things I didn't know and the lack of deep research into why the one-off failed. I want to avoid the epistemic trespass discussed previously.

Hence, I almost always pass.

A few final points on alternatives.

Unlike ETFs and mutual funds, alternative investments are private funds with accredited limited partners—mainly wealthy investors and institutions. They do not have mandatory SEC reporting requirements and are not legally obligated to disclose their performance publicly. Unlike public investments, alternative investments are free to keep their track records private.

Survivorship bias is inherent in whatever reported results you see for alts. Any fund that is underperforming can simply choose to skip reporting that quarter or year. Funds doing poorly are missing from the aggregate results.[393]

Like everything else, Sturgeon's Law—90% of everything is crap—applies to the universe of alts. A small number of alpha generators and a lot of expensive under-performers. If you have a billion dollars and you're well connected, or someone you know can make a phone call on your behalf to get you into the top decile of alternatives, then great (lucky you!). But most of us don't have that access, and the ones you can get into easily tend not to be the top-performing funds.

I'm reminded of the words of the great Groucho Marx, who wrote in his autobiography, "*I don't want to be a member of any club that would have me.*"[394] Who knew that one of the Marx Brothers was an alternative investing genius?

Next, we look at the spending scolds you will encounter when spending your hard-earned dollars. And some smarter ways to spend your money.

PLEASE BUY YOURSELF A NEW CAR

TO MANAGE YOUR personal finances properly, you need only follow three rules:

No. 1. Spend less than you earn.
No. 2. Prioritize investing for your future.
No. 3. Figure out what matters to you, then spend accordingly.

Most spending advice involves paying down debt and not buying things. If you are young and broke, that applies. However, if you are deep in credit card debt and a *spendaholic*, you know what you have to do. Follow these simple rules, and you can ignore the spending scolds like Suze Orman and Dave Ramsey.

Hell, just follow rule #1: Spend less than you earn.

The spending scolds have a history of inappropriate and misleading advice. They finger-wag *everything*, warning of the dire consequences for anyone foolish enough to spend and enjoy their money. At nearly every level, their complaints are absurd, and the arguments they present in support are silly.

Like this exaggeration: "Buying new cars is like taking $40,000 and setting it on fire."[395] Each year, between 14 and 17 million new cars are sold in the US. Lighting your cash on fire leaves you a pile of ash; buying a new car gets you a safe, reliable, efficient form of transportation.

One thing I have learned from 30 years of working in finance: *People sure can be weird about money.*

Never mind the countless anecdotes I could cite; the entire field of behavioral economics is based on this. Our weirdness is demonstrated by the foolish financial decisions we make each day, the unsupported beliefs

PART 4: GOOD ADVICE

we hold dear, and the odd pronouncements we make whenever the subject of spending comes up.

Some examples of this include:

- You're flushing money down the toilet if you drink a latte.[396]
- It's financial suicide to own a house.[397]
- Never buy a boat or a sports car.[398]
- Don't pay for your kids' college.[399]

Underpinning all these warnings is a fundamental misunderstanding about the difference between a) spending and b) spending *beyond your means*. The former is how we consume the goods and services we need to go about our daily lives, acquiring the things we want because we enjoy them; the latter is an error in judgment, a behavior fraught with risk that really does have the potential to lead you down the path of financial ruin.

Simply saying no to consumption is lazy and thoughtless. Personal spending should be determined by the totality of the buyer's financial circumstances, needs, desires, and goals.

Spending scolds are not only wrong, they are tedious bores. They invariably cite a wealthy person who lives frugally, implying that you, too, can acquire great sums of money just by being cheap. This is, of course, a deeply flawed argument that totally misunderstands the most basic issues of how household budgets work.

A favorite silly story of thrift involved National Basketball Association (NBA) star Kawhi Leonard.[400] He had signed a three-year $103 million contract with the Los Angeles Clippers but was still driving a 20-year-old SUV. Yet here's the thing: You could skip buying a new car for the rest of your life, and you will still never be as rich as Leonard because you are not a two-time NBA champion, six-time All-Star, and one of the greatest two-way players in NBA history.

Driving an old car is not a budget-conscious virtue—it is *reckless and irresponsible for a professional athlete*. A modest accident that damages Leonard's knees or wrists could derail—or even end—his entire career. "Wasting" money on a new car with all the latest safety features will reduce the odds of a catastrophic injury that prematurely cuts his playing career short.

That 20-year-old car? It does not have:

- Lane-departure warning
- Lane-keeping assist
- Collision avoidance systems
- Electronic stability control
- Adaptive cruise control
- Blind-spot warning
- Seatbelt pretensioners
- Forward-collision warning
- Crumple zones
- Automatic emergency braking
- Bluetooth.

A question for the rest of us who can neither dunk nor hit the open man cutting to the hoop: Don't you want the latest, greatest safety equipment protecting you and your family? That 20-year-old car has 20-year-old actuators for its 20-year-old airbags, which have 20-year-old sealed gas canisters that are supposed to inflate instantly. Would you, in Los Angeles traffic, bet a $103 million contract on them?

The key that the spending nags all seem to fail to understand is that budgets are about living within your means, not living like a pauper, whether you have to or not.

Merely saying "no" is not financial advice; it is a form of blind risk avoidance. The problem with such advice is twofold. First, it misunderstands the purpose of money. Second, it fundamentally misses out on the best way to make intelligent financial decisions.

Money is misunderstood by many. The problem is people and how they behave around money. Money is not the root of all evil; the Bible references "the pursuit of money." Money is merely a tool, a medium of exchange.

At its most basic level, money allows sustenance and security: Food, housing, clothes, medical care, and transportation. Get a little more of it, and you can pay for your kids' education and take a nice vacation now and again. Freedom from worry is a nice benefit of having enough to cover the above. If you're fortunate enough to have more than enough, you have options: Entertainment, hobbies, travel, philanthropy, or whatever catches your fancy.

This brings us back to the boat mentioned above.[401] Assuming you have enough cash and/or credit, using some of it to buy a boat is simply an option, one that should be considered intelligently.

Let's start with the costs. There is the purchase price, which my experience as a boater teaches is the cheapest part of boating. Where will you keep it—at a marina slip (most expensive but most convenient), a mooring (cheaper but less convenient), or a trailer (cheapest but least convenient)? You might own a dock, but that means you spent a lot of money on related real estate. Maintenance and repairs are not cheap, especially if you are out in saltwater (as opposed to freshwater lakes and rivers). There are issues of winter storage if you live in the north, and then prep for boating season. Fuel and insurance are costs, as are snacks and beer.

These are all easily calculable by anyone with a spreadsheet or even a pencil and paper. You should be able to determine what a boat will cost you; assuming you have a household budget (what do you mean you don't?!), then you should also know how much boat you can afford.

How much are you going to use it? What friends and family will accompany you? Who else do you know that boats? What other time demands do you have? Think about these and other questions, and you can determine (a) if you can afford a boat and (b) if it's worth it to you.

Boating has the upside of creating memories that last a lifetime with friends and family. Being out on the water enjoying a beautiful summer day is hard to beat—but only if you can afford what you purchased.

We can run through the same exercise for just about any expenditure, from that latte to a vacation home. Just saying no is lazy and misses the point of money as a tool. Let me suggest better advice than *never ever buy a boat*: Don't buy things you cannot afford, won't actually use, and that will cause you more pain than pleasure.

I'm a boater, and I have many friends who are boaters. One bought a

14-foot kayak and is out each morning weather permitting for a robust paddle. His blood pressure is down, his outlook is sunny, and he enjoys the solitude on the water. Another friend bought a 55-foot behemoth. It's a floating hotel that he hardly ever used—and sold it at a big loss after two years.

My advice for people considering buying a boat is to recognize four key issues: costs, skill, experiences, and psychology. For any wannabe boater or anyone making a major purchase, you need to:

- Understand what you are getting into.
- Consider all of the costs of ownership.
- Only buy what you can afford.
- Make an intelligent decision about using your limited time and money.

The formula is simple: Spend less than you make. Make intelligent decisions. Don't pretend to be something you are not by spending more than your income justifies. You do not need a business degree from Wharton to figure this out.

Merely saying "No!" to anything with a price tag attached is lazy and useless.

—

Next, some caffeinated advice: *Buy yourself a f*^king latte.*

BUY YOURSELF A F*^KING LATTE

IT'S THE CLICHÉ that refuses to die: Personal finance nag Suze Orman warned investors that if they "waste money on coffee, it's like 'peeing $1 million down the drain.'"[402]

I disagree. If the difference between success and failure is *the cost of a cup of coffee*, you have much bigger financial problems. A daily $5 latte does not amount to much in the grand scheme of life.

Mind you, I am aware society can be too materialistic.[403] But we need to be honest about the actual challenges facing us; the latte bullshit is a distraction from genuine financial issues in society.*

Here is what really gets me annoyed: Orman tells her audience that "Your Daily Coffee Habit Is Costing You $1 Million," with this calculation:

> Let's say you spend around $100 on coffee each month. If you were to put that $100 into a Roth IRA instead, after 40 years the money would have grown to around $1 million with a 12% rate of return.

Nope. This calculation is nonsense, and worse, it is intellectually dishonest. The actual real numbers are almost 75% less.

Let's consider five reasons why you should occasionally treat yourself to that cup of Joe.

---

* Special thanks to Heleine Olen, who has written about this extensively, both in her book *Pound Foolish* and online. As a guest on Masters in Business, she went off on the "gurus, pundits, self-anointed experts, crackpots, cranks, and outright frauds who populate the backwaters and slipstreams of American finance." You definitely want to hear what she has to say about Orman…

HOW NOT TO INVEST

1. The numbers don't add up

So, 12% annual returns for 40 years? That's 50% better than what the markets give you. I *literally* have $5 billion for anyone who can get my clients fat 12% returns annually for the next 40 years.

Historically, equities return 8% annually (with dividends reinvested) over the long term. Maybe less when valuations are higher (like they have been lately).[404] If you invested $100 per month for 40 years (that's $48,000), the compounded returns would be somewhere between $300,000 to 350,000.[405]

But 12% annually? *PUH-leeze*. If you promised that in a mutual fund advertisement the SEC would throw your ass in jail.

2. Inflation adjust it

Note that the $350,000 is in nominal, not inflation-adjusted dollars. By the year 2065, assuming a modest 2–3% inflation rate, $300k won't be all that big of a number.

For some perspective, back in the 80s, the median house cost about $62,000 (it's over $420,000 today), and the median income was under $20,000 (it's $80,610 today). In 2065, you should expect $300,000 to be about $90,000 in 2025 dollars.

Inflation-adjusting the returns of not buying yourself a cup of coffee every day for 40 years reveals it is not a lot of money. Maybe you can buy yourself an okay car—assuming anyone is even buying cars in 2065…

3. Remove the denominator blindness

Numbers out of context are misleading, and this one is no exception. Instead, frame it via its relationship with other related items. In this case, that six-figure latte compounded appreciation should be put into context relative to the rest of your earnings and/or portfolio appreciation.

It requires a meaningful denominator.

Over the next 40 years, a moderate-sized portfolio plus contributions and appreciation can add up to millions of dollars. And a person's lifetime earnings? If you earn the median income of $80,610—and never receive a raise for 40 years—that adds up to $3,224,400. If you get a mere 3% raise annually, that's over $6.5 million ($6,531,280); 5% annual raises lead to over $11 million in cumulative gross earnings.[406]

Comparing $350,000 (or $90,000 inflation-adjusted) out of $5 or $10 million lifetime earnings shows how insignificant a daily cup of cappuccino is.

4. Focus on large fixed costs, not small discretionary ones

Many Americans do not earn enough money, and therefore cannot save enough. More than a few will be in trouble come retirement.

Here is where the coffee nonsense gets called out for the bullshit it really is: Prior to the pandemic, wages were flat for three decades; economic mobility was near all-time lows. Healthcare costs keep going up; college has become an economic hardship for many. These are significant issues to most Americans; a $5 cup of coffee is not.

The problem with your fixed costs is that they are, well, *fixed*. They are often impossible to cut back on. Housing, healthcare, and education are all expensive; coffee, even good coffee, is not. (The same goes for avocado toast.) Please excuse my lack of enthusiasm for fretting over $5 lattes while we ignore 30-plus years of limited real wage gains for so many people.[407]

5. Mental bandwidth

Regardless of your view of the Stanford marshmallow experiment and delayed gratification, there is validity to the claim that willpower is finite.[408] All of us have more important issues to exhaust our willpower on than this.

There are much bigger economic issues in everyone's life. Any of these are far larger and more consequential than modest spending. All of us have better things to worry about than denying ourselves the occasional cup of fresh, hot java.

Go enjoy a $5 latte. While you sip that warm, delicious brew and enjoy its health benefits, ponder the enormous challenges facing millennials, future retirees, boomers—anyone who is not fortunate enough to find themselves in the top third of the American economic strata. It's obvious that penny-wise, pound-foolish solutions miss the bigger picture.

Since failure is inevitable, we need to discuss how to fail better. That's next.

FAIL THEE WELL

WE HAVE SPENT a lot of time discussing errors, mistakes, and failures. Since failure is inevitable, we would all benefit from learning how to fail better.

On a trading desk, you are taught to expect to be wrong. Surprisingly, that attitude is rare elsewhere in finance. This is a shame because a healthy outlook on failure benefits businesses, governments, and just about everyone.

High stakes make aviation an excellent subject for the study of failure. In other fields, errors may be subtle, and the results may not be recognized for years. When there is a flying failure, planes fall out of the sky, and footage of the wreckage is on the evening news.[409]

Matthew Syed points this out in *Black Box Thinking*.[410] Aviation is an open, data-rich system, with statistics going back a century: In 1912, the US Army had 14 pilots, and even before the war, more than half (eight) would die in crashes. The Army (this was before there was a US Air Force) set up an aviation school to teach pilots how to fly more successfully. The school had an unfortunate 25% mortality rate.

Fast-forward a century. Syed observed that in 2013, there were 36.4 million commercial flights worldwide carrying 3 billion passengers. That year, there were only 210 commercial aviation fatalities. For some context, 1 million flights resulted in 0.41 accidents—an average of 2.4 million flights were needed for just one single accident. In 2017, there were *zero* commercial airline passenger deaths; none in 2022, 2023, or 2024 (up to the time of going to press). That is an astounding improvement over the course of a century.

How did the industry achieve this? By being self-critical and learning from every accident. The industry extensively studies each crash or near miss. The Federal Aviation Administration (FAA) mandates a cockpit voice recorder and flight data recorder. This creates a comprehensive and objective data set to study any failure, including a wealth of insights into why planes go down.

Even the famed black box flight recorders are subject to review and improvement. Today, black boxes are *orange*, making them easier to spot in difficult terrain or underwater. They also have submersible locator beacons to aid in their detection and retrieval from the deep ocean. The fact that "black boxes" are orange may be the perfect metaphor for how intensely the industry thinks about safety.

Compare this with a closed system, such as healthcare and hospitals. That industry takes a very different approach to dealing with errors; not surprisingly, it produces vastly inferior results.

How different? Syed notes the remarkable contrast between air travel and preventable medical errors: After heart disease and cancer, medical errors are the third leading cause of death in America. As many as a half-million fatalities in the US, at a cost estimated at $17 billion a year, are due to errors.[411] Peter Pronovost, a clinician at Johns Hopkins Medical School, wondered how we would respond if two 747 jumbo jets fell out of the sky each day, killing roughly 900 people.[412] That's how many people die daily from medical mistakes.

Why is health care so different from aviation? First, there is little publicly available data and no standardized review process when errors occur. Whatever self-examination takes place is private, sealed, and not readily available for public scrutiny. Some people believe doctors are infallible saviors, creating a reluctance to admit error. Insurance costs, litigation, and protecting reputations reduce the industry's desire for public accounting. In short, healthcare is everything that aviation is not.

Investing straddles the two approaches. There is a great deal of data, but it isn't the most open system. SEC rules mandate disclosures by mutual funds but require much less from hedge funds, venture capital, private equity, brokers, and registered investment advisors.[413]

Silicon Valley, technology, and the venture capital business model do a better job with failures. Entrepreneurs and venture funders alike wear their misses like a badge of honor. Many venture capitalists even post their biggest fails on their websites. They recognize their model is to make a lot of losing bets in pursuit of finding the next humongous winner. Equity

PART 4: GOOD ADVICE

investors don't have quite the same model, but they would benefit from a similarly humble approach to recognizing their own limitations.[414]

The stigma surrounding failure needs to go. The surest way to avoid future failure is to embrace it and learn from past failures.

I learned to fail better from Ray Dalio. He is, by any conceivable measure, wildly successful. The founder of Bridgewater Associates (one of the world's largest hedge funds) is also one of the world's 100 wealthiest people.[415]

Bridgewater has been called the fifth most important private company[416] in America; his book *Principles: Life and Work* was a *New York Times* bestseller. Given all of these accomplishments, you may be surprised to learn that Dalio attributes the secret of his success to *failure*.

He started Bridgewater in 1974; eight years later, a new bull market was just getting underway. However, Dalio's research found problems in the credit markets. Earlier in the year, he had warned that emerging market bank debt could potentially pose a major risk to the economic recovery. When Mexico defaulted in August 1982, Dalio was hailed as an economic seer and market wizard.

His reputation grew, and in November 1982, he appeared on *Wall Street Week* with Louis Rukeyser, the most important financial news program of its time. Dalio "confidently declared we were headed for a Depression." But that's not what happened; months earlier, timely central bank interventions had a positive effect on emerging market banking, and Dalio's disaster forecast never materialized.

However, it was a disaster for Bridgewater Associates, and the firm almost went bankrupt. He had to lay off all his employees and borrow money from his father to support his wife and two young children. He wrote, "I am still shocked and embarrassed by how arrogant I was."

But from failure comes rebirth: Dalio rebuilt his firm from scratch; he looked at failures—from ordinary flops to major disasters and every error in between—as fodder for future gains. Each error was an opportunity to learn something new and get better as an investor. "Principles" are what came out of his public failure.

Dalio insists the key to his turnaround was in discovering new wisdom from mistakes. He created a broad set of rules to "fail well":

- View mistakes as opportunities to improve. He calls this "mistake-based learning."
- Own your errors. Never hide them, but bring them forward to create a learning opportunity.
- Pain + reflection = progress. The "pain of failure" should lead to reflection, from which your wisdom derives.
- Track what you do; keep systemizing what you learn from your mistakes.

Embracing failure was the key to Dalio's success. It can also be the key to yours.

What is in your control? What's not? Understanding the difference is our next chapter.

UNDERSTAND WHAT YOU CONTROL

ONE OF THE secrets to failing well is understanding what is and is not in your control.

If you read the financial press or watch FinTV, take note of what the majority of coverage is about: Things you have absolutely no agency over. It's what I call *financial weather*. The daily noise, the *Sturm und Drang*, the angst-producing warnings are all about subjects beyond your control.

There is always scary news *somewhere*. The typical viewer response is an overreaction, such as "What do I do? What should I do?" This is the wrong approach. During periods of market volatility and stress, you should step back and consider the bigger picture. The most important thing you can learn—whether you are a trader, strategist, investor, or entrepreneur—is to recognize what you can and cannot control.

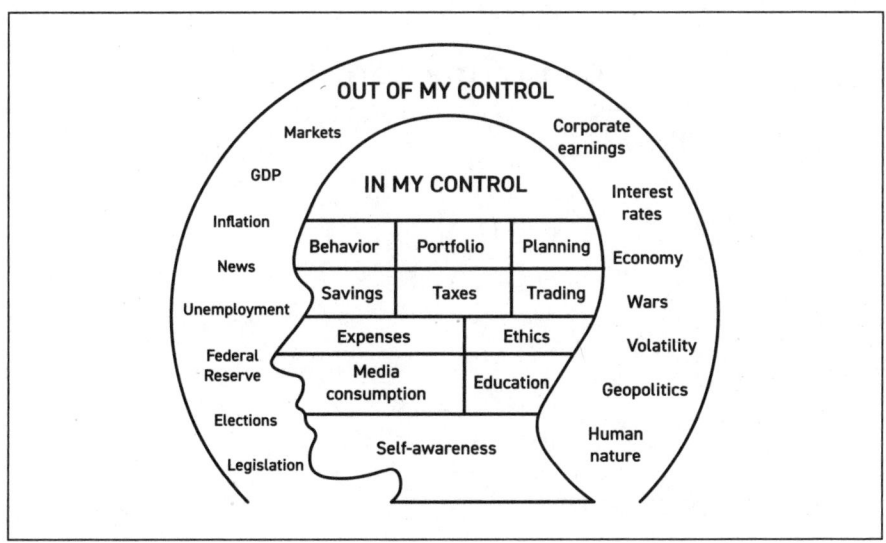

My experience has been to focus on what I can control and roll with the punches for what I cannot. When I do that, everything vastly improves.

Consider the following two lists—these are what is in and out of your control:

Within your control

1. Financial plan
2. Portfolio asset allocation
3. What you watch (or don't watch) on TV
4. Understanding your own emotions (and emotional state)
5. Choosing what to read and what to skip
6. Recognizing the value of empirical evidence and data
7. Furthering your education
8. Honoring your buy and sell discipline
9. Maintaining your own ethical standards
10. Buying excellent legal, tax, estate, and financial counsel
11. Pursuing a career that is deeply satisfying
12. The people you associate with professionally
13. Your behavior.

That *other* list:

Out of my control

1. Federal Reserve
2. GDP
3. Geopolitics
4. Market volatility
5. Interest rates
6. Consumer spending
7. Elections
8. Corporate earnings
9. War
10. Unemployment rates

PART 4: GOOD ADVICE

11. Legislation
12. Media coverage; front page news
13. Human nature and the crowd's reactions and panic.

Investors should avoid the emotional roller coaster, develop an intelligent long-term plan, and execute it. Focus on what you can control; do not stress over what you cannot control. It may be rainy or sunny out, but there isn't much you can do about it other than carry sunscreen or an umbrella.

Or as our friend Carl Richards explains:

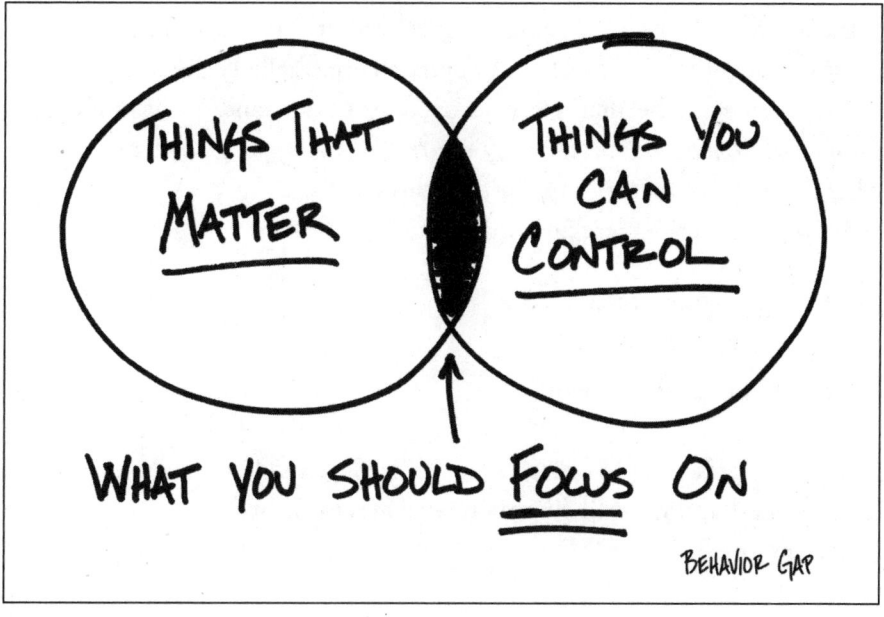

In our last chapter, I *finally* explain how to get rich in the markets!

HOW TO GET RICH IN THE MARKETS

GLOBAL CAPITAL MARKETS—stocks, bonds, private investments, and real estate—are worth over $100 trillion.

There are many ways to capture some of that fortune. But you need to recognize where the odds of each approach are stacked against you.

To get rich in the markets, you need to understand a few important things. These are not secrets; they are *truths*. I am going to share 10 ways where you can score really big in the markets.

But—*plot twist!*—these are ranked on three factors:

1. Degree of difficulty.
2. Likelihood of success.
3. Time needed to work.

These are presented in order, from the hardest and least likely to succeed to the easiest and most likely way to accumulate a fortune.

Let's get wealthy.

1. Find the next Apple or Nvidia or whatever

What could be easier? Find a small company that's unloved and undiscovered, then *buy, buy, buy*! Once you identify that one future Nvidia, you have to convince lots of other people to buy it, too (but only *after* you own it).

The hard part? Holding these until the rest of the world figures out what you know. As these gems enjoy enormous growth and profits, their stock prices will soar!

PART 4: GOOD ADVICE

- Degree of difficulty: 10/10
- Likelihood of success: 1/10
- Time required: 2–20 years

2. Innovate

Over the past few decades, there has been enormous innovation in markets. Whether it's ETFs, direct indexing, free trading apps, private credit, cryptocurrencies, or any manner of fintech ideas, the world of investing has become rife with clever new ways to do it faster/cheaper/better than ever before.

All you need to do is invent one of these! Build a company around your innovation, monetize it, and then sell out to a bigger firm.

- Degree of difficulty: 9/10
- Likelihood of success: 2/10
- Time required: 2–7 years

3. Jump on the next bubble (but jump off before it pops)

There are bubbles everywhere, and to profit from them, you only need to do four things: 1. Identify them as they ramp up; 2. Buy into them (even if pricey); 3. Figure out when they peak; 4. Sell your holdings before the collapse.

- Degree of difficulty: 8/10
- Likelihood of success: 3/10
- Time required: 1–5 years

See also: Trade stock options.

4. Short stocks/markets

The flip side of bubble trading is to identify wildly overvalued companies or markets and then bet against them. Sure, the crowd is right most of the time, but when they are wrong, it's spectacular.

You will need a steel gut to deal with the short squeezes and vitriol that come your way—this is why short sellers have become an endangered species—but surely it's worth it.

- Degree of difficulty: 9/10
- Likelihood of success: 4/10
- Time required: 6 months to 3 years

Bonus points: Identifying the frauds the regulators missed…

5. Time the market

Markets go up, markets go down, how hard can it be to be on the right side of the trend?

- Degree of difficulty: 7/10
- Likelihood of success: 3/10
- Time required: Whenever the next major reversal occurs.

6. Provide a valuable service

Now, we're getting into some heavy lifting. Figure out how to provide some sort of service, be it research, execution, asset management, or simply identifying the things everybody else has missed. Then, monetize that service.

- Degree of difficulty: 7/10
- Likelihood of success: 7/10
- Time required: 5–10 years

PART 4: GOOD ADVICE

7. Become a great salesperson

I was never a good salesperson, but I was always in awe of those who were. If you can get people to purchase whatever you are selling (regardless of its value) and charge a substantial markup and/or commission on that product, you can make a killing in this business. You don't even have to be right—you just need to be confident and earn the trust of your clients.

- Degree of difficulty: 5/10
- Likelihood of success: 9/10
- Time required: However long it takes you to start closing.

8. Index

Buy the entire market, hold it for years, and enjoy your retirement. The challenge is that your own instincts and behavior will work against you the whole time. While this should be a 1 out of 10 in terms of degree of difficulty, unfortunately, your wetware makes it harder than it need be.

- Degree of difficulty: 4/10
- Likelihood of success: 10/10
- Time required: 10–20 years

9. Dollar cost average

DCA is yet another way to all but guarantee accumulating a fortune, but only if you stick to it over time. Doing this with indexes or broad markets is the preferred way, but it's been done with individual stocks (primarily blue chips).

- Degree of difficulty: 3/10*
- Likelihood of success: 9/10

---

* If you automate this—automatically tap your paycheck so you don't see it—the degree of difficulty drops to 1...

- Time required: 5–25 years

10. Compound forever (aka rarely sell)

In markets, time is your friend; the longer you have investments compounding (especially if you reinvest dividends or interest), the better off you'll be. If it's good enough for Warren Buffett, it's good enough for you.

- Degree of difficulty: 2/10
- Likelihood of success: 10/10
- Time required: between now and forever.

Investors are confronted with endless choices, but it all boils down to this: Do you want to do this the easy way, or do this the hard way? All you need is the patience to get rich slowly.

———

Coming up, the last word…

CONCLUSION

YOU MADE IT! Congratulations for plowing through all 444 pages of my inner monologue. I hope you found the book entertaining and useful.

I had a lot more fun writing this than I expected. It was very rewarding revisiting a lot of the discussions I have previously had on investment topics in *The Washington Post*, Bloomberg, TheStreet.com, and from my blog, The Big Picture.

It's taken me decades to accumulate the stories, insights, and wisdom you have just consumed. I am extremely confident that if you implement these ideas, you will become wealthier, happier, and much less stressed about your financial circumstances.

Sometimes, you put something out into the world, and you don't get the response you were hoping for: "Maybe that's true, but I still think Cisco is a great stock." It is very gratifying to find out 25 years later that many of the outlier positions and arguments I have previously made turned out to be (mostly) right.

Hopefully, 25 years from now, *this* book will still be useful to investors.

Until then, I want to hear from you: If this book helped you, and how, what you want more color on, what was confusing, and anything else you want to learn more about.

Thank you for reading this. Please reach out to me with any questions or suggestions at HNTI@RitholtzWealth.com.

Barry Ritholtz

ACKNOWLEDGMENTS

THIS BOOK WAS made possible only via the generosity, shared insights, and outright assistance of so many people.*

Morgan Housel (of *The Psychology of Money* fame) and Craig Pearce (Harriman House) gently prodded me over the past few years to write this particular book. They both insisted it would be a fast and easy review of all of my previous ideas, commentaries, and columns. They were mistaken. Thank you for this white lie.

Craig was a delight to work with as an editor: a firm but gentle hand was exactly what this material required. I found the writing joyous and the editing process painless. What more could you ever ask for from a publisher?

A few other editors whose influence can be seen in these pages: Kelly Johnson at *The Washington Post* helped me find my voice speaking to Main Street investors. Thomas Donlan from *Barron's* showed me how to excise all of the fat, leaving only sinew and muscle for readers. Tim O'Brien and David Shipley for bringing me to Bloomberg. Most of all, James Greiff taught me how to weave data with opinion, respect the readers' time, and get to the damned point already. (Jim, I have stopped my throat clearing, except perhaps for the first section in the first part of the book.)

The team at Ritholtz Wealth Management is a perpetual source of ideas, data, context, insight, and wisdom. You see many references to the RWM folk, as they have been a large source of feedback and refinement of my own investing philosophy. This book would have been so much less rich without them. Ben Carlson, Michael Batnick, Josh Brown, Nick Maggiulli, and Callie Cox all deserve a special shout-out. Their voices were echoing in

---

* I apologize in advance if I accidentally omit anyone.

my head as I wrote this. The Tax Bills—Bill Sweet and Bill Artzerounian—were enormously helpful to everything tax-related. Ben, Michael, and Callie, along with the rest of my investment committee, including Taylor Hollis and Blair duQuesnay, also deserve mention for their sage counsel and insights. Matt Cerminaro makes all of our charts look great, and his work is seen throughout this book.

My partners, Kris Venne and Jay Tini, have taught me so much over the years about what good advisors do for their clients. If you found the Good Advice section useful, credit them (if not, blame me for failing to learn what they taught). They also work with our amazing team of 30 CFP advisors, who do incredible work for our clients every day.

Everyone quoted, cited, or written about in the book deserves special thanks. However, a few standouts truly influenced me: The behaviorists David Dunning, Dick Thaler, Bob Shiller, Thomas Gilovich, and the late, great Danny Kahneman, have all profoundly shaped my thinking.

Additionally, the people I have been privileged to get to know beyond a few hours of Masters in Business interview time have been intellectual mentors (whether they knew it or not). Ray Dalio on learning from our mistakes, Howard Marks on second-level thinking, Scott Galloway on carving your own path, and Cliff Asness for maintaining a sense of humor throughout. Ed Hyman and Ed Yardeni have deeply affected how I think about the relationship between the economy and markets.

Jeff Weitzman, Jonathan Miller, Dave Nadig, Josh Frankel, Michael Batnick, Brian Hamburger, and Ralph Sevush have given me endless sage counsel over the years. Their insights are reflected in mine. Nobody has given me more love, support, and insight than my wife Wendy.

Whom else might I have forgotten? I guess one final thank you is needed: To Wall Street, whose avarice, incompetence, and recklessness made this book both possible and necessary. I could not have done any of this without you...

ENDNOTES

1 Charley Ellis, "The Loser's Game," *Financial Analysts Journal* (July–August 1975), pp. 19–26.
2 Charley Ellis, *Winning the Loser's Game* (McGraw-Hill, 1985).
3 Prashant Gopal, "Billionaire Sam Zell Says Recession Likely in Next 12 Months," Bloomberg (December 16, 2015).
4 Morgan Brennan, "The Investment Zen Of Sam Zell: Inside The Grave Dancer's $4 Billion Business Empire," *Forbes* (October 6, 2013).
5 Edward Lee Thorndike, "The Constant Error in Psychological Ratings" (1920). Thorndike was an American psychologist and professor at Columbia University.
6 Phil Rosenzweig, *The Halo Effect (and Other Business Delusions That Deceive Managers)* (Free Press, 2007).
7 Jeff Cox, "'We're Heading for Recession,' Zell Predicts for Economy," CNBC (October 2, 2012).
8 All references in this book to US recessions are based on the Business Cycle Dating by National Bureau of Economic Research (NBER). See nber.org/research/business-cycle-dating.
9 "Real Estate Developer and 'Grave Dancer' Sam Zell: 'It's All about Supply and Demand'," Knowledge at Wharton (September 19, 2007).
10 Andy Greene, "The 50 Worst Decisions in Movie History," *Rolling Stone* (September 25, 2023).
11 Trung Phan, "The LEGO Star Wars Inception," *Saturday Post* (April 26, 2024).
12 IMDbPro Box Office Mojo, "Top Lifetime Grosses," boxofficemojo.com/chart/top_lifetime_gross/?area=XWW.
13 Marcos Franco, "The 10 Most Lucrative Movie Merchandise Franchises, from 'Star Wars' and 'Batman' to 'Frozen' and 'Cars'," *IndieWire* (August 6, 2023).
14 Molly Allen, "I visited the world's last Blockbuster, and the video-rental store took me back to my childhood," Business Insider (April 2, 2023); and Wendy Lee, "How Netflix survived the streaming wars to stay the subscription video king," *Los Angeles Times* (March 6, 2024).
15 Robert H. Frank, *Success and Luck: Good Fortune and the Myth of Meritocracy* (Princeton University Press, 2017).
16 Robert H. Frank and Philip J. Cook, *The Winner-Take-All Society: Why the Few at the Top Get So Much More Than the Rest of Us* (Free Press, 1995).

17 Michael J. Mauboussin, *The Success Equation: Untangling Skill and Luck in Business, Sports, and Investing* (Harvard Business Review Press, 2012).

18 The Beatles, allmusic.com.

19 Bob Seawright, "Eyes Wide Open: The Beatles and Their Critics," *The Better Letter* (February 1, 2024). See also: Cary Schneider "What the critics wrote about the Beatles in 1964," *Los Angeles Times* (February 9, 2014).

20 Bob Seawright, "Eyes Wide Open: The Beatles and Their Critics," The Better Letter (February 1, 2024).

21 See also Steve Silverman, "Early Criticism of The Beatles," *Useless Information* (February 11, 2016).

22 Billboard Hot 100™, billboard.com/charts/hot-100/1964-02-01 (February 1, 1964).

23 Richard Harrington, "The Birth Of Beatlemania: 25 Years Ago Today, That Sullivan Show," *The Washington Post* (February 9, 1989).

24 Derek Thompson, *Hit Makers: The Science of Popularity in an Age of Distraction* (Penguin Books, 2017). It was first published as: Derek Thompson "The Four-Letter Code to Selling Just About Anything," *The Atlantic* (January/February 2017).

25 Ted Gioia, "Why Did the Beatles Get So Many Bad Reviews?" The Honest Broker (January 30, 2023).

26 Elvis Costello, "100 Greatest Beatles Songs," *Rolling Stone* (April 10, 2020).

27 Danny Boyd, "When you hire stunt guys to direct the movie," CinemaStix, YouTube (April 1, 2023).

28 IMDbPro Box Office Mojo: John Wick (2014) $86,081,850, boxofficemojo.com/title/tt2911666.

29 IMDbPro Box Office Mojo: John Wick: Chapter 2 (2017) $174,348,632, boxofficemojo.com/title/tt4425200.

30 IMDbPro Box Office Mojo: John Wick: Chapter 3—Parabellum (2019) $328,349,908. boxofficemojo.com/title/tt6146586.

31 IMDbPro Box Office Mojo: John Wick: Chapter 4 (2023) $440,157,245, boxofficemojo.com/title/tt10366206.

32 Todd Spangler, "'Squid Game' Is Decisively Netflix No. 1 Show of All Time With 1.65 Billion Hours Streamed in First Four Weeks, Company Says," *Variety* (November 16, 2021).

33 Dasl Yoon and Timothy W. Martin, "Netflix's 'Squid Game' Is the Dystopian Hit No One Wanted—Until Everyone Did," *The Wall Street Journal* (October 4, 2021).

34 Steven Malanga, "The Retirement Crisis That Wasn't," *City Journal* (January 10, 2024).

35 Chloe Berger, "Older boomers won the pandemic after becoming a whopping $14 trillion richer, Fed data reveals—and Gen X is losing the race," *Fortune* (December 22, 2023).

36 Ben Carlson, "The Luckiest Generation," A Wealth of Common Sense (August 25, 2023). Ben Carlson is director of Institutional Asset Management at Ritholtz Wealth Management (RWM).

ENDNOTES

37 Barry Ritholtz, "Who Is to Blame for Inflation, 1-15," The Big Picture (June 28, 2022).

38 Philip Aldrick, "Larry Summers Says US Needs 5% Jobless Rate for Five Years to Ease Inflation," Bloomberg (June 20, 2022).

39 Paul Graham, "How to Be an Expert in a Changing World," paulgraham.com (December 2014).

40 James K. Glassman and Kevin A. Hassett, *Dow 36,000: The New Strategy for Profiting from the Coming Rise in the Stock Market* (Crown Business, 1999).

41 Michael P. Regan and Bloomberg, "Remember 'Dow 36,000'? The 'most spectacularly wrong investing book ever' is finally right—22 years later," *Fortune* (November 1, 2021).

42 Michael Lewis, *The Big Short: Inside the Doomsday Machine* (W.W. Norton & Company, 2010).

43 Jeremy Salvucci, "Michael Burry's net worth: How the 'Big Short' investor got rich," TheStreet.com (April 2, 2024).

44 Adam Khoo, Founder and Chairman of Piranha Profits, a Singapore based trading school. He describes himself as a professional investor and trader. adam-khoo.com.

45 @adamkhootrader, twitter.com/adamkhootrader/status/1691397274524631040 (August 15, 2023).

46 Joe Keohane, "That guy who called the big one? Don't listen to him," *Boston Globe* (January 9, 2011).

47 Barry Ritholtz, "Maybe the Coronavirus Didn't End the Bull Market," Bloomberg (April 1, 2020).

48 Robert Kiyosaki, *Rich Dad, Poor Dad* (Warner Books, 1997).

49 Ben Carlson, "Rich Author, Poor Readers," A Wealth of Common Sense (December 15, 2023).

50 Ben Carlson, "Rich Author, Poor Readers," A Wealth of Common Sense (December 15, 2023).

51 Robert Kiyosaki @theRealKiyosaki *twitter.com/theRealKiyosaki/status/1733976936945459411* (10:28 pm December 10, 2023).

52 Robert Kiyosaki @theRealKiyosaki *twitter.com/theRealKiyosaki/status/1441994336850251780* (6:13 am September 26, 2021).

53 Robert Kiyosaki @theRealKiyosaki *twitter.com/theRealKiyosaki/status/1321438606959931394* (1:08 pm October 28, 2020).

54 Robert Kiyosaki @theRealKiyosaki *twitter.com/theRealKiyosaki/status/1251111793885278208* (12:34 pm April 17, 2020).

55 Robert Kiyosaki @theRealKiyosaki *twitter.com/theRealKiyosaki/status/994655292674764800* (8:07 pm May 10, 2018).

56 Robert Kiyosaki @theRealKiyosaki *twitter.com/theRealKiyosaki/status/638746651796967424* (5:14 pm September 1, 2015).

57   Robert Kiyosaki @theRealKiyosaki *twitter.com/theRealKiyosaki/status/602096655500873730* (2:00 pm May 23, 2015).

58   Robert Kiyosaki @theRealKiyosaki *twitter.com/theRealKiyosaki/status/56008841162272770* (4:02 pm April 7, 2011).

59   Helaine Olen, "Rich Dad, Poor Dad, Bankrupt Dad?" *Forbes* (October 10, 2012). See also: "'Rich Dad, Poor Dad' Author Files for Bankruptcy for His Company," ABC News (October 12, 2012).

60   William J. Bernstein, *The Investor's Manifesto: Preparing for Prosperity, Armageddon, and Everything in Between* (Wiley, 2009).

61   Anthony Robbins, *Awaken the Giant Within: How to Take Immediate Control of Your Mental, Emotional, Physical and Financial Destiny!* (Simon & Schuster, 1991).

62   Bennett W. Goodspeed, *The Tao Jones Averages: A Guide to Whole-Brained Investing* (Dutton Adult: First Edition, 1983).

63   John Maynard Keynes, *The General Theory of Employment, Interest and Money* (Palgrave Macmillan, 1936).

64   Philip E. Tetlock, *Expert Political Judgment: How Good Is It? How Can We Know?* (Princeton University Press, 2005).

65   Howard Marks, *The Most Important Thing: Uncommon Sense for the Thoughtful Investor* (Columbia Business School Publishing, 2011). And recounted in Howard Marks, "Risk Revisited," Howard Marks Memo (September 2014).

66   Howard Marks, twitter.com/HowardMarksBook/status/1044964993127649280 (September 26, 2018).

67   Stephen Kellert is a philosopher of science at Hamline in Minnesota. The quote is from *In the Wake of Chaos: Unpredictable Order in Dynamical Systems* (University of Chicago Press, 1993).

68   George Soros, *The Alchemy of Finance: Reading the Mind of the Market* (Wiley, 1994).

69   Theodor Reik, *Curiosities of the Self: Illusions We Have about Ourselves* (Farrar, Straus & Giroux, 1965), Essay 3: "The Unreachables: The Repetition Compulsion in Jewish History," p.133 (verified with scans). This is often misattributed to Mark Twain, but there is no evidence he ever said or wrote those words: See "History Does Not Repeat Itself, But It Rhymes," Quote Investigator (January 12, 2014).

70   Richard Feynman, speaking at a Caltech graduation ceremony, via MIT's Andrew W. Lo, "Warning: Physics Envy May be Hazardous to Your Wealth!" ssrn.com (March, 2010).

71   Andrew Feinberg, "How to Build an Entire Financial Channel That Mainly Loses People Money," slate.com (February 19, 2024).

72   Joshua M. Brown, "In which Downtown Josh Brown saves the mutual fund industry," The Reformed Broker (December 14, 2016). Josh Brown is CEO at Ritholtz Wealth Management.

73   Neal Frankle, *Why Smart People Lose a Fortune* (Just Write, 2004).

ENDNOTES

74   TTI @TikTokInvestors. Quotes are via DMs on Twitter; they remain anonymous as they work in the finance industry and are not authorized to speak publicly on behalf of their employer.

75   None of these TikTok influencers sells securities to clients, so they do not fall under the regulatory oversight of the Securities and Exchange Commission (SEC). But my firm does, and we spend a lot of time and money making sure every single thing we publish meets all SEC requirements.

76   TTI @TikTokInvestors, "Max out your 401K could be the dumbest advice that I've ever heard for anyone that wants to take financial control" (August 25, 2020).

77   TTI @TikTokInvestors, "Turn $100 into a million" (May 4, 2024).

78   TTI @TikTokInvestors, "A sneak peek of one of our top-secret trading strategies" (January 17, 2021).

79   TTI @TikTokInvestors, "Live on the water during tax season" (April 17, 2024).

80   TTI @TikTokInvestors, "House Depreciation" (December 12, 2023).

81   IRS, "The Truth About Frivolous Tax Arguments—Section III," irs.gov (March, 2022). See also: "Part III—Administrative, Procedural, and Miscellaneous Frivolous Positions—This notice lists positions identified as frivolous for purposes of section 6702(c) of the Code. Notice 2008-14, 2008-4 I.R.B. 310, modified and superseded," irs.gov.

82   TTI @TikTokInvestors, "Teach your home-schooled children to day trade" (April 20, 2024).

83   TTI @TikTokInvestors, "Why invest in index funds when you can just pick the top individual stocks?" (April 18, 2024).

84   Andy Serwer, Irene Gashurov and Angela Key, "There's Something About Cisco," *Fortune* (May 15, 2000).

85   Cliff Edwards, "Commentary: Sorry, Steve: Here's Why Apple Stores Won't Work," *BusinessWeek* (May 21, 2001).

86   Nearly a decade and a half later, those naysayers were recounted here: Ana Swanson, "How the Apple store took over the world," *The Washington Post* (July 21, 2015).

87   Jerry Useem, "Apple: America's best retailer," *Fortune* (March 8 2007).

88   Seth Fiegerman, "Apple Has Twice the Sales Per Square Foot of Any Other U.S. Retailer," Mashable (November 13, 2012).

89   Chance Miller, "Apple again found to be the world's top retailer in sales per square foot," 9TO5Mac (July 29, 2017). See also: Marianne Wilson, "The most profitable retailers in sales per square foot are...." *Chain Store Age* (CSA) (July 31, 2017).

90   Jon Fortt, "Forget the iPhone: BlackBerry is still the one to beat," *Fortune* (August 24, 2007).

91   "Nostalgia calling: BlackBerry had a good quarter, but it had nothing to do with phones," chartr.co (June 30, 2023).

92   Bruce Upbin, "The Next Billion," *Forbes* (October 26, 2007).

93   "Microsoft to acquire Nokia's devices & services business, license Nokia's patents and mapping services," Microsoft News Center (September 3, 2013).

94   Paul Graham, "How to Be an Expert in a Changing World," paulgraham.com (December 2014).

95   Jack Hough, "Apple to Hit $1 Trillion in Market Value in 2018," *Barron's* (December 23, 2017).

96   Michael Crichton, "Why Speculate?" International Leadership Forum, La Jolla, California (April 26, 2002).

97   Anna Hirtenstein and Akane Otani, "The Worst of the Global Selloff Isn't Here Yet, Banks and Investors Warn," *The Wall Street Journal* (March 22, 2020).

98   Matt Phillips, "Can Investors Trust the Stock Market Rally?" *The New York Times* (April 20, 2020).

99   Harry Dempsey, "Investors show little faith in 'bear market rally'," *Financial Times* (May 19, 2020).

100   Ian Cassel, Twitter (March 3, 2024).

101   Horatio Alger Association, "Elizabeth Holmes, Visionary Silicon Valley Entrepreneur and Passionate Advocate for Female Engagement of STEM Curricula to Receive 2015 Horatio Alger Award." PR Newswire (December 4, 2014).

102   Kimberly Weisul, "How Playing the Long Game Made Elizabeth Holmes a Billionaire," *Inc. Magazine* (October 2015).

103   April Witt and Peter Behr Washington, "Dream Job Turns Into a Nightmare: Skilling's Success Came at High Price," *The Washington Post* (July 29, 2002).

104   As I detailed in: Barry Ritholtz, *Bailout Nation: How Greed and Easy Money Corrupted Wall Street and Shook the World Economy* (Wiley, 2009).

105   Eddy Elfenbein, *twitter.com/EddyElfenbein/status/1788246336430653843* (5:35 pm May 8, 2024).

106   William Shakespeare, *As You Like It*. "All the world's a stage, And all the men and women merely players; They have their exits and their entrances; And one man in his time plays many parts." (c.1599).

107   As inflation was spiking in 2022, I tried to assess its causes. My list included at #5, "Consumers (overspent without regard to cost)." See: Barry Ritholtz, "Who Is to Blame for Inflation, 1–15," The Big Picture (June 28, 2022).

108   Carl Gustav Jacob Jacobi, "Invert, always invert" (German original: *"man muss immer umkehren"*). See: Hugh Chisholm, *Encyclopaedia Britannica Eleventh Edition* (Cambridge University Press, 1911, Vol. 15, p. 117).

109   Oliver Burkeman, *Four Thousand Weeks: Time Management for Mortals* (Farrar, Straus and Giroux, 2021).

110   Another 2 million get self-published. See: Steven Piersanti, "The 10 Awful Truths about Book Publishing," *Berrett-Koehler Publishers* (March 1, 2023).

111   Bob Sutton, "Strong Opinions, Weakly Held," Work Matters (July 17, 2006).

112   Charles Darwin, *The Descent of Man, and Selection in Relation to Sex* (1871).

ENDNOTES

113 David McRaney, *How Minds Change: The Surprising Science of Belief, Opinion, and Persuasion* (Portfolio, 2022).

114 Marcus Aurelius (a Roman emperor who lived from AD 161 to 180), *Meditations* (the first recorded mention of *Meditations* is believed to be CE 364 by Themistius).

115 National Consortium for the Study of Terrorism and Responses to Terrorism (START), University of Maryland.

116 Garrick Blalock, Vrinda Kadiyali, Daniel H. Simon, "Driving Fatalities After 9/11: A Hidden Cost of Terrorism," researchgate.net (December 5, 2005).

117 Insurance Institute for Highway Safety / Highway Loss Data Institute, "Fatality Facts 2022: Yearly Snapshot," iihs.org (June 2024).

118 CDC Centers for Disease Control and Prevention, Heart Disease, "Heart disease in the United States," cdc.gov. See also: Max Roser, "Causes of death globally: what do people die from?" Our World in Data (December 7, 2021).

119 W. Kip Viscusi and Richard J. Zeckhauser, "The Denominator Blindness Effect: Accident Frequencies and the Misjudgment of Recklessness," ssrn.com (October 2002). The paper looked at the impact of this phenomenon on jury awards for punitive damages. As you might guess, this bias played a significant role. But the concept is just as applicable to economics, markets, and portfolio management.

120 Dan Gardner, *Risk: The Science and Politics of Fear* (Macfarlane Walter & Ross (September 29, 2015).

121 Barry Ritholtz, "Don't Be Blinded By Big, Scary Numbers," Bloomberg (October 14, 2015).

122 Gus Lubin, "49 Former NASA Scientists Send A Letter Disputing Climate Change," Business Insider (April 11, 2012).

123 Ihor Gawdiak with Helen Fedor, *NASA Historical Data Book, Volume IV* (NASA Resources, 1969–1978).

124 US Bureau of Labor Statistics, Employment Situation Summary, bls.gov.

125 Sam Ro, "Mind the anecdata," tker.co (January 22, 2023). See also: Sam Ro, "Don't be misled by no-context reports of big tech layoffs," tker.co (November 15, 2022).

126 Justin Aquino, "From Estate Tax to Death Tax: How to Change Public Opinion Overnight," coolcommunicator.com.

127 In 2021, there were 3,464,231 deaths—up substantially from 2019 levels pre-Covid of 2,854,838. That fell to 3.27 million deaths in 2022, and have continued falling since. I am rounding down to only 3 million (but it could be more). National Vital Statistics Reports Volume 70, Number 8, "Deaths: Final Data for 2019," cdc.gov (July 26, 2021). See also: National Center for Health Statistics, "Deaths and Mortality," cdc.gov.

128 Kathryn Miles, "Cause of Death: Selfie," *Outside* (April 16, 2019). Selfie deaths in 2015 include people falling to death (4), a live hand grenade, hit by a train, electrocuted (2), shot themselves (2), fell from a bridge, fell down the stairs at the Taj Mahal. See also: Barry Ritholtz, "Fixing Your Clients' Behavior—The Biggest Problem Never Solved," The Big Picture (January 23, 2017).

129   CDC National Center for Health Statistics, National Vital Statistics System, Mortality Statistics, cdc.gov (2017).

130   Ellen Huet, "Google I/O 2014: Keynote Live Blog," *Forbes* (June 25, 2014). See also: io.google/2024.

131   A few other threats to consider: Armed toddlers kill 21 people per year (and rising). *Autoerotic asphyxiation* is 150 deaths each year. Two people die each year because vending machines fall on them ("Be less stupid" means not rocking these back and forth to get your candy). Seventeen people died climbing Mount Everest. Twenty-eight people died skateboarding. Why are these numbers a concern? They were a blip out of the 2,813,503 deaths in the United States in 2017, according to the Centers for Disease Control and Prevention. See also: Daniel D. Cowell, MD, MLS, CPHQ, "Autoerotic Asphyxiation: Secret Pleasure—Lethal Outcome?" *Pediatrics* (November 1, 2009).

132   Jordan Ellenberg, *How Not to Be Wrong: The Power of Mathematical Thinking* (Penguin Books, 2014).

133   Edwin J. Elton, Martin J. Gruber, and Christopher R. Blake, "Survivorship Bias and Mutual Fund Performance," *The Review of Financial Studies*, Vol. 9, No. 4 (winter, 1996), pp. 1097–1120 (24 pages).

134   "Why Worry About Survivorship Bias?" dimensional.com (October 12, 2020).

135   Barry Ritholtz, "Mediocre SPAC Returns Shouldn't Be a Surprise," Bloomberg (October 22, 2020).

136   Bank of America even offers a service to provide wealthy customers with solutions for collectors and institutions while helping to navigate the complex art world. "Art Services Art Services for Collectors and Institutions," privatebank.bankofamerica.com.

137   Fan Fei, "Monet's 'Haystack' sells for record $110.7m at auction," *Financial Times* (May 14, 2019). Note I am not including the cost of insurance, storage, security, and transport for rare artwork, which adds considerably to its total cost of ownership.

138   Katya Kazakina, "Mnuchin's Art-Dealer Dad Nabs $91 Million Record Koons Bunny," Bloomberg (May 16, 2019).

139   Liddy Berman, "Eleven Works from the S.I. Newhouse Jr. Collection Come to Christie's May Auctions," AD (May 6, 2019).

140   Avantika Chilkoti, "The Best Investments of 2018? Art, Wine and Cars," *The Wall Street Journal* (December 31, 2018).

141   Barry Ritholtz, "Transcript: Bill Bernstein," The Big Picture (April 21, 2019). See also: Katya Kazakina, "Steve Cohen Outed as Mystery Buyer of $91 Million Koons Bunny," Bloomberg (May 21, 2019). See also: Frederik Balfour, "Billionaire's Secrets on How to Make a Bundle in Art," Bloomberg (May 7, 2018).

142   Hagerty Price Guide Index, hagerty.com. The Hagerty Price Guide Indexes—first published in 2009 (dating back to 2006)—are a series of stock market-style indexes. Hagerty Price Guides track 1,400 vehicles in four different conditions. These indexes are updated quarterly and provide an overview of how these segments of the collector car market are performing overall, as well as relative to each other.

143   JVL, "The Numbers," The Triad.

ENDNOTES

144 Barry Ritholtz, "Why Economists Missed the Crises," The Big Picture (January 5, 2009).

145 Barry Ritholtz, "Unintended Consequences, Part II: What if LTCM Was Not Rescued in 1998?" The Big Picture (April 17, 2020).

146 Josh Zumbrun, "Economists Believe a Recession Is Likely Within Next Four Years," *The Wall Street Journal* (October 13, 2016).

147 In the 70+ years since World War II ended, there have been 12 recessions. That is a recession every 5.9 years. "US Business Cycle Expansions and Contractions," NBER.

148 Larry Swedroe, "Why you should ignore economic forecasts," *MoneyWatch* (November 26, 2012).

149 Barry Ritholtz, "The Next Recession Is Coming. Big Deal," Bloomberg (October 14, 2016).

150 O. Emre Ergungor, "Recession Probabilities," Federal Reserve Bank of Cleveland (August 23, 2016). See also: Weiling Liu and Emanuel Moench, "What Predicts U.S. Recessions?" Federal Reserve Bank of New York, staff reports (September 2014).

151 I first wrote about how ridiculous the 96% claim was that month, so let's use that date for our framework. But it works regardless of your start and end points. Try it on Nick Maggiulli's S&P 500 calculator: ofdollarsanddata.com/sp500-calculator.

152 Nick Maggiulli, "S&P 500 Historical Return Calculator [With Dividends]," Of Dollars and Data. A sum of $1,000 invested in the S&P 500 with dividends reinvested would return 10.23% annualized, and from April 1917 to July 2023 would be worth $30,761,431.21.

153 Wealth, instagram.com/p/CopP4exp3Vx.

154 Federal Reserve Bank of St Louis, "Employed full time: Median usual weekly nominal earnings."

155 Shri Khalpada, "How Far Does $1 From 1999 Go Today?" PerThirtySix (December 10, 2023).

156 Nick Maggiulli, "$1 in the S&P 500 with dividends reinvested grew 6.94% annualized; over that 24-year period it would have grown to $5.00," in "S&P 500 Historical Return Calculator [With Dividends]," Of Dollars and Data.

157 If instead of the S&P 500, you had purchased a conservative 60/40 portfolio of stocks and bonds (e.g., Fidelity Balanced Fund, FBALX) with dividends reinvested, this would have grown at 6.30% annualized. Or, the Vanguard Total Market (VTI) garnered about 7.8% annually over the same period. Data returns from Nick Maggiulli's US Stock/Bond Historical Return Calculator.

158 Federal Reserve Bank of St Louis, "All Employees: Total Nonfarm." Commonly known as Total Nonfarm Payroll, this is a measure of the number of US workers in the economy that excludes proprietors, private household employees, unpaid volunteers, farm employees, and the unincorporated self-employed. This measure accounts for approximately 80% of the workers who contribute to GDP.

159 Monty Python, "Dead Parrot," youtu.be/4vuW6tQo218?feature=shared

160 Ernest Hemingway, *The Sun Also Rises* (Charles Scribner's Sons, 1926).

161   Paul Volcker, "Think More Boldly," *The Wall Street Journal* (December 14, 2009).

162   Daniel Kahneman, *Thinking, Fast and Slow* (Farrar, Straus and Giroux, 2011).

163   Amos Tversky and Daniel Kahneman, "Availability: A Heuristic for Judging Frequency and Probability," The Hebrew University of Jerusalem and the Oregon Research Institute, *Cognitive Psychology*, Vol. 5, Issue 2, pp. 207–232 (Science Direct, 1973). See also: Amos Tversky and Daniel Kahneman, "Judgment under Uncertainty: Heuristics and Biases," *Science New Series*, Vol. 185, No. 4157, pp. 1124–1131 (American Association for the Advancement of Science, 1974).

164   Peter Benchley, *Jaws* (Doubleday, 1974).

165   "Preventable Tragedies: Unintentional Shootings by Children," Everytown Research and policy (last updated: April 26, 2023). See also: Suzy Khimm, "Children unintentionally shot and killed at least 157 people last year, Everytown says," NBC News (March 18, 2024).

166   Raymond Wolfinger (1931–2015).

167   David Smith, "The plural of anecdote is data, after all," *Revolutions* (April 6, 2011).

168   Joshua M. Brown, "A Field Guide to Stock Market Corrections," The Reformed Broker (August 20, 2013).

169   Barry Ritholtz, "Looking at the Very Very Long Term," The Big Picture (November 6, 2003). I am anticipating criticism of my definition as "a rationalization of the current overpriced environment." However, the definition was first developed in 2003, in the opposite environment—with the Nasdaq Composite Index down almost 80%, and a full-on bear market raging.

170   Barry Ritholtz, "This Bull Market Has Room to Run: Many of the conditions are in place for long-term gains in stocks," Bloomberg UK (November 4, 2016).

171   S&P 500 Earnings by Year, multpl.com.

172   Note: We don't inflation adjust when comparing ratios like price-to-earnings (P/E), because it is pointless, as both the price (numerator) and earnings (denominator) are equally affected.

173   Barry Ritholtz, "How Expensive Are Stocks—Really?" Bloomberg (March 3, 2017). See also: Nir Kaissar and Barry Ritholtz, "How to Know When Stocks Are Properly Valued: A Debate," Bloomberg (June 26, 2017).

174   The 1982–2000 era is worthy of its own book. My favorite is Maggie Mahar's, *Bull: A History of the Boom and Bust*. The patterns she describes regularly repeat.

175   Sometimes there are false starts. The 1966–1982 era looked like it was over in 1980, only to see a 28% slide to the 1982 lows. This is a very imprecise science.

176   Carmen M. Reinhart and Kenneth S. Rogoff, "Is the 2007 U.S. Sub-Prime Financial Crisis So Different? An International Historical Comparison," *The American Economic Review*, Vol. 98, No. 2 (January 14, 2008). See also: Barry Ritholtz, "5 Historical Economic Crises and the U.S." The Big Picture (February 9, 2008).

177   Stephen J. Dubner, "When Barry Ritholtz Talks, People Listen," Freakonomics (March 11, 2009).

ENDNOTES

178   Jurrien Timmer, "Is the secular bear market ending for stocks?" Fidelity Viewpoints (January 27, 2013).

179   Barry Ritholtz, "Significance of secular market should not be underestimated," *The Washington Post* (November 7, 2014).

180   Heinrich Schwabe first noted this in 1843. See also: "The Solar Cycle," NASA (October 27, 2011).

181   Heather Gillers, "Pension Funds' Dilemma: What to Buy When Nothing Is Cheap?" *The Wall Street Journal* (January 1, 2018).

182   MSCI ACWI "captures large and mid cap representation across 23 Developed Markets (DM) and 24 Emerging Markets (EM) countries."

183   Nick Maggiulli is Chief Operating Officer and Data Scientist at Ritholtz Wealth Management.

184   Nick Maggiulli, "Just Keep Buying," Of Dollars and Data (April 11, 2017).

185   My Bloomberg colleague Nir Kaissar and I debated this issue in 2017. See: Nir Kaissar and Barry Ritholtz, "How to Know When Stocks Are Properly Valued: A Debate," Bloomberg (June 26, 2017). See also: Barry Ritholtz, "Judging the Staying Power of Record Markets," Bloomberg (April 27, 2017); and Barry Ritholtz, "How Expensive Are Stocks—Really?" Bloomberg (March 3, 2017).

186   Keith Wibel, "Preparing for Low Returns," *Barron's* (August 29, 2005).

187   Mark Hulbert, "If Profits Grow, How Can the Market Sink?" *The New York Times* (February 6, 2005).

188   "Trouble Ahead," *Barron's* (August 29, 2005).

189   Barry Ritholtz, "Off the Charts," The Big Picture (July 31, 2020).

190   Barry Ritholtz, "Big Tech Drives the Stock Market Without Much U.S. Help," Bloomberg (July 13, 2020).

191   Gemma Tarlach, "The 5 Mass Extinctions That Have Swept Our Planet," *Discover* (September 12, 2022).

192   Gary B. Smith, "Looking to the Past for Guidance," TheStreet.com (September 15, 2001).

193   Barry Ritholtz, "Maybe the Coronavirus Didn't End the Bull Market," Bloomberg (April 1, 2020). Every rally or bust has large counter moves that may not be a real break from underlying trends.

194   Michael Batnick, "The Fastest Bear Market Ever," The Irrelevant Investor (March, 2020).

195   Barry Ritholtz, "Pick Another Day to Celebrate the Bull Market's Birthday," Bloomberg (March 9, 2018).

196   Bob Fernandez, "Yield-Curve Pioneer Says This Recession Warning Is Real," *The Wall Street Journal* (May 23, 2023).

197   Howard Marks, *The Most Important Thing: Uncommon Sense for the Thoughtful Investor* (Columbia Business School Publishing, 2011).

198   Barry Ritholtz, "Forecasting & Prediction Discussions," collected writings, The Big Picture.

199   Philip E. Tetlock, *Expert Political Judgment: How Good Is It? How Can We Know?* (Princeton University Press, 2005).

200   Philip E. Tetlock and Dan Gardner, *Superforecasting: The Art and Science of Prediction* (Crown, 2015).

201   Ben Carlson, "How to Predict a Market Crash," A Wealth of Common Sense (July 23, 2021).

202   Barry Ritholtz, "Apprenticed Investor: The Folly of Forecasting," TheStreet.com (June 7, 2005).

203   Leslie P. Norton, "Barry Ritholtz and Josh Brown Won't Predict The Market, But They'll Talk About Anything Else," *Barron's* (December 18, 2020).

204   Michael Batnick is Managing Partner at Ritholtz Wealth Management.

205   Hendrik Bessembinder, Te-Feng Chen, Goeun Choi and John Wei, "Do Global Stocks Outperform US Treasury Bills?" ssrn.com (July 9, 2019).

206   Bessembinder is also the managing editor of *The Journal of Financial and Quantitative Analysis*, a position he's held since 2003.

207   The authors note: "The finding that most stocks underperform US Treasury bills does not contradict the evidence that returns to broad stock markets handily outperform returns on Treasury instruments." See for example: E. Dimson, P. Marsh, and M. Staunton, *Triumph of the Optimists: 101 Years of Global Investment Returns* (Princeton University Press, 2002).

208   Luke Kawa, "Alliance Bernstein: Passive Investing Is Worse for Society Than Marxism," Bloomberg (August 23, 2016).

209   Simone Foxman, "Paul Singer Says Passive Investing Is 'Devouring Capitalism'," Bloomberg (August 3, 2017).

210   Luke Graham, "Morgan Stanley: Passive investing boom is creating a 'frightening' risk for markets," CNBC (July 10, 2017).

211   Akepanidtaworn Klakow, Rick Di Mascio, Alex Imas and Lawrence Schmidt, "Selling Fast and Buying Slow: Heuristics and Trading Performance of Institutional Investors," ssrn.com (September 1, 2019).

212   Barber and Odean, "The behavior of individual investors," in *Handbook of the Economics of Finance*, Vol. 2, Part B (Elsevier, 2013), pp. 1533–1570. See also: D. Grosshans, F. Langnickel, and S. Zeisberger, "The Role of Beliefs in Trading Decisions," (2018).

213   Ben Carlson, "What if You Only Invested at Market Peaks?" A Wealth of Common Sense (February 25, 2014). See also a similar idea from email discussions with Gaspar Fierro, a reader in Spain (who sent along a spreadsheet): "El mejor inversor de la historia" (June 25, 2014), ritholtz.com/blog/wp-content/uploads/2014/08/Best-timer-returns.xlsx.

214   David Mikkelson, "Einstein and Compound Interest," snopes.com (November 6, 2006).

215   Patrick O'Shaughnessy, *Millennial Money: How Young Investors Can Build a Fortune* (St. Martin's Press, 2014).

ENDNOTES

216   Farnoosh Torabi, "Why I Caved And Altered My Retirement Portfolio," Bloomberg (July 18, 2020).

217   Markus Glaser and Ludwig Maximilian, "Why Inexperienced Investors Do Not Learn: They Do Not Know Their Past Portfolio Performance," *Finance Research Letters*, Vol. 4, No. 4 (November 15, 2007).

218   "Wall Street Still Doesn't Understand Apple, Ritholtz Says," Bloomberg Surveillance (August 24, 2021).

219   Since that sale, Apple's stock split 4-for-1 on August 28, 2020, 7-for-1 on June 9, 2014, and 2-for-1 on February 28, 2005. Each share sold in 2003 would have been 56 shares today. Source: Apple Investor Relations, apple.com.

220   Barry Ritholtz, "Lessons from Our Origin Story," The Big Picture (September 17, 2021).

221   Bruce Newman, "Apple's lost founder: Jobs, Woz and Wayne," *Mercury News* (June 2, 2010).

222   Steve Wozniak with Gina Smith, *iWoz: Computer Geek to Cult Icon: How I Invented the Personal Computer, Co-Founded Apple, and Had Fun Doing It* (W.W. Norton & Company, September 17, 2006).

223   Wired Editorial staff, "101 Ways to Save Apple," *Wired* (June 1, 1997).

224   Katya Kazakina, "Founding Apple Contract Jobs Signed Sells for $1.6 Million," Bloomberg (December 13, 2011).

225   Dan Simon, "The gambling man who co-founded Apple and left for $800," CNN (June 24, 2010).

226   David Benoit, "Eleven Years in the Making: Breaking Even on JPMorgan's Purchase of Bear Stearns," *The Wall Street Journal* (December 25, 2019).

227   Marks, *The Most Important Thing*.

228   Ray Dalio, *Principles: Life and Work* (Simon & Schuster, 2017).

229   Meir Statman, *What Investors Really Want* (McGraw-Hill, 2010).

230   Upton Sinclair, "I, Candidate for Governor and How I Got Licked," *Oakland Tribune* (December 11, 1934).

231   Eric Balchunas, "How the Vanguard Effect Adds Up to $1 Trillion," Bloomberg (August 30, 2016).

232   Marvin Howe, "Arthur Belfer, 86, Philanthropist And Head of Petroleum Concern," *The New York Times* (May 4, 1993).

233   Lay was found guilty on six counts of securities and wire fraud. He was also found guilty of four additional counts of fraud and making false statements. Skilling was found guilty on 19 counts of conspiracy, fraud, false statements, and insider trading. Shaheen Pasha and Jessica Seid, "Lay and Skilling's Day of Reckoning," CNN Money (May 25, 2006).

234   Leslie Eaton and Geraldine Fabrikant, "Enron's Collapse: The Losers," *The New York Times* (December 5, 2001).

235   Erin E. Arvedlund, "Don't Ask, Don't Tell: Bernie Madoff Attracts Skeptics in 2001," "Bernie Madoff is so secretive, he even asks investors to keep mum," *Barron's* (May 7, 2001).

236 Joshua Oliver, "Enron, Madoff and now FTX: New York's Belfer family strike out again," *Financial Times* (January 15, 2023).

237 "The Man Who Figured Out Madoff's Scheme," CBS News 60-Minutes (February 27, 2009).

238 *See* e.g. 08-1789—Securities Investor Protection Corporation v. Bernard L. Madoff Investment Securities, LLC. et al., www.govinfo.gov/app/details/USCOURTS-nysb-1_08-ap-01789; Case: 12-2557 Document: 96-1 Page: 1 11/07/2012 762747 www.madofftrustee.com/document/dockets/003137-fishmanmotion12-2616docket77.pdf; Case 1:15-cv-01151-PAE Document 21 Filed 05/27/15

239 Joshua Oliver, "Enron, Madoff and now FTX: New York's Belfer family strike out again," *Financial Times* (January 15, 2023).

240 "Victim recoveries brought to a minimum 91% of fraud losses MVF has paid $4.221 billion directly to victims," Department of Justice Asset Forfeiture Distribution Program, Madoff Victim Fund, madoffvictimfund.com.

241 Dietrich Knauth and Brendan Pierson, "FTX's new CEO helped bolster Enron victims' recovery," Reuters (November 15, 2022).

242 "FTX Files Consensus-Based Plan of Reorganization: 98% of FTX Creditors to Receive At Least 118% of Allowed Claims in Cash within 60 Days of Effectiveness," PR Newswire/FTX (May 7, 2024).

243 Even if it were 1995, a $1m with dividends reinvested would have appreciated 530%, grown at an annualized rate of 9.6%, becoming $6,295,391. Nick Maggiulli, "S&P 500 Historical Return Calculator [With Dividends]," Of Dollars And Data.

244 Tamim Elyan and Manus Cranny, "This Billionaire Says He's Put Half His Net Worth Into Gold," Bloomberg (May 1, 2018).

245 The Bloomberg Billionaires Index is a daily ranking of the world's richest people: www.bloomberg.com/billionaires

246 I beat gold to death in "12 Rules of Goldbuggery," The Big Picture, April 16, 2013.

247 Henry Sanderson, "Egyptian billionaire Naguib Sawiris to launch new gold investment vehicle," *Financial Times* (November 27, 2017).

248 Barry Ritholtz, "Gold Miners Index Down 30% Since 1993 Inception," The Big Picture (November 12, 2015).

249 Barry Ritholtz, "Gold Miners Are No Longer a Proxy for the Metal," The Big Picture (July 23, 2015).

250 Barry Ritholtz, "A Billionaire Makes a Classic Investing Error: Concentrating in a single asset class can be an invitation to trouble," Bloomberg (May 3, 2018).

251 Thomas Gryta, "Retirement Shock: Need to Find a Job After 40 Years at General Electric," *The Wall Street Journal* (April 22, 2018).

252 Barry Ritholtz, "How to Avoid a Retirement Disaster," Bloomberg (April 23, 2018).

253 Nick Maggiulli, "U.S. Stock/Bond Historical Return Calculator," Of Dollars And Data.

254 Aswath Damodaran, *The Corporate Life Cycle: Business, Investment, and Management Implications* (Portfolio, 2024).

255 "Never stop buying lottery tickets," xkdc.com.

256 Julie Flaherty, "'Buy and Forget' Pays Off Big," *The New York Times* (December 3, 2000).

257 "Man buys $27 of bitcoin, forgets about them, finds they're now worth $886k," *Guardian* (October 29, 2013).

258 The family would have done better if they'd put their wealth in a low-cost index fund. Devon Pendleton, Dasha Afanasieva, and Benjamin Stupples, "Secretive Dynasty Missed Out on Billions While Advisers Got Rich," Bloomberg UK (August 13, 2024).

259 Jason Zweig, "A Couple Won the Powerball. Investing It Turned Into Tragedy," *The Wall Street Journal* (July 12, 2024).

260 Jason Zweig, *Your Money and Your Brain: How the New Science of Neuroeconomics Can Help Make You Rich* (Simon & Schuster, 2007).

261 Pablo S. Torre, "How (and Why) Athletes Go Broke," *Sports Illustrated* (March 23, 2009).

262 Barry Ritholtz, "Congratulations! You just signed a $325 million deal. Now what?" *The Washington Post* (November 21, 2014).

263 Barry Ritholtz, "Professional athletes need to learn to keep their finances in good shape," *The Washington Post* (May 31, 2014).

264 Orianna Rosa Royle, "Peloton's former billionaire CEO says he's lost all his money and had to sell his possessions," *Fortune* (August 27, 2024).

265 Lydia Moynihan, "Ex-Peloton CEO John Foley gets real about company crash: And his unexpected venture into home décor," *The New York Post* (August 23, 2024).

266 Joshua M. Brown, *You Weren't Supposed to See That: Secrets Every Investor Should Know* (Harriman House, 2024).

267 Wikipedia: Great Wealth Transfer, en.wikipedia.org/wiki/Great_Wealth_Transfer

268 "Cerulli Anticipates $84 Trillion in Wealth Transfers Through 2045," Cerulli Associates (January 20, 2022).

269 See: "For the love of money is a root of all kinds of evil" (1 Timothy 6:10) and "You cannot serve both God and money" (Matthew 6:24).

270 Lizzie Johnson, "An alleged $500 million Ponzi scheme preyed on Mormons. It ended with FBI gunfire," *The Washington Post* (February 1, 2023).

271 Barry Ritholtz, "Navigating Financial Disasters (Updated)," The Big Picture (August 22, 2024).

272 Swensen even wrote a book explaining how to be like Yale's endowment: David F. Swensen, Pioneering Portfolio Management: An Unconventional Approach to Institutional Investment (Free Press, 2009).

273 John Harvard's Journal, "Money-Manager Transition," *Harvard Magazine* (March–April 2005).

274 Marcia Vickers, "The Money Game," *Fortune Magazine* (October 3, 2005).

275   Beth Healy, "Harvard ignored warnings about investments Advisers told Summers, others not to put so much cash in market; losses hit $1.8b," *The Boston Globe* (November 29, 2009).

276   Zachary M. Seward, "Alum Donor Blasts HMC," *The Harvard Crimson* (February 10, 2004).

277   Stephanie Strom, "Harvard Money Managers' Pay Criticized," *The New York Times* (June 4, 2004).

278   Andrew M. Duehren and Daphne C. Thompson, "A Guide to Harvard's Endowment," *The Harvard Crimson* (September 23, 2016).

279   Beth Healy, "Harvard ignored warnings about investments Advisers told Summers, others not to put so much cash in market; losses hit $1.8b," *The Boston Globe* (November 29, 2009).

280   Dan Primack, "Harvard: Great school, lousy investor," *Fortune* (October 31, 2013).

281   I try to avoid sports metaphors, but I published an earlier version of this essay in *The Washington Post* in 2016 two weeks before the Super Bowl. Barry Ritholtz, "You're obsessed with outcomes. Here's why attention to process pays off," *The Washington Post* (January 23, 2016).

282   Annie Duke, *Thinking in Bets: Making Smarter Decisions When You Don't Have All the Facts* (Portfolio, 2018).

283   Barry Ritholtz, "Transcript: William J. Bernstein," The Big Picture (March 7, 2021).

284   Efficient Frontier Advisors, www.efficientfrontier.com

285   William J. Bernstein, *The Delusions Of Crowds: Why People Go Mad in Groups* (Atlantic Monthly Press, 2021).

286   Michael Mauboussin, "What Have You Learned in the Past 2 Seconds?" Frontiers of Finance, Credit Suisse, First Boston (March 12, 1997).

287   There is a longer conversation to be had about the tax consequences in nonqualified accounts. The simple math is that you have to overcome the big hurdle of long-term capital gains at 23.8% (20% plus 3.8% Affordable Care Act's Net Investment Income Tax) just to break even…

288   Daniel Elkind, Kathryn Kaminski, Andrew W. Lo, Kien Wei Siah, and Chi Heem Wong, "When Do Investors Freak Out? Machine Learning Predictions of Panic Selling," *The Journal of Financial Data Science* 4(1) (Winter 2022).

289   Larry Swedroe, "Men are more likely to panic than women," The Evidence-Based Investor (March 22, 2022).

290   Barry Ritholtz, "Why politics and investing don't mix," *The Washington Post* (February 6, 2011).

291   Alexander J. Shackman, Andrew S. Fox, and David A. Seminowicz, "The cognitive-emotional brain: Opportunities and challenges for understanding neuropsychiatric disorders," *Behavioral and Brain Sciences* 38(86) (June 8, 2015).

292   Magdalena Ewa Krol and Wael El-Deredy, "When Believing is Seeing: The Role of Predictions in Shaping Visual Perception," *Journal of Experimental Psychology* 64(9) (September 1, 2011).

ENDNOTES

293   Michael J. Boskin, "Obama's Radicalism Is Killing the Dow," *The Wall Street Journal* (March 6, 2009).

294   Barry Ritholtz, "The Danger of Dogma," The Big Picture (July 27, 2003).

295   As I discussed in *Bailout Nation*, other conditions were forming that would also hasten the end of the sell-off. Markets were not only deeply oversold, but once again the Fed was cutting rates—this time, rates went down to zero. Congress forced the accounting rule-making body to be more accommodating to the banking sector. FASB 157, as it is known, ended "mark-to-market accounting," allowing banks to hide their bad loans.

296   Callie Cox is Chief Market Strategist at Ritholtz Wealth Management.

297   Barry Ritholtz, "WSJ Jumps the Shark," The Big Picture (January 22, 2010).

298   Donald Luskin, "Quit Doling Out That Bad-Economy Line," *The Washington Post* (September 14, 2008).

299   Six months after this was published, I looked back and annotated the column. I found 55 specific sentences that were either factually false or made predictions that turned out not to be true. Other than the September 14 date on the column, there was literally nothing in it that proved to be accurate. Barry Ritholtz, "REVIEW: Quit Doling Out That Bad-Economy Line," The Big Picture (March 13, 2009).

300   Donald Luskin, "11 Reasons to Buy Now," www.dowjones.com/smartmoney (November 30, 2007).

301   Donald Luskin, "Even Worse Than the Great Depression," www.dowjones.com/smartmoney (March 6, 2009).

302   Donald Luskin, "Stocks Slide—It's About Time," www.dowjones.com/smartmoney (May 10, 2010).

303   Donald Luskin, "The 2013 Fiscal Cliff Could Crush Stocks," *The Wall Street Journal* (May 4, 2012).

304   Donald Luskin, "OpenFund closes its doors," CNN (August 2, 2001).

305   "Donald Luskin: Stupidest Man Alive," Grasping Reality on TypePad, by Brad DeLong (December 5, 2005).

306   Reade Pickert, "Republican Voters Bet on Stocks After Trump Win. Dems Didn't," Bloomberg (October 1, 2018).

307   Justin Wolfers, "Debate Night Message: The Markets Are Afraid of Donald Trump," *The New York Times* (September 30, 2016).

308   Barry Ritholtz, "Would you let a mystic manage your investment portfolio?" *The Washington Post* (November 28, 2015).

309   As of this writing, gold has risen to $2,600, or up about 650% since 1985; the S&P 500 is at 5859, up 3,700% over the same period.

310   E.S. Browning, "Exorcising Ghosts of Octobers Past: Despite Housing Slump, Crashes Such as in 1987 Likely to Stay Memories," *The Wall Street Journal* (October 15, 2007).

311   "Bernanke Believes Housing Mess Contained," *Forbes* (May 17, 2007).

312   Scott Patterson, "How the 'Flash Crash' Echoed Black Monday: May 6 Selloff Had Parallels to 1987; Electronic Trading Magnified Selling Pressure This Time," *The Wall Street Journal* (May 17, 2010).

313   Charles Duhigg, "Stock Traders Find Speed Pays, in Milliseconds," *The New York Times* (July 23, 2009).

314   In both cases, troubles first appeared in the stock futures market, precipitating a decline in the regular "cash" market. The two created a feedback loop, dragging both markets lower.

315   Spock also served as a Captain, Admiral in Starfleet, and Federation ambassador.

316   Due to this mixed-species heritage Spock had to be removed from Amanda's body and raised in a test tube for two months, during which time Vulcan scientists made subtle chemical adjustments to the fetus to ensure its survival. The fetus was returned to Amanda's body to complete the human gestation period, then put in an incubator for four months to complete the Vulcan gestation period. He is the first such mixed-race child to survive.

317   If you want to learn the history of Vulcan philosophy, begin with Surak, "the most important philosopher in the history of the planet Vulcan."

318   By awarding the Nobel Prize to both Fama and Shiller, Stockholm recognized this schism. Fama's thesis was that the pricing mechanisms of markets were so efficient that they were difficult (if not impossible) to beat; Shiller's data overwhelmingly showed that markets could be as irrational as the humans who traded them. Bubbles form, prices detach from reality, then crash back to Earth. Refer also to Barry Ritholtz, "How Shiller helped Fama win the Nobel," *The Washington Post* (October 18, 2013).

319   Refer to Barry Ritholtz, "The kinda-eventually-sorta-mostly-almost Efficient Market Theory," The Big Picture (November 20, 2004).

320   Not to be confused with the trading game of the same name—Spock Market—which was similar to fantasy football, only with Star Trek characters during reruns and a sort of drunken bingo: "The Spock Market is actually kind of fun. You set up an account and are given 15,000 Federation Credits or FDR. You can then buy and sell different 'stocks' based on characters and items from the show. For instance, my portfolio is composed of Scotty (SCT), Chekov (CKV), Communicator and Communications, Inc (COM), Federation Costume and Uniform (FCU), Dilithium Mining and Mineral (DMI), and Red Shirt (RDS). The object is to be one of the top 6 Traders."

321   Callie Cox, "Running the numbers: Some stats on how the stock market moves," OptimistiCallie (August 30, 2024).

322   Luke Kawa, "Bernstein: Passive Investing Is Worse for Society Than Marxism," Bloomberg (August 23, 2016).

323   Matt Levine, "Are Index Funds Communist?" Bloomberg (August 24, 2016).

324   Myles Udland, "Jobs Week is Here," Business Insider (March 28, 2016).

325   Simone Foxman, "Paul Singer Says Passive Investing Is 'Devouring Capitalism'," Bloomberg (August 3, 2017).

326   Michael Sheetz, "Jeffrey Gundlach says passive investing has reached a 'mania': Investors should avoid index funds," CNBC (December 17, 2018).

ENDNOTES

327   Luke Graham, "Passive investing boom is creating a 'frightening' risk for markets, Morgan Stanley says," CNBC (July 10, 2017).

328   Christopher Joye, "Passive investing is lobotomised investing," *Financial Review* (May 5, 2017).

329   James Ledbetter, "Is Passive Investment Actively Hurting the Economy?" *The New Yorker* (March 9, 2016).

330   Michael Brush, "Opinion: Your love of index funds is terrible for our economy," MarketWatch (December 10, 2018).

331   Kopin Tan, "The Passive Investing Bubble Could Soon Pop," *Barron's* (March 25, 2017).

332   John Divine, "Has Passive Investing Become Fraught With Risk?" *Money* (November 14, 2019).

333   David Tuckwell, "Vanguard's ETF investors are buying the dip," ETF Stream (March 11, 2020).

334   Caleb Silver, "Individual Investors Calmly Buy Stocks During Sell-Off," Investopedia (March 11, 2020).

335   Bill McNabb, Masters in Business podcast, Bloomberg Radio (May 2015).

336   Barry Ritholtz, "Don't Mourn the Death of Stock-Picking Just Yet," Bloomberg (April 5, 2017).

337   Barry Ritholtz, "The Death of Active Management Has Been (Somewhat) Exaggerated," The Big Picture (April 5, 2017).

338   Richard H. Thaler, *Misbehaving: The Making of Behavioural Economics* (Penguin, 2016).

339   He literally wrote the foundational book in the field, *Behavioral Game Theory* (Princeton University Press, 2003). Additionally, he is the editor of *Advances in Behavioral Economics* (Princeton University Press, 2003).

340   Colin Camerer, Masters in Business podcast, Bloomberg Radio (November 2024).

341   Dr. Anna Lembke, *Dopamine Nation: Finding Balance in the Age of Indulgence* (Dutton, 2021).

342   Terry Gross, "In 'Dopamine Nation,' Overabundance Keeps Us Craving More," NPR Fresh Air (August 25, 2021).

343   Opioids, cocaine, and amphetamines generate an increase of 10 times above baseline dopamine production, overwhelming the brain's pleasure circuits. This has an obviously enormous impact on decision-making. "How an Addicted Brain Works," *Yale Medicine* (May 25, 2022).

344   Justin Kruger and David Dunning, "Unskilled and Unaware of It: How Difficulties in Recognizing One's Own Incompetence Lead to Inflated Self-Assessments," *Journal of Personality and Social Psychology* 77(6) (December 1999).

345   The film was based on Chuck Palahniuk's 1996 novel, *Fight Club*. The exact language spoken by Tyler Durden, the character played by Brad Pitt: "The first rule of Fight Club is: you do not talk about Fight Club. The second rule of Fight Club is: you DO NOT talk about Fight Club! Third rule of Fight Club: someone yells "stop!",

goes limp, taps out, the fight is over. Fourth rule: only two guys to a fight. Fifth rule: one fight at a time, fellas. Sixth rule: No shirts, no shoes. Seventh rule: fights will go on as long as they have to. And the eighth and final rule: if this is your first time at Fight Club, you have to fight."

346   "Daniel Kahneman on Bias," socialsciencespace.com (January 4, 2013). Full quote: "Well undoubtedly there is bias in science, and there are many biases, and I certainly do not claim to be immune from them. I suffer from all of them. We tend to favor our hypotheses. We tend to believe that things are going to work, and sometimes we delude ourselves in believing our conclusions."

347   Benjamin Graham (updated by Jason Zweig), *The Intelligent Investor: The Definitive Book on Value Investing* (First published in 1949). Latest edition, Harper Business, 3rd Edition, 2024.

348   Nathan Ballantyne, "Epistemic Trespassing," from Nathan Ballantyne, *Knowing Our Limits* (Oxford University Press, 2019). See also: Nathan Ballantyne, "Epistemic Trespassing," *Mind*, vol. 128 (April 2019).

349   Nathan Ballantyne "Epistemic Trespassing."

350   Matan Mazor and Stephen M. Fleming, "The Dunning-Kruger effect revisited," nature.com (April 8, 2021).

351   Julia Bönisch, "Déformation professionnelle: Beruflich bedingte Missbildung," Süddeutsche Zeitung (May 21, 2010).

352   Mixingmemory, "The 'Illusion of Explanatory Depth': How Much Do We Know About What We Know?" ScienceBlogs (November 16, 2006).

353   Stephen J. Dubner and Matt Hickey, "How to Change Your Mind," Freakonomics (May 29, 2019).

354   Steven Sloman and Philip Fernbach, *The Knowledge Illusion* (Pan Macmillan, 2018).

355   Leon Festinger, Henry Riecken, and Stanley Schachter, *When Prophecy Fails: A Social and Psychological Study of a Modern Group That Predicted the Destruction of the World* (1956); and Leon Festinger, *A Theory of Cognitive Dissonance* (Stanford University Press, 1st edition, 1957).

356   *Introduction to Psychology*, Chapter 7: Thinking and Intelligence, Lumen Learning.

357   John Kenneth Galbraith, "Came the Revolution; The General Theory of Employment, Interest, and Money. By John Maynard Keynes. 403 pp. New York: Harcourt, Brace & World. Paper, $2.95." *The New York Times* (May 16, 1965).

358   Andrew Clark and Jill Treanor, "Greenspan: I was wrong about the economy. Sort of," *Guardian* (October 24, 2008).

359   Barry Ritholtz, "Don't Blame Dodd-Frank for the Slow Recovery," Bloomberg (October 7, 2015).

360   Cullen Roche, "The Fear Trade Has Been Demolished," Pragmatic Capitalism (July 19, 2013).

361   Outside the US, the book is titled *The Heretics: Adventures with the Enemies of Science*.

ENDNOTES

362 Haidt is the author of *The Righteous Mind: Why Good People Are Divided by Politics and Religion* (Pantheon, 2012).

363 Morgan Housel, "A Message From the Past (Thoughts on Nostalgia)," Collaborative Fund (October 14, 2024).

364 J.P. Morgan Asset Management, "Guide to the Markets," jpmorgan.com.

365 "35 facts not likely found on ARKK yet unreleased 12/31/2022 factsheet," @ChrisBloomstran, January 21, 2023. Bloomstran also tweeted that Woods appeared on CNBC 23 times, which helped drive ARKK assets to a peak of $29 billion, while charging $300 million in fees. Someone, please remind me never to upset Chris…

366 Ian Salisbury, "Cathie Wood's ARKK Investors Missed the Big Gains and Ate Huge Losses, New Data Show," *Barron's* (August 20, 2024).

367 Barry Ritholtz, "How you, the amateur investor, can beat the pros," *The Washington Post* (November 8, 2015).

368 Jason Zweig, Charles Ellis, "Wall Street's Wisest Man getting rich off stocks is simple, says Charles Ellis. Here's how," CNN Money (June 1, 2001).

369 Barry Ritholtz, "No matter what, the long-term investor comes out ahead of the short-term trader," *The Washington Post* (August 10, 2014).

370 Michael Batnick, "Gradual Improvements Go Unnoticed," The Irrelevant Investor (March 20, 2017).

371 Advisor's Alpha, advisors.vanguard.com/advisors-alpha

372 See: William D. Cohan, "Finra Arbitration Case Offers a Peek Into a Murky World," *The New York Times* (June 3, 2016); Andrew Welsch, "Stiffed Investors Win Arbitration Cases, but Never See a Dime. Do Regulators Have a Fix?" *Barron's* (October 18, 2021); Michael A. Perino, "Report to the Securities and Exchange Commission Regarding Arbitrator Conflict Disclosure Requirements in NASD And NYSE Securities Arbitrations," sec.gov (November 4, 2002); Benjamin Lesser and Elizabeth Dilts, "Wall Street's self-regulator blocks public scrutiny of firms with tainted brokers," Reuters (June 12, 2017).

373 See William D. Cohan's Bloomberg series: "Wall Street Justice System Is a Kangaroo Court," Bloomberg (January 12, 2012); "Wall Street's Captive Arbitrators Strike Again," Bloomberg (July 8, 2012); "Wall Street's Kangaroo Court Gets a Black Eye," Bloomberg (July 29, 2012); "Don't Let Brokers Keep Watch on Themselves," Bloomberg (March 13, 2014); "Wall Street's Overlords Always Win," Bloomberg (April 27, 2014).

374 Eric Balchunas, "How the Vanguard Effect Adds Up to $1 Trillion," Bloomberg (August 30, 2016).

375 Hendrik Bessembinder, Te-Feng Chen, Goeun Choi and John Wei, "Do Global Stocks Outperform US Treasury Bills?" ssrn.com (July 5, 2019).

376 Barry Ritholtz, "Winner-Take-All Phenomenon Rules the Stock Market, Too," Bloomberg (July 29, 2019).

377 "SPIVA Global Mid-Year 2024," S&P Global (October 7, 2024).

378 Larry Swedroe, "After-Tax Performance of Actively Managed Funds," Alpha Architect (December 1, 2023).

379   It almost doesn't matter which one you choose—S&P 500 (SPY), Vanguard (VTI), or Blackrock (ITOT) total market indices. All three have been within a few percentage points of each other since inception.

380   Regret theory traces its academic history to 1982, and was developed independently by numerous researchers, notably by Graham Loomes, Robert Sugden, David E. Bell, and Peter C. Fishburn.

381   These two possibilities—a 10-fold increase versus a 90% drop—are roughly symmetrical in terms of math (but probably not probabilities). Both were possible; neither was analyst consensus at the time. The latter turned out to be what occurred.

382   This isn't about loss aversion but regret-decision theory. Investment decisions are probabilistic exercises using imperfect information about an unknowable future. But that leaves out the human side of the equation. The potential emotional response of regret, when new information (e.g., price) becomes available, can be a crippling experience.

383   Administrative concerns include enormous monthly brokerage account statements, endless pages of annual reports, notifications for every corporate action or announcement, and many other minor annoyances.

384   Once trading costs dropped to zero, a large cost impediment to DI disappeared.

385   When substituting one individual stock for another, the replacement needs to be similar in terms of numerous elements such as value, market cap, volatility, sector, liquidity, growth, revenue, earnings, trading characteristics, etc. Canvas allows that sort of granularity.

386   Special thanks to Ari Rosenbaum, who helped me analyze the specific data around the tax issues for RWM clients; and to Patrick O'Shaugnessy, who has been the driving force of Canvas, and has continually helped to incorporate new features and services for Canvas.

387   I was a seed investor with Eric Golden when he launched Canopy; The Compound Capital, RWM's fintech fund, is also an investor.

388   "Hedge fund market to reach $13tn globally by 2032," Hedgeweek (March 21, 2024).

389   Simon A. Lack, *The Hedge Fund Mirage: The Illusion of Big Money and Why It's Too Good to Be True* (Wiley, 2012).

390   James Chanos, Masters in Business, Bloomberg Radio (August 2014).

391   Peter Madigan, "The Inexorable Rise of Private Credit," BNY Mellon (June 27, 2024).

392   "MiB: Private Equity," The Big Picture (April 20, 2023).

393   Although limited partners in funds are always entitled to receive audited returns, third parties that gather quarterly and annual numbers for comparisons are left to wheedle, cajole, beg, and plead for voluntary data disclosure.

394   Groucho Marx, "Groucho and Me," Bernard Geis Associates (January 1, 1959).

395   Jared Dillian, "The road to riches is this simple: Drive a crappy car," Mauldin Economics (June 21, 2019).

ENDNOTES

396 Suze Orman, "If you waste money on coffee, it's like 'peeing $1 million down the drain,'" CNBC (March 28, 2019).

397 James Altucher, "It's Financial Suicide To Own A House," JA.com (October 9, 2015).

398 Michael Taylor, "Never buy a boat," *San Antonio Express* (July 31, 2015).

399 James Altucher, "Don't Send Your Kids to College," JA.com (February 25 2013).

400 "Drive a crappy car," ibid.

401 "Never buy a boat," ibid.

402 Suze Orman, "If you waste money on coffee, it's like 'peeing $1 million down the drain,'" CNBC (March 28, 2019).

403 Both Thomas Gilovich and Alan Kreuger have written that experiences bring greater happiness than material goods. See Daniel Kahneman and Alan B. Krueger, "Developments in the Measurement of Subjective Well-Being," *Journal of Economic Perspectives* 20:1 (Winter 2006).

404 We really have no idea what the level of reinvested dividends will be for the next four decades—they have been falling for the past four decades, so $350k looks to be a very high guess.

405 According to the Securities and Exchange Commission's compound interest calculator, that works out to about $350,000.

406 I understand a straight-line percentage raise of median income does not reflect the complex reality of how most workers' earnings' curve behaves, but it is a good ballpark figure to show some context for that denominator blindness.

407 Sallie Krawcheck, CEO and co-founder of Ellevest, points out how much bigger of an issue the gender pay gap is versus latte prices: "Just buy the f***ing latte," Fast Company (May 6, 2019). Note: Fast Company stole my headline!

408 Walter Mischel and Ebbe B. Ebbesen, "Attention in delay of gratification," *Journal of Personality and Social Psychology* (1970), 16(2), pp. 329–337.

409 Jordan Ellenberg, *How Not to Be Wrong: The Power of Mathematical Thinking* (Penguin, 2014).

410 Even before there was a commercial aviation industry, the military kept records on aircraft accidents. Matthew Syed, *Black Box Thinking: Why Most People Never Learn from Their Mistakes—But Some Do* (Portfolio, 2015).

411 Sarah Kliff, "Medical errors in America kill more people than AIDS or drug overdoses. Here's why," VOX (April 22, 2015). There are several studies of preventable, fatal medical errors and the results vary widely. The studies include: The American Institute of Medicine, which estimated the range at 44,000 to 99,000 a year; The Harvard study, which places the figure at more than 120,000; and *The Journal of Patient Safety*, which placed the figure at 400,000. Other deaths from improper care at nursing homes, pharmacies, outpatient clinics, and private offices could bring the figure to more than 500,000 a year.

412 Sarah Klein and Douglas McCarthy, "A Conversation with Peter Pronovost About Patient Safety."

413   The collapse of Bear Stearns eventually led me to write *Bailout Nation*. When Bear collapsed in March 2008, it wasn't merely a harbinger of the coming financial crisis; it was a reminder that no company was immune from existential failure. Public companies are reluctant and often strongly resist attempts to document and openly assess their failures. Perhaps they are not the ideal model to look to when thinking about failure.

414   Jeff Bezos, founder and chief executive officer of Amazon.com Inc., is one of the few executives who discusses failure openly. "To invent you have to experiment, and if you know in advance that it's going to work, it's not an experiment. ... Invention requires a long-term willingness to be misunderstood. Companies that don't embrace failure and continue to experiment eventually get in the desperate position where the only thing they can do is make a Hail Mary bet at the end of their corporate existence."

415   Bloomberg Billionaires Index.

416   "The 25 Most Important Private Companies," *Fortune* (2017).

INDEX

A

Abbey Road: 20
Academy Awards: 13
Acampora, Ralph: 173
American international Group: 237, 314
Apple: 235, 239–240
Apple Store: 69, 70
Arca Gold Miners Index: 271
Archduke Franz Ferdinand: 189
Arizona State University: 358
Arizona State University Carey School: 213
Artificial intelligence: 21
Augustus Investments Group: 384
Austerians: 105

B

Bartiromo, Maria: 337
Bates, Kathy: 13
Batnick, Michael: 207, 223, 390, 415, 447, 448
Bear Stearns: 237, 244–246
Bear markets: 60, 165, 191, 208
Bearce, Stephen: 244
Behavioral finance
  Avoiding emotional investing pitfalls: 296–297
  Cognitive biases: 300, 350–351
  Emotional Decision-Making: 350–351
  Financial Mistakes: 121–134
  Psychological Barriers: 167–170, 350–351
Belco: 262–263
Belfer
  Center: 263
  Corporation: 262
  Court: 263
  Hall: 263
  Research Building: 263
Belfer, Robert: 262, 263
Belfer, Rochelle: 265
Benchmark Capital: 420
Berkshire Hathaway: 216, 357
Bernstein, Bill: 362
Bernstein, William: 38
Bessembinder, Hendrik: 213, 401
Bezos, Jeff: 270, 275
Bianco, Jim: 173
Bianco Research: 173
Black Monday: 324
Bloomberg
  Aggregate Bond Index: 249
  Barclays: 386
  Billionaires Index: 268
  Radio: 57
  Terminal: 55
Bloomstran, Chris: 384
Bogle, Jack: 217, 401
Bonds
  Duration and risk considerations: 275
  Role in portfolio: 408
  Risk/reward balance: 407
Boston Globe: 33
Boyd, Danny: 21
Bridges, Jeff: 13
Bridgewater Associates: 435
Brown University: 359
Brown, Josh: 59, 89, 281, 447
Buffett, Warren: 141, 248, 252, 270, 290, 357
  (See Berkshire Hathaway (pages 216, 357))
  (See Munger, Charlie (pages xii, 2, 109, 215))
Bull market: 28–29, 165–169, 191
Burkeman, Oliver: 110

Burry, Michael: 33
Business Week: 60–61

C

Caan, James: 13
Cambria Funds: 417
Carlson, Ben: 25, 35, 37, 53, 89, 201, 242, 447
Cassel, Ian: 88
Chanos, Jim: 420
Cisco Systems: 66
Cognitive dissonance: 361
Colas, Nicholas: 246
Cold War: 328
Columbia Business School: 304
Columbia Pictures: 13
Compounding
    Advantages for long-term investing: 214
    Role in wealth building: 121, 296
Cooley, Professor Thomas: 368
Cornell Medical College: 263
Costello, Elvis: 20
Counterpoint Global: 15, 304
Cox, Callie: 311, 334, 447, 448
Cramer, Jim: 404
Cro Magnons: 309
Crossing Wall Street: 245
Cryptocurrency: 265, 421
Culkin, Macaulay: 150
Cyclical markets: 174–177

D

Dalio, Ray: 145, 247
Danoff, Will: 252
Darwin, Charles: 114
Dent, Arthur: 306
Dexter, Dave: 17
Disney, Walt: 14
Diversification
    Key to reducing risk: 274–275
    Reducing volatility in portfolios: 275
Dong, Hwang: 23
Dotcom Bubble: 319
Dow Jones Industrial Average: 28, 44, 124, 131, 172, 272, 324
Duke, Annie: 293

E

Economic Innumeracy
    Avoiding numerical misunderstandings: 119
    Decision-making challenges: 283
Einstein, Albert: 224
Elfenbein, Eddy: 107
Ellis, Charles: xi, 385, 448
Enron (See Madoff, Bernie (pages 263, 264–267)) (See Lehman Brothers (pages 12, 105, 218, 237, 272, 274, 314))
    Historical fraud impact: 217, 262–266
    Lessons from financial failure: 233, 265

F

FTX: 265
Faber, Meb: 417
Fail, Will: 69
Fama, Eugene: 327
Federal Reserve: 44, 86, 141, 144, 173, 250, 322, 370, 438
Feinberg, Andrew: 58
Festinger, Leon: 361
Feynman, Richard: 451
Financial Times: 83, 265, 270
Foley, John: 281
Foothills Asset Management: 181
Forbes: 46, 60–61
Fox Studios: 14
Franklin Templeton: 226

G

Gardner, Dan: 124
Gates, Bill: 270
General Electric: 218, 269, 272
General Motors: 218
Glaser, Markus: 231
Goldman, William: 21
Goldstein, David: 69
Goodspeed, Bennett: 40
Goudet, Olivier: 276
Graham, Benjamin: 252
Graham, Paul: 27, 76
Gramm, Phil: 105
Grand Canyon: 155
Great Depression: 12, 141, 315, 323

INDEX

Great Financial Crisis: 41
Great Recession: 319

H

Haidt, Jonathan: 368
Hamline University: 47
Harf, Peter: 279
Harrington, Richard: 449
Harvard
  Business School: 278
  Kennedy School: 263
  Law School: 262
  Management Co.: 290
  Medical School: 100
  University: 26
Hassett, Kevin: 28
Holmes, Elizabeth: 100
Housel, Morgan: 107, 371
Houston Natural Gas Corporation: 262
Hughes, Howard: 413
Hyman, Ed: 89

I

Index funds
  Advantages over active management: 400
  Lower costs and better outcomes: 399
Internet Research Agency: 149
Ivy League: 290

J

Jane Street Trading: 115
Jesus Christ: 285
Jobs, Steve: 69, 155, 270
Johansen, Bob: 112
John Wick: 21, 22
Jordan, Michael: 39
Judd, Jeffrey: 285

K

Kahneman, Daniel: 256, 328
Kallasvuo, Pekka: 74
Keene, Tom: 89, 235
Kellert, Stephen: 47
King, Stephen: 13

Kipling, Rudyard: 375
Kiyosaki, Robert: 450
Koons, Jeff: 136
Korean War: 262
Kynikos Associates: 420

L

Lay, Ken: 262
Lehman Brothers: 12, 105, 218, 237, 272, 274, 314
Lewis, Michael: 31, 32, 115
Lincoln Center: 263
Lindzon, Howard: 236
Loewy, Raymond: 19
London Business School: 46
Long Term Capital Management: 193
Loomes, Graham: 465
Los Angeles Clippers: 425
Luskin, Donald: 313
Lynch, Peter: 248, 252, 290, 401

M

Mack, Consuelo: 90
Madoff, Bernie: 263, 264–7
Maggiulli, Nick: 179, 447, 457
Malanga, Steven: 25
Malkiel, Burton: 201
Marcus Aurelius: 209
Market behavior
  Emotional responses: 328
  Predicting downturns: 227
Market crashes: 334
Market cycles: 175
Markopolos, Harry: 264
Marks, Howard: 115, 197, 245
McRaney, David: 116
Metropolitan Museum of Art: 137, 263
Meyer, Jack: 288
Miller, Jonathan: 89
Modern Finance Theory: 305
Monet, Claude: 136
Montgomery, Paul Macrae: 77
Morgan Stanley: 15, 304, 415
Munger, Charlie: xii, 2, 109, 215
Musk, Elon: 270, 275

N

Nadig, Dave: 89, 238
National Basketball Association: 280, 425
National Economic Council: 26
Neff, John: 252
New York Times: 134, 216
New York University: 273
Newsweek: 19, 60–61
Nokia: 74
Northern Telecom: 75
Norton, Edward: 356

O

Oaktree Capital Management: 245
Obama, Barack: 318
Orascom Group: 268
Orman, Suze: 424, 429

P

Palo Alto Institute: 112
Pearl Harbor: 189, 192
Picasso, Pablo: 413
Pitt, Brad: 356
Planning
    Financial goal setting: 395
    Tax-aware strategies: 410
Presley, Elvis: 18
Price, Thomas Rowe: 252
Pronovost, Peter: 434
Pryor, Richard: 266

Q

Quantitative easing: 173

R

Rams, Louis: 280
Ramsey, Dave: 424
Reagan, Ronald: 49
Reeves, Keanu: 21, 332
Richards, Carl: 381, 439
Risk: 260, 274
Risk Management
    Behavioral impact: 293
    Denominator blindness: 122–129
    Opportunity cost: 134–135
    Survivorship bias: 131–135
    Understanding and mitigating risk: 260, 274, 408
Ritholtz Wealth Management: 50, 57, 398
Ro, Sam: 89, 127
Robbins, Tony: 38
Robertson, Julian: 252
Robinhood: 199, 227, 236
Robinson, Joan: 122
Rosenau, Sue: 277
Rosser, Barkley: 122
Roubini, Nouriel: 33
Rubenstein, David: 90
Rukeyser, Louis: 90, 435

S

Sahm, Claudia: 89
Salisbury, Ian: 384
Samuelson, Paul: 105, 404
Santa Clara University: 248
Sawiris, Naguib: 268
Seaport Securities: 324
Secular markets: 167, 170–175
Shiller, Robert: 327
Silicon Valley: 101, 239
Silicon Valley Bank: 404
Simons, Jim: 290
Skilling, Jeff: 262
Slok, Torsten: 89
Sloman, Steven: 359
Sommers, Jeff: 216
Soros, George: 47
South Sea Bubble: 319
Sports Illustrated: 280
State Street: 340
Statman, Meir: 248
Stern School of Business: 273
Stocks
    Historical performance insights: 214
    Concentration in wealth creation: 216
Storr, Will: 367
Strategies, Investing
    Active vs passive management: 295, 350–351
    Diversification: 350–351

INDEX

Dollar-cost averaging: 226
Index funds: 350–351
Market timing: 226, 334
Valuation multiples: 167–168
Sugden, Robert: 465
Sullivan Theater: 18
Summers, Lawrence: 25–27
Suttmeier, Stephen: 175
Syed, Matthew: 433

T

Takahashi, Dean: 288
Taleb, Nassim: 201, 292
Tall Paul: 156
Templeton, John: 252, 401
Tetlock, Philip: 201
Thaler, Richard: 256, 347
The Beatles: 17, 18, 19, 20
The Big Picture: 1, 85, 394
Thompson, Derek: 19
Thorndike, Edward: 11
Torabi, Farnoosh: 227
Trump, Donald: 317–8
Tulip Bubble: 319
Tversky, Amos: 159, 328,
Tyson, Mike: 241

U

United States: 27, 105, 130, 153, 213, 261, 307
United States Army: 262

V

Vanguard Group: 340
Venne, Kris: 410
Vietnam War: 27, 171

W

Wald, Abraham: 133
Wall Street: 1, 15, 55, 59, 60, 89, 170, 226, 227, 229, 264, 281, 285, 296, 329, 338, 340, 363, 365, 375, 394, 403
Wall Street Journal: 62, 83, 89, 143, 244, 278, 315, 323
World War I: 147
World War II: 26, 27, 132, 143, 192
Washington Post: 285, 309, 313, 314
Wayne, Ronald: 239
Weimar Republic: 320
Weisberg, Ted: 324
Wells Fargo: 238, 244
Wharton Neuroscience: 351
Wharton School: 12
Wibel, Keith: 181
Wild West: 63
Wolfe Research: 245
Wolfinger, Raymond: 160, 455
Wong, Michael: 324
Woods, Cathie: 383
World Series: 293
Wozniak, Steve: 239

Z

Zell, Sam: 11
Zuckerberg, Mark: 78
Zweig, Jason: 62, 89, 256